Re
N6
25
E53
1983b
V.2

P9-BJB-271

THE ENCYCLOPEDIA OF VISUAL ART

VOLUME TWO
HISTORY OF ART
Roman Art - Early Christian Art

GROLIER EDUCATIONAL CORPORATION
DANBURY, CONNECTICUT 06816 USA

138028

ROMAN ART

A bronze statuette of a household god, adapted from a Hellenistic prototype
c31 BC–AD 14. Ashmolean Museum, Oxford (see page 178)

ROMAN Art—strictly speaking—is the art of the city of Rome, or at least art executed by or for Romans. Such a definition is, however, too narrow and ignores the great cultural achievements of the *pax romana*. Between the 1st century BC and the 4th century AD diverse traditions, Hellenistic, Italic, Celtic, Berber, Levantine, and Egyptian interacted and acquired a distinctively Roman stamp, at once diverse and unified. In the later Empire, contemporaries did not find it incongruous that the Empire was ruled from Trier, Milan, Nicomedia, or Constantinople. In a famous encomium, Rutilius Namatianus an early 5th-century aristocrat from Gaul, wrote that "because Rome has given the conquered equal rights under her Law she has made a City out of what was once a world".

The character of Rome's cultural achievement is often misunderstood. To some extent this is a legacy of the Roman literary tradition. Cicero (106–44 BC) in his prosecution of Gaius Verres, Governor of Sicily (and notorious art-thief), in 73–70 BC contrasted the Greek love of statues and painting with the near indifference of the average Roman. Yet Cicero was a noted connoisseur and Philhellene, whose passion for art was no doubt equal to that of his Greek clients. Virgil (70–19 BC) writing a Latin epic, the *Aeneid*, to rival Homer,

conceded Greek supremacy in the arts; the Roman mission was "to impose the way of peace, to spare the conquered and crush the proud". If the popular image of Roman civilization lays emphasis on the might of her legions, the cruelty of her rulers, and the vulgarity and decadence of her arts and morals, this reputation stems from such persuasive (and biased) writers as Petronius, critic and satirist (*fl.* mid 1st century AD), Seneca, moralist and embittered poet (*c*4 BC–AD 65), Tacitus, historian and enemy to the pretensions of the Julio-Claudian and Flavian dynasties (*c* AD 56–*c* AD 115).

Of course some truth lies in their perception, if the population of the empire is to be rigidly divided into "conquerors" and "conquered" and the name "Roman" taken in the narrowest of all senses. But such over simplification ignores the Roman army's part in bringing and encouraging Mediterranean art styles in distant corners of the Empire. Consider, for example, the delightful Antonine reliefs set up by the legions of Britain in southern Scotland to mark the completion of a new frontier (*c* AD 143), or the distinctive tombstones carved in military workshops around all the borders of the Empire. It ignores the restraint of so much Roman architecture—the Market at Leptis, the little round temple at Tivoli, and even the Imperial fora at Rome—whose effectiveness derives more

The Roman Empire with some places mentioned in the text

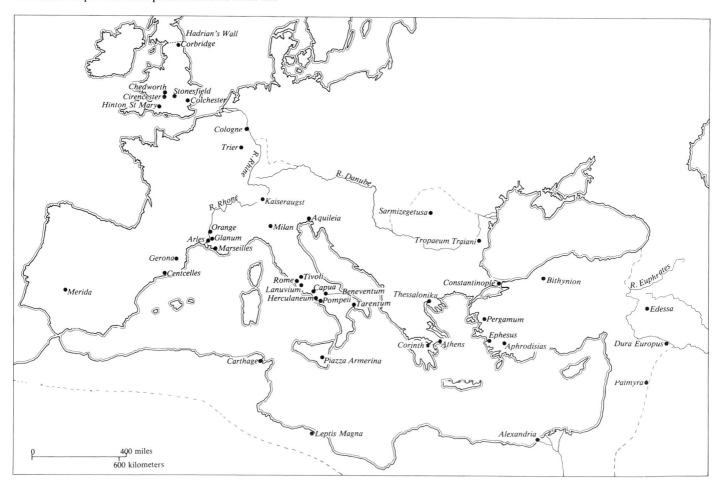

from skillful planning, from the positioning of buildings in organic relationships to others, and from the natural environment, than simply from sheer size. Even if Trimalchio in the *Satyricon* misused refinement, it certainly exists in the chastity of the best sculpture, painting, silverware, gems, and glassware. Any prolonged study of Roman art must emphasize the links with Classical and Hellenistic Greece, with a culture manifestly living and vital.

A second difficulty in assessing Roman art arises from the nature of classicism itself. Sculptors and painters of the 5th and 4th centuries BC are known to us by name, and their individual innovations were recorded at some length by such writers of the Roman age as the Elder Pliny (AD 23–79) and Pausanias (*fl.* mid 2nd century AD). Unfortunately our sources look backwards in their attitudes—Pliny dismisses the creative High Hellenistic Age (296–156 BC) in one short sentence: "Then Art stopped." Judged by such standards, copying and pastiche were the only respectable approaches, and although Pasiteles in the 1st century BC achieved some fame as a classicizer in both sculpture and toreutics, it must have been hard for artists to achieve distinction. The ways of representing the human body, its musculature and gestures had been learned. All that was left was to combine figures in a meaningful way, symmetrically, as in the *nymphaeum* of Herodes Atticus at Olympia (mid 2nd century AD), or dramatically, as in the grotto at Sperlonga (1st century AD). What had been perfected by the masters could not be improved. Copying was a craft, like milling or shoemaking, and like them its products were seldom signed.

Fortunately the artists came from different backgrounds, and so did not treat the Classical heritage in the same way. They were challenged by new political ideologies—and produced a fine tradition of Imperial State relief; by new techniques—and developed the crafts of the mosaicist and stuccoist; by new religious ideas—and created the symbolism of the various mystery cults.

Roman art was both varied and constantly changing. Who could deduce the hieratic symbolism of the base of the obelisk of Theodosius (AD 390) at Constantinople from the free-figure groups of *Ara Pacis*, so obviously modeled on the Parthenon frieze? And do the little niche mosaics at Herculaneum (1st century AD) give any real premonition of the great 4th-century vault at Centcelles near Tarragona, perhaps the mausoleum of the Emperor Constans who died in AD 350? How free the painting of the Villa of the Mysteries, Pompeii (1st century BC) seems alongside the formal row of Orantes from the Lullingstone house-church (British Museum, London; 4th century AD). The art of the Roman period not only bridged Antiquity and the Middle Ages but was an era of staggering achievement in its own right.

The Republic (*c*500–31 BC). Early Republican art was basically Etruscan. Latium lay between the important centers of northern and southern "Etruria" and was influenced by both. In the early 5th century BC Vulca, the great sculptor in ter-

racotta from Veii, was summoned to make the cult-image of Jupiter for the temple on the Capitoline Hill. The southern Etruscan enclave around Praeneste was noted for its bronze-work; a fine engraved casket, the Cista Ficoroni (4th century BC; Villa Giulia, Rome), carries a Latin inscription on its handle: "Novios Plautios made me in Rome; Dindia Macolnia gave me to her daughter."

Before Rome became a Mediterranean power early in the 2nd century BC, Greek influence was experienced largely at second hand via Etruria. This did not imply indifference to the arts: Fabius Pictor, from the renowned *gens* of the Fabii and, as his name implies, a painter, decorated the temple of Salus (Health) in 304 BC. A painting of battle and treaty scenes from a tomb on the Esquiline may give some idea of his somewhat archaic style (*c*200 BC; Museo Capitolino, Rome).

Art was, no doubt, largely practical. A famous passage in Polybios (*c*200–*post* 118 BC) describes Roman funerary rites:

> they place a portrait of the deceased in the most prominent part of the house, enclosing it in a small wooden aedicular shrine. The portrait is a mask which is wrought with the utmost attention being paid to preserving a likeness in regard to shape and contour ... When a prominent member of the family dies, they carry them in the funeral procession, putting them on those who seem most like the deceased in size and build.

This attention to the features of the dead is typically Etruscan, suggesting that Roman attachment to *verismo* portraiture and the idea of the portrait bust itself must be of Italian origin, however much their forms were transformed by new materials and techniques from the Hellenistic east.

A relief in the Museo Capitolino from Rome is carved in the coarse local travertine. It shows the busts of Blaesius and his wife Blaesia within a rectangular frame. No attempt has been made to model the upper parts of their bodies, and their heads are frontal, icon-like masks similar to those on the reclining figures of Etruscan sarcophagi. We observe the same rounded faces, prominent lips, and (in the case of Blaesius) large ears. The relief dates from *c*75 BC. Similar in general design, but probably about 30 years later, the tombstone of L. Ampudius Philomusus, his wife and daughter, now in the British Museum, London, marked a considerable advance in technique. The wrinkles on Philomusus' face bring to mind a bust in the Museo Torlonia, Rome, which depicts an old man, as well as the portraits on coins of C. Antius Restio (*c*46 BC).

The more integrated structure of these heads springs from contact with the Greek world, demonstrated by the head of a priest from the Athenian Agora, where the marks of age are treated with the same simple dignity as on the Museo Torlonia Bust. Indeed, many late Republican portraits from Italy were doubtless the works of immigrant sculptors. Instead of low quality travertine they used marble, which allowed sculptors to model with greater precision than had previously been possible. Native traditions were never forgotten—a marble statue of Augustan date in the Museo Capitolino, Rome, depicts a Roman with the busts of two ancestors, as though he were a participant in the funerary ceremony described by

Polybios. It is easy to see strong Hellenistic influence in the drapery and in the figure's head, but the subject is undeniably Roman.

Two reliefs, possibly from the same monument (the Altar of Domitius Ahenobarbus) but certainly of the same date, show that at least two styles of relief were current in mid-1st-century Italy. The relief in Munich (Staatliche Antikensammlungen) shows the marriage of Peleus and Thetis in a marine *thiasos*—reminiscent of work from western Asia Minor. The other slab, in the Louvre, Paris, depicts a Roman official taking a census and a state sacrifice, in the prosaic "matter-of-fact" manner of the Esquiline painting. If the gestures of the figures—magistrates, soldiers, and priests—appear somewhat stiff, it is because they were the first step towards mastering historical relief, achieved barely half a century later in the *Ara Pacis*.

The art of painting was well established in Etruria as well as among the Greek cities of Magna Graecia. Despite the existence of a local tradition epitomized by the Esquiline tomb-painting and inferred from the literary descriptions of tableaux displayed at military triumphs, the main line of development in the late Republic came from the Hellenistic world.

As early as the 4th century BC, plaster relief based on architectural forms, such as cornices or wall-facings imitative of marble, were employed at Athens and Olynthos. The Masonry style became common throughout the Hellenistic world, for example at Pergamum, Delos, and the cities of southern Italy. In Campania, where elaborate architectural compositions are to be found in the House of the Faun, Pompeii, and in the Samnite House, Herculaneum, it is frequently called the First Pompeian style.

The decorative potential of such walls was, of course, limited and attention was frequently centered on elaborate polychrome floor mosaics. These again emphasize the Greek origins of Romano-Campanian decoration, whether in the case of the great Battle of Issus pavement from the House of the Faun (Museo Archeologico, Naples) based on a painting by Philoxenos of Eretria (*fl.* end of 4th century BC) or in that of a winged Dionysos seated upon the back of a snarling tiger, an *emblema* in the House of Dionysos, Delos. One of the most famous mosaics from Pompeii (Museo Archeologico, Naples) depicts a group of wandering musicians and exploits the late Hellenistic skill in genre scenes. It is signed by Dioskourides of Samos (*fl.* early 1st century BC) and is thus certainly of eastern inspiration whether Dioskourides was resident in Italy or exporting small, fully-assembled pavements from the Greek Islands.

From *c*70 BC a major change in interior design becomes evident, but because of lack of evidence outside Italy it is not possible to know whether the Second style originated in Italy or resulted from outside impetus. As Rome was now the major center of artistic patronage in the Ancient world there is much to be said in favor of the first possibility, although many of the artists involved were doubtless Greek.

The Second style was a logical extension of the First. Instead of the room being enclosed by blocks of imitation stone, a skillful use of perspective produced a world of receding vistas, which allowed full play to the imagination. In the House of the Labyrinth at Pompeii, a *tholos* (circular pavilion) is glimpsed just beyond the garden wall. Similar *tholoi* are shown in the *triclinium* of a recently excavated villa at Oplontis and in the *cubiculum* of the villa of Publius Fannius Synistor, Boscoreale (paintings now in the Metropolitan Museum, New York). They probably had a funerary significance and can be compared with such monuments as the Mausoleum of the Julii at Glanum in Provence or the mausoleum called *La Conocchia* (the distaff) at Santa Maria Capua Vetera. At Boscoreale the wall of the room includes fanciful representations of buildings as well as landscapes and garden scenes which introduce a sense of space. However, the presence of the so-called "Adonis gardens", broken pots from which herbs are growing, suggests that the owner had a special interest in the Adonis myth and in the ideas of rebirth connected with it.

This theme is developed in a cult-room containing paintings, some of which are now in New York (Metropolitan Museum) and some in Naples (Museo Archeologico). The figures boldly painted on a red ground almost certainly contain representations of Adonis and Aphrodite (Venus), but some details, including a Macedonian shield, suggest that the fresco was adapted from a Hellenistic original.

The Villa of the Mysteries, just outside Pompeii, also has a cult-room similar in general conception and probably of the same date (*c*40 BC). Round the room, as though on a stage, preparations are being made for an initiation; it ends in a marvelous detail of Ignorance attempting to whip the neophyte. She, however, is protected by Initiation and beyond her we observe a Maenad dancing in ecstasy, symbolizing the successful accomplishment of the ordeal. Dionysos and Ariadne preside over the ceremony. The cult of Dionysos (Bacchus) had achieved certain notoriety earlier in the Republic (*c*186 BC) but came to be an accepted part of Roman religion, bringing as it did the promise of salvation.

Not all Second style painting is strictly religious. A frieze in the Vatican Museums, Rome, from a house in Rome shows scenes from the *Odyssey*. Individual figures are identified by name (in Greek characters); it is possible that the artist based his work on an illustrated scroll of the work. There is nothing small scale, however, in the rocky landscapes of the country of the Lestrygonians, the mysterious house of the enchantress Circe, or the almost medieval horror of the tribulations of the damned in Tartarus.

Perhaps the most successful surviving painting in the Second style is the luxuriant wild garden depicted in an underground room of a villa at Prima Porta near Rome (paintings now in the Terme Museum, Rome). The house was built in the third quarter of the 1st century BC for Livia, wife of Octavian (who was later known as Augustus) and the painting can

Right: Panel II from the cubiculum of the villa of Publius Fannius Sinistor, Boscoreale; height 244cm (96in). Metropolitan Museum, New York

A luxuriant wild garden: a Second style painting from Livia's villa at Prima Porta; height 300cm (118in). Terme Museum, Rome

probably be dated to *c*25 BC. In place of the somewhat stylized vistas of the Boscoreale bedroom we seem to have unimpeded access to a garden in which all manner of trees, shrubs, and flowering plants—laurels, oleanders, cypresses, quinces, roses, periwinkles, poppies—grow in luxuriant profusion. Beautiful birds fly amongst the foliage adding to the general impression of peace and harmony. Actual gardens which may have approximated to the Prima Porta "ordered wilderness" have been revealed by excavation (for example at the Palace of Fishbourne, Sussex, England, from the late 1st century AD, perhaps the residence of a local client king called Cogidubnus). The virtuosity of this painting is matched by that of the

A still-life composition from the house of Julia Felix, Pompeii.
Museo Archeologico Nazionale, Naples

marvelous still-life compositions showing bowls of fruit, eggs, thrushes, silver vessels, and pieces of textile in the House of Julia Felix, at Pompeii (Museo Archeologico, Naples). Like the Prima Porta fresco, which reveals a truly Roman taste for nature, they provide rare examples of Roman inventiveness which does not seem to look back to Greek precedents.

The molded elements of First style walls were forced upwards in the decorative schema of Second style rooms, and in late Republican lunettes and vaults achieved a high level of accomplishment. In the House of the Griffins, Rome (*c*70 BC), a pair of spirited confronted Griffins fill one lunette and a plant motif the other. The style of these devices is reminiscent of decorative sculpture used widely at this time for garden furniture. Greater originality is shown in the vaults of the House of the Cryptoporticus, Pompeii (*c*40 BC), which are enriched with coffers containing devices in relief: plants, items of armor, objects connected with Bacchus. In these ceilings the use of color was avoided (as, indeed, on contemporary floors with their monochrome mosaics), so that attention might be focused on the walls.

Although the Second style displayed an orderly and consistent strength in planning it soon gave way to a more truly decorative fashion. In the vault in one room of the House of the Cryptoporticus there are fanciful pairs of animals confronting each other. Similar conceits are found on the walls of Livia's villa in Rome, the Farnesina House, which can be very little later than the Prima Porta house. The organic unity of the walls was finally broken. Small panel pictures were divided from each other by purely decorative elements which do not betray any idea of function. The design of the vaults followed the same scheme: panels between fanciful ornament.

Vitruvius, a contemporary writer on architecture (*fl.* late 1st century BC) complained that

> those subjects which were copied from actual realities are scorned in these days of bad taste. We now have fresco paintings of monstrosities, rather than truthful representations of definite things. For instance, reeds are put in place of columns, fluted appendages with curly leaves and volutes, instead of pediments, candelabra supporting representations of shrines, and on top of their pediments numerous tender stalks and volutes growing up from the roots and having human figures senselessly seated upon them; sometimes stalks having only half-length figures; some with human heads, others with the heads of animals. Such things do not exist and cannot exist and never have existed ... For how is it possible that a reed should really support a roof, or a candelabrum a pediment with its ornaments, or that such a slender, flexible thing as a stalk should support a figure perched upon it, or that roots and stalks should produce now flowers and now half-length figures? (*Vitruvius, the Ten Books on Architecture*, trans. Morgan, H.M., Harvard University Press, 1914.)

The most delightful examples of this style of elegant conceit may be seen in Naples and New York. They come from the Villa of Agrippa Postumus (12 BC–AD 14) at Boscotrecase. Here we find floral motifs reminiscent of those on the *Ara Pacis* and light architectural frames which merely serve to emphasize the solidity of the walls. However, the sense of illusion so prominent in the great Second style cycles of painting is not absent. Mythological and sacro-idyllic landscapes encapsulate the natural world in the same small-scale ways as do the watercolors of early-19th-century landscape artists. Pliny mentions a painter, probably named Ludius or Studius (the text is corrupt)

> active during the time of the Divine Augustus ... who first instituted that most delightful technique of painting walls with representations of villas, porticoes and landscape gardens, woods, groves, hills, pools, channels, rivers, coastlines.

However artificial works of the Third style are in general effect, individual elements were well observed. Thus the swags in a room of the Farnesina House, Rome, contain a profusion of different sorts of fruit recalling the swags carved on the inner screen wall of the *Ara Pacis*, the unique Caffarelli Sarcophagus (Staatliche Museen, Berlin) and numerous altars and ash-chests of the time.

These normally portray garlands suspended from *bucrania* (bulls' skulls) by ribbons, which billow out in accordance with the demands of symmetry, not the wind. On the four sides of the ash-chest of Aelia Postumia (Fitzwilliam Museum, Cambridge) a pair of birds is shown beneath each swag and either a bird or a Gorgoneion above. An altar from the theatre at Arles (Arles Museum) depicts swans holding garlands in their beaks. Delightful as such artifice certainly is, Vitruvius could not have approved. Yet the sculptors of the late 1st century BC and the early 1st century AD were capable of such *tours de force* as Livia's garden room at Prima Porta. An altar in the

Terme Museum, Rome, has a couple of crossed plane branches portrayed on its front face. The curl of the leaves and the perceptible variety in their shapes suggest that they were sculpted from nature, although the arrangement of the composition as a whole remains artificial.

The early Empire (31 BC–AD 193). The reign of Augustus (31 BC–AD 14) does not mark a watershed; so it is not very helpful to contrast the late Republic with the Augustan Age. Only in the sphere of propaganda and state art can a new sense of purpose be discerned.

> We have reached the last era of Sibylline Song. Time has conceived and the great sequence of the Ages starts afresh. Justice, the Virgin, comes back to dwell with us, and the rule of Saturn is restored (trans. E.V. Rieu).

So wrote Virgil in his famous fourth Ecologue.

Graphic expression is given to these lofty thoughts by the *Ara Pacis*—the Altar of Peace—which is both the culmination of Republican Hellenism and the masterpiece of Augustan art. It was erected, according to its own propaganda, to celebrate the major achievement of the regime: the restoration of peace to the Roman world after more than a generation of violence and civil war. The site was consecrated in 13 BC and the structure finished in 9 BC.

The altar itself is ornamented with a very small frieze which recalls a similar frieze in the temple of Apollo Sosianus (*c*20 BC). Here we observe the Suevotaurilia (sacrifice of bull, ram, and pig), and a number of priests and vestal virgins who await Augustus as the officiating magistrate. All the awkwardness of the Altar of Domitius Ahenobarbus has gone; instead we discern a minute gem-like precision which suggests the influence of cameo-carving, which had achieved a peak of technical virtuosity. The famous *Gemma Augustea* belongs to the early 1st century AD (Kunsthistorisches Museum, Vienna), but other masterpieces of glyptic art are known to have originated in court studios at an even earlier date.

At the corners, decorative griffins and sprays of acanthus recall the ornamental garden furniture of the late Republic, perhaps carved by artists from Asia Minor (from Pergamum?). We have noted similar motifs on stucco in the House of the Griffins, Rome.

The long sides of the outer screen walls are divided into two registers. (Inside, the hanging swags and *bucrania* already mentioned recall the original ceremony on the site in 13 BC when a temporary fence was erected to shield the officiating priests from sights of ill-omen.) The lower, an intricate conceit of acanthus combined with other plants and flowers and inhabited by birds and small creatures, closely recalls the Third style in painting. The swans, which perch on tendrils too slender for them, bring to mind one of the motifs on the Farnesina stucco, as well as the device on the Arles altar. They allude to Augustus' veneration for the god Apollo, to whom swans were sacred. Above this decorative band is a procession led by Augustus himself, doubtless inspired by the Parthenon frieze but modified according to the factual character of Roman

On the Altar of Peace, erected to celebrate peace in the Roman world: Italy, or Mother Earth, between personifications of air and water

historical relief. As in actual life, not everyone is intent on the ceremony. For example, the children of members of the Imperial family are more concerned about not getting lost and grasp the garments or hands of their parents; Augustus' sister Octavia has to rebuke her daughter Antonia who is talking to her husband Lucius Domitius Ahenobarbus as the sacred rites are about to begin.

A different treatment is accorded to the end walls which contain the entrances. Above the acanthus register are carefully chosen neo-Attic reliefs, which recall the private commissions rich people in the late Republic kept in their houses (for example, Dionysos visiting a poet who reclines on his couch in front of a rich architectural background, on a slab in the British Museum, London). The only difference here is that the devices chosen serve the ends of State propaganda. The best preserved of these reliefs are the Sacrifice of Aeneas in front of a temple of the Penates at Lanuvium, and Italy (or Mother Earth) between personifications of air and water. The latter figure can be compared with Tellus as portrayed on the breast-plate of the Prima Porta Statue of Augustus, certainly of eastern origin, and based on clear Hellenistic precedents.

Few compositions so clearly challenge us with the basic problems of Roman art as the *Ara Pacis*. It is supremely harmonious, and marries baroque and classicizing tendencies with great skill. It is the consummate expression of the Roman mission, "to spare the conquered and put down the proud". The historical context of its erection is known. Yet, for all that, it is the work of Greeks and *unknown* Greeks at that.

Gems and silver plate also frequently carry propaganda devices. They are often of high quality and engraved gemstones are often signed by the artists responsible. The compliments paid to the Emperor and his family are extremely fulsome and recall the adulation bestowed on Hellenistic kings. Of course this was only possible because they were intended for courtiers who were not hostile to the frankly monarchic ambitions of the Caesars.

An intaglio (now in the Museum of Fine Arts, Boston) depicts Octavian (Augustus) as Neptune driving a chariot pulled by sea horses. It presumably refers to his victory over Marcus Antonius and Cleopatra at Actium (31 BC). A pair of gems show the Emperor in the persona of the god Mercury (private collection, London), and Octavia his sister, as the goddess Diana (British Museum, London). The style in each of these cases matches the signed work of the gem-cutter Solon in its baroque intensity.

One of Augustus' signet rings, mentioned by both the Elder Pliny and by Suetonius, carried his own portrait and was cut by a certain Dioskourides (not, of course, the mosaicist mentioned above). This gem does not survive but several others by Dioskourides are extant. The best is perhaps the one at Chatsworth, Derbyshire, England, which shows Diomedes stealing the Palladium from Troy, a popular theme also tackled by other gem-cutters such as Gnaios (Chatsworth) and Felix (Ashmolean Museum, Oxford). An intaglio by Dioskourides, in Naples (Museo Archeologico), depicts Achilles wearing the armor of Thetis. The neoclassicism of these gems recalls the

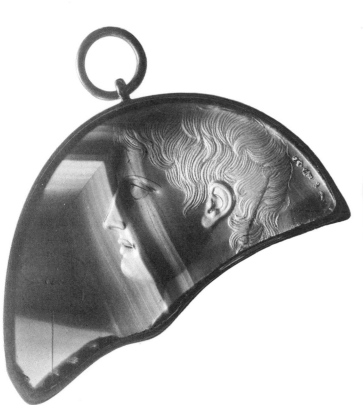

The Emperor Augustus as Mercury: an agate intaglio; mount modern. Ionides Collection

Octavia as Diana: an agate intaglio. British Museum, London

work of the sculptor Pasiteles, and gives us considerable insight into Augustus' own tastes. The Achilles gem in particular may have been intended to compliment the Emperor's supposed heroic qualities. It is noteworthy that we are told that prior to using his own portrait he employed a signet depicting Alexander the Great, a known admirer of Achilles.

Certainly a silver cup from a chieftain's grave at Hoby, Denmark (National Museum, Copenhagen) depicts Achilles, with the features of Augustus, confronting a submissive Priam. The artist, a certain Cheirisophos, was making a subtle allusion to Rome's magnanimity to the barbarian world, specifically to Parthia in the east. The cup should be compared with one of a pair found at Boscoreale, dating from the reign of Tiberius (AD 14–37; Rothschild Collection, France) which depicts Augustus receiving the submission of a native chieftain. It is executed in the same matter-of-fact style as most Roman state reliefs but the relative positions of the two key figures (Emperor and barbarian) are the same as on the Hoby cup.

The most famous Roman cameo is probably the *Gemma Augustea* (Kunsthistorisches Museum, Vienna). It dates from the end of Augustus' reign (*c*AD 12) when Tiberius had been adopted as heir. Augustus is shown as if still in the prime of youth. A Capricorn, his birth-sign, above his head, the goddess Roma seated beside him, and other features identify the Emperor as no ordinary mortal but the beloved companion of the gods. Tiberius, however, steps naturally enough from his triumphal chariot in order to pay his respects. The everyday world intrudes—it is the *numen* (spiritual power) of Augustus, not his body, that is incorruptible; the Imperial power not the Emperor's that is continuous and eternal.

This use of allegory is derived from Hellenistic art and may be seen on the *Tazza Farnese* (Museo Archeologico, Naples). Though it has been variously explained, J. Charbonneaux suggested that it glorifies Cleopatra I (Regent 181–176 BC) in the persona of Euthenia-Isis, wife of the Nile, and that the youthful figure beside her is her son, Ptolemy VI, as Harpokrates. It is possible that this fine cameo was brought to Italy as a spoil of war after the Battle of Actium (31 BC). A piece of silver plate, found at Aquileia (Kunsthistorisches Museum, Vienna) might be dated to just before the battle if the key figures represented are Marcus Antonius as Triptolemos and Cleopatra as Demeter. As on the *Tazza Farnese*, the seasons are personified and the earth goddess, Tellus, also appears.

The silver cup from Hoby. National Museum, Copenhagen

Some scholars assign the work to the reign of Claudius, but his features are not resembled by those of Triptolemos.

Political and eschatological allegory have much in common. The Portland Vase, a blown glass vessel in two layers cut as a cameo, now one of the treasures of the British Museum, London, has been interpreted as portraying Augustus as Peleus and Livia as Thetis, though there are simpler, perhaps more cogent, explanations. Certainly, both Peleus and Thetis are shown on the vase and also, to follow Professor Ashmole's explanation, Achilles and Helen of Troy resting after death on the White Island in the Euxine Sea. The meaning of both scenes is that heroic souls achieve felicity after death. A vase in Naples, produced by the same method, portrays cupids gathering grapes and again alludes to the idea of resurrection within the context of generalized Dionysiac belief. Fallen capitals shown on both the Portland Vase and the Blue Vase have counterparts in the discarded drinking vessels below a pair of centaurs playing musical instruments on the funerary altar of the Imperial freedman Amemptus dating from the reign of Tiberius (AD 14–37; Louvre, Paris). The meaning is surely

The Portland Vase; height 25cm (10in); 1st century AD. British Museum, London

connected with the discarding of earthly things in favor of the joys of the other world.

The art of the Julio-Claudian period (AD 14–68), at least until c AD 60, continued to be fashioned in the same Augustan mold. Thus the portraits of Tiberius (AD 14–37), Gaius (AD 37–41), Claudius (AD 41–54), and other members of the *Domus Divina* (including a formidable company of Imperial women such as Livia and Agrippina I) are shown with much the same features as those of Augustus and his contemporaries. In general their traits are idealizing but individual. See, for example, the details of coiffure or prominence of jaw or nose. The portraits are Greek in conception and some of the best examples come from the East (for example, the veiled head of a Julio-Claudian prince, dated c AD 29, in the site Museum, Corinth).

The Prima Porta statue of Augustus from Livia's suburban villa (Vatican Museum, Rome), is a posthumous work as the bare feet common to gods and deified mortals testify. It combines a typical Julio-Claudian portrait with a body taken from the famous Doryphoros of Polykleitos. However, what might have been incompetent pastiche is given vibrancy and power by an adaptation of the gesture so that the right arm is held out in an attitude of command; by the adoption of the dress of a Roman general; and even by the support—a cupid on a dolphin which provides a reference to the descent of the Julii from Venus Genetrix. Most fascinating of all is the breastplate which is reminiscent of the art of state cameos and silver plate as well as of the *Ara Pacis*. The central motif is the return of a Roman Eagle captured from Crassus by the Parthians. Other figures represent conquered provinces, one of which is Gaul, and we also observe personifications of Earth and Sky.

An altar similar to the *Ara Pacis*, the *Ara Pietatis*, was begun in AD 22. Two of its scenes survive showing figures standing in front of buildings (Villa Medici, Rome). Although the groupings are somewhat mannered, the introduction of architecture as an important element in the background of Roman reliefs was an advance, and looks forward to the complex scenes of Trajan's Column. One of a pair of silver cups from Boscoreale showing state scenes has been mentioned; the other portrays Tiberius in a triumphal chariot and the sacrifice of a bull, very similar to the sacrifice on one of the *Ara Pietatis* slabs. Continuity with the past is also reinforced by a state cameo, almost as famous as the *Gemma Augustea*, the *Grand Camée de France* (Cabinet des Médailles, Paris). Tiberius now occupies the dominant position, seated in majesty as the "earthly Jupiter". Beside him is his mother, Livia, and in front of them stands Germanicus, returned from campaigning on the northern frontier and about to depart for the east (AD 17). Above the mortal members of the Imperial house are the deceased members who have become gods (*divi*), foremost among them Augustus, holding his scepter. Both the *Gemma Augustea* and the *Grand Camée* show representations of conquered barbarians in a subsidiary lower register. The flowing hair of the unfortunate captives and the sense of rhythmic order are in the High Hellenistic manner, which flourished in the Greek world during the 2nd century BC, and it is very clear that this style still had its admirers.

The most interesting and, perhaps, significant development of these years (at least in the Roman west) occurred in southern Gaul. It would be hard to credit the fact that the Arch at Orange was erected and carved in the same decade as *Ara Pietatis* if epigraphic evidence had not fixed its dedication to AD 26. Above the side passages is an assortment of Celtic arms which seems highly appropriate in a structure marking the refoundation of a colony of legionary veterans. Names of Gaulish origin appear on the shields, either as a record of the conquered chieftains or, more probably, as signatures of the artists who carved these impressive panoplies. It has been suggested that the words "Voillus/avot" on one shield mean "Voillus fecit"—"Voillus made it" (although both "Voillus" and "Avot" could be different names). If so, the arch gives valuable testimony to the existence of skilled artists who were not Greeks. In the light of this, it is all the more of a shock to realize that the brilliant illusionism of the relief derives from such compositions as the balustrade of the temple of Athena Nikophoros at Pergamum and not from a study of contemporary Gaulish ethnography. A similar antiquarianism is to be seen in the panels of naval spoils above them. They are shown because it was appropriate that a victory monument in the Pergamene tradition should contain such allusions. Ever since the Battle of Actium Rome had been undisputed mistress of the seas.

The reliefs in the attic of the arch were quite unlike anything in Rome at the time: magnificent battle scenes involving a grand melée, clearly related to the sort of composition found on the frieze of the temple of Artemis, Magnesia (in Asia Minor) in the 2nd century BC (Louvre, Paris). But they are not unique because similar battle scenes concerned with events from Greek mythology ornament the base of the mausoleum of the Julii at Glanum, a work dating from the late 1st century BC, mentioned above in connection with *tholoi* in Second style frescoes. Here, and in other major sculptural groups from southern Gaul, such as the trophy of Saint Bertrand-de-Comminges, there existed a full-bloodied version of High Hellenistic art which had not been watered down by the classicizing tendencies of the Pasiteleans. It must be remembered that Marseilles (Massilia) was still Greek in culture and had strong links with Magna Graecia as well as with areas even further to the east.

In the reign of Nero (AD 54–68) and to an even greater extent in Flavian times (AD 69–96), these baroque tendencies manifested themselves in Italy. The change can be seen first in painting where the Third style gave way to the Fourth, which was illusionistic and, like the Second style, aimed to open out the wall. However, unlike these earlier paintings the vistas do not allow any true escape from the room but merely present a progression of theatrical *scaenae*. Although the idea of the style came from Greece, it was championed by Emperor Nero whose court artist Famulus is one of the few Roman as opposed to Greek artists whose names have come down to us.

A coin of Nero

Pliny tells us that

he was grave and severe in his person, while his painting was rich and vivid ... He painted for a few hours only in the day, and treated his art seriously, always wearing the toga, even when mounted on scaffolding. The Golden House [Nero's palace] was the prison of his art, and hence not many examples of it are known.

Although buried beneath later structures, some of the rooms in Nero's Golden House have survived. Others were preserved until the time of the Renaissance, when the fanciful paintings from underground grottoes gave rise to the word "grotesque".

The reopening out of the wall reached its apogee at Pompeii in decoration executed after the earthquake of AD 62. The scenes of Atys amongst the nymphs and of Iphigenia in Tauris in the House of the Gem-engraver Pinarius Cerialis present tableaux taken direct from the theater. A series of paintings from the basilica at Herculaneum (Museo Archeologico, Naples) depicts mythological episodes with an educational theme, again with a *trompe l'oeil* setting. A vivid portrayal shows Theseus after he has slain the minotaur receiving the salutations of the children he has rescued. The difference between the hero and his companions is emphasized by the contrast in their ages, in the great difference of size between Theseus and the boys, in his much darker coloring, and in his bold "heroic" gesture. Theseus as Savior-hero (*Soter*) has little to do with ordinary humanity, but the work tells us a great deal about how the later Greeks regarded their gods, their heroes—and their rulers.

The work is a masterpiece, as are others in the Basilica such as the centaur Chiron teaching Achilles the lyre, copied from a Hellenistic sculpture (the type is also known on engraved gemstones). The originality of the composition springs from the accurate portrayal of nuances of gesture and expression, and from an extraordinary sense of depth, making the most of what was then known about perspective. Another picture based on an earlier prototype is that showing Hercules finding Telephus suckled by a hind in Arcadia. Arcadia is shown as a female personification, reminiscent of a Roman portrayal of a province such as Britannia, or Hispania. The same subject can be seen on the Telephos frieze of the Great Altar of Zeus from Pergamum; although there Telephos is suckled by a lioness. The Herculaneum picture seems to be a free adaptation of the Pergamene work.

Of course the means by which such baroque devices in painting reached Italy are not altogether clear. A marble pilaster from the Aventine (now in the Uffizi, Florence) and considered to be of Domitianic date (AD 81–96) is covered with

The House of the Menander

The terrible eruption of Vesuvius in AD 79, which destroyed the cities of Pompeii and Herculaneum, has enabled antiquaries from the 18th century onwards to recover many details of the daily life and and artistic tastes of men and women of all classes living in Campania during the last century of the Republic and the first century of the Empire. The House of the Menander, so named from a painting of this great Greek writer of comedies (who worked in the 4th and 3rd centuries BC) in an *exedra* (recess) opening off from the peristyle (garden colonnade), belonged to a member of the local gentry called Quintus Poppaeus. The family achieved considerable eminence during the reign of Nero (AD 54–68) whose second wife was the notorious Poppaea Sabina.

Although the house was originally fairly small, with the main rooms grouped around the *atrium* (hall), it was enlarged and replanned in the middle of the 1st century BC when the great peristyle was constructed, with luxurious rooms painted in the naturalistic Second style opening off it. A fine example is to be seen in an *exedra*, whose walls seem to be pierced by ovoid windows, giving us a view of plants and birds beyond. The decorative scheme recalls that of the "garden room" in the house of Augustus' wife Livia at Prima Porta near Rome. Another room has a fine mosaic pavement showing pygmies in boats

in a landscape of the Nile, a theme found on a much larger scale in the temple of Fortuna at Praeneste (Palestrina) which must have originated in Hellenistic Alexandria.

Most of this decoration was swept away after an earthquake, which struck Pompeii in AD 62, damaged the house. The new, Fourth style paintings are arranged more formally as panels. Apart from the fresco of Menander holding a scroll, they include a series of scenes connected with the fall of Troy, in a room off the *atrium*, all painted with considerable verve. Especially dramatic is the moment when the unwitting Trojans drag the wooden horse into their city.

Most owners of houses in Pompeii had had time to remove their valuables when the eruption of 79 began; but the House of the Menander was still being renovated when disaster struck. The slave or freedman steward called Eros, who felt he lacked the authority to remove the family's silver and jewelry and was unwilling to abandon his responsibilities, died in his room. The valuables lay undisturbed in a cellar until this century.

▲ The recess painted in the naturalistic Second style

▼ The mosaic pavement of pygmies in boats on the Nile

▶ A dramatic Fourth style panel-painting in the House of the Menander: the unwitting Trojans drag the wooden horse into their city

◀ A silver mirror with a bust, possibly of the goddess Diana, chased in relief on its back

The silver plate consisted of 118 items and included a mirror with a bust, probably of a woman (the goddess Diana?) chased in relief on its back, as well as a number of drinking cups including two showing the Labors of Hercules, for example the hero taming the horses of Diomedes and plucking apples from a tree guarded by a serpent in the garden of the Hesperides.

Amongst the jewelry were a number of gold rings in the beautiful and simple form current through the 1st century AD. The wearing of gold rings was limited to members of the aristocratic senatorial and equestrian orders, additional confirmation, if any were needed, of the high social rank of the owners of the property. The rings are set with engraved gemstones cut in intaglio for use as signets. These miniature masterpieces of the jeweler's art would have been more highly prized than the frescoes on the wall or even than the family's silver. The best is a garnet cut with a representation of a charioteer watering his horses. Another gem, a green jasper, portrays a herdsman with his goat. Like almost all the treasures found in this house, they reveal a sense of taste and style far removed from the vulgarity which, rather unjustly, in the minds of many people, is the hallmark of Roman art.

MARTIN HENIG

Further reading. Maiuri, A. *La Casa del Menandro e il suo Tesoro di Argenteria*, Rome (1933).

◀ A Fourth style portrait of Menander holding a scroll

▼ A scene on a drinking cup: Hercules fighting a centaur

Below A gold ring set with a garnet shows a charioteer watering his horses

Theseus after slaying the Minotaur, from Pompeii; 1st century AD. **Museo Archeologico Nazionale, Naples**

arms and armor that resemble those carved on the Orange Arch and thus provide one piece of evidence linking the Flavian baroque with the Hellenism of southern Gaul. There are hints of late-1st-century chiaroscuro in the reliefs of a lioness and her cubs and of sheep in a rocky landscape (now in the Kunsthistorisches Museum, Vienna) which can probably be ascribed to the late Julio-Claudian period. What is certain is that by the reign of Domitian (and probably earlier) the new pictorialism had become widely disseminated. The fine sphinx carved in local stone, from a cremation cemetery in Colchester (Colchester and Essex Museum, Colchester), has wings comparable with those of a Domitianic winged Minerva (or Minerva conflated with Victory) from a gate in Ostia, or the more famous Victory of Brescia (Museo Romano, Brescia). The rich detail of reliefs from the tomb of the Haterii (Lateran Museum, Rome) with its graphic portrayal of a crane worked by a treadmill and of a richly ornamented temple tomb employs the same essentially Hellenistic techniques, although many details—especially the ceremonies connected with the deceased and the little busts in their niches—bespeak a strong

Italian influence, which is perhaps to be ascribed to the wishes of the patron.

The most famous Flavian reliefs are those carved on the Arch of Titus, erected by Domitian (AD 81–96) in memory of his brother. The display is much simpler and more restrained than the decoration on the Orange Arch, and the main sculptures are confined to the single passageway. In Antiquity the Arch of Titus was hemmed in by the Porticus of Nero and the Temple of Jupiter Stator; and despite the conventional but finely detailed little frieze around the entablature and the spirited victories in the spandrels, the traveler passing through the arch was not prepared for the rich effect of the passageway. The veristic illusion produced by an imaginative treatment of light and shadow allowed genuine participation in Titus' achievement in quelling the Jewish revolt in Palestine (AD 66–70). On the south side we see the spoils from the temple of Jerusalem in a tableau that gives life to Josephus' description of the triumph. Josephus mentions

> a gold table weighing many talents, and a lampstand, also made of gold, which was made in a form different from that which we usually employ. There was a central shaft fastened to the base; then arms extended from this ... and on the end of each of these a lamp was forged. There were seven of these, emphasizing the honour accorded to the number seven among the Jews.

On the north side Titus is shown in his triumphal chariot, accompanied by a Victory, his horses guided forward by the goddess Roma. Above the two reliefs and linking them is a fine coffered vault with a small relief in the soffit of Titus being carried up to the heavens by an eagle. Such a scene involving a viewpoint from an unusual angle was well suited to Flavian baroque art. We may compare the stucco rendering of the *Rape of Ganymede*, in the underground basilica by the Porta Maggiore, Rome. The purposeful flight of the winged genius (who here replaces the usual eagle) is contrasted with the relaxed, passive body of the shepherd boy surrendering himself to his fate as the cupbearer of Jupiter (Zeus). Such a comparison of active and relaxed forms was a favorite subject of Pergamene sculpture in the 2nd century BC. However, other scenes which treat themes from Greco-Roman legend as well as those portraying life in school and gymnasium are more restrained in their classicism.

There were, of course, many links between Julio-Claudian and Flavian art, for many artists continued to work in their accustomed manner. When a pair of reliefs were found in the area of the papal Palazzo della Cancelleria (Vatican Museums), one of which clearly portrays Vespasian and his younger son, the other Domitian setting out to campaign in Germany, the restrained, classicizing style came as a great

A scene on the Arch of Titus: Titus in his triumphal chariot. Rome

surprise to scholars who regarded the Arch of Titus as the typical Flavian monument. But Rome was conservative so it is not so puzzling to find the art style of *Ara Pietatis* still in vogue in the Rome of the 80s. In any case, although the illusionistic shadows and highlights are missing, the subject matter—especially of the *profectio* (departure) of Domitian—marks a definite change of emphasis. Gods and personifications appear alongside the Emperor as they do indeed on the Arch of Titus (and on Julio-Claudian cameos) but they imply a concept of Empire to which Augustus and Tiberius would hardly have risked giving public expression. Under a thin veil of the Republican decencies we breathe the heady air of oriental monarchy.

The Cancelleria Reliefs are of considerable interest in illustrating the factors that governed a commission. Most surviving state sculptures come from monuments that were both completed and successfully served a purpose. But here the artist was engaged on an important work at the time an unpopular Emperor was assassinated and thus faced a problem. On the *profectio* relief, instead of Domitian setting out to campaign in Germany we see the aged Nerva who succeeded him: but Nerva (AD 96–8) never went on such an expedition during his brief tenure of the Imperial throne and even a cursory glance at the relief shows that the head is in fact a recarved head of Domitian. In the event, both pieces were considered unsatisfactory and unsuitable as state propaganda. So the artist put them aside for the future in his mason's yard where they became covered with earth and rubbish, lost and forgotten for 1,800 years. They were rediscovered just before the Second World War.

A true fusion between classical and baroque tendencies was not achieved until the erection of Trajan's Column a century and a half after the Altar of Domitius Ahenobarbus. Under Trajan's successor, Hadrian (AD 117–38), this conscious classicism, combined with a baroque freedom in the portrayal of emotion or scenes of violent action, continued to hold sway. Then, in the Age of the Antonines, there was a decisive return to Flavian illusionism, and a decline in classical influence.

The second century AD marked the acme of Roman Civilization:

> If a man were called to fix the period in the history of the world during which the condition of the human race was most happy and prosperous, he would without hesitation, name that which elapsed from the death of Domitian to the accession of Commodus.

Edward Gibbon was not thinking here especially of the visual arts, but in them it is possible to sense a creativeness in counterpart to soaring optimism and general confidence in the Empire. In part it reflected a more cosmopolitan attitude. The Greeks were accepted into partnership in the Empire in quite a new way or, in other words, the Roman Empire assumed most of the characteristics of a commonwealth. Aelius Aristides (*fl.* 2nd century AD) wrote the most fulsome defence of the Roman Empire; Marcus Aurelius, the Emperor (reigned AD 161–80), composed a volume of philosophical ideas in

Greek. Nor must we forget the satirist Lucian (*fl.* 2nd century AD), a sculptor manqué who put in the form of a dream the rival attractions of sculpture and literary culture, so telling us how an educated man regarded the arts. Sculpture, which could almost be an hereditary craft, promised fame and moderate wealth without wandering abroad while Literature counters with the gibe that a sculptor would always rank as a common craftsman. Greek and Roman attitudes to such things were in truth very much the same. Hadrian, the greatest of Rome's philhellene Emperors, must take much of the credit for creating the 2nd-century Empire, both politically and culturally, but the roots of the new polity lie further back, with Trajan (AD 98–117).

A number of important state monuments can be associated with Trajan, but whilst the *Tropaeum Traiani* at Adamklissi (Rumania) is incompetent provincial work the Great Trajanic Frieze, largely incorporated in the Arch of Constantine at Rome and the Arch of Trajan at Beneventum, are in large part (if not entirely) Hadrianic. The column in Trajan's Forum and the architectural works surrounding it are his finest memorial. The column, which dates from AD 113, is a hollow shaft of Parian marble, about 100 ft (30 m) high, standing on a plinth. A continuous spiral scroll, carved with scenes from the Dacian Wars of AD 101–2 and 105–6 winds up it, in a band about 3 ft (1 m) in width. Like Trajan's market and the forum it was doubtless planned by the architect Apollodorus of Damascus (*fl.* late 1st/early 2nd century AD). On the base are Dacian arms disposed in a manner already familiar to us from the Arch at Orange although some of the details no doubt come

Trajan's Column: part of the battle. Rome

from actual observation of Dacian arms and armor which were probably new to Roman artistic tradition.

In the frieze, scene succeeds scene in a manner reminiscent of the Vatican *Odyssey* landscapes although here the hero is not a mythological figure but Trajan, the *Optimus Princeps*, shown with his companions—both generals and soldiers. Indeed, it was important that the Emperor was not shown as a figure different *in kind* from his comrades either in size or in the character of his uniform. As in Julio-Claudian art, the gods hardly appear. However, when battle scenes are shown, Roman achievement called for the sort of artistic response found in the attics of the Orange Arch and common to the baroque tradition. So the accurate representation of men and buildings coexisted with a more heightened and poetic approach.

The story begins at the bottom with the watchtowers of the Roman *limes* and a personification of the Danube (apart from Jupiter Tonans helping the Romans in a battle, the moon goddess Luna informing us that a battle was taking place at night, and a Victory with a shield, the only non-human figure in the composition). It proceeds to the Emperor's council of war, a religious ceremony, and Trajan's harangue to the troops, and then onwards through the events of the first war. The successful conclusion of that campaign is shown by the victory mentioned above, an adaptation of the Flavian "Victory of Brescia" type. The renewed outbreak of hostilities and the campaign leading to the assault on Sarmizegetusa are graphically shown. The culminating point is a great set piece, the death of Decebalus, where the baroque language of the Hellenistic battle scene (celtomachy or gigantomachy) is combined with the matter-of-fact observations of the Roman war artists with such skill that an original masterpiece was created. This can now be shown thanks to the recent discovery, near Philippi in northern Greece, of the tombstone of Tiberius Claudius Maximus (*ob.* AD 116) who came upon Decebalus at the moment he was committing suicide and carried his head to the Emperor. He had the earlier episode carved as his own memorial (Archeological Museum, Kavalla). As a work of art it is poor, but is surely a more reliable record of the event than the dramatic, heroic posing of Decebalus and his Roman enemies on the column.

The sympathy shown for Decebalus, which is also to be found in some freestanding statues of Dacians, such as the so-called *Thusnalda* (in the Loggia dei Lanzi, Florence), is no doubt, in part, a response to the vaunted "spirit of the age" found, for example, in the letters of the younger Pliny, but it also springs from the admiration of the noble savage (usually a Celt) already seen in Pergamene art.

Another important early-2nd-century monument is the Arch of Trajan at Beneventum. This was voted by the Senate before Trajan departed to campaign in Parthia (AD 114) but references to Hadrian's sensible, but inglorious, retrenchment in the east show that it was not finished until the reign of his successor. Its debt to the Arch of Titus is obvious, especially in the use of passageway reliefs and the richly coffered vault,

again with a figural device in the soffit (Victory crowning the Emperor with a wreath). However, the main faces of the Beneventum arch are carved with reliefs as well, their theme being the benefits Trajan conferred on the Empire. As on the Cancelleria Reliefs, the world of the gods and of men is made to seem close and friendly but, in this instance, without the pedantry and overglorification of the Emperor which disfigures the Flavian sculpture. Trajan talks to a recruit, to foreign embassies, founds colonies, fosters trade. In the passageway he inaugurates a new road and distributes bread to needy families. Only the little entablature frieze is strictly triumphal; it shows a procession of captive Dacians and the treasure of Decebalus.

The emphasis on public works rather than warfare upon the arch is Hadrianic: where Trajan was a great soldier and conqueror, Hadrian was a consolidator, with a strictly practical approach to the management of the legions. In his frontier policy he can be likened to Augustus in the latter part of his reign. He believed that the boundaries of the Empire were finite and, in consequence, that within them Romanization should be vigorously pursued. He was greatly interested in architecture (he is said to have quarreled with his architect, Apollodorus of Damascus) and may have been personally responsible for the rebuilt Pantheon with its fine dome. In Athens he completed the great temple of Olympian Zeus and built a library; and at Tivoli he planned and built an extensive country palace.

A gold coin of Hadrian

Much the most famous type in Hadrianic art is that of Antinous, although unfortunately—in common with most of the works of the Roman period—we do not know who created it. Hadrian met Antinous during a visit to Bithynia in Asia Minor, perhaps in AD 124, and thereafter the young provincial was accepted as a member of the Imperial entourage. Although much salacious gossip has accrued to the nature of the relationship between the Emperor and his young favorite none of it is contemporary. But it is reasonable to guess that Hadrian, himself the son of a minor aristocrat from a western city (Italica in Spain), was attempting to honor a member of that same curial class from an eastern town and perhaps even toying with the idea of involving someone of Greek birth in the succession, and ending the political monopoly of the Latin-speaking West in the government of the Empire.

Unfortunately Antinous was drowned in the Nile in AD 130 and Hadrian's grief—widely shared in the eastern provinces—resulted in the growth of a new hero-cult. Statues of Antinous equate him with Apollo, Dionysos, Hermes, Asklepios, and Silvanus—savior gods or vegetation deities. Pausanias tells us there were fine paintings of Antinous as Dionysos at Mantineia, the mother city to his native Bithynion. The type of Antinous with its cascading hair, delicate features, and expression of brooding melancholy is unforgettable, blending the Classical ideal with something more individual and particular. A large number of the extant statues and reliefs are works of very high quality. The Antinous Farnese in Naples is carved in Greek marble and presents the subject as Hermes, guide of souls. Here the contours of the face are particularly well modeled and the curls of hair formed into an especially pleasing pattern. The face evokes great intensity of feeling, partly through the device of outlining the pupils of the eyes—a practice beginning to enter portraiture at this time. The colossal head in the Louvre, Paris, the Antinous Mondragone, combines the physiognomy of the young Bithynian with the general form taken from a 5th-century Apollo. Winckelmann called it "the glory and crown of sculpture in this age as well as in all others". A relief found near Lanuvium and now in the Instituto dei Fondi Rustici, Rome, depicts Antinous in the persona of Silvanus. It is signed by Antonianos of Aphrodisias, and is carved in the richly pictorial style so characteristic of Asia Minor. Antinous stands in relaxed pose under a spreading vine and in front of an altar. His hound stands beside him. The skill manifest in this relief, which recalls earlier Greek tombstones, was to find a ready outlet in the carved sarcophagi which appeared from this time onwards.

Hadrian wrote a poem to a departing soul, usually taken to be his own, though he may have been addressing Antinous. This more personal sense of individual identity may have been a leading factor in the reemergence of inhumation as a burial rite and of the sarcophagus as an art form, although no fundamental religious change can be discerned. Many of the ash-chests and grave-altars of the 1st century AD manifest a strong belief in the afterlife.

In the east, sarcophagi stood in the open or in the center of open tomb-chambers and are carved on all four sides; but in the west where they were placed against the walls of the tombs, the back was left uncarved. In some respects it is valid to talk of "Eastern" and "Western" sarcophagi, but it must be remembered that in all instances the artists were of Greek origin.

The early (Hadrianic) sarcophagi were designed with a strong sense of form and proportion. Overcrowding was avoided and individual figures never allowed to dominate the total impression by such over-dramatic devices as standing too far in front of the background. Details were skillfully carved—the sculptor had not yet adopted the bad habit of rendering details by means of a host of drill-made borings. During the 2nd century the freshness of these Hadrianic sarcophagi was lost. We should compare the Pashley Sarcophagus from Crete (Fitzwilliam Museum, Cambridge), which shows the triumph of Bacchus, with a sarcophagus depicting

A statue of Antinous as Apollo. Delphi Museum

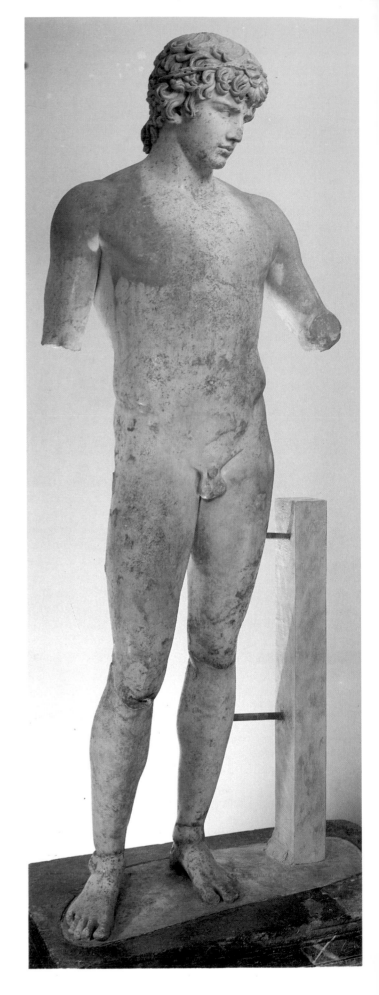

the same subject, carved a century later, now in the Metropolitan Museum, New York. In the former, the cortege of the god has power, life, and dignity. Figures are disposed along its length singly or in natural groups, moving forward in a real procession. In the early-3rd-century example, the carving is awkward and the figures bunched together in order to create a textured screen of highlight and shadow.

Some sarcophagi show scenes from classical mythology—gigantomachies; Orestes revenging himself on Clytaemnestra and Aegisthus; the destruction of Niobe and her children by Apollo and Artemis. Others, following the tradition of the ash-chests (and of the unique, Augustan, Caffarelli Sarcophagus, Staatliche Museen, Berlin) have decorative garlands held by putti, satyrs, or some other figures, though the space above the garland sometimes contains a scene such as the myth of Actaeon or Diomedes seizing the Palladium from Troy, the former recalling the ravening power of death and the latter expressing the ancient ideal of heroism as the true purpose of human endeavor.

A very attractive group of "Eastern" sarcophagi show full size amorini (cupids) representing the happy immortality of the soul in paradise. They no longer support garlands but play musical instruments, dance, and generally behave as young children. The majority have been found in Greece and, indeed, Athens, may have been the center of production.

Amorini are also figured on the highly ornate and accomplished pilasters from the Baths of Aphrodisias (Istanbul Museum) where they inhabit well-cut, fleshy acanthus scrolls together with Herakles and members of the Dionysiac thiasos. Other reliefs from the building include a frieze with a city goddess (Tyche) and a male equivalent (perhaps the demos) reclining and holding horns of plenty. Female torsos, springing from acanthus are, appropriately enough, closely paralleled in a relief above the entrance to the cella in the Temple of Hadrian, Ephesus, carved by artists of the same school. They are immediately reminiscent of figures from a frieze in the Temple of Venus Genetrix, Rome (similarly combined with vegetal elements) but the tradition can be taken back to the eccentricities of the early Third style as well as forward to Severan works at Leptis Magna and from Torre Annunziata (Museum of Fine Arts, Boston).

Hadrian's Palace at Tivoli gave full scope to the Emperor's aesthetic tastes. Buildings of complex plan, displaying idiosyncracies of design, from different parts of the Empire, housed a varied art collection. The sculpture galleries of the world are full of works said to have been unearthed on the site. Many are reproductions of such Greek statues as the Erechtheion Caryatids, happily in situ as part of the surround of an ornamental pool, the Canopus. Here they demonstrate the way in which the Romans could find new uses for well-known types and dispose them in different relationships to each other. In the case of the Caryatids it may be noted that Augustus had previously used copies to ornament his forum. Other sculptures from Tivoli are more baroque in tradition, such as the pair of centaurs, copies by Aristeas and Papias of Aphrodisias,

based on Pergamene or Rhodian work of c150 BC (Museo Capitolino, Rome). It should also be noted that ten representations of Antinous have been found in the Palace. In addition to the sculptures, there are a number of mosaics including an emblema of doves drinking from a bowl, based on a work by Sosos of Pergamum (fl. 2nd century BC) and a more violent composition of a male centaur revenging himself on wild beasts who have killed his wife (Museo Capitolino, Rome).

The Hadrianic achievement is summarized by the coin series that shows personifications of the varied provinces of the Empire. The effect recalls the arch at Beneventum, with its stress on the Emperor as restorer and benefactor. It was appropriate that Hadrian's successor, Antoninus Pius, should place idealized sculptures of the provinces in the Temple of Divus Hadrianus in Rome (c AD 145). Here the Roman world appears as a voluntary federation of cities and provinces, partaking of a common culture. The classicizing mode of representation, calm and urbane, reinforces this happy theme to which Aelius Aristides gave voice, in a panegyric at about the same time.

You have made the word "Roman" apply not to a city but to a universal people. You no longer classify peoples as Greek or barbarian ...there are many people in each city who are no less fellow citizens of yours than of those of their own stock, though some of them have never seen this city ...The whole world, as if on holiday has turned to finery and all festivities without restraint. All other competition between cities has ceased, but a single rivalry obsesses every one of them—to appear as beautiful and attractive as possible.

In the light of these words, it is fitting that the best series of state reliefs of the reign of Antoninus Pius should be not from Rome but from Asia Minor, at Ephesus. The altar with its reliefs (now mainly in the Kunsthistorisches Museum, Vienna) was set up c AD 140 and depicts the adoption of Antoninus Pius and Marcus Aurelius in AD 138. In general design the altar owes a great deal to the Great Altar of Zeus at Pergamum, though it is less complex. Reliefs were set up around three sides of the monument. On the right there were generalized scenes of combat, in style similar to the Great Trajanic Frieze (incorporated in the Arch of Constantine) or the battle scene on the strongly Hellenistic Amendola Sarcophagus from the Via Appia outside Rome (AD 150; Museo Capitolino). On the left side this is balanced by goddesses, including an Apotheosis of Diva Plotina, through whose agency Hadrian was helped to the succession. The longest and most important side was set between them and shows a personification of Ephesus (perhaps also a personification of Alexandria); a cuirassed emperor, presumably Trajan, mounting a chariot accompanied by Nike (Victory), Virtus, and Helios. Then the great scene of sacrifice attended by the Antonines and Hadrian, presents the monument's raison d'être. An intriguing possibility is that a youth in the background with long curling hair is indeed Antinous. His presence here, neither as a divus nor as a mortal (for he had been dead eight years), would have served to remind the population of Asia

Minor that the Empire (and its ruler) was not interested in the west alone. In the event the younger of the two adopted Antonines, Marcus Aurelius, was to become very much of a Greek both in his thought and in his writings.

The impact of the east is very marked on the base of the Column of Antoninus Pius (AD 138–61) which was set up in his memory by Marcus Aurelius (AD 161–80) on a site in the Campus Martius (Vatican Museum). The great Apotheosis relief shows the same subtle blend of historical and allegorical as the Altar of Ephesus, and epitomizes the hold Hellenistic tradition had by now achieved in Rome. The illusionistic tendencies begun in Rome under the Flavians had triumphed and would last for as long as a healthy organic development continued in Roman art, that is until the late 3rd century AD.

There had been earlier scenes of Apotheosis (including one on the *Grand Camée de France*, and another on the Arch of Titus, mentioned above), but for our purpose the closest parallel is a Hadrianic relief from the demolished *Arco di Porto-gallo* showing a winged female figure (*Aeternitas*) carrying Sabina, Hadrian's wife, up to the heavens while Hadrian looks on (Palazzo dei Conservatori, Rome). In the Antonine relief, the general composition is similar to the one on the Hadrianic Apotheosis, and was probably inspired by it. A male figure reclines on the left, personifying the Campus Martius. On the right, occupying the same position as Hadrian in the Conservatori relief, sits the goddess Roma. The surprise comes with the flying figure, which has been turned into a youth with long hair and majestic pinions which sweep the heavens while his feet almost touch the body of Campus Martius or the Egyptian obelisk (the so-called *Gnomon* of Augustus) which he is carrying and which indeed stood in the Campus Martius. The identity of the figure is established by the globe set with crescent and stars and the serpent he holds. He is *Saeculum Aureum*, the Golden Age, and represents renewal and eternity. Above him Antoninus Pius and Faustina are enthroned as Jupiter and Juno, looking down on the hap-

The Apotheosis relief on the base of the Column of Antoninus Pius. Vatican Museums, Rome

piness of a world that was fostered by them and will be maintained by their successors. Few reliefs in Roman baroque style ever managed to rival this in power of execution or majesty of design.

The other carved side of the base is a relief showing a funerary *decursio* of the praetorian guard and various members of the Roman nobility. The figures are seen in what may be termed bird's eye perspective, with more distant figures raised above those in front. This device was not new in the 160s (it is found on Trajan's Column), but it was to become much more common in late Antonine and Severan times. The somewhat stumpy little figures mark a regression from the careful rendering of anatomy in the Apotheosis, but the relief appeals to those who admire the primitive in art.

The Arch built to commemorate Marcus Aurelius' wars on the Danube (AD 168–76) no longer exists, but 11 sculptures from this period survive, eight in the attic of the Arch of Constantine and three in the Palazzo dei Conservatori, Rome. The use of large reliefs is reminiscent of Trajanic and Hadrianic work at Beneventum. As might be expected, the cutting is rich and deep; figures tend to stand clear of their background which is generally carved with architectural details. Thus events and ceremonies are each shown in a definite setting.

In a scene of triumph, Marcus stands within his triumphal chariot, which is about to swing round through an arch (as on the famous processional scene in the Arch of Titus, although *there* the chariot itself lacks this focus: it was left to Marcus' sculptors to combine the chief elements of the two scenes). Other episodes include a sacrifice, a *durbar* at which captives are pardoned, the giving of a new king to the Quadi, and the donation of a largesse to the citizens. The general impression is of dignity and a lack of conflict, even when the theme is a military one.

However, the wars of Marcus Aurelius' time ended the calm order of Antonine civilization and the column (which was begun in his own reign but finished during that of his unworthy son Commodus (AD 180–92) makes the point unconsciously, but all the more poignantly, by being closely modeled in its external features on Trajan's Column. But whereas, on the latter, soldiers go about their tasks with order and decorum, here both Romans and barbarians display emotional instability. The figures, smaller and more contorted (resembling those on the base of the column of Antoninus Pius), are frequently disposed in tight little bunches. They reflect perfectly the beginning of what Professor Dodds has called an "Age of Anxiety". One scene is especially moving. The rain is succouring Roman troops and throwing their enemies into confusion, but instead of a straightforward portrayal of this "miracle", the sculptor has introduced a strange, dominating being, partially composed of long streaming hairs (of rain). The British reader is reminded of the water-deity whose head appears in the center of the temple pediment at Bath (Bath Museum), instead of a Gorgoneion. In both cases we perceive one of those glimpses, alas all too rare, of daring originality in

Roman art.

Sculpture was produced for private patrons throughout the 2nd century. The fountain building or *nymphaeum* erected by Herodes Atticus at Olympia, built in the form of a hemicycle, and set with statues of members of the donor's family as well as with Imperial images, continued the tradition of arranging sculpture in symmetrical relationships which may be observed at Tivoli and in the Pantheon (whose niches originally contained statues of the gods). Portrait sculpture also demonstrates a certain conservatism. The Italic features of the Flavian portrait and the high "pompadour" *coiffures* of the ladies gave way to a more restrained style under Hadrian. Female heads could almost be confused with portraits of Julio-Claudian date but those of their husbands are universally distinguishable by virtue of their "philosophers'" beards—a fashion that must have owed much to Hadrian. At first they were short and fairly closely clipped but under Antoninus Pius and even more under Aurelius the beards became both long and straggly.

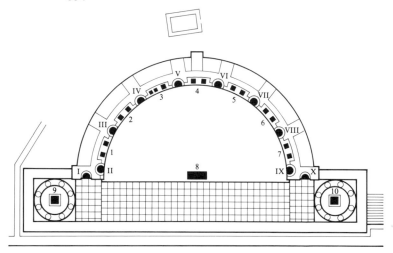

II	Sabina	5	Son/Son-in-law of Herodes and Regilla
I	Nerva (?)		
1	Grandfathers of Regilla	VII	Lucius Verus
III	Hadrian	6	Mother/Father of Herodes
2	Mother/Father of Regilla	VIII	Faustina the Elder
IV	Children of Marcus Aurelius	7	Grandfather/Granddaughter of Herodes
3	Youngest Children/Daughters of Herodes and Regilla		
V	Faustina the Younger	IX	Antoninus Pius
4	Regilla/Herodes	X	Trajan (?)
VI	Marcus Aurelius	8	Bull
		9	Hera (?)
		10	Zeus (?)

The fountain building of Herodes Atticus at Olympia

Such beards were, of course, worn by men portrayed on Antonine sarcophagi. More important changes made were an ever increasing depth in relief, the employment of the drill to give the effect of detail, and a more mannered approach to composition. These features can be observed in the Medea Sarcophagus in the Terme Museum, Rome, where three scenes of increasing dramatic impact (showing first Medea contemplating the children she is about to murder, then the deed itself, and finally her escape in a chariot drawn by dragons)

Detail of the corner of a vault in the tomb of the Pancratii

establish a continuous style which is nevertheless far less visually satisfactory than the integrated design of a generation earlier. The fussy elaboration of some of the detail makes for heaviness. A similar criticism could be made of the Casali Sarcophagus in Copenhagen (National Museum) where various deities gather on either side of Bacchus and Ariadne. The most successful Antonine sarcophagi, at least those of "Western" type, display battle scenes. Although the Via Tiburtina Sarcophagus in the Terme Museum, Rome, is so full of figures that individual identities are submerged, the piece is essentially honest in its approach to a battle and indeed it follows on from the tradition of Hellenistic battle scenes. Sarcophagi of "Eastern" type frequently show statuesque figures set against a background of columns and niches. Outstanding amongst these are the Melfi Sarcophagus (c AD 170; Palazzo Pubblico, Melfi), and the even more elaborate one in Velletri (late Antonine; Antiquarium, Velletri). The design of these works was influenced by temples, nymphaea, and theaters—especially those of the Greek east—in which sculpture was integrated with an architectural setting.

A similar effect was sought by stuccoists, who took their art to a very high level of achievement in Antonine times. The Tomb of the Valerii under St Peter's depicts various deities and members of the owner's family as well as figures from the Bacchic thiasos. Polychrome (including gilding) is used in place of the plain white stuccos of earlier times. In the Tomb of the Pancratii in the Via Latina, mythological episodes, for example, the seizure of the Palladium, Priam before Achilles, the Judgment of Paris, all executed in stucco, alternate with paintings. Here the decoration continues over the entire vault, creating an amazingly lavish impression on the visitor. Even when ceilings were decorated with simple, nonfigurative stucco, as in the Tomb of the Ax under S. Sebastiano with its rosettes within roundels, a very beautiful effect was obtained, remarkably like that achieved by some 17th-century ceilings in England.

Unfortunately the Antonine achievement in painting is less impressive. After Pompeii and Herculaneum had been overwhelmed by Vesuvius in AD 79, it becomes harder to pursue the development of painting in detail. Though it is clear from examples in Italy, such as the figures shown against colored backgrounds in a house in the Via dei Dipinti, Ostia and the Toilet of Venus in the Baths of the Seven Sages in the same city, as well as from others in the provinces, such as figures and decorative details in Leicester and Verulamium (St Albans), England, that the use of perspective, so outstandingly good in the Herculaneum basilica, had been in large measure abandoned. Few Antonine paintings of high quality are known. There are exceptions, for example the Mithraeum at Capua where the emotional intensity of the best Antonine sculpture was transferred to painting. In the center of the composition we observe the elemental struggle between Mithras and the bull on which the eyes of the sun, moon, earth, and ocean, shown in human guise, are fixed. The sun and moon are especially fine. The former appears in the persona of a charioteer wearing a red cloak fastened over his shoulder by means of a gold brooch. His hair is wild and wind-swept, his eyes stare with vivid intensity at the central action. There is more than a reminiscence of Alexander the Great as he appears on the mosaic from the House of the Faun. Luna (the moon) is almost equally compelling, recalling the figure of Arcadia in the Pergamene-inspired "finding of Telephos" fresco from the Herculaneum basilica.

The importance of eyes in middle- and late-imperial art cannot be overstressed. They were regarded in Neoplatonic theory as the link between the outward body and the inner mind of man. Panel-paintings on wood or linen, both in encaustic—a wax-based paint rather like oils—and in tempera have been found attached to mummies in Roman-period cemeteries in the Fayum, Egypt; for example at Hawara. They provide graphic instances of this. Although there was considerable stylistic development here between the 1st and 4th centuries, almost all these portraits were designed frontally and fix their eyes firmly on the onlooker. (Note the fine examples in the British Museum, London; the Royal Scottish Museum, Edinburgh; and Fogg Art Museum, Cambridge, Mass.)

The elemental struggle of Mithras and the bull in the Mithraeum at Capua

The Later Empire. Under the Severan dynasty (AD 193–235) emotion—the hallmark of Antonine art—appears to have given way to formalization. In the case of state art, this meant the expression of a more hierarchical relationship between the ruler and the inhabitants of the Empire. In sarcophagi the gods confront mortals across a similar divide; even the Christian frescoes in the Roman catacombs were not untouched by the new hieraticism (witness the "Orans" figure in the cemetery of Priscilla, Rome).

A painting in tempera executed upon a wooden panel from Egypt (now in Staatliche Museen, Berlin), provides a good introduction to early-3rd-century art. It represents Septimius Severus (193–211), his wife Julia Domna, and his sons Caracalla and Geta. They wear special clothes, and jeweled diadems which mark them out as distinctive. They stare outwards, as though interrogating the onlooker. It is true there is much individual characterization—even Severus with his forked beard looks vaguely Antonine, but he could not be mistaken for Marcus Aurelius. Here is no kindly philosopher but a stern and absolute ruler.

Severus and his wife are also depicted on the Arch of the Argentarii in the Forum Boarium, Rome. Once again they seem to be distant and "posed". The ornamental surround to the scene is reminiscent of the intricate detail found on Flavian tomb-altars (not the only case of Severan sculptors in Italy harking back to work of a century earlier). The Arch of Severus (AD 203) which dominates the Forum is a sad disappointment, as the sculptures are so battered, but it is clear that the style of composition with its little groups of stunted figures has much in common with the Column of Marcus Aurelius. Certainly the large panoramic scenes with their out-of-scale figures present an alarming contrast to relief sculpture of the 2nd century, but part of this divergence is simply that the Arch of Severus in Rome is rather badly carved. Septimius Severus lavished his greatest care on his home town Leptis Magna, and it is there that the best and most typical sculptures of his reign can be found. The attics of the contemporary triumphal arch at Leptis contain a magnificent scene of triumph in which the Emperor stands facing the spectator from the platform of his chariot. The other figures around him are rigidly frontal as on the scene of sacrifice. An almost Byzantine aesthetic prevails here, accentuated by the deeply carved folds of the drapery. Earlier emperors had built Imperial fora at Rome; characteristically Severus built his great basilica and public square at

A 2nd-century panel portrait of a woman. Royal Scottish Museum, Edinburgh

Leptis, and brought in Aphrodisian sculptors to decorate it. The pilasters at the entrance to the basilica with their inhabited scrolls recall earlier Hadrianic prototypes in Asia Minor.

The increasingly "Royal" style of the emperor and his family opened up opportunities of patronage for gem-engravers and other craftsmen. A cameo in the British Museum, London, conflates Julia Domna with Juno Caelestis and shows her riding in a chariot drawn by two bulls, while another in Kassel (Staatliche Kunstsammlungen) gives her the attributes of Victory. An intaglio from Castlesteads, Cumberland (now lost), depicted Severus as the Egyptian god Serapis. All the members of the Imperial family (Septimius Severus, Julia Domna, Caracalla, and Geta) appear on a fine cameo in Paris (Cabinet des Médailles). Other gems, such as the Bear Cameo from South Shields (Newcastle Museum) carved on Indian sardonyx, make no direct reference to state propaganda, but were possibly the products of state workshops. Presumably only the very wealthy or influential would wear such jeweled settings in their brooches. All these gems are distinguished by the same rather two-dimensional carving as we find in sculpture on a larger scale.

Linearity and frontality were just two aspects of the provincial art in the eastern provinces of the Empire which came to influence Roman sculpture and painting as a whole. The deities carved on stone beams from the temple of Bel, Palmyra, exemplify this to a marked degree as early as AD 32 (site museum). The idea was apparently to bring the gods into a closer relationship with living men, rather than to stress the divide between the two worlds, as the Romans were later to do. A similar notion was responsible for the practice of employing frontally disposed portraits to seal ossuaries in tombs. These display strong Greco-Roman influence in the modelings of their features, and yet they could not be confused with western sculpture. In the case of female portraits, such as the masterpiece in Copenhagen (Ny Carlsberg Glyptotek) called *The Beauty of Palmyra* (early 3rd century AD) this is partly a matter of the lavish use of jewelry but in all cases, not only at Palmyra but also at Hatra beyond the Imperial frontiers, and at many lesser centers, line and pattern were more important than volume.

An interesting example of how Palmyrene art reached the west is presented by two tombstones from South Shields (site museum) carved by a Palmyrene, in one case for a Palmyrene patron called Barates who was burying his British-born wife Regina, and in the other for Victor, a Moor from north Africa. The movement of artists even on a small scale in the Empire would have been sufficient to spread various modes of representation. At the end of the 3rd century tetrarchic sculpture seems to reflect the workshop traditions of the north Balkans, unfortunately less refined than those of Asia Minor or of Syria.

Painting and mosaic were increasingly subject to local in-

Left: Septimius Severus and his family, a painted panel; early 3rd century. Antikenabteilung, West Berlin

A decorated pilaster on the basilica of Severus at Leptis Magna

A stone bust of a roman from Palmyra. Ny Carlsberg Glyptothek, Copenhagen

fluences. Many of the finest mosaic pavements of the middle Empire are to be seen in north Africa, especially in Tunisia where the use of bold, contrasting colors set against simple, generally white, grounds together with developed intricate decorative borders produced an unusually lively response to the problems of two-dimensional design. A floor from La Chebba (Musée National, Tunis) has, as its centerpiece, a roundel showing Neptune rising from the sea in a chariot drawn by sea horses. Around this *emblema* are delicate personifications of the seasons as young women holding appropriate attributes, each enclosed in a light vegetal frame, and vignettes of men pursuing various seasonal activities. Equally attractive is a floor from Oudna, also in Tunis, with a central scene of Bacchus giving the vine to Icarius in Attica, and a surround comprising a luxuriant vine in the midst of which cupids are gathering grapes. A pavement found at Acholla (Musée National, Tunis) presents a Marine *thiasos* with nereids seated on dolphins and sea creatures of various kinds, as well as vegetal motifs, combined with human figures. The centerpiece is a "Triumph of Bacchus" which alludes to the salvation of the soul from the powers of death, presumably in the Islands of the Blessed on the other side of Ocean, through the lifegiving beneficence of the god of wine. The mosaic of Rural Labors at Cherchel (site museum) presents an overall carpet design in rich polychrome, with men amongst vines which are neither in the foreground nor the background but act as rhythmic interruptions of the human activity. As at Leptis pattern was more important than naturalism.

The frontally disposed formal group of soldiers in a fresco showing a scene of sacrifice in the temple of the Palmyrene

A mosaic floor from La Chebba. Musée National du Bardo, Tunis

gods at Dura Europus (Yale University Art Gallery, New Haven) is, however, closer to the Leptis Arch in feeling and cannot be many decades later in date. Instead of a presiding emperor, the chief figure here is the tribune of the local garrison, Julius Terentius, who is pouring a libation on the altar.

The most remarkable paintings from Dura are the biblical scenes adorning the synagogue (National Museum, Damascus) which must have been executed prior to AD 245 as the building was destroyed at that time by fortifications hurriedly erected against the Persians. Samuel, depicted on a larger scale than other Israelites, anoints David who stares passively in front of him in the company of a group of men who stand as rigid as statues. To take another example, in the *Vision of Ezekiel*, the *manus dei* descends from the heavens (an anticipation of Byzantine iconography) and seems to manipulate the strange trousered men below, whose faces are equally blank and impassive. At their feet lie the little doll-like bodies and parts of bodies belonging to those yet to be resurrected. This scattering of objects in the field is also seen in the synagogue in the shattered paraphernalia from the Shrine of Dagon and, of course, goes back to a Hellenistic pavement by Sosos. But many of the other details, such as the dress and the frontal rigidity of the figures, are certainly Oriental. A fine series of mosaics ornamenting the floors of tombs at Edessa date to a period shortly after the Romans had established control (late 2nd/early 3rd century AD). They depict local notables with their families, in a style very close to the Dura paintings. Various groups of trousered men and long-robed women are disposed in fixed frontal attitudes, with their heads and arms as formally posed as in Victorian photographs, and provide further striking confirmation that the tendencies which are—in the west—first made manifest in the Marcus column had their source along the eastern borders of the Empire.

The apparent prosperity of the Empire under Severus and even his immediate successors gave no hint of the turmoil of the 3rd century which in many areas (including Rome) had serious repercussions on the arts. The production of state reliefs, so important in the previous age, almost ceased, for rulers had neither time nor money for expensive monuments. In order to obtain a consistent picture of 3rd-century propaganda we must turn to coins, struck in large numbers and debased metal (as well as in gold, although gold coins are admittedly very rare). Every new claimant to the Imperial throne hoped he would fare better than his predecessors and avoid being killed either by the Persians or in civil war, and realized that it was vital that the populace of the Empire should be able to recognize him and accept his propaganda. Thus the quality of portraiture was never higher: in their coins we see the taut, worried features of the Emperors, for example Macrinus (217–18), Decius (249–51), and the stylish Gallienus (253–68), his hair and beard carefully combed; the good-natured Postumus (259–68), a Gaulish usurper whose portrait is deliberately reminiscent of the Antonines; the rugged head of Carausius (287–93) with his thick bull neck

whose image gives the appearance of energy, and the mask-like features of the joint-Augusti Diocletian (284–305) and Maximian (285–305) which are in line with the general later Roman tendency of stressing the divide between Emperors and their subjects.

A coin of Carausius

The failure of the Empire in foreign wars was eloquently expressed by reliefs set up by Persian monarchs to show their victories over Severus Alexander (AD 232), Philip the Arab (AD 244), and Valerian (AD 260). In choice of setting—the sides of rocky gorges—the reliefs harked back to much earlier Achaemenid prototypes, and this is especially notable in the highly formalized composition from Darabgird showing Ardashir (224–41) accepting a Roman submission in the 230s (?232). This style was nevertheless sometimes influenced by art from the west, notably in a relief at Bishapur, dated to c AD 260 and possibly the work of Roman prisoners settled in Iran, which depicts Shapur (AD 242–72) triumphing over the Roman Emperors, one of whom is certainly Valerian who was actually captured by the Persians. The faces and equipment of the defeated Roman troops are considerably more naturalistic than was normally the case in Persian art, and the Roman Emperor, humbled and kneeling, is a figure of sympathy.

To see an emperor in triumph we must turn to a private work—a sarcophagus showing a Roman general on horseback riding forth from a melee of writhing figures. The general has been identified as the Emperor Hostilian who reigned, briefly, in AD 251 and this is presumably his coffin (Terme Museum, Rome). We may note the persistent use of the drill, making for an interesting trellis-like pattern, though the carving of individual figures is rather mechanical.

The Hellenistic tradition of Antonine days flowered again in the cultivated court of Gallienus, which also provided a home for philosophers, for example Plotinus (AD 205–70). Indeed, to judge from the persistence of certain types of sarcophagi showing philosophers and the "Gallienic" style of the rival "Gallic" Emperor Postumus, the "Gallienic Renaissance" was fairly widespread. The term "Renaissance" is something of a misnomer as the artists did not have to learn their craft anew, but the revival of patronage was a significant milestone in 3rd-century art.

A baroque head from the Theater of Dionysos, Athens, has long curling locks which cascade down the nape of the neck, somewhat like the hair of Antinous. The carefully trimmed beard seems to be consciously modeled on Hadrian's. It is not surprising that some scholars have dated this piece and others like it (such as a head in Dresden) to late Hadrianic or Antonine times. However, the eyes have strongly outlined pupils, appearing to gaze into the distance, and the expression is far

The triumphant Hostilian: a scene from the Ludovisi Sarcophagus; marble; height 145cm (57in); mid 3rd century. Terme Museum, Rome

less calm than any Antonine portrait. It is exactly matched on another splendid head in the Terme Museum at Rome which has much shorter hair and can be compared very closely with Gallienus' coin portraits. The Athens head bears some likeness to the head of Alexander the Great found at Pergamum (Istanbul Museum) and dated to the 2nd century BC; it may represent Gallienus in the guise of Alexander. If so, the comparison was hardly a happy one as Gallienus, whatever his other qualities, lacked military success. The reference to Hadrian was both apt and deliberate, no doubt to draw attention to the fact that like his forebear he was a hellenizer and philosopher.

The Sidamara Sarcophagus (Istanbul Museum) was carved in Asia Minor at about this time and has reliefs on all four sides. The most striking of these is an enthroned philosopher in profile, reading from a scroll. Beside him is his wife and they are accompanied by Artemis and the Dioscouri. In the background is a rich architectural framework but, as opposed to earlier "Eastern" sarcophagi, the figures are far more dominant. A similar and equally fine philosopher sarcophagus may be seen in Rome (Lateran Museum).

Gallienic in style, although conceivably later in date, are the reliefs from the *Arcus Novus* which seem to belong to the 260s rather than to the 280s (tetrarchic period). Most of them are now in the Boboli Gardens, Florence, but an important fragment is in the Villa Medici, Rome, showing a Victory inscribing vows for the emperor's safety on a circular shield. The subject matter of the pedestals in Florence is traditional—captive barbarians, Victories, and the Dioscuri. But the bold cutting, high relief, rich plastic textures of the Victories' hair and draperies, and the fine proportions of all the figures take us back to the High Antonine style of the Arch of Marcus Aurelius. The conscious pursuit of beauty is, indeed, very apparent and is matched exactly in the Athens Gallienus. It is not surprising that these reliefs were copied in the reign of Constantine although the result, to be seen on Constantine's Arch, was of very low quality.

The only public sculpture of the tetrarchic age of much merit when judged by the standards of the Greco-Roman past is the Arch of Galerius at Thessalonica whose original form was that of a quadrifons (four-way arch). Only two of the original four piers survive, each with four superimposed layers of relief, which were in part derived from the designs on sarcophagi. The scenes of battle are fairly effective from a distance, and the thin bands of vegetal ornament separating the various zones were cut with the panache we have come to expect from the sculptural school of Aphrodisias in Asia Minor.

Scenes of Imperial audiences, with the Emperor frontally seated and quite immobile amongst his equally impassive subjects, mark further acceptance of an Oriental aesthetic since the time of Severus, but one by no means unexpected to anyone who has looked at art from Palmyra or Dura Europus. The most famous sculpture from the tetrarchy is the portrait group of the complete college of four emperors, now in St Mark's Square, Venice (AD 285–305), but once in Constantinople. The work was carved in Egyptian porphyry, a purple stone used only for sculptures of members of the Imperial family. Each emperor is indistinguishable from his fellows; they have identical mask-like faces, jeweled daggers and diadems. Their personal characteristics are not of interest; all that matters is their status (and so, their large eyes proclaim, they are less human than forces of mediation between the gods and men). Similar porphyry sculptures, for example the figures of Diocletian and Maximian in the Vatican, the head of Constantius I (?) in the British Museum, London, and the bust of Licinius (from Athribis) in Cairo, are equally harsh, equally untouched by ordinary emotion. The humanistic traditions of the Greco-Roman portrait here gave way to the all-seeing eye of the Imperial icon.

To understand the origins of late Roman or Byzantine art we must consider the Roman attitude to the gods and the supernatural. The forms of state art did not, and were not meant to, fulfil an emotional need though it was widely believed that it was both wise and well-mannered to observe *Pax Deorum*. The army regularly initiated official acts of worship and it is not surprising to find that the late Roman fort at Luxor in Egypt contained a shrine and magnificent paintings of emperors and their bodyguards, now unfortunately lost—destroyed by Egyptologists in their scramble for pharaonic reliefs below. Here the *numen*, the divine spirit as opposed to the earthly body, of the emperor and the gods of the Roman state were venerated with fitting pomp.

For private worship men turned to whichever deities most attracted them: Aelius Aristides, the apologist of the 2nd-century Empire to Asklepios; Apuleius (*c* AD 123–late 2nd century) to Isis; and presumably the owners of the great Dionysiac (Bacchic) pavement in Cologne to Dionysos (late 2nd century). Sometimes the cults were relatively new importations, such as Mithraism, but by no means always. Worshipers at the temple of Mithras in London venerated the Iranian god, but the best sculpture from it is a head of the Egyptian Serapis of late Antonine date, while a small votive group of Dionysos and his *thiasos* offers "life to wandering men" in an accompanying inscription. This is unlikely to antedate the 3rd century. As in the Hellenistic world, people expected their gods to be saviors, and it is in this capacity that Dionysos and Hermes are shown on sarcophagi.

Emperors who brought security, for example Diocletian and Maximian, were hailed as having "Jovian" or "Herculean" characteristics; from here is was a short step to regarding them as different from the rest of humanity. It might have been thought that Christianity, which became the religion of the Roman state under Constantine, would have abolished such pretensions. Instead, it further established them by attributing to the Emperor the function of God's deputy on earth. The enormous marble head of Constantine, now in the Palazzo dei Conservatori in Rome, is impressive and mask-like, scanning the world through great drilled eyes in approximation to the divine ruler of the universe (*Cosmocrator*). A parallel may indeed be noted in the Christ painted in the Catacomb of Commodilla in Rome.

The old human values had not been forgotten; at its lowest level the reuse of pillaged Hadrianic and Antonine sculpture in the Arch of Constantine (and the inept Victories, river gods, and captives of contemporary date) display an awareness of earlier traditions. A ceiling painting from the Imperial Palace at Trier (Bischöfliches Museum, Trier) shows female members of the Imperial family, which are highly accomplished portraits in their own right, and a cameo in the Hague portrays

Head of the Egyptian deity Serapis. Museum of London

Constantine, his mother Helena, his wife Fausta, and his son Crispus in a chariot pulled by centaurs. The workmanship, if a little heavy, is classical enough to have led the great German scholar Adolf Furtwängler to suggest that it was a Julio-Claudian work showing the British triumph of Claudius. In some measure, of course, it *is* based on a 1st-century state cameo just as some of Constantine's coins attempt to suggest that he was the new Augustus Caesar.

To a greater extent than before, Roman art in the 4th century was eclectic. For the most part, though not exclusively, the freer, classicizing works are associated with paganism and the hieratic formalism of the Conservatori head or the little friezes on the Arch of Constantine (showing the Emperor elevated and separated from his subjects) with Christianity and the Imperial Court.

Aristocratic patronage is well represented in the many examples of 4th-century silver frequently unearthed in hoards. Silver plate tends to be very conservative in appearance, and the range of pagan subject matter suggests a far from moribund interest in the old cults. A picture-dish from Ballana, Nubia, probably looted from Roman Egypt (Egyptian Museum, Cairo) shows a deity who combines the attributes of

Apollo with those of Hermes, Dionysos, and other deities such as Ares and Hephaestos. The plate illustrates the tendency to "syncretize" the gods and to see them all as the manifestation of a greater whole.

The great Oceanus Dish in the Mildenhall Treasure (British Museum, London) depicts Dionysos with his *thiasos*, satyrs, maenads, Pan, and Hercules, dancing around an inner register of nereids and tritons. At the center is the mask of a sea-god which has given the dish its name. Although found in Britain with several other splendid pieces of silver it was not manufactured there, but imported from the Mediterranean area. Another British find, from Corbridge (Alnwick Castle Collection) is a *lanx* (rectangular dish) which depicts a group of deities, notably Apollo, worshiped on Delos. It was probably made to celebrate the emperor Julian's visit there in AD 363. Julian was a convert from Christianity to the old religion and his "apostasy" may have given considerable encouragement to pagans, even after his untimely death fighting against the Persians (later that year). The hope of a future pagan revival lingered at least until the end of the century.

Instead of the saints of Christianity, the pagans venerated their heroes, especially Achilles. The Achilles dish from Kaiseraugst (Römermuseum, Augst) has a central *emblema* which portrays the hero disguised amongst the daughters of Lycomedes, and, on the rim, a number of other scenes from the early life and education of the hero. It is certainly 4th century in date, and the didacticism of the piece can be regarded as a deliberate counterblast to the teaching aspects of Christian art, for example the silver flask found at Traprain Law near Edinburgh (Museum of National Antiquities of Scotland, Edinburgh) or sarcophagi from the Les Aliscamps Cemetery, Arles, or the Church of S. Felix, Gerona, with scenes from the Old and New Testaments.

Similar aristocratic patronage may have been responsible for the "Rothschild-Lycurgus" cup in the British Museum, London, which belongs to the type of glass vessel known as *diatreton*. These were beakers, laboriously cut out in two layers; essentially a cameo-cutting technique used on the Portland Vase, though no doubt it required even greater technical expertise virtually to separate the two strata. The Rothschild cup depicts Lycurgus, one of the enemies of Dionysos, being strangled by the nymph Ambrosia, whom he had been pursuing and who had conveniently been metamorphosed into a vine. Other *diatreta* were purely decorative and were cut in such a way that the outer layers present a trellis of geometric forms. Magnificent examples have been found both at Cologne and Trier.

An art that made considerable headway in the 4th century was that of the mosaicist. Hitherto his form of decoration had been principally confined to floors, but now it invaded vaults as well. The church of S. Constanza was built as a mausoleum for Constantina, Constantine's eldest daughter (*ob.* mid 4th century AD). As yet there was nothing specifically Christian about its mosaics, indeed the art was studiously neutral. The various emblems of immortality were scattered around the

The Achilles dish from Kaiseraugst; 4th century. Römermuseum, Augst

annular vault as on Sosos' "unswept floor" mosaic (of which a copy from the Aventine is to be seen in the Vatican). Here are shells, peacocks, and pomegranates which most directly bring to mind the voyage of the soul over the sea to the islands of the blessed, the journey of the soul to the sky and immortality, and the Persephone myth with its promise of future resurrection. Another vault mosaic depicts amorini treading grapes and vintaging, a reference to Dionysos. No doubt a Christian could have accepted these symbols indeed, vintaging cupids are shown on a porphyry sarcophagus from the church (Vatican Museums, Rome), presumably Constantina's. Another contemporary mausoleum, perhaps that of Constans, one of Constantine's sons, at Centcelles near Tarragona in Spain, had a complex vault decoration which is admittedly Christian in part but also has some lively hunting scenes which are reminiscent of hunt mosaics from Utica and Carthage (British

A diatreton (cage cup); c300 AD

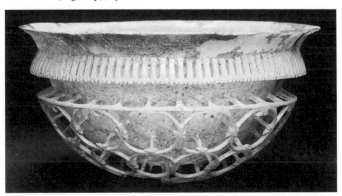

The Hinton St Mary Mosaic

The mosaic discovered at Hinton St Mary, Dorset, England, in 1963, and now in the British Museum, London, measures 28 ft 4 in by 19 ft 6 in (8.6 m by 6 m). It covered the floor of a square room with its vestibule which comprised part of a country house dating from the early 4th century AD.

Dominating the room is a roundel containing the bust of a man, clean-shaven and endowed with large, staring eyes. On either side is a pomegranate, symbol of immortality, and behind his head the sacred Christian monogram, the *Chi-Rho*, composed of the first two letters of Christ's name in Greek. There is little doubt that the figure is Our Lord although the placing of *signum Salvatoris Christi* on floors was specifically forbidden by an imperial decree of AD 427, which perhaps implies that such an abuse was known earlier. It is probable that the design of the pavement was originally intended for a mosaic vault of a type found surviving in late Roman churches of the Mediterranean area, for example the one in the apse of the Cappella di S. Aquilino in the church of S. Lorenzo, Milan, which also portrays a youthful Christ. Certainly the scenes in the lunettes, three of which show hounds chasing deer and a fourth, the Tree of Life, as well as busts occupying the corners of the panel (and presumably derived from wind deities or seasons although they have been bereft of pagan attributes and might now symbolize the Evangelists), could only all be viewed the right way up at the same time if the vault explanation for the composition is adopted.

The central motif in the vestibule is a roundel showing the hero, Bellerophon, mounted upon the winged horse Pegasus, holding a spear in his right hand with which to pierce the monstrous Chimaera. Unfortunately the figure of Bellerophon was damaged and patched in the later 4th century, and the mosaicist has shown the Chimaera as a gamboling feline with a rather lifeless goat-head emerging from its back and an equally unconvincing serpent as a tail. Nevertheless, the composition is relieved by a bold linear sense and an attractive control of color. The legend is fairly common in ancient art, and indeed was the motif on a Greek pebble-mosaic from Olynthos dated to the 4th century BC. In late Antiquity it assumed a Christian significance as the victorious struggle of Good against the powers of Evil. It was found on a mosaic at the nearby villa at Frampton (which incidentally also had a *Chi-Rho* device) as well as at Lullingstone in Kent, a villa with a Christian painted chapel. A fragment of bronze sheeting in the Historisches Museum der Pfalz, Speyer, displays the motif in relief alongside another roundel containing portraits of the family of Constantine, the first Christian Emperor, while a signet ring found at Havering-atte-Bower, Essex, which also shows Bellerophon and the Chimaera, is certainly of late Roman date, when Christianity was the official religion of the Empire.

▼ From the Hinton St Mary Mosaic: Bellerophon on his winged horse Pegasus slays the monstrous Chimaera. British Museum, London

▼ In the church of S. Lorenzo, Milan: the youthful, beardless Christ in the apse of the Capella di S. Aquilino

► From the Hinton St Mary Mosaic: the Head of Christ. The pomegranates on either side are symbols of immortality. British Museum, London

On either side of this scene is a rectangular panel which, like the three lunettes already mentioned, show hounds and deer. They may be interpreted either as continuations of the Bellerophon theme, the struggles of the Christian life, or as symbolizing the joys of Paradise. Similar hunting scenes are recorded elsewhere in Christian contexts—for instance in the Basilica of Cresconius, Djemila—although once again the theme was adapted from the common repertory of secular art (for instance, the *Little Hunt* at Piazza Armerina).

The style of the mosaic is almost identical with that found in other mosaics from the same area and especially the example from Frampton already mentioned. It was laid by a highly original school of mosaicists which almost certainly had its headquarters at the nearby town of Dorchester (*Durnovaria*). Clearly this was no ordinary villa dining room but must have been a small chapel with a narthex containing the Bellerophon scene, symbolizing the Christian's struggles against the evil of the world, and the cult-room itself, dominated by the sublime figure of Christ as *Cosmocrator*—Ruler of the Universe.

MARTIN HENIG

Further reading. Painter, K.S. "The Design of the Roman Mosaic at Hinton St Mary", *Antiquaries Journal* vol. LVI, (1976) pp49–54. Toynbee, J.M.C. "A New Roman Mosaic Pavement found in Dorset", *Journal of Roman Studies* vol. LIV, (1964) pp7–14.

◄ From the villa at Lullingstone, Kent: another example of Bellerophon and the Chimaera (*in situ*)

▼ The Little Hunt at Piazza Armerina. Villa Romana del Casale, Sicily

Museum, London) and of the Little Hunt floor mosaic at Piazza Armerina in Sicily.

Hunting was an activity that cut across religious differences. At Piazza Armerina we see not only the normal activities of the chase where the quarry was boar or deer, but also a great mosaic which shows ferocious lions, leopards, and other exotic fauna being captured alive for exhibition in the Roman arena. The presiding magistrate in his rich robes has been identified as the Emperor Maximian, but it is possible that the floor was laid at a later date, perhaps the mid 4th century. Obviously, the owner of the great country estate centered on Piazza Armerina was immensely rich, but so were several members of the late Roman aristocracy, such as Q. Aurelius Symmachus, who was known to have had specific responsibility to put on shows for the Roman people. The pagan nature of other floors at Piazza Armerina depicting Hercules, the myths of Lycurgus and Ambrosia, and of Ulysses blinding Polyphemus, is not in doubt.

As in the case of silver plate much valuable evidence comes from Britain—in the 4th century a land with many large villas, some no doubt owned by members of the native aristocracy and others by men whose fathers and grandfathers had fled Gaul in the civil unrest and invasions of the 3rd century. Of course silver plate could be imported, but mosaics had to be laid on the spot. Firms of mosaicists thus grew up in the towns of the province. At Cirencester there was a workshop with a particularly robust sense of color, line, and pattern. Indeed, one example of a Corinian pavement has been found at the capital city of Trier. An especially notable floor depicting Orpheus and the beasts was laid at the palatial residence at Woodchester—did it belong to the governor of Britannia Prima? Orpheus occupies a central roundel, which is encircled by an inner register of birds and an outer one of quadrupeds. A similar but simpler mosaic was laid in the villa at Barton Farm, just outside the walls of Cirencester (Corinium Museum). Mosaics from Chedworth, Gloucestershire, and Stonesfield, Oxfordshire, portrayed Dionysos. The latter, known only from an engraving, showed the god with his panther in a circular medallion surrounded by a rich border (incorporating a running scroll which appears to issue from the head of Neptune). The Chedworth mosaic can be presumed to have been the centerpiece of a floor which retains part of its octagonal, segmented surround containing vigorous portrayals of nymphs and satyrs. All these mosaics have decorative motifs in common, for example the Stonesfield scroll is also found at Chedworth and Woodchester.

The Corinium mosaics display a well-mannered paganism, which, as in S. Constanza, would not have been obnoxious to Christians. Indeed Christian and pagan motifs are combined in mosaics from Frampton (no longer extant) and Hinton St Mary (British Museum, London), both laid by the firm of mosaicists from Dorchester, Dorset. Both depict the Christian *Chi-Rho* and the latter the head of Christ as well; but they also portray Bellerophon on Pegasus slaying the Chimaera, and at Frampton the head of Neptune, and figures of Bacchus

The Hare mosaic from a house in Cirencester. Corinium Museum, Cirencester.

and Venus and Adonis are shown as well.

Some of the best Romano-British mosaics depict genre scenes like the chariot race at Horkstow, Lincolnshire (British Museum, London), the leopard leaping on to a gazelle from the villa at Dewlish in Dorset, which demonstrates an interest in wild animals similar to the Piazza Armerina mosaic, and the hare mosaic from Cirencester, showing a much quieter approach to nature.

The late Roman aristocracy had scholarly pretensions and in Taunton Museum, a mosaic from Low Ham, Somerset, England, shows episodes from the *Aeneid* dealing with the wanderings of Aeneas and his sojourn at Carthage. It is probable that this floor was actually copied from an illuminated manuscript such as the *Vergilius Romanus* in the Vatican Library, which with its bold, linear outlines and rich colors seems to belong to a Romano-British or Romano-Gaulish milieu. More conventionally Classical in feeling, but less imaginatively drawn, the *Vergilius Vaticanus* (also in the Vatican Library) shows how the neoclassical style could survive in the minor arts through the medium of copying. A translation into ivory of a couple of pictures of priestesses pouring libations (Victoria and Albert Museum, London; Musée Cluny, Paris) demonstrates that a real understanding of Classical canons of beauty could be kept alive by craftsmen in the circle of wealthy aristocrats, like Quintus Aurelius Symmachus and Nichomachus Flavianus who commissioned the ivory diptych cited above to celebrate their children's wedding in AD 393/4.

A remarkable late Roman pagan shrine in the Via Livenza,

Rome, has a fine fresco portraying the goddess Diana hunting in a woodland setting, and a mosaic floor discovered in the Kornmarkt at Trier seems to come from a room of similar function as Jupiter and Leda with their offspring, Castor, Pollux, and Helen of Troy, appear together with a number of votaries of a cult (Landesmuseum, Trier). For the most part the religion of the last pagans was a private and small-scale affair. The philosopher Proclus in Athens (AD 411–85) who dreamed that the goddess Athena had asked him to give her sanctuary as she had been ejected from her home in the Parthenon, is a good example of late Antique piety and of the essentially quietist nature of the faith of the last champions of the Greek and Roman gods.

Unlike the dividing point between "Greece" and "Rome" (the occurrence of which is a matter for debate since in the east there was complete cultural continuity) the religious and social fabric of life was now threatened. The public celebration of cult acts was forbidden by Theodosius (AD 391) and temples were pillaged throughout the Empire by undisciplined mobs. It is a mistake to think of the "barbarians" merely as an external threat when temples and the academies of classical learning were under attack from illiterate peasants such as the *Circumcelliones* in north Africa. Nor did it make any difference that this "vandalism" was perpetrated in the name of a Christian emperor.

The old cults had dwindling numbers of adherents in the towns—few people could match up to the bravery of Hypatia, martyred by a rabble of monks in Alexandria (AD 415). Insofar as it survived under the protection of rich senators or eminent philosophers, the Hellenic faith belonged to the sort of coterie we glimpse in Macrobius' *Saturnalia*. Elsewhere worship of the gods lingered in the countryside which was less touched by Christianity than the towns. In Britain there are examples of rural shrines at Lydney in Gloucestershire (which even had a fine mosaic commissioned by an official of the temple) and at Maiden Castle near Dorchester, Dorset. Thus, the ancient cults of whatever origin became known to posterity as "Paganism", the religion of the *pagani*—countrymen.

The art of the court which we contrasted with that of the aristocracy continued to follow in the formal, nonclassical traditions of the Arch of Constantine and the Conservatori head. The bronze head of Constantius II in the Capitoline reminds us of the historian Ammianus Marcellinus' description of that Emperor seated immobile on his horse and looking neither right nor left. The style became even more rigid and a head found at Constantinople showing the Emperor Arcadius portrayed even the hair as a kind of extension to the diadem. Empresses followed suit, as we may see on the Rothschild Cameo (Rothschild Collection, France) with its portraits of Honorius and his wife Maria (although other identifications have been proposed; not surprisingly for it is almost impossible to tell 4th-century emperors apart). In the whole parade of 4th-century portraits it is only with those of the Pagan Julian (and on coins, Procopius his kinsman and Eugenius who was trying to take power at the end of the century with pagan support) that we find any real individuality. Here an attempt was made to return to Antonine prototypes but the sculptors and die-engravers were not sure how to give life to the face and injected rather too much of 4th-century stiffness and formalism into their basic designs. The cleanly "chiseled" beard on Julian's portraits and his philosophic mien, however, add variety to what is otherwise the depressing end of one of Rome's greatest art forms.

A coin of Constantius II   A coin of Julian

The Emperor Constantine built a new Imperial Capital on the Bosphorus. Although there had been a Greek city—Byzantium—on the site, the massive scale of the new works made Constantinople a place unencumbered by the trammels of pagan tradition. Here was a "New Rome" in every sense.

A number of works of art were gathered from sites where they had been venerated for ages and here set up as mere secular embellishments to the city. The bronze tripod from Delphi standing on a base of three entwined snakes was thus reerected in the hippodrome where part of the base survives. Rather different was the case of the Column of Arcadius which set out to imitate the forms of Trajan's Column and the Column of Marcus Aurelius. Only a small fragment remains, but fortunately some fine drawings of it were executed in the 16th century. Here the past was being manipulated to serve the turn of imperial propaganda. The ruler sits in state and is adored by his subjects. He does not *lead* his soldiers into battle as their comrade and friend, like Trajan or Marcus, but rather *presides* over the exploits of his army.

An Egyptian obelisk brought, like the tripod, to the hippodrome from elsewhere stands on a sculptured base that depicts Theodosius presiding at the horse races. He stands in a special box, a head taller than his companions, other members of the Imperial family. Outside the box we see his entourage and bodyguard. Below are the Roman people ranked in monotonous and unvarying frontality. Again, one feels, the Roman tradition of state relief has nothing left to say. Byzantine sculpture—screens, pulpits, sarcophagi, columns—can be charming but it is for the most part purely decorative.

Mosaic did not lapse into triviality, but had to find a new iconography, except where, for example, classical personifications could be useful. Victories became angels, and river-gods could represent the Jordan in baptisteries. In the Mausoleum of Galla Placidia in Ravenna we can still discern a link between Christ the Good Shepherd amongst his flock and the old Greco-Roman pastoral.

There are admittedly certain surprising survivals even in court circles, such as the 5th- or 6th-century floor mosaics in the Great Palace at Constantinople, showing men at their rural labors, and various animals and birds. Greco-Roman secular art struggled on, but without the beliefs that gave it sustenance. Compromise was impossible between the ever stricter Christian beliefs of the emperors and the ethos of the last pagans—"Not by one path alone can man attain so great a mystery" proclaimed the great Symmachus (AD 382) in trying to persuade Emperor Valentinian II to give the Altar of Victory back to the Senate.

A large silver plate found near Merida in Spain was evidently a costly gift celebrating the 10th anniversary of the reign of Theodosius (AD 388; Archaeological Museum, Madrid). It shows the earth goddess disporting herself with three amorini. She is similarly placed to the goddess on the Aquileia patera of early Imperial times, and even recalls Tellus on the *Ara Pacis*. However, above her there is no enactment of the Demeter myth nor affirmation of public missions; instead we see Theodosius enthroned between his sons, Valentinian II and Arcadius, within the confines of a shrine-cum-palace. They appear unapproachable, "like lizards" in the apt metaphor of Hypatia's pupil, Synesius (AD 370–413). Beside them are their bodyguard, of whom the same author writes

> their faces and foreheads are bathed in sweet perfume; they carry golden shields and golden spears. Their presence announces the appearance of the prince, just as the first, faint morning light heralds the rising of the sun.

The Roman achievement and its legacy. The Roman achievement was vast, but it depended less on individual artists and movements than in the fact that Greek and Hellenistic art did not perish, as have so many traditions of the human past, but were taken—by Rome—to distant corners of Europe and the Levant where they struck deep roots. Romanesque art was heavily influenced by the surviving monuments of the Empire and International Gothic saw the emergence of a classical style (at Chartres, Reims, and elsewhere) under the chisels of men who could never have looked upon a Greek statue. In the east, Byzantine art—different as it is from what went before— showed a constant awareness of its origins.

The similarity in the linear design of a tombstone from Murrell Hill, Cumberland, England (Tullie House Museum, Carlisle) and the figures of the Evangelists in the Lindesfarne Gospels (British Museum, London) has been pointed out by George Henderson. The portraits of Virgil in the *Vergilius Romanus* (Vatican Library, Rome) are even closer, and perhaps all three works of art taken together show how a local style in one province could effectively survive the Dark Ages.

But even beyond the possibilities of immediate survival, Roman art was one of the sources of direct inspiration to the Renaissance. Instead of copying and adapting the work of the Middle Ages, there were Roman statues to emulate and adapt. Donatello created his David in the image of Antinous, a cupid was closely based on an ancient bronze of Atys (such as the fine figurine that is one of the treasures of Trier Museum). The Laocoön, a rather overblown work of late Hellenistic times, apparently the statue praised by Pliny as "a work to be preferred to all that the arts of painting and sculpture have produced" turned up in Rome in 1506 and helped to mold the art of Michelangelo and his contemporaries. From statues it was but a short step to rediscovering the human body and its true proportions.

In the past century and half, enthusiasm for Rome has declined before new knowledge of Greek art in all its phases, and some well-known writers on art are extremely harsh in their judgment on Rome's achievement. Perhaps we are now beginning to see that this is unfair, and while some Roman sculptures and paintings are indifferent copies of Classical masterpieces commissioned by people with more money than taste, others are highly refined and subtle attempts to build on the labors of the Greek past. In particular we may single out the great sculpture workshops of Asia Minor and the inventors of Roman illusionistic painting. It should always be remembered that when Petronius wrote of Trimalchio's vulgarity and lack of taste, he was not describing a typical "Roman" but inviting us to laugh, with him, at the follies of the parvenu outsider.

MARTIN HENIG

Bibliography. Boëthius, A. *Etruscan and Early Roman Architecture*, Harmondsworth (1979). Boëthius, A. and Ward-Perkins, J.B. *Etruscan and Roman Architecture*, Harmondsworth (1970). Brown, P. *The World of Late Antiquity*, London (1971). Painter, K.S. *The Wealth of the Roman World*, London (1977). Pollitt, J.J. *The Art of Rome c 753 BC–AD 337*, New Jersey (1966). Strong, D. *Greek and Roman Gold and Silver Plate*, London (1966). Strong, D. *Roman Art*, Harmondsworth (1976). Toynbee, J.M.C. *Death and Burial in the Roman World*, London (1971). Vermeule, C. *Roman Imperial Art in Greece and Asia Minor*, Cambridge, Mass. (1968).

CELTIC ART

Celtic bronze flagons with coral and enamel inlay found at Basse Yutz
height 39cm (15in). British Museum, London (see page 216)

IN the eyes of the ancient world the Celts were a nation, though a nation made up of many tribes loosely grouped together, and always liable to break up into smaller bands. When and how the Celtic language arose is not known, but the archaeology of 2nd-millennium Europe gives some hints as to how this particular "nation" was consolidated. In the later 2nd millennium we find in much of central and western Europe an amalgamation of pastoralists and settled agriculturists. The pastoralist tradition brought with it the custom of burying the chieftain in isolated splendor with his weapons and other finery, and sometimes with his slaves and womenfolk. The other tradition appears more egalitarian, with large cemeteries of urn-burials, all much on a level of wealth. There may also have been small groups of warlike conquerors from further east who welded the older inhabitants into well-organized aggressive tribes. The pattern of barrow-burials, grouped around a defended hill site, found on the upper Danube, the middle Rhine, and in Bohemia, suggests the tribal center of a chieftain or even a minor king commanding a fixed territory.

A rather similar dichotomy existed during the 5th and early 4th centuries BC when the first truly Celtic art appeared. There was one zone of rich burials, known as the Zone of Chieftains' Graves, which spread in an arc from the eastern Alps through the middle Rhine and Moselle into Champagne, with extensions into southwest Bohemia and to the Loire. The burials were generally under tumuli and often held imported treasures, as well as fine work from local craftsmen. Beside this, and only slightly later in its beginnings, lies a second zone characterized by cemeteries, some very large, of flat inhumation graves, which probably started in central Switzerland, with a minor extension into Burgundy in the west and a major extension eastwards through southwestern Germany to north Bohemia, Moravia, and the borders of Hungary. In Champagne the zones overlap. It is from this Flat-grave Zone with its poorer burials and more uniform social structure that the main Celtic expansion took its greatest impetus. A historical watershed comes c400 BC. By then some bands of Celts had already crossed the Alps into Italy, but the great expansion followed around, or soon after, 400 BC, taking one band to sack Rome in 379 BC and others a little later into Transylvania and the Balkans, till about 100 years later still Celts were looting Delphi and crossing the Hellespont into Anatolia.

The society that had grown up in the Celtic heartland, mainly the Chieftains' Graves Zone, by the 6th century BC, just before the appearance of La Tène art, was tribal, aristocratic, bellicose, and prosperous. This is seen especially in the richest burials, made in wood- or stone-lined chambers, usu-

Distribution of main sites mentioned

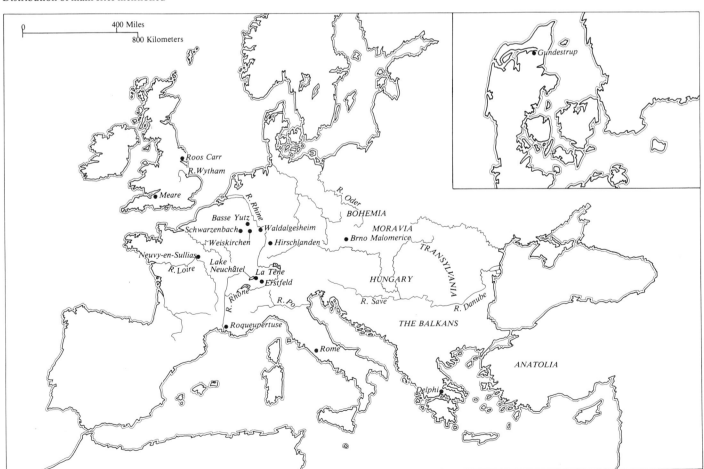

ally under round barrows. The cart, hearse, or later two-wheeled chariot, in which the dead were carried to the grave, was buried too, and the body was accompanied by weapons, ornaments, and other prized possessions, all of which were richly ornamented. The graves were grouped round fortified hill sites, and on top of one, at Hirschlanden in Württemberg, there stood for a few years an almost life-size, naked stone warrior (Württembergisches Landesmuseum, Stuttgart).

The rich gear placed in the graves included bronze tableware, Etruscan flagons, Greek vases, and even ivories from the Levant and silk from the Far East. Through these exotic imports Celtic craftsmen were first brought into touch with the products of Classical Mediterranean workshops, which they were to transform and make their own. The presence of these well-dated imported objects helps to date the beginning of early La Tène art. The new style appeared in the first half of the 5th century BC, but for a little while it ran parallel with the outgoing "Hallstatt" tradition. This aristocratic element, with its improved tribal organization, added to a heavier agricultural use of the land and, in a few places, overpopulation also contributed to the Celtic expansion at the end of the 5th century.

La Tène art. It is arguable that Celtic La Tène art was the first authentic art style to have arisen in Europe since the Upper Paleolithic. It is named after an underwater site on Lake Neuchâtel in Switzerland from which a quantity of bronze, iron, and other weapons were dredged, many decorated in a new, flowing linear style, unlike the earlier arts of Europe and equally alien to the Classical styles of the Mediterranean. La Tène now usually means the art produced by the Celts while they were still independent of Roman and other conquerors. It is generally speaking a small-scale art created for a warrior aristocracy that, in Stuart Piggott's words, "demanded flamboyant display from its head-hunting, charioteering chieftains and their petty courts; or somber trappings and imagery in the forest sanctuaries of a religion in which human sacrifice and the cult of the severed head played an important part. It is strange and unfamiliar to us as it was to the Greeks and Romans. So much of the finest work comprises small, intense and exquisite pieces of intricate workmanship in gold, silver or bronze, which capture and concentrate preciousness, virtuosity, symbolism and beauty". It was among the 6th- and early 5th-century BC Celtic-speaking inhabitants of the land lying northward of the Alps that this art was invented, for invention it was. There is no single source, native or foreign, and no gradual unfolding. In fact it is rare to find an art style so different from anything that went before, whose archaeological setting can be studied and understood, yet which itself remains profoundly elusive and unpredictable.

In describing La Tène art it is still best to use the system of styles and names worked out by Paul Jacobsthal in 1944, in spite of his Western bias, which excluded some important Hallstatt-based geometric material from the more easterly branch of the Chieftains' Zone, for Early style is in fact the art

The sandstone statue from Hirschlanden; height without feet 150cm (59in). Württembergisches Landesmuseum, Stuttgart

of the Chieftains' Graves. It was the suddenness of the appearance of this art that led Jacobsthal to formulate his three roots: the Classical art of the Mediterranean, received generally through Etruscan intermediaries; Oriental art, principally Scythian and Persian; and a native root, from the Hallstatt style of geometric decoration. In Early style the sources can still be discerned without much difficulty, but it was followed in the 4th century BC by a second or Waldalgesheim style which, though still receiving inspiration from Classical and Etruscan decorative motifs, is far more radical in its transformations. This in turn was followed by a heavier, three-dimensional, Plastic style; and running partly parallel with it, a more linear Sword style. British insular art began later than continental La Tène, but had a not dissimilar development.

The Classical root of the First or Early style has been studied more closely than the others. Palmettes, lotus buds, and

The Gundestrup Caldron

From the end of the last Ice Age votive offerings were made in the Danish bogs and meres. The most extraordinary is probably the silver caldron found in 1891 at Gundestrup near Børremose, Jutland. As discovered it was dismantled and has been reconstructed with the help of small portions of rim and an iron hoop. The sides are formed by seven outer panels placed back to back with five larger inner panels. They do not make a good fit and one outer panel may be missing. There is also a roundel at the base. All are decorated in high relief, hammered from below and chased above. The outer panels and base were originally covered with thin gold foil. At least three different artists worked on the panels and the author of the base was the most sophisticated.

Ever since its discovery there has been controversy over this magnificent vessel. It has been claimed as Celtic work on the strength of the iconography, and as Thracian or Dacian on style and technique; but there is some agreement on its date. The busts of the outer panels appear to represent male and female gods surrounded by their emblems, attributes, and elements of myth. They are dignified, formal, and static, their features tending to abstract pattern but in a manner not specifically Celtic. An exception is an uncomfortable female with attendants. The inner panels are alive with circular movement. An antlered god squats between a stag and a wolf, holding a "torque" and a horned serpent, and has been claimed to be a Celtic god; elephants, winged griffins, the combat of man and lion, and a person astride a dolphin (or more probably a Black Sea sturgeon) are ultimately Oriental or Hellenistic.

Another scene shows a tree of life, dividing spurred and helmeted horsemen from foot-soldiers, with three trumpeters blowing in-

◄ The silver Gundestrup Caldron, reconstructed; height 42cm (17in); diameter 69cm (27in). National Museum, Copenhagen

Below left An inner panel of the Caldron; 20×42cm (8×17in)

▼ An outer panel of the Caldron; 20×25cm (8×10in)

struments that ancient authors called *carnyx*. The Celts are known to have terrified their enemies with the hoarse sounds reverberating from their animal mouthpieces, and this *carnyx*, which was used by the Galatians in Asia Minor as well as by the western Celts, is the only exclusively Celtic object represented. The towering figure at the other end of the panel may be performing a sacrifice or else dipping a dead warrior in the caldron of revivification known in Irish legends.

The search for the stylistic ancestry of the Gundestrup Caldron begins near the Caspian in northern Persia where a wealth of gold and silver work was produced, especially in "Amlash" and at Marlik in the 12th century BC, in a peculiar "Animal style" which is a provincial version of Babylonian and Assyrian art. This style, which is quite unlike Scythian, can be followed westwards to the kingdom of Urartu in eastern Anatolia, to the Phrygians of the central plateau, and finally to the Thracian population of the Balkans. The lopsided drawing of antlers and the "hanging feet" of animals on gold work that is Urartian, though found in a 6th-century Scythian tomb at Kelermes in the Kuban, are conventions followed by Gundestrup, while in 4th-century Thrace, still independent though under strong Greek influence, the

local Thracian style of beaten goldwork looks even more like Gundestrup. Since this was the art of provincials its divergence from Greek and Persian-Achaemenian court art is explained. Certain medallions or horse *phalerae* found from south Russia to the Channel Islands show the style surviving into the 1st century AD.

Considerations of style and technique lead us to look for the Gundestrup workshop in a place where Thracian versions of ancient Orientalizing art were still executed, and where silver was readily available, which narrows the field to the Carpatho-Danubian region and the Transylvanian and Balkan silver mines. If the stylistic argument is preferred to more subjective interpretations of iconography, there is still the problem of

how the caldron reached the Baltic, and how it acquired its Celtic characteristics. There was a long tradition of northern contact with central Europe which continued through the last centuries BC. From *c*218 BC a Celtic kingdom existed in Bulgaria, but from this advanced position the Celts were soon driven back to their central European homeland, so that refugee metalwork found its way to the north as well as to western Europe. However, a western origin for the caldron still has its advocates.

N.K. SANDARS

► Animals on the gold sheathing of a battle ax handle from a 6th-century Scythian tomb at Kelermes in the Kuban. Hermitage Museum, Leningrad

Far right A stylistic ancestor of the Gundestrup Caldron: a silver beaker, probably from Marlik, Persia. Minneapolis Institute of Arts

▼ The base roundel of the Caldron; diameter 24cm (9in). The bull's horns are lost

► 4th-century Thracian metalwork: the top of a silver-gilt greave from Vratsa, Bulgaria; height 46cm (18in). National Museum, Sofia

tendrils, the stock-in-trade of the Classical repertoire, were taken to pieces by Celtic craftsmen and reassembled into still coherent but quite unclassical patterns. The gold openwork bowl from a grave at Schwarzenbach in the Hunsrück, Germany, is a good example (Staatliche Museen, Berlin). The eastern root is more elusive, for though objects in the Scythian style have been found in Hungary and even further west, the orientalizing root of La Tène art is more indebted to Persian (Achaemenid) objects which did not get further into Europe than Bulgaria. For some scholars all these oriental elements were filtered through Etruscan intermediaries, but they could have come by way of the Persian occupation of Thrace between 513 and 479 BC. This orientalizing takes the form of fine decorated drinking horns (never popular in the Classical world), in a taste for monsters, and for backward-looking heraldic pairs like those on a belt-clasp from Weiskirchen, Saarland (Rheinisches Landesmuseum, Bonn). The native (Hallstatt) root was probably a good deal stronger than used to be thought. Its importance appears in the Early style of the eastern Chieftains' Graves Zone with stamped decoration, and compass-based geometric motifs that take the place of the flowing designs of the west, though both are based on a Classical floral motif. Intersecting arcs and circles are built up into patterns that certainly owe something to the Hallstatt tradition. But there were some less rigid native arts surviving from an earlier phase of the late Bronze Age which may also have had a part in the genesis of Celtic art. In an astonishingly short time the diverse elements—floral, geometric, orientalizing, and classical—were fused together into a consistent style which is unlike any one of them alone.

Gold ornaments from the chieftain's grave at Waldalgesheim. Rheinisches Landesmuseum, Bonn

The gold openwork bowl from Schwarzenbach; diameter 13cm (5in). Antikenabteilung, Staatliche Museen, West Berlin

La Tène art, especially in its early phase, was the art of a warrior society. The styles were used in the decoration of weapons, parts of war chariots, and all the bowls and flagons necessary for serving wine in Barbarian versions of the symposium, adopted, along with the wine itself, from Mediterranean lands; as well as on personal ornaments: torques, bracelets, and belt-clasps. Celtic artists made their own version of the Etruscan and Oriental beaten bronze flagons with animal-shaped handles. Perhaps the most accomplished, as well as the most oriental, are the pair found at Basse Yutz in Lorraine, France (British Museum, London). The handle and rim animals, with their characteristic spiral motif for ears and joints, have their nearest relatives in the Urals where we find both at Pazaryryk, which is broadly contemporary, while earlier eastern examples are known in wood and bone. Technically these flagons with their enamel inlay are as fine as anything produced in Classical or Oriental workshops. A chance find of gold neck-rings and bracelets from Erstfeld, Canton. Uri, in Switzerland, though certainly of Celtic workmanship, contains four neck-rings in the most Oriental style of any yet found, with intertwining animal, human, and floral subjects. They may be allied to some of the more orientalizing ornament in Rhenish Chieftains' Graves, but they are quite unlike Etruscan work and their origin remains a problem.

The second style of La Tène art has been named after one of the last of the great Rhenish princely chariot burials found at Waldalgesheim, Kreuznach, Germany. It is probably early to mid 4th century BC, and so a generation later than the majority of the Chieftains' Graves. Like many rich Celtic burials it held the body of a princess, with her gold bangles and finely decorated bronze chariot fittings, and also an imported Italian bronze situla. The decoration of this was used by the native craftsman who worked with a new freedom, and an audacious, rather wayward attitude towards design which is also new. This second style appeared almost as suddenly as the first. There was no gradual transition, except perhaps on the Marne, France. It is markedly absent from the Zone of Chieftains' Graves and belongs to that of the Flat Graves in Switzerland, southwest Germany, and eastern France. This was the style that the Celts who had gone down into Italy, adopted in the early to mid 4th century BC, and which was also carried eastwards into Transylvania and to the Balkans. Throughout this vast region there was contact and exchange between workshops. One characteristic of the style, which was carried over into much later work, is a particular sleight of hand, by means of which designs that appear asymmetric in fact depend on the reversing and transposing of symmetric elements, to form a whole which partakes of both. The subtlety with which compass-work is disguised, and the linear twinings and convolutions that are made to appear organic and floral, but which turn out when examined to be abstract and inorganic, all belong to a peculiarly Celtic species of ambiguity.

Plastic style, which developed in the late 4th century BC, owes almost as much to the Early style as to the Waldalgesheim, a feature made possible by the chronological overlap between the two. It inherited from Early style the transformations of men and monsters and the visual punning. But there was a new treatment of man and animal in which mass and contour, body and limb became three-dimensional patterns with their own inner coherence, which is not that of the natural creature. The simplified swirl of contour is shown admirably on bronze openwork fittings of unknown function that were found at Brno Malomerice in Moravia, Czechoslovakia (Moravian Museum, Brno). There is also an abstract version of Plastic work which was used on bracelets and bangles from the Pyrenees to Bulgaria.

Sword style, or sometimes Hungarian Sword style, is so called because it was first recognized on scabbards and iron swords of the 3rd century BC, in Hungary and Switzerland. It shows a tendency, exactly opposite to that of Plastic style, towards flat, linear, often asymmetric designs of great elegance and sophistication. It had a very wide currency, and its source lies in the convoluted Waldalgesheim tendril and other abstract, sometimes asymmetric, motifs. The delight of the Hungarian swordsmiths in transverse patterns and in sym-

Bronze shield found in the River Witham; diameter of inlaid center roundel 15cm (6in). British Museum, London

Limestone Janus heads from Roquepertuse; height 22cm (9in). Musée Borely, Marseilles

metric, as well as asymmetric, designs owes most to an eastern Danubian Waldalgesheim, but the equally popular motif of a lyre in the guise of confronted dragon pairs with spiral twisted tails may have a western origin and was much used on Swiss swords. Tendril interlace seems to be a new development in this style, which also appears on spears and other metalwork.

Celtic religion did not require natural representations of the gods, or of the otherworld and its supernatural beings. This does not mean that religious ideas are not expressed in abstract and decorative designs. The large number of votive offerings found in sanctuaries, rivers, and meres suggests that they were. In monumental carving in stone and wood the religious dimension became explicit. Here again there are opposing tendencies, towards both the abstract and the natural, and there is a concentration on the head, severed or attached, as there is in Celtic literature and legend. A group of life-size and larger-than-life stone heads and figures from the Rhineland and Württemberg probably stood on the tops of mound graves. In a sanctuary at Roquepertuse in Provence, France, there are Janus heads with a characteristically sardonic physiognomy (Musée Borely, Marseilles); also friezes and seated figures, in which classical models can be recognized. Bronzesmiths also occasionally worked on a monumental scale, and one of their masterpieces is the boar, 1.26 m (4 ft 2 in) long, found in a sanctuary at Neuvy-en-Sullias on the Loire, and probably of the 1st century BC (Musée Historique et Archéologique de l'Orléanais, Orléans). Figures like this (especially boars) were carried as standards. Bronze caldrons were also beaten out with ornamental panels, though the most spectacular, a silver caldron found at Gundestrup in Denmark, owes virtually nothing to La Tène art.

La Tène art reached the British Isles at a late date and was in great part due to the arrival of the Belgae from northern Gaul. Before this time there was virtually nothing that could be called art in the British Isles, neither in domestic pottery nor metalwork, though there was a high level of technical accomplishment in the making of weapons and in the ornaments made by Irish goldsmiths; the work of the wood-carver is virtually unknown apart from the Roos Carr figures from Holderness, Yorkshire. But when the La Tène style of art did at last arrive it enjoyed an extraordinarily prolonged life. A few continental objects may have come independently of any settlement as early as the 5th century BC. Early style stamp-decorated pottery, and a little corresponding metalwork, was the immediate inspiration of the British Iron Age pottery found at sites like Meare in Somerset, and also for some of the decoration on the earliest British La Tène bronzework. There cannot have been any great interval between this and the continental models. Such comparisons give the needed link between the rich, inventive, continental workshops of the early 4th century BC (not all of them in the west), and insular art of the 3rd and 2nd centuries BC.

As on the continent, the finest workmanship was lavished on the warrior's panoply, and especially on shields, helmets, and horsebits, as well as the more usual swords, sheaths, spears, and bangles. The shield boss from the River Wytham is one of the finest (British Museum, London). Then, quite late, at the turn of the 1st century BC, mirror-backs were decorated with compass-based designs of great intricacy. An insular version of the Plastic style, using animal and human heads and animal handles, was developed, and there is abstract plastic ornamentation on heavy gold bangles. Many designs show an obsessional preoccupation with birds seen in profile, dismembered, or disjointed. There also grew up a deliberate use of the voids within a design for decorative purposes, which was developed to such a degree that negative and positive have equal weight. Basketry, sometimes done with a rocked graver, was

preferred as a filling motif to continental pouncing; and a crinkly line was reproduced by tapping along a ridge in place of filigree or beading. In Ireland this art survived during the Roman occupation of Britain where, as all over the continent, it was driven underground, only to reemerge in the rich aftermath of early Christian Celtic art, when many of the same designs reappeared and underwent yet another transformation.

From the 2nd, and still more the 1st, century BC onwards, Celtic tribes minted their own coins, based on the Macedonian gold *stater*. But the Celtic delight in misreading Classical subjects and employing them decoratively, became a vice and, by distorting naturalistic motifs, led to confusion and anarchy.

La Tène craftsmen inherited from Late Bronze Age metalwork-shops a superlative technique: great precision, control, and clean design. What had been lacking was breadth of treatment and subject matter, invention and variety. This deficiency was made good by the new artists who were masters of all the goldsmith's techniques except granulation. The use of the compass in the layout of designs was sophisticated and subtle, from 5th-century-BC Early style to masterpieces of ambiguity like the British mirror-backs of the turn of the 1st century, where an extraordinarily complicated deployment of the geometry of compass-arcs gives an illusion of flowing freehand draftsmanship.

In potting, the fast wheel was new to western Europe beyond the classical world, while some of the painted designs belong to the same decorative schools as the metalwork. Success in monumental sculpture shows that its rarity, and the concentration on small ornaments and personal gear, came from social causes, not lack of skill. Some have seen the hands of individual artists, but the point is hard to prove; certainly workshops had their individual styles. It is above all the peculiar sort of ambiguity of subject, the delicacy of techniques, the equilibrium and consistency, and its professionalism which ensure La Tène art a unique place among the art styles of the world. It possessed moreover a toughness which allowed it to dominate over much of Europe during four centuries, and to survive another four underground and on the peripheries (such as Ireland) until its second flowering in the early Middle Ages.

N.K. SANDARS

Bibliography. Cunliffe, B. *The Celtic World*, London (1979). Duval, P.-M. *Celtic Art in Ancient Europe*, London (1976). Duval, P.-M. *Les Celtes*, Paris (1977). Filip, J. *Celtic Civilization and its Heritage*, Wellingborough (1977). Hatt, J.-J. *Celts and Gallo-Romans*, London (1970). Jacobsthal, P. *Early Celtic Art*, Oxford (1944). Megaw, J.V.S. *Art of the European Iron Age*, Bath (1970). Powell, T.G.E. *The Celts*, London (1980).

13

PARTHIAN AND SASSANIAN ART

An Indo-Parthian bronze rhyton from the Indus region; height 25cm (10in)
Ashmolean Museum, Oxford (see page 220)

THE Parthians. Towards 238 BC the nomad chief Arsaces and his successors, founders of the Arsacid dynasty of Parthia, at the head of their followers, the tribes of the Parni and Dahae, entered northeastern Iran from the Caspian steppes. By 148 BC under Mithradates I, they had wrested most of the Iranian Plateau from the hands of the Seleucids, the Macedonian successors of Alexander the Great. Arts and technology of Greek derivation, mixed no doubt with recollections of the Achaemenid past, must at this time have been widely diffused in the urban centers. Naturally Seleucid art reflected the well-known forms of Classical Greece and the familiar deities of Classical mythology, represented according to the anthropomorphic conventions of the Greeks. The enormous wealth obtained by the Macedonians from captured Achaemenid treasures, or accumulated from later tribute, will have made possible the creation of noteworthy monuments, of which literary sources give hints, but of which next to nothing survives.

Such antecedents are reflected in the earliest Parthian constructions and artifacts. This first phase is represented, in particular, by finds from Soviet excavations at Nisa in Turkmenistan. The large number of ivory drinking-horns (*rhyta*) recovered from this site reflect Hellenistic influences in their decoration, though the form and origin of such vessels is Iranian, together with certain religious nuances.

In architecture, easily obtainable mudbrick was preferred as a building material, rather than stone. The peristyles of stone columns traditional in Greek, and in modified form in Achaemenid architecture, gave way to compound piers of mudbrick masonry, or to engaged piers attached to the wall face. In the latter arrangement, further visual relief was pro-

vided by alternating niches. The decorative details of the facades were rendered no longer in marble but in carved gypsum plaster, a medium capable of most ornate effects. The trabeate roof elements of earlier periods were replaced by the architectural arch, a major innovation, which had probably evolved at Babylon soon after Alexander. The Parthian arch, like the Roman, was semicircular. Its introduction was followed by the barrel vault, which effectively consisted of a series of juxtaposed arches, and took the place of timber roofing.

The development of the barrel vault in turn led to that of the *aivan*, a barrel-vaulted portico open to the front, which usefully provided shelter from the high midday sun, yet relieved the winter chill by admitting the slanting rays of morning, or of midwinter. A favorite ground plan of Parthian times, and constantly influential in succeeding centuries, was the rectangular enclosure with four interior *aivans*, one serving also as the entrance passage. By the close of the 1st century AD the mudbrick dome made its appearance for roofing a square chamber. The underlying square was accommodated to the circular dome by the bridging of its corners with arches to form a squinch. That this innovation was of Parthian date is confirmed by its appearance at Ribat-i Safid in Khurasan, where a fire temple of the subsequently classical "quadruple-arch" design is dated to the 2nd century AD on the evidence of associated structures. The palace of the Sassanian, Ardashir I, at Firuzabad, near Shiraz (c AD 224) used several domes, and though the work of the succeeding dynasty, must have been started under Parthian rule.

In sculpture, Hellenizing subjects progressively gave way (towards AD 50, a trend that has been associated with the

Distribution of important centers

Statue of Sanatruq, lord of Hatra; height 220cm (87in); 1st–2nd century AD. Iraq Museum, Baghdad

Detail of a fresco from the Mithraeum at Dura Europus showing, possibly, Zoroaster. Yale University Art Gallery, New Haven

prolonged revolt from the empire of the Hellenized city of Seleucia-on-the-Tigris) to a new insistence on themes that emphasized Iranian life and customs: equestrian feats, archery and hunting, with the typical Iranian costume of overshirt and baggy trousers, the latter essential for a life on horseback. In scenes of court life the garments were splendidly jeweled and brocaded. Princely figures wore a decorated "tiara" or an exotic crown. Already in Hellenistic art, profile representation had been increasingly replaced by three-quarter renderings made possible by the artists' increasing command of perspective. By the 1st century AD, a mechanical frontality became typical of provincial Parthian schools of sculpture, such as those of Bard-i Nishande in Elymais, or at Dura Europus and Palmyra. This was partly the consequence of technical developments; partly desired in the context of religious sculpture to focus the attention of the worshiper; and eventually a mere

fashion of the period, by which Parthian work and Parthian personalities are instantly recognizable. On Arsacid coinage, where legitimate successors followed the precedent of the founder, Arsaces, and placed their portrait to the left, the facing bust was usually an indication of rebellion.

The supreme medium of Parthian art was originally painting, but of the numerous illuminated manuscripts and frescoes that must have existed relatively few remain. The paintings of Kuh-i Khwaja (in Sistan), and of Miran in eastern Turkestan (the last more specifically Kushan, but showing details in Parthian style) give an indication of its quality. The Old Testament frescoes of the Synagogue at Dura Europus show Jewish subjects, but many figures are in Parthian costume. In the *Mithraeum* at Dura, the hunting fresco shows a typical Parthian scene. There are also many vividly sketched graffiti of Parthians sacrificing at an incense altar, hunting on horseback, or riding in cavalry armor. The Greek philosopher Philostratus in his *Life of Apollonius* describes palace frescoes at Babylon under Vardanes (AD 42). The heresiarch Mani (AD 215–73), the founder of Manichaeism, whose syncretic doctrines reflect the Parthian culture in which he was born, is said to have been greatly skilled at manuscript illumination, a craft pursued with devotion by his medieval followers.

The great Parthian rock sculptures at Bisitun, Sar-i Pul (Hulwan), and at Shimbar, Izeh, and Tang-i Sarvak in Elymais, employed flattish, low relief, with surface textures ren-

The life-size bronze statue of a Parthian chief from Shami, near Bard-i Nishande. Iran Bastan Museum, Teheran

dered in hatching—techniques borrowed from the draftsman and the painter, rather than typical of the sculptor. There were few sculptures in the round, although there is a marble head of a Parthian queen from Susa and a magnificent life-size bronze of a Parthian chief found at Shami. Especially splendid were the 2nd-century AD statues of princes at Hatra.

In the minor arts, marked differences prevailed between the various regional styles, for example between those of Babylonia and the Iranian Plateau. In the former district, pottery with greenish glaze is found in the shape of *amphorae*, and the typical "slipper-sarcophagi". Further east there are reddish, unglazed wares of well-fired clay. Spouted jugs, pilgrim flasks, vessels with zoomorphic handles and even a spouted *rhyton-amphora* were found at Shahr-i Qumis. Other sites of the period are barely investigated: but hemispherical drinking bowls of hard red pottery ("clinky" or cinnamon ware) with parallel forms in metal, have occasionally been reported, and may have evolved from the Hellenistic "Megarian bowls". In the Indo-Parthian region (Afghanistan, Punjab) pedestal cups are typical, usually in yellowish ware with horizontal burnishings. At Taxila and elsewhere, related forms in silver, horizontally fluted, prove the introduction of the metalworker's lathe. In glass, the typical form is again a hemispherical bowl (mold-blown), with wheel-cut facets.

Few textiles of Parthian date have been recovered (but notably at Germi in Persian Gilan, decorated with key, swastika, and chequer patterns). Arsacid coinage, in silver and copper, has somewhat stereotyped themes, with the recurrent reverse type of the Royal Archer. It is, however, of great historical interest, since the large silver issues are often dated not only to the year, but also to the month. Parthian seal-engraving, unlike that of other Iranian dynasties, is sparse and obscure, but a number of clay impressions are known from Nisa and Shahr-i Qumis.

An art style derived from that of Parthia prevailed also in the Arsacid "frontier kingdoms", where feudatory rulers maintained local courts (Elymais, Characene, Persis, Hatra, Adiabene, and Iberia/Georgia, besides Armenia, which, nominally a condominium, was subject to frequent and forceful Roman interference). Also Parthian in culture though politically independent was the kingdom of the Indo-Parthians (AD 25–60), whose Emperor Gondophares is said to have entertained the Christian Apostle Thomas. Here Iranian, Indian, and Classical influences were intermingled. After AD 60 the region was overrun by the Central Asian Kushans, under whose rule the "Greco-Buddhist" art of Gandhara made its appearance (*see* Indian Art).

The Sassanians. Towards AD 224 the dynasty of the Arsacids was overthrown by the Sassanian family, originating from the southern province of Fars (Persis). Though the capital of the new empire, like that of its predecessor, was soon established at Ctesiphon on the Tigris in Babylonia, the new rulers lavished special attention on their home province. The founder, Ardashir I (ruled AD 224–41) built there the circular city of

Ardashir I: part of a relief at Firuzabad; length 18m (59ft)

Gur, later known as Firuzabad. His son, Shapur I (ruled AD 240–72), founded Bishapur, further to the north. The greatest Sassanian city of the province, Istakhr, had long stood close to the ruins of Achaemenid Persepolis. All three cities are the sites of notable rock sculptures, some of the best-known monuments of Sassanian art. Those at Firuzabad immortalize the victory and coronation of Ardashir. The first, a scene of equestrian combat, in particular, employs the flat relief reminiscent of Parthian times.

The reign of Shapur I was celebrated for the overthrow of three separate Roman emperors: Gordian III (AD 238–44) slain on the Euphrates, Philip I ("the Arab") forced to sue for peace soon afterwards, and Valerian (AD 253–9) captured and carried away to Persia. In art, Sassanian kings are easily distinguished by their tall and bulbous individual crowns, which also appear on coinage. Roman emperors are generically recognizable by their gilded wreaths, but the identification of individuals is less certain. Panels showing the overthrow of one, two, or three Emperors by Shapur I may be seen at Naqsh-i Rustam (near Istakhr), at Bishapur, and also at Darabgird, south of Shiraz.

Bahram II (AD 276–93) and his chief priest Kardeir are prominent in sculptures at Naqsh-i Rustam (acclamation, equestrian combats); also at Sar Mashhad where a magnificent composition of a lion-hunt stands, no doubt with allegorical reference to their Roman antagonist Carus (AD 282–3). At Bishapur, Bahram's triumph over the Arabs is represented; at Naqsh-i Bahram, an enthronement scene. On the most probable interpretation, the newly discovered sculpture at

Tang-i Qandil, near Bishapur, depicts the same ruler's betrothal while still a prince, possibly to Shapurdukhtak, granddaughter of Shapur I. A similar subject appears at Barm-i Dilak near Shiraz. An equestrian combat sculpture of Bahram II at Rayy near Tehran is known to have been destroyed during the 19th century.

Later sculptures at Naqsh-i Rustam are an investiture attributed to Narseh (AD 292–302), an equestrian combat of Hormizd II (AD 302–9) with an unknown opponent; and perhaps Shapur II (AD 309–79) overthrowing the Roman Julian the

Bahram II (center) hunting lions: part of an allegorical relief sculpture at Sar Mashhad

Sassanian Silverware

Magnificent silverware was especially typical of the Sassanian period, and was much in demand for the banquets of the court, in particular the great festival of Mithra, the Mihrgan. On some occasions the plate may have subsequently been presented to the guests, especially to foreign envoys or influential tribal chiefs. During the 3rd and 4th centuries AD the prevalent shape was the *calotte*, a shallow segment of a sphere, standing on a foot-ring. The usual method of manufacture for the body of the bowl was by spinning on a lathe, a process often revealed by traces of horizontal striations. On the grandest examples the decorative figures were in high relief, shaped separately by the repoussé method, and attached to the interior of the vessel. Often, there was a separate inner shell which carried the figures. On simpler pieces, ornament was limited to incised decoration. Highlights of the relief were frequently gilded by the use of mercury

◄ A 4th-century silver bowl with high-relief decoration of the goddess Nana sitting on a lion. British Museum, London

Below left On a *c* AD 360 plate: Varahran II Kushanshah hunts boars; diameter 28cm (11in). Hermitage Museum, Leningrad

▼ On a 5th-century AD Sassanian silver bowl: Peroz hunts gazelles; diameter 22cm (9in). Metropolitan Museum, New York

amalgam. Later, during the 5th and 6th centuries AD, more varied shapes are attested. They include drinking-horns (*rhyta*) adorned with human busts or the foreparts of animals, plain elliptical bowls, lobed dishes, jug-like ewers, and flasks.

There are two main groups of decorative subjects. The first consists of representations of the Sassanian kings, either enthroned, or more frequently engaged in their favorite sport of hunting, usually on horseback. The individual personal crowns of the kings can in some cases be recognized from their coinage, as can those of one of the governors of Bactria (northern Afghanistan), princes who bore the title of Kushanshah. Several other unrecognized crowns may be those of unrecorded princes. The characteristic Sassanian dress consisted of long shirt and full trousers, with the streaming ribbons from neck and ankles that were indicative of royalty. Unlike the cavalry of the Middle Ages, the Sassanians rode without the use of stirrups, and their composite bow was drawn with the fingers, the arrow laid on the left side of the bow as in European archery. On the earliest group of pieces (4th century AD) the hunter-prince engages two formidable creatures, lions or wild boar. During the 5th and 6th centuries, the commonest quarry is a larger flock of innocuous herbivores, *mouflons*, or gazelles. The second main group of subjects consists of stylistically modified copies of the inconography of classical silverware. Dionysiac themes are prevalent, with frequent emphasis on the whirling forms of the maenads, female devotees of the god. It is likely that booty from Roman temples came to be dedicated in the Zoroastrian sanctuaries of the Sassanians, and later copied, with such modifications as a Zoroastrian interpretation of the figures might suggest.

The vast prestige attaching to the Sassanian court silverware led to the production of imitations in provincial centers, notably on the Caspian coast; and, with recognizable modifications of style, in most of the adjoining states, particularly in Sogdia beyond the Oxus and among the Kidarite Huns who occupied Afghanistan after c AD 380. Despite their religious inhibitions, the Muslim Arabs who conquered Sassanian Iran after AD 651 accumulated huge quantities of silverware, and their triumphant paladins occasionally indulged in banquets and wassail in the Sassanian manner. There are even a few bowls that can be dated on internal evidence to the period of Arab ascendancy, and others showing that the tradition was revived under Muslim Iranian princes, such as Adud al-daula, Prince of Shiraz (AD 949–83), the Samanids of Bukhara, and the Seljuk Turks. Inevitably, the appearance of antiquarian forgeries has been suspected in recent times, but their detection has depended in the main on stylistic judgment. Problems of authenticity have evoked a lively discussion in cases where a well-established provenance was lacking.

A.D.H. BIVAR

Further reading. Carter, M. and Grabar, O. *Sasanian Silver*, Ann Arbor (University of Michigan) (1967). Erdmann, K. "Zur Chronologie der Sassanidischen Jagdschalen", *Zeitschrift der Deutschen Morganländischen Gesellschaft* Vol. XCVII, 2, (1943) pp239–83. Ettinghausen, R. *From Byzantium to Sasanian Iran and the Islamic World*, Leiden (1972). Porada, E. *Ancient Iran*, London (1965).

▲ A 6th–7th century silver-gilt flask with scenes of a grape harvest. British Museum, London

Above right A female head and buffalo head decorating a 5th- or 6th-century *rhyton*. Cleveland Museum of Art

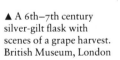

► On a Sassanian-style bowl produced under Muslim rule: an Islamic hunter; 8th century AD. Hermitage Museum, Leningrad

Apostate (AD 355–63). At Taq-i Bustan, near Kirmanshah, in northwest Iran, was a game park, pool, and grottoes decorated with sculptures of Shapur II (309–79) and Shapur III (AD 383–8), Ardashir II (AD 379–83), and Khosrau II (AD 591–628), all in investiture scenes. The last is rendered in high relief, with all the details of his splendid costume; and again below on his charger in full armor, perhaps on the eve of his invasion of the Byzantine Empire. This whole corpus of sculptures provides a notable record of the ideology, costume, and history of this dynasty, whose full significance is only gradually emerging.

Sassanian architecture developed logically from the forms which had been brought into being under the Parthians. Arch, barrel vault, *aivan*, and dome were established from the beginning in the palace of Ardashir at Firuzabad. However, the characteristic profile of all these forms was no longer semicircular, but elongated into an ellipse. Greater height and flexibility were made possible by the modification. Materials used in monumental structures included sun-dried brick, baked brick (appearing on the Plateau only towards AD 540, but earlier in Babylonia), or pebbles and rubble set in gypsum mortar. Squared (ashlar) masonry was used only in the most formal structures. Characteristic Sassanian building plans included the "quadruple-arched" fire temple, which was a square chamber, roofed with a dome on squinches, with open archways in each of the four walls. More elaborate fire temples were provided with a square (or cruciform) sanctuary, domed, and often opening into a large *aivan*, and thence to the courtyard. This plan had a notable influence on the evolution of the Persian mosque. An elaborate complex of Sassanian religious buildings, representing the fire temple of Adhurgushnasp, has been excavated at Takht-i Sulaiman in Azarbaijan. Structures at Firuzabad in Fars are still under investigation.

Caravanserais and forts were generally rectangular enclosures, with circular towers at the corners, and occasionally in

A leaping bear: a stucco panel from Ctesiphon

the middle of each wall. These towers were characteristically of "stilted" plan, so as to increase the projection of the tower from the wall line, and achieve more effective flanking fire. Occasionally, for example at Turang Tepe, the towers were given an elliptical plan, resembling the profile of the arches. Their lower stories were regularly built solid, for defence.

The most celebrated of Sassanian palaces is the Taq-i Kisra, at Ctesiphon, near Baghdad. The ruins of this complex, ascribed by some to Shapur I though traditionally the work of Khosrau I are said to cover 29 acres (11.7 ha). Its main surviving feature is the elliptical *aivan* vault, 84 ft (25.6 m) in span. Exterior walls are varied with engaged columns and niches. Other surfaces were richly ornamented with molded and carved stucco, which (here and at other Sassanian sites) employed geometrical motifs, hunting scenes, royal portraits, and heraldic "devices" in great profusion. Smaller palaces near Veramin, and at Damghan, probably of the early 5th century AD, possessed especially fine stuccos. Other palace complexes existed at Qasr-i Shirin, near the Persian border with Iraq, and at Dastagerd on the Iraq side of that frontier.

Another important vehicle of Sassanian art was luxury silverware, required for the exuberant banquets that were a feature of the period. The impression made by these magnificent vessels was often stressed in later Arabic and Persian literature. The open bowls were usually manufactured by turning on the lathe. Decorations were made separately by the repoussé method, and later slotted and soldered into place. The finest pieces often employed very high relief. Simpler works were merely incised or inlaid, and during the 3rd century the use of niello is found. Finished work was enhanced by gilding, which also served to cover joins resulting from the first method.

Such silverware was so greatly admired by later generations that more or less convincing imitations have been produced in every succeeding period. Products of the Islamic Middle Ages are usually recognized by anachronisms of technical detail and social custom, costume, and equipment. The characteristic crowns are inaccurately rendered on "post-Sassanian" works, or adopt the devolved forms perpetuated by certain Muslim rulers (the Buyids, Samanids etc). There is no reliable rule of thumb to distinguish modern antiquarian forgeries, though laboratory tests have provided some indications.

The most important early class of Sassanian silverware was the circular bowls depicting Sassanian kings (and several princes) hunting. Two groups have been distinguished, on the grounds of composition: in the earlier the king vanquishes two ferocious creatures and in the later the quarry is a whole flock of timid herbivores. There is literary evidence that silver bowls (especially no doubt of these kinds) were used by rulers and princes as diplomatic presents. Their manufacture may have been a monopoly of special court workshops. Less strictly ceremonial are a class of bowls, flasks, and ewers bearing subjects which allude to viticulture or revelry, and reflect the Dionysiac motifs of the classical world. These were no doubt appropriate for convivial occasions. Several other pieces display adaptations of subjects from Greco-Roman mythology, for example the girl carried off by the eagle on the bowl from Tcherdin in the USSR, originally inspired by the classical myth of Zeus and Aegina. Or the bowl in the Metropolitan Museum (New York) depicting two youths with winged horses, a subject variously interpreted as derived either from the Dioscuri, or from Belerophon with Pegasus. A later phase is exemplified by the numerous flasks with dancing or standing female figures, musicians, or the heraldic *senmurv* (griffon), a subject also carved on the robes of Khosrau II at Taq-i Bustan, and considered almost as an official badge of his kingdom. Many of these themes were echoed in various styles under the medieval Muslim rulers of Iran, for whom the prestige of the Sassanian tradition, and the appeal of its courtly splendor, outweighed the Islamic prohibition on figured representation.

Among textiles of the Sassanian period, it is above all the magnificent silk brocades that have survived, or have been perpetuated through the decorative tradition of later schools from Byzantium to Japan. Iran occupied a strategic position between China and the Roman world, and was thus able to capture the supplies of silken yarn, or to control the flow of silk thread, and of fabrics made from it, to the Mediterranean world. By the mid 4th century, important silk-weaving establishments had been founded in Iran, especially in the province of Khuzistan, and their ornate fabrics of highly characteristic designs were winning worldwide celebrity. Most typical was the use of animal and bird forms, within circular medallions, surrounded by borders of white bezants representing pearls. Several examples have been preserved with relics in the cathedral treasuries of Europe; others, now at the Louvre, Paris, or in Lyons, were recovered from a graveyard at Antinoe in Egypt. Typical motifs are the boar's head, Pegasus, the diademed ram, and the *senmurv*—all significant for Sassanian iconography. Hunting scenes are not attested in the surviving work; but imitations in the later derivative styles of medieval Iran suggest that hunting scenes must also have been used in Sassanian textile factories. The weave used in textiles of the Sassanian period is the "compound twill" technique. It is only in the ornate derivatives of Sassanian figured silks manufactured under the later Islamic dynasties in Iran that the more elaborate "lampas" weaves were introduced. The Sassanian figured textiles with their circular "medallions", followed by these later imitations, were imported to Byzantium, and also influenced the development of textile design in Europe.

Two lesser arts which attained distinction under the Sassanians were coinage and seal-engraving. The obverse type of the coins was throughout the bust of the reigning king, distinguished by his individual crown. The details of dress and ornament are rendered with meticulous care. On the reverse, with very few exceptions, the fire altar appears, symbolizing the Zoroastrian religion of the dynasty. Because of the fine style, issues from the first century of the dynasty have the greatest aesthetic appeal. Those of its last century (AD 551–651) on the other hand, offer the greater historical value, since they are inscribed with both date and mint-abbreviation. Silver

A fragment of silk decorated with a senmurv, a fabulous winged creature; height of roundel 36cm (14in); 6th or 7th century.
Musée des Arts Décoratifs, Paris

A silver drachm of Shapur I. British Museum, London

pieces, of thin, spread fabric, constitute the bulk of the coinage. Gold was struck only for rare presentation pieces, probably used at coronations. Sporadic issues are known in billon, bronze, and even lead. The east of the empire, in central Asia and Afghanistan, was ruled until AD 360 by viceroys of the Sassanian family, who issued separate coinage. Their distinctive crowns differ in construction from those of the suzerain rulers. In the east gold coinage circulated widely, as it had under the previous dynasty in that region, that of the Kushans. It was only in the reign of Khosrau I Anushirvan (AD 531–79) that really large volumes of silver coinage came into circulation in Iran, and rural economy passed on to a cash basis. For this reason, coins of the later reigns are relatively common.

Seal-engraving attained a high standard under the Sassanians, and output was copious—evidence no doubt that seals were required everywhere for legal and official transactions. Engraved gems are almost indestructible, and have therefore preserved a larger and more representative range of motifs than any other medium. The portrait bust is the most common subject, with headgear appropriate to the owner's rank—magus, scribe, official, or prince. The domed tiara was typical of the nobles, sometimes distinguished by a linear "device". Such marks originated as cattle brands, but were used to designate high office and membership of the chief aristocratic families. Human or divine figures are often found, singly or in groups. Gems showing a couple holding a ring between them are usually thought to come from wedding rings.

In the huge variety of other subjects, animal forms are numerous. Lions, camels, bulls, and stags are typical, but the wolf suckling twins is evidently reminiscent of the "Romulus and Remus" theme popular in Roman art, here probably rein-terpreted as a reference to Zoroastrianism. Particularly attractive is the wide range of fabulous creatures—Pegasus, sphinx, and griffon. Birds, of good omen in Zoroastrianism, are common, and there are also flowers and plants, and religious scenes showing fire altars and priests. Sometimes a seal was engraved with a "device" alone, and most of the finer specimens bear the name and title of the owner, carefully engraved in Pahlavi script. There is evidence that the Sassanian lapidaries were able to engrave on hard stones such as emerald and sapphire; even, it is alleged, on diamond. The majority of surviving pieces are on colored quartzes such as cornelian and onyx. After AD 500 jasper, rock crystal, and garnet become popular. Many of the stones were shaped as ring-bezels, some of remarkable size. Separate stones had the form of ellipsoids, and later, domes. In some cases an entire ring is carved out of a large block of quartz. More bizarre in style are the medical and magical amulets, recognizable by their subjects and the fact that the inscriptions are not reversed to read correctly from an impression.

A.D.H. BIVAR

Bibliography. Bivar, A.D.H. *Catalogue of W. Asiatic Seals in the British Museum, Stamp Seals II, the Sassanian Dynasty*, London (1969). Colledge, M.A.R. *Parthian Art*, London (1977). Ghirshman, R. *Iran: Parthians and Sassanians*, London (1967). Godard, A. *The Art of Iran*, London (1962). Harper, P.O. *The Royal Hunter: Art of the Sasanian Empire*, New York (1978). Herrmann, G. *The Iranian Revival*, London (1977). Herzfeld, E. *Archaeological History of Iran*, London (1934). Pope, A.U. *A Survey of Persian Art* vol. 1, Oxford (1938). Sellwood, D. *An Introduction to the Coinage of Parthia*, London (1971).

14

STEPPE ART

A bronze stag pole-top from the Ordos Desert; Han period
206 BC–AD 221. British Museum, London (see page 235)

THE term Steppe Art has come to be used for a certain group of interrelated styles illustrated by finds made mainly from the 18th century onwards in the excavation of tombs on the Eurasian steppe or near it. Some of the finds are of metal, bone, or wood, though not of stone. They served as ornaments, badges, or symbols on the clothing and equipment of mounted nomad warriors on the Eurasian steppes from Hungary to Manchuria. But sometimes figures in the same style occur on larger surfaces, such as textile fabrics, or on pieces of worked-and-dyed leather. These must have decorated the tents of nomads during their lifetimes, but they have been preserved for centuries afterwards by the accidental effects of the climates to which they were exposed in certain regions. Not all the materials mentioned were represented in any one place, but it is reasonable to assume that in most of the best-equipped burials all of them existed together before natural decay destroyed some or plunderers removed others.

The styles are thought to have prevailed during a period which began shortly after 700 BC and lasted into the early centuries of the Christian era, for different lengths of time in different places. In spite of their variety, they have a common feeling which is not that of civilized art, and a common origin among nomad peoples living beyond the steppes; but in their later phases they were subject to various outside influences.

The most characteristic manifestation of Steppe art is the well-known Animal style, as M. Rostovtzev first called it. Originally established *c*500 BC, the style represents animals, birds of prey, and certain monsters—particularly griffins—in a distinctive way. Remoter foreign influences also appear in the introduction of animals unknown on the steppes, such as lions and large serpents. But the tame animals on which the nomads lived are absent from the Animal style, except that it is not always clear whether horses found fairly frequently are tame or wild. There must have been a pervasive reason behind this preference for wild animals. The same nomads from time to time represented the human forms of warriors and hunters, and even of goddesses, but these are rare. Vegetation is found as a background in some pieces, mostly in ones known from the eastern steppes which seem to represent scenes from well-known legends. These pieces may be regarded as marginal to nomad art.

Though other peoples have created styles representing animals, these nomad styles are distinctive. The Animal style appearing in them was created by the white nomads—Indo-Europeans of the Iranian branch, who inhabited the western half of the steppes, extending from the Danube basin and south Russia in the west to Zungaria and the Pamir in the east. Tribal migrations also carried forms of it further eastward to regions within the range of Chinese influence. In its earliest and undeveloped form it is represented by small carvings in bone of the 8th and 7th centuries BC as at Zabotin in south Russia; the material limited both size and shape, and made necessary a certain degree of contortion. But the tradition that arose continued in such things as the metal plaques of the developed style.

The main development evidently resulted from contacts, peaceful or warlike, in the 7th century BC with the civilized peoples of the Near East, but it still resulted in a barbarian art. The effects of these contacts were spread far and wide, as if over an inland sea. The strongest influence in development beyond the earliest stage appears to have come from Iran, which, as R. Ghirshman argues, had such strong links with the steppes that these should be named "Outer Iran", particularly as before the Turkish expansion from Mongolia kindred languages were spoken in both regions. Iranian culture, apart from its own character, received much influence from Assyria

The Eurasian steppes

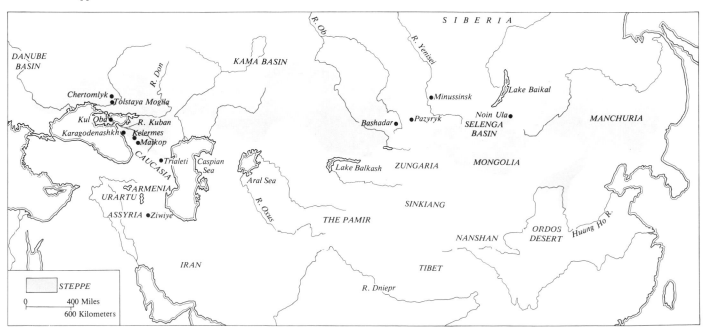

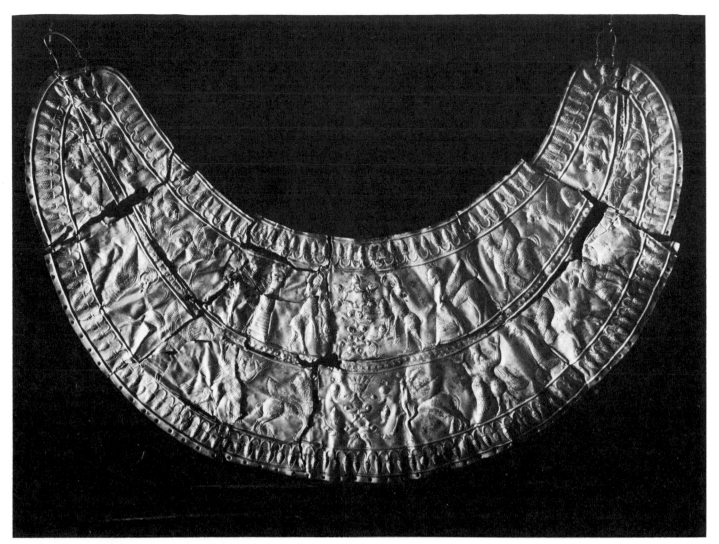

A gold pectoral from the treasure of Ziwiye. Archaeological Museum, Teheran

and from the ancient kingdom of Urartu in Armenia. The nomads were affected by both these older cultures whether by direct contact or by mediation through Iran. Direct contact often took the form of raiding and the carrying off of civilized craftsmen to work for nomad masters.

The spread of styles and techniques would still have been furthered by the perpetual movements of peoples on the steppes, particularly in times of disturbance. These movements could cross and intermingle and sometimes be reversed, making new patterns as currents in an estuary do at change of tide.

It is time to describe the various styles, region by region. The best known, and perhaps the oldest in its full development, is the Scythian style of the Pontic Steppe in south Russia. A Near Eastern prelude to this style is apparent in the treasure of Ziwiye in Kurdistan, a hoard of goldwork and other objects perhaps collected by a Scythian chief during the Scythian invasion (Iran Bastan Museum, Teheran). Two objects from this may be picked out. One is a lunate sheet of gold probably once worn as a pectoral ornament by the chief. It shows in two registers symmetrical processions of Phoenician and Assyrian monsters converging on a Tree of Life, in each case a small feline beast of prey of purely Scythian style bringing up the rear. The other is a piece of beaten gold plate bearing a repetitive design, in the manner of modern wall-

paper, in which stags and ibexes are represented entirely in the Scythian manner, each animal enclosed in a network of branches. The vegetation in both pieces is in Urartian style.

Scythian metalwork of just this kind, with features added from Urartu, was found in the great Scythian kurgans of the Kuban and the Dniepr. The stag with thrown-back antlers and drawn-up legs, prominent here, was a widespread emblem of Scythian origin, used on plaques decorating shields, bowcases, ax-handles, and pole-tops used as standards. A common feature, as in Siberia, is the beveled junction of two slanting surfaces, used to represent the rounded body or haunches of an animal. It is likely that this originated in woodcarving.

One southern animal subject was the lion, not a native of south Russia or Caucasia. It is a sign of Near Eastern influence. This influence appears again in such a creature as the panther figured on a gold plaque from Kelermes in the Kuban Basin (Hermitage Museum, Leningrad). It has hollows in its ears and paws which must once have been filled with cloisonné inlay, a feature of polychrome style as continued later in a Sarmatian work of an Asiatic tradition. From the illustrations it will be seen how vivid and lifelike the Animal style can be, careless though it often was of proportion and natural posture.

Among human figures, where they appear, the commonest are those of the Great Goddess, as found at Karagodenashkh

Goldwork from the Kuban: a panther-shaped blazon of a shield.
Hermitage Museum, Leningrad

in the Kuban, attended by her priests, and those of warriors carrying the severed heads of enemies.

Some of the goldwork from the Kuban and the Dniepr shows Greek influence from the Pontic colonies. Some later examples, such as the plaque and ornaments from Kul Oba in the Crimea, and a silver gilt vase from the rich burial of Chertomlyk on the lower Dniepr, are actually Greek work (both in the Hermitage Museum, Leningrad). Most striking of the

Greek work carried out for Scythian masters is a gold pectoral ornament from Tolstaya Mogila in the Ukraine (Hermitage Museum, Leningrad). Its outer rim shows a lion and a griffin attacking horses, and a lion attacking a boar, while its inner rim shows among other things a cow suckling a calf, two Scythian bondmen milking a ewe, and two other Scythians mending a shirt. All these representations are entirely Greek in style. Greek influence indeed contributed sometimes so powerfully to the native art as to destroy its original Scythian quality either in style or even in theme.

At the eastern end of Iran nomad presence during the same period may be assumed but actual evidence only emerges a little later, after the Median Empire had fallen to the kindred Persians. It is contained in the Oxus treasure, a large collection of goldwork of various dates, the earliest belonging to the height of the Achaemenid Empire or even a little earlier (British Museum, London). While many of the objects are in Persian style, some are so close to nomad styles that they may

Two griffins attack a horse on a gold pectoral from Tolstaya Mogila. Hermitage Museum, Leningrad

be taken to be the work of the Sakas of central Asia. Other specimens of Saka styles so far discovered are comparatively few and not striking. Large tombs discovered in this part of central Asia have proved to be empty. Otherwise we should have better examples of the styles of the Massagetae, the Saka people against whom Cyrus the Great fell fighting after he had conquered the rest of his empire.

Another, remoter link with Achaemenid Persia has been found north of the Saka territory in the frozen tombs of Pazyryk in the High Altai (5th century BC), which are also crucial for the understanding of nomad art in eastern Asia. A Persian tapestry from the fifth tomb, the oldest tapestry known, shows embroidered figures of women apparently performing a sacrifice. From their attire these should be Persian royal ladies. The same tomb contained the oldest known Persian carpet bordered with a procession of stags, and outside this another of walking grooms and mounted horsemen in Achaemenid style.

These imported textiles are of great interest as signs of contact with the Persian Empire, but they are not nomad art any more than the Greek and oriental metalwork earlier described. More remarkable and characteristic of the steppes is a felt hanging from the fifth tomb, decorated with appliqué felt in bright colors, showing a horseman in tight trousers and a short cloak riding up to a seated figure who holds in one hand something that may be a Tree of Life (Hermitage Museum, Leningrad). The seated figure appears to be female but completely bald under a heavy fur cap, while her chair is of Assyrian pattern. The figure is likely to be a local form of the Great Goddess. A strange monster in colored appliqué felt which appears on another hanging from this tomb is a human-headed sphinx with an animal body, wings, and apparently horns. The Near Eastern influence still seems to be present, but these hangings are unique.

The Animal style in appliqué felt and also in wood carving has a close resemblance to the Scythian, but the suggestion of formal monumentality which hangs over the Scythian figures is gone. Illustrations of these finds from the Altai show wilder and more bounding animals for the most part, sometimes with twisted bodies possible in a cat or weasel, but not in horses as represented. The style was making new departures. A wavy and rippling character is particularly noticeable in a relief on the side of a coffin at Bashadar in the central Altai (6th century BC)—the animal figures are tigers carrying prey. This quality appears even more in some Sarmatian work from the steppe north of the Black Sea (Hermitage Museum, Leningrad).

In the fifth tomb of Pazyryk further links with civilization are shown in a canopy decorated with figures of swans very much in Chinese style. The canopy once belonged to a carriage of Chinese form also found there. At this date the Persians of the Achaemenid period were not acquainted with the Chinese, but these nomads seem to have been in contact with both. Indeed, from a far earlier period, the Karasuk culture of Minussinsk (12th century BC) which had connections with

A winged lion attacks an ibex: an appliqué felt saddle-cloth decoration from Pazyryk. Hermitage Museum, Leningrad

A tiger carved on a cedarwood coffin from Bashadar. Hermitage Museum, Leningrad

Shang China, is regarded by some scholars as having contributed to the Animal style, after the advent of nomadism (8th–7th centuries BC).

Much longer known than the art of the Altai, but equally striking, are the gold plaques collected from tombs in southern Siberia in the 17th century by Russian prospectors and settlers on the initiative of Peter the Great and carefully preserved by his order. The actual sites from which these pieces came are not known though they came from the region of Kazakhstan, so that nothing can be said about the other contents of the tombs. Nor were the rich sources of gold in Siberia used in ancient times by civilized peoples ever traced. The subjects of Peter were interested only in amassing the gold, which they had intended to melt down. It was Peter himself who had sufficient appreciation of the art of these Scythian pieces to forbid the melting.

Like the art of the Altai, that of these south Siberian plaques was more full of life than the art of the Pontic Steppes and more varied in its choice of subject. The figures seem to mirror the outward life of the nomads and beyond that their imaginations and beliefs. Pieces with imaginative content show ferocious combats of wild beasts and monsters. There are also other kinds of plaque which have been called anecdotal because they seem to represent particular episodes in legend and story. In technique there is much use of hollows, as in some of the Scythian pieces. These contained brightly colored stones, and show affinities with pieces from the Oxus treasure which were probably made by the Sakas (British Museum, London). There are also affinities with Chinese art. Another eastern feature is the openwork form in which many of them are cast.

A good example of animal combat in this west Siberian style, dated to the 4th century BC, shows a lion-griffin, with small wings indicated on its shoulders, biting through the neck of a collapsing horse (Hermitage Museum, Leningrad). Like other animal victims of beasts or monsters, as sometimes also in the Altai, the horse is so twisted that its hind legs reach upwards and its forelegs and muzzle downwards. This twist is hardly found in Scythian work. Another plaque shows a more or less equal battle between a tiger and a griffin, in which both creatures seem likely to be mauled to death. Some of these animal figures reappear further east in the art of the Ordos Desert (3rd century BC), but in bronze, even if cast in copies of the same molds that had been used for the gold. The relation of these pieces and those of the Ordos shows the wide diffusion of this Steppe culture. The style is so intensely dramatic, that some powerful myth may be supposed to underlie it.

The anecdotal pieces again seem to be a new departure, representing episodes in the life of some nomad hero. Figures of ordinary mortals do appear in Scythian art, carrying the heads of enemies, but these human figures are different and far more interesting. One for instance represents a hunter on the forested edge of the Siberian steppe with drawn bow pursuing a powerful boar from which another rider has taken refuge by climbing a tree, while his horse seems to be trying to climb after him. A more mysterious piece likewise shows a forested scene, where a warrior lies with his head on the lap of a woman squatting on the ground and wearing a headdress like a Turkish *tarbush*, while a groom squats near them holding the reins of two horses. Such narrative scenes seem to be exclusive to the Sarmatian style in Siberia; they have not yet

been found among Sarmatian remains further west in south Russia or the Danube Valley. The figures of two wrestlers that appear in this art are known also in Scythian art. This seems to show that the Turkish and Mongol love of wrestling had a long ancestry among nomads. One apparently Far Eastern theme was the curled animal with mouth to tail, found from the Pontic Steppe to the Ordos Desert.

The Ordos Desert, in fact, is the next important region to consider. Though it lies on the southern side of the great bend of the Huang Ho and has usually been reckoned part of China, its people usually belonged with the nomads to the east and north of them beyond the Great Wall. Its style of nomad art was mostly an eastern continuation of the Sarmatian, but showed in many places a strong influence from China. The Chinese influence blended much more easily with the recipient nomad art here than did the Greek with Scythian art at the other end of the steppe. Indeed, further inside China pieces have been discovered in which Chinese and nomad characters are inseparably blended like the colors on shot silk. This is the so-called Huai style of Chinese art, just south of the basin of the Huang Ho. This shading of Chinese art into nomad might be better compared to the shading of Persian into Saka art which is seen in the Oxus treasure.

The Ordos bronzes are often difficult both to date and classify for Chinese and western scholars alike, since, as with the Sarmatian goldwork, their places of origin are not exactly known. But they cover the period when the Indo-European tide moving eastward across the northern steppes was halted and reversed by the Altaic current which is much better known in history. The critical moment in this process was *c*160 BC, when Giyu, ruler of the Hsiung Nu confederacy inflicted a crushing defeat on the rival confederacy of the Yueh Chih under its Iranian rulers, and drove them westward from their pastures by the Nan Shan into Zungaria and Sinkiang.

A forest scene with men and horses, in gold. Hermitage Museum, Leningrad

A gold curled panther from western Siberia; 6th century BC. Hermitage Museum, Leningrad

This appears to have happened during the period of the Ordos bronzes, which perpetuated an originally Iranian tradition under new masters, the Hsiung Nu. Like the Yueh Chih, the Hsiung Nu were a variegated confederacy, and it has been remarked that many of their tribes were white. It was perhaps these white tribes, probably speaking a Turkic language, who carried on the western tradition of nomad style in altered circumstances, and under some influence from the Chinese.

The pieces from the Ordos are plaques, belt-ornaments, belt-clasps, pole-tops, knives, daggers, and axes with some ornamentation, and occasionally human figures, even mounted ones. The Scytho-Sarmatian ancestry of the animal figures is clear to see both in style and in some cases in the suggestion of ruthless ferocity. But some figures, animal and human, are playful or grotesque in a manner not known elsewhere on the steppes; this is perhaps part of the Chinese influence. Within their sequence an earlier group is attributed to a time before the rise of the Han power in China in the 3rd century BC, and a later one to the period of continual warfare between the Han and the Hsiung Nu.

In the intervals of warfare the Hsiung Nu not only plundered northern China in an irregular fashion, but also traded with the Chinese. Traces of both kinds of contact are clearly seen among the contents of the tombs of Noin Ula in the Selenga basin south of Lake Baikal and east of the Altai, where Chinese goods, particularly textiles, are found along with specimens of nomad art (Hermitage Museum, Leningrad). There are also suggestions of another style of nomad art distinct from the Sarmatian. The name Noin Ula in Mongol means "Lords' Hill" and was doubtless given because the Mongols saw that many chiefs of peoples who had held power earlier than themselves were buried in this valley. Modern scholars are content to link the excavated tombs with the Hsiung Nu at the time of their greatest power and widest contacts. The chiefs were buried in strong coffins placed within timber chambers, very much in the Scythian manner. Two hundred and twelve were located in P.K. Kozlov's expedition, but less than 20 have been excavated. If the remainder are eventually excavated, there will be great gains for the history of the Hsiung Nu and later nomads of this region.

As the contents of the Pazyryk graves were preserved in ice, so the finds of Noin Ula were kept intact by water which had soaked through the ground and prevented alternation of drying and wetting. This was particularly advantageous because so many of them were rugs and carpets and other textiles, often Chinese, such as women's cloaks and bonnets. There were also some metal pieces similar to those from the Ordos. On one carpet a winged monster like a wolverine is shown attacking a bellowing elk; on another, less well executed, a yak faces a monster hard to identify (Hermitage Museum, Leningrad). The yak sometimes appears in Sarmatian metalwork further west, but was evidently an important animal for the makers of this art, for a silver plaque shows a yak with characteristic horns, and hair on its belly (Hermitage

A silver plate from Noin Ula decorated with a yak. Hermitage Museum, Leningrad

Museum, Leningrad). The head is shown frontally, not in profile as in Sarmatian pieces, and the feet of the animal show little relation to the rocks on which it stands against a background of trees. This piece seems to be of native inspiration, not in the Sarmatian manner.

More remarkable so far eastward is a tapestry showing two moustached faces of central Asian Turkic type, perhaps south Russians. Purely Chinese on the other hand is a tapestry representing turtles swimming among water plants (both in the Hermitage Museum, Leningrad). The stages in the decay of the Animal style in Mongolia may be further documented when more of the tombs of Noin Ula have been opened.

Our survey has carried us right across the northern steppes, where mounted nomads, at first all of them Indo-Europeans, practised the Animal style and others connected with it even in some parts east of Zungaria after 700 BC. Certain earlier traditions of art appearing, for instance, in the gold and silver figures of bulls from Maikop in the northern Caucasus and in the embossed vessels of Trialeti in Transcaucasia, were indeed continued in some of the regions included, but have been passed over because of their early date before the rise of mounted nomadism. But it is worth noting that the art of Maikop was deeply indebted to the arts of early Iran and Mesopotamia, and that of Trialeti to some traditions in Anatolia, before in each case links with the southern civilizations were broken off. Scythian art shows a revival of these southern links in new circumstances.

During the Scythian period the arts of Ananyino in the Kama basin and of Tagar in the Minussinsk basin of Siberia were strongly influenced by the animal art and weapons of the nomads but were not practised by nomads.

In south Russia the Scythians were succeeded in the 3rd century BC by the Sarmatians, whose art as known from Siberia has been described. In present usage the name of Sarmatian is used for Iranian nomads scattered over an immense area east of south Russia as far as the borders of China. In ancient usage the nomads of south Russia and the Danube Valley were sometimes called Sarmatians, but the name has no wider connotations. The Sarmatian nomads of eastern Europe fell under the rule of the Huns, who appear not to have used any form of the Animal style in the west, even if their ancestors had done so in eastern Asia. Under the next domination of the Danube Valley, that of the Avars, there appears to have been a certain revival of the Animal style during the late Avar period from AD 670 onwards, when the Avars were less influenced by Byzantine art than they had been in the first generations after their arrival. Their belt-plaques and belt-clasps, and the pieces of metal hanging from their belts to indicate rank, show a crude form of the Animal style, particularly in the figures of griffins, which it is natural to attribute to a revival of Sarmatian tradition, whether of local origin or carried westward from Asia. This tradition faded out early in the Middle Ages.

The Turks of Mongolia and central Asia did not, so far as is known, use art of the Scythian and Sarmatian traditions during their great age of expansion when they ruled most of the remaining Indo-European nomads. Elsewhere in Asia the Animal style survived for a time in northern Tibet, but is not otherwise known. In Europe the art of the Germanic tribes for some centuries contained traces of the Animal style, as might be expected from the several centuries of close contact between Germans and Sarmatians.

It remains to offer a few remarks on the significance of the Animal style. This element in nomad art may be regarded as aristocratic, for it has only been found in the graves of chieftains and important warriors. It may be compared to the coats of arms adopted much later in medieval Europe, which were likewise the marks of a warrior caste. As in the Middle Ages armorial bearings were of more than local significance, so in nomad society plaques, badges, and pole-tops in the Animal style are likely to have been symbols of warrior bands made up from the chieftain's families of various tribes who might join in common enterprises of migration or war. The ferocity that appears so often in the animal figures could symbolize the spirit of these bands. The content of the scenes of animal combat, ultimately of Assyrian origin but which had traveled to the east, has been variously interpreted. That they symbolize struggles between light and darkness or good and evil seems unlikely, for which animal is which of these? It is more probable that the animals are tribal totems in conflict: animals akin to the tribe and never killed or eaten by its members except in special circumstances. But totemism seems a shade more primitive than this nomad art. To take another age, we do not regard the fighting lion and unicorn or other heraldic animals of the Middle Ages as totems. However, there is an analogy between these animal figures and the wolf, and the doe inherited from a remoter past and regarded as ancestors in Turkish and Mongol belief. Other writers regard the animals as protective spirits taking animal form, such as appear in shamanistic belief as guides to the shamans or others on visits to the world of spirits, or as a development of hunting magic, such as inspired the paleolithic cave-painters. It cannot be said that we fully understand the significance of nomad art.

The beauty of some of these figures is surely incidental to their main purpose, if that was magic or shamanistic cult. Their quality, especially when grouped in scenes, is entirely barbaric, in spite of influences from the southern civilizations. This was not civilized art, but represented a special world and a special cast of mind, inimical to civilization, as Herodotus saw. An analogy can be seen in the different but equally distinctive art of the Celtic peoples of the same centuries (see Celtic Art), most strikingly illustrated in such work as the decoration of the celebrated caldron from the bog of Gundestrup in Denmark dated c100 BC (National Museum, Copenhagen) with its human and animal figures of unapproachable wildness.

†E.D. PHILLIPS

Bibliography. *Frozen Tombs: the Culture and Art of Ancient Tribes of Siberia*, (British Museum) London (1978). Jettmar, K. *The Art of the Steppes*, New York (1969). Minns, E.H. "The Art of the Northern Nomads", *Proceedings of the British Academy*, London (1942). Minns, E.H. *Scythians and Greeks in South Russia*, Cambridge (1913). *Or des Scythes: Trésors des Musées Soviétiques*, Paris (1975). Rice, T.T. *The Scythians*, London (1957). Rudenko, S.I. (trans. Thompson, M.W.) *Frozen Tombs in Siberia: the Pazyryk Burials of Iron Age Horsemen*, London (1970).

15
INDIAN ART

Radha and Krishna in a Grove, a Kangra school painting; 27×18cm (11×7in); c1820–5
Victoria and Albert Museum, London (see page 272)

NDIAN Art can be understood in a restricted or a wider sense: it can refer to the art produced in the South Asian subcontinent—comprising the present Republics of India, Pakistan, and Bangladesh—or it can also be taken to include the spheres of Indian cultural influence—Kashmir, Nepal, Tibet, and Ceylon. The development of art in the South Asian subcontinent may be conveniently divided into three periods: the first—the Buddhist, Jain, and Hindu art of the ancient period—came to an end in the north with the Muslim conquest of India in 1210, although it continued in the south until the 20th century. The second, the Indo-Islamic period, lasted until 1757 when British power was established in India. From that time until now is the third period of the westernization of India.

The civilization of the Indus Valley (c2500–1500 BC). The earliest evidence of Indian art and architecture is found in the two ancient cities of Mahenjo-daro and Harappa (c2500–1500 BC) in the Indus Valley in the northwest. Apart from the material remains very little is known about the inhabitants, because their script remains undeciphered even today. Their remarkable achievements were the two cities, based on precise grid plans and served by an advanced drainage system, unrivaled in the ancient world until the Romans' 2,000 years later.

In India, cities based on grid plans and oriented strictly in the four cardinal directions have a continuous tradition, at-

Important centers mentioned in the text

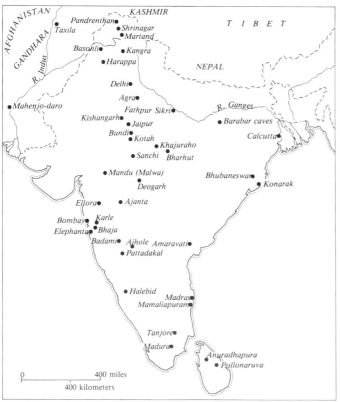

tested by architectural manuals as well as by the Hindu city of Jaipur. Unlike Egyptians and Sumerians, with whom they traded, Indus people had no taste for monumental sculpture: they preferred small-scale sculptures, human and animal. The famous torso (National Museum of India, New Delhi), whose antecedents are unknown, shows not only a mastery of the human form but foreshadows later sculpture in the loving treatment of soft, warm flesh. Entirely different in style is the aborigine girl (National Museum of India, New Delhi) treated with verve and spirit, whose anklets and bangles remind us of rich personal ornaments depicted by later Indian sculptors. No less impressive are the animal reliefs on seals, especially the naturalistic bull with its exquisitely carved dewlaps (National Museum of India, New Delhi)—yet again a reminder of the achievements of the later period.

When the two flourishing cities fell before the advancing Aryans from the north, art disappeared for over a millennium (1550–300 BC). No art from the Vedic period (1500–1000 BC) has been discovered; possible exceptions are literary references to sacrificial altars which may be regarded as early exercises in the art of design and building. We may ask why Vedic mythology, whose gods have similarities with Greek gods, did not encourage a similar development of narrative art. It was much later that *Puranic* gods provided inspiration for narrative art. One reason offered is that Vedic elemental gods like Fire or Wind did not lend themselves easily to visual representation. An alternative explanation may be that the Vedic sacrificer's contractual relation with divinity did not require an elaborate pantheon. Nor did worshipers concern themselves with images except for their limited use in Vedic ritual. Admittedly the pastoral Aryans were socially less complex than the urban Indus people, but their literature shows a deep love of nature eloquently expressed in lyric hymns of great beauty and feeling.

Buddhist art from c 3rd century BC to c 12th century AD. Indian society had evolved from tribal societies into republics and kingdoms with flourishing cities as their capitals by about the 5th century BC—a period famous for intense intellectual activity, above all debates on metaphysical questions. The Buddha (c563–483 BC) founded the first great world religion, soon to spread all over Asia. His message was attractively simple and directed to the average householder; it demanded neither costly Vedic sacrifices nor painful austerities but urged him to lead a moderate, virtuous life. The message was powerful enough to draw many people; it also provided the first major impulse for art in the historic period. Grateful for showing them the moderate eightfold path, wealthy merchants of ancient cities like Vidisha or Kashi flocked to him; it was they who searched for appropriate monuments to venerate his sacred memory.

As in many other religions, existing popular objects of worship were taken over by the Buddhists and invested with sacred meaning. *Yakshas* and *Yakshis*, popular semidivine beings, who still figure in folklore, were made to serve the religion of the Buddha. Age-old worship of the tree enclosed by a fence now came to be a reminder of the great Teacher's attainment of enlightenment under the Bodhi tree. Thus the *stupa*, originally a tumulus placed over burial ashes of a monarch or other important person, emerged as the first Buddhist sacred architecture. Relics of the Buddha were generally placed in *stupas*. We know that a battle between different tribes took place over Buddha's mortal remains. The great Emperor Ashoka is said to have built many *stupas*; the ones that remain intact or even in fragments from the early period are Bharhut, Sanchi, Bodh Gaya, Amaravati, Jaggayapeta, Manikyala, and Butkara (Swat).

The most impressive as well as the best preserved of the early *stupas* is the great *stupa* at Sanchi, which allows us to study its form in some detail. The fact that Sanchi was an important religious center for both Buddhists and Hindus is borne out by archaeological evidence covering a millennium. Its special importance must be explained partly by its close proximity to Vidisha, a major ancient city. It also lay at the meeting point of arterial trade routes. The great *stupa* was not conceived as a single unified piece of architecture but grew in stages over centuries, attaining its final form in the 1st century BC. The original modest hemispherical solid mound of earth covered by bricks, dating from Ashoka's reign, was enlarged to twice its size and enclosed in dressed ashlar masonry.

As it stands today it consists of several parts. The main hemispherical part, called the *anda* (egg) and embodying the universal symbolism of the cosmic egg, rests on a very high base (*medhi*). The swastika-shaped ground plan suggests its origin in a solar cult, similar to common stone cist-graves in India, as in Brahmagiri. Buddhists, who compared the Buddha with the sun, reinterpreted the original circular plan as the Buddhist "wheel of doctrine", but the worshiper was still required to conform to the solar cult and to go around the shrine in a clockwise direction. The whole *stupa* was surrounded by a stone railing of massive proportions and marked by four elaborate and beautiful gateways. In keeping with solar symbolism there are precisely 120 uprights. On top of the hemispherical dome was the sacred relic, once again guarded by a stone fence. The shaft that pierces the dome in the center right down to the ground is crowned with three stone umbrellas celebrating the Buddha as the universal emperor of the spiritual world. In contrast to the deliberate simplicity of the main dome, the four gateways are richly adorned with narrative sculpture.

When the *stupa* was one of the great centers of Buddhist religion it left an impression far removed from the one created by its present ruined state. It was painted a brilliant white and decorated with gay festoons and banners on festival days. In Amaravati, on the Kistna in south India, we can gather from the remaining fragments and from the replica left to us that the idea of a white *stupa* was brilliantly realized through the use of limestone to cover the drum of the *stupa*.

The second type of Buddhist architecture was the rock-cut *chaitya*, which, unlike the *stupa*, could accommodate people inside and thus met the need for a meeting place for the congregation. Since it is the earliest surviving form of building or shelter, properly speaking, it gives us an idea about ancient Indian architectural practice. From the Greek ambassador Megasthenes' account we know that Ashoka's grandfather Chandragupta Maurya had built a splendid three-storied, pillared hall of wood and stone, whose foundations have recently been discovered. From this evidence we can certainly guess that wooden architecture was advanced in this period. But we still do not know how the buildings were constructed.

The *chaitya* form arose in order to house *stupas*. When Buddhist *stupas*, most of which were small and quite unlike Sanchi in scale, began to be covered with roofs, so that the faithful could circumambulate them in all weathers, the choice of the material—stone—was as simple as it was ingenious. Unlike wood or even brick, stone was durable and abundant. This solution may have taken some time to reach, for early *chaityas* were close copies of wooden buildings. But in matters of religion, convenience can never be the only criterion, and we are in danger of oversimplifying faith if we overlook symbolic associations of carving the temple of god out of the very heart of the living rock.

The *chaitya* was generally part of a whole complex of buildings forming a Buddhist monastery. The monks and nuns, who needed shelter in the rainy season when they were in retreat, lived in *viharas* or pillared halls with living cells all around them. It was they as well as the laity who paid their respects to the *stupa*, the most important symbol of the faith. The rock-hewn *chaitya* or a simple covered hall with a *stupa* at one end thus arose to cater for their needs. The earliest ones are in the Barabar caves in Bihar, but the rock-cut *stupa* form developed here spread to other parts of India. They are however mostly concentrated in the Western-Ghat mountains near Bombay, notably in Bhaja, Kondivte, Kondane, Nasik, Bedsa, Pitalkhora, Aurangabad, Ajanta, Kanheri, and Karle.

The Lomash Rishi is an early *chaitya* and displays a brilliant finish on the stone, a characteristic feature of the Maurya period c 2nd century BC. Although it is not a Buddhist cave, we can clearly see the basic *chaitya* plan set out here. The long hall is separated from the circular room, which contains the *stupa*, by a wall with a door in the middle. The roof of the circular room is hemispherical to accommodate the *stupa*, while the ceiling of the hall is in the form of a barrel vault. The shape of the ceiling is echoed outside in the horseshoe-shaped facade of Lomash Rishi, a feature that was to become universal in *chaityas*. The striking feature of Lomash Rishi is that although it is a stone building it reproduces rafters, laminated planks, tie rods, and other elements from wooden buildings—not only on the exterior but in the interior as well. As the *chaitya* form evolved, increasing use was made of stone, but in many cases actual wood was used along with stone, and wood continued to be used in late examples.

The climax in *chaitya* building was reached in Karle, not the latest but the grandest in conception, rivaling some of the greatest Hindu temples of the later period. Therefore in Karle

The chaitya at Karle, 2nd century AD; a side view of the entrance

we can study the main architectural features of the early *chaitya* quite well. Built in the 2nd century AD, it was an ambitious project in which the whole community took part—we even know the name of one donor, Bhutapala. Karle is in the form of a main hall with a lofty ceiling, flanked by two narrower halls with lower ceilings on either side. The main hall is separated from the two smaller ones by means of rows of robust columns, whose capitals contain human and animal sculptures. The entrance to the rock-cut hall is through three doors in the profusely sculptured facade set in a recess cut out of the surrounding virgin rock. The horseshoe-shaped window, which cleverly solves the problem of illuminating the interior with natural light, dominates the whole facade by its design and size. The shape of the horsehoe window is carried on in the interior ceiling, undoubtedly the most spectacular feature of this monument. The closely packed wooden arches, which give the vault the shape of an inverted boat, rise slightly above the two massive rows of columns. The way they are cunningly placed, slightly back from the pillars, creates the impression that they are floating in space. This, together with the unusual height of the ceiling and the slight outward curve of the supporting arches, produces the impression of the lofty vault of heaven, a boldness of architectural vision quite unrivaled in this period. A close scrutiny of Karle will reveal that the actual height of the ceiling is only 45 ft (13.7 m)—certainly less than that of Notre Dame of Paris. The sense of height and elegance of Karle owes a great deal more to the careful proportions of the different parts skillfully deployed than to its actual dimensions. At the farthest end of the *chaitya* is the *stupa*; the columns that separate the main hall from the aisles continue around the *stupa*, but behind it they become undeco-

rated octagonal ones. A further elaboration of Karle from earlier prototypes is the intermediate area between the front entrance and the main hall, which helps us to adjust our vision from the bright sunlight outside to the quiet grandeur of the interior. *Chaityas* continued to be built; cave XIX at Ajanta belongs to the 5th century. The decoration has become richer and the sun-window turns into a perfect circle, but the boldness and the impetus of Karle is absent.

As in architecture, the most powerful impulse to sculpture came from Buddhism and the earliest examples are from the reign of the great Buddhist Emperor, Ashoka (c269–232 BC). The aftermath of the bloody Kalinga war led to his conversion to nonviolence and subsequent resolution to conquer nations by moral persuasion instead of war. There already existed in India the tradition of freestanding pillars representing the *axis mundi* or marking royal graves, a tradition common to the whole of the ancient world. Ashoka turned them into powerful instruments for disseminating his humanitarian ideas all over his Empire, so that today they are invariably associated with him. These freestanding pillars, whose lower parts are buried deep into the ground, rise generally to a height of 40 to 50 ft (12 to 15 m) terminating in a bell-shaped capital.

An especially fine example is the Rampurva Bull capital, whose abacus is decorated with the honeysuckle and palmette motif derived from western Asia (Presidential Palace, New Delhi); other capitals often show animal and bird motifs alternating with symbolic wheels. These capitals were surmounted by animals and crowned with large representations of the Buddhist Wheel of Law. The Rampurva Bull shows the reassertion of Indian mastery of the animal form, last seen in the Indus. The most important reason why these pillars were identified as Ashokan was the Emperor's use of the pillar surface to inscribe his spiritual message, a practice also extended to rock surfaces. This feature, together with other western motifs, and the knowledge of Persian and Greek expansion into the northwestern frontiers of India led scholars to attribute Persian and Classical origins to Ashokan art. In fact India borrowed motifs such as honeysuckle or the heraldic lion from the common cultural pool of western Asia in the same way as Persians and Greeks did, long before the actual Persian invasion of India. Trade links which went back to the Indus civilization probably encouraged a continuous flow of artistic motifs to India. A striking feature of animal sculpture from Ashoka's times is the high mirror-like finish which seemed to disappear with the Mauryas.

Actual Buddhist narrative art appeared after Ashoka on the surface of the Sanchi gateways and in Bharhut and Bodhgaya. The *Jatakas*, popular stories, taken over by Buddhists as vehicles of instruction because of their powerful hold over ordinary people, are to be found depicted at Sanchi in places where they could be prominently seen. In the days of restricted literacy, the narrative friezes, whether in medieval Europe or in ancient India, were the chief means of reminding the faithful of the basic tenets of their faith. Sanchi also celebrates the personal spiritual triumph of the Buddha by depicting the various stages of his life that could remind his followers of his great achievement and message. But because the Buddha discouraged the worship of his person, which would have distorted his precept of personal moral responsibility, his followers carefully avoided representing him in human form. Instead he is symbolized by an empty throne, a tree, or a *stupa*.

A typical example of Sanchi sculpture is the north gateway in three tiers, each containing in the central parts continuous narratives derived from Buddha's life as well as from the *Jatakas*. The most impressive are the wide range of animals and birds decorating the gateway. The representation of these different subjects shows the considerable skill of the sculptors in telling stories that involve the use of many figures. The depiction of distance is avoided in the reliefs: the areas between figures are filled with huts, houses, and trees. The narrative art in Sanchi received further elaboration in Amaravati, where the figures show greater movement, grace, flexibility, and expression, partly because of the use of limestone. In general the sculptures of Sanchi and Amaravati tell us a lot about contemporary secular life including some depiction of the prevalent wooden architecture, little of which has survived.

In the early centuries of the Christian era Buddhist art began to seek different subjects, as Buddhism itself was moving away from the earlier *Hinayana* form into the *Mahayana* order which looked upon the Buddha as a divine, savior figure to be actively worshiped. This new attitude encouraged the need for a sacred image of the great teacher. In fact the emerging *Bhakti* movement, which sought a transcendent god to whom the worshiper was bound by personal devotion, was not confined to Buddhism alone. In the 2nd century Krishna emerged as the great transcendent god of the Hindus in the mystical poem *Bhagavad Gita*, where he appears as a god who demands absolute devotion. If we look to the Classical world a little earlier, transcendental deities in various mystery religions, notably the god Dionysos, had come to dominate the spiritual life of the period. In the West the different syncretic faiths eventually coalesced within Christianity, the most powerful religion to emerge in this period.

The human form of the Buddha, created partly under the influence of *Mahayana* Buddhism, evolved in two centers of the Kushan Empire, Gandhara and Mathura. The Kushans, originally from central Asia, set up an eclectic empire based on Classical and Indian civilizations and became the most important patrons of Buddhism since the days of Ashoka. Gandhara, lying in the northwest corner of India with its capital Takshashila (Greek: Taxila), came under successive Persian and Greek influence, especially after Alexander's incursions into these parts. Fragments of the Corinthian order, Greco-Roman sculptural pieces and coins have been discovered here which suggest the presence of artists and craftsmen from the west. It is significant that when the need arose for the sacred image of the savior, in both Christianity and *Mahayana* Buddhism in Gandhara, the sculptors naturally turned to an artistic tradition prevalent in the Roman Empire. It is thus evident that

craftsmen serving both religions had been trained in the watered-down version of Roman art, suggesting a remote connection with the metropolitan center. Both Christ and the Buddha were presented wearing the *pallium*, the robe worn by ancient Greek philosophers, because of their role as great spiritual teachers. The Roman derivation of Gandharan art may also be seen in the narrative cycles of the life of the Buddha which are similar to Roman reliefs and unlike the Sanchi reliefs. In Gandhara the episodes are broken up on the panel, unlike the Sanchi treatment of the stories in the form of a continuous narrative. Although Gandhara Buddhas have been rightly criticized for being crude, provincial Roman works which failed to capture the serene spiritual triumph of the great master, the finest examples certainly combine the best of the two worlds—the vivid naturalism of the Classical and the idealized beauty of the Indian.

In Mathura, the other center of the Kushan Empire, the more robust type of the standing and seated Buddha figures drew inspiration from the indigenous tradition of the colossal *Yakshas*. The enormous Bodhisattva from the 2nd century AD,

A painted Buddha at Gandhara

Relief Sculptures at Sanchi

The relief sculptures on the great *stupa* at Sanchi represent the first important period in the history of Indian narrative art. The didactic requirements of Buddhism, the world's first major evangelical faith, gave rise to these dramatic reliefs. The faithful, already familiar with stories from the Buddha's life and preaching, were meant to "read" them when they visited the *stupa* to pay homage to the great teacher. Although the early *stupas* at Bharhut and Bodh Gaya represented Buddhist scenes, it was in the Sanchi great *stupa* that a project was undertaken on an unprecedented scale in the 1st centuries BC and AD, based on subscriptions raised from the community, as attested by inscriptions on the *stupa*. The *stupa* itself remained unadorned until the very end: but decorative ornaments of beautiful women; animals, floral, foliate, and geometrical motifs; and series of narrative sculptures in relief celebrating the life and spiritual achievements of the Buddha cover the curved architraves and pillars of the gateways.

Significantly, this great Buddhist cycle only show Buddha through symbols recalling his

◄ Narrative sculpture on the north gateway at Sanchi

▼ Flowing narrative on the bottom architrave of the north gateway

spiritual progress. Some 60 themes were treated here and repeated according to their importance; their arrangement on the four gateways in the four cardinal directions suggests that the most "meaningful" stories faced the faithful as they approached the gateways. In contrast to earlier, flat treatment of reliefs, including deeper undercutting to convey distance, Sanchi sculptors use a "pictorial" convention, showing recession by reducing the size of distant figures. Instead of Bharhut's bare background, we have here clearly depicted forests and towns, with their recognizable balconies and vaulted roofs, surrounded by moats; and unlike earlier, stiff, frontal poses we now have animated figures in many poses. The sculptors adopt two narrative conventions: the first is a continuously flowing narrative, as seen in the *Vessantara Jataka* (north gate, bottom architrave, front and back), a story dealing with the Buddhist doctrine of *dana* (charity), a story so familiar that the faithful had no difficulty in following its course along the architrave, from the front through to the back. The second convention is seen in the *Battle for the Relics of the Buddha* (south gate, back, middle architrave), one of the most dramatic scenes in Sanchi. The central panel depicts the great tumult of the battle, the town as background, while next to it is the scene showing the victorious kings departing with relic caskets. In other words, scenes representing two successive points of time are here presented simultaneously or synchronically. The most striking feature is the treatment of the crowd by the artists, who subordinate the individual features of figures in favor of capturing the great din and bustle, the general rhythm and movement of the crowd. We also see the range of expressions, from the beautiful *Yakshis* to the exploration of the grotesque and humorous in the representations of the demon hosts of Mara who tempt the Buddha. No less impressive is the treatment of animals, notably elephants and water buffaloes, confirming the Buddhist view of the unity of all living creatures.

PARTHA MITTER

Further reading. Marshall, J.H. *The Monuments of Sanchi* (3 vols.), Calcutta (1913–14).

◀ The great *stupa* at Sanchi, showing the positions of the gateways

Below Adjacent successive scenes, as used on the middle architrave on the back of the south gateway at Sanchi

Bottom The middle section of the lowest architrave on the back of the north gateway at Sanchi

dedicated by the monk Bala (Sarnath Museum), is an impressive example of the style and may be contrasted with Gandhara Buddha. Both scale and gesture are heroic and the expression is full of latent energy. The close-fitting robe which leaves the right shoulder bare reveals rather than conceals the powerful frame. The serene beauty of the Gandhara Buddha is not aimed at; instead the sculptor chooses to represent him as the great spiritual conqueror. The seated Buddhas too have an air of immediacy about them and a scorn for physical beauty. When Jains, the other great dissident sect, fashioned the sacred image of their leader, they naturally turned for inspiration to Buddhist art, and there is no stylistic difference between the image of the Buddha and Jina. The Jains, however, differed from Buddhists with regard to iconography. The Jain ideal of the teacher who had conquered all worldly cravings, including sexual, was realized in the fully naked Jaina images—the only totally nude figures in Indian art.

The ideal form of the Buddha, which partially emerged in the formative phase of the Gandhara and Mathura schools, attained technical perfection and conceptual maturity in the Gupta period (AD 320–540). When the physical beauty of Gandhara and the spiritual strength of Mathura came together to produce the finest Buddha images—images that provided the iconographic and aesthetic norm for Buddhist art all over Asia, right up to Japan. The Gupta period, named after the Imperial family, which ruled most parts of India in this age, represents the supreme cultural achievement of ancient India, made largely possible by political unity.

With the Guptas is associated ancient India's greatest poet, Kalidasa (c5th century AD). Rules about good living were formulated and standards of criticism set. The early-5th-century Chinese traveler Fa Hsien has left us a vivid account of his own impressions of great peace and security in India under the Guptas. The sculptors of this age, who were given the task of presenting the spiritual triumph of the Buddha over worldly cravings, chose to represent this through a new type of physical beauty. The Sarnath Buddha (Sarnath Museum), one of the great examples of this style, expresses in his gently enigmatic smile the serene, inner confidence that denies the anguish of worldly existence. The power of this beautiful image can be seen all over Asia for it soon became the great ideal for all Buddhists to emulate. The Indian norms of beauty—perfect oval face, lotus eyes, and lion-like torso—as well as iconographic rules such as the third eye, top knot, webbed fingers, and the nimbus became well-established. The nimbus which appeared behind Gupta Buddhas was delicately carved with decorative motifs.

This period also witnessed the supreme achievement in the field of painting in ancient times. The spirit of the Gupta age informs much of the Buddhist paintings in the *chaityas* and *viharas* of Ajanta, although the actual area was outside the immediate sphere of Imperial hegemony. We know very little about the origins of this tradition apart from the information available from early-1st-century caves (IX, X). But most of the important paintings belong to the 5th century and deal with

A Gupta-style Buddha at Sarnath; sandstone; height 160cm (63in); 5th century AD

stories from Buddha's life and Buddhist legends. Although the context is religious, the world revealed before us is the secular, vivacious one of 5th-century India, so memorably described by the poet Kalidasa.

The particular approach chosen by the artists was naturalistic, and even trivial everyday subjects came under their close scrutiny—beggar with bowl and stick, hunter with dog, cook preparing meal, seafaring ships, and other themes of human interest are constantly interwoven with the major religious stories from *Jatakas*. Everything from internal and external architecture, indigenous and foreign people and their different costumes, and patterns of textiles, flora, and fauna, are all captured in warm, glowing colors which have until recently resisted the ravages of time. Foliate, floral, animal, and geometrical decorative patterns are to be seen in great profusion, especially on ceilings.

Ajanta artists used colors based on organic substances which were mixed with water and gum and applied on a treated, plastered surface. Two of the best-preserved and most famous subjects are the Bodhisattvas or Buddhist saviors from Cave I, resplendent in their bejeweled, princely costumes, epitomizing earthly beauty. The face of the Bodhisattva, who holds the lotus, represents the traditional Indian ideal of beauty with the lotus eyes and perfect oval face seen in the sculpture of the Gupta Buddha. Here the painter sought to convey the sense of solidity by the use of highlights and shading, reinforced by means of a dark brown outline.

Form in Ajanta is defined more by light and shadow than line, however, and the pictorial surface is dominated by a series of closely related tones of grays and browns that avoid pure colors. The Ajanta artists loved to use many figures which they arranged in complex patterns in a continuous narrative all around the walls. Another famous subject in Cave I, the renunciation of his Kingdom by Mahajanaka, related in the *Jataka*, is a typical example of their approach. Here the painter has chosen the moment when, according to ancient custom, he was ritually washed with water before leaving his kingdom. Mahajanaka, who in his renunciation was seen as prefiguring the Buddha, is shown here seated in a similar pose. The whole scene taking place in his palace shows careful observation of contemporary interior architecture and other details, such as the deer throne, the servants, and the women who surround him.

The important achievement of Ajanta was not allowed to be forgotten; all over Asia up to China and Japan, Buddhists took Ajanta to be their ideal and modified, elaborated, and interpreted Ajanta art in the light of their own experience. In India, paintings slightly later and similar to Ajanta were produced in Bagh and Ellora, fragments of which remain. Wallpaintings were continued in the south, and as late as 1540 we find an impressive series of paintings in the Lepakshi temple in the Vijayanagar, the last great Hindu kingdom, notably the famous boar hunt.

Hindu art from c 5th century AD to c 17th century AD. In the reign of the Guptas in the 5th century, Buddhist art reached great heights both in sculpture and painting. This was also the first great age of Hindu art, exemplified by the evolution of the temple. In the Hindu temple, architecture and sculpture are related by a common principle; but for the sake of convenience they will be treated separately here. The same spirit of *Bhakti* which led to the development of the image of the Buddha also brought about changes in Hinduism. In the period of the Vedic sacrifice temples were unnecessary. Their rise followed the establishment of the two important groups within Hinduism, the worshipers of Shiva and Vishnu, who built temples to their own supreme personal gods. When Hindus searched for the appropriate architectural form to adopt they did not have to look far, for they already had important examples before them.

Architects had reached a very high level in the art of building in the Gupta period and they naturally applied their experience in Buddhist buildings to the new requirements of Hindu art. Thus we see in the early Hindu temples clear traces of the *chaitya* form. From the very beginning the requirements of the two faiths were entirely different, and this is seen in the arrangement of the early temples. The Buddhist sacred building, the *chaitya*, was designed to accommodate a large gathering; the Hindu temple was above all the house where the particular god resided. Initially this did not need more than a cell for the sacred image. The basic form was also from the outset profoundly affected by cosmological symbolism, the most important aspect of which was implicit in the word applied to the cell, "garbha griha" (womb-house). Religion also required the temple to be correctly oriented in four cardinal directions and to face the east, a principle generally adhered to except where the geographical peculiarities of the site demanded necessary changes.

Unlike Buddhist architecture, the ideal shape of the temple was the square, the symbol of eternity, standing outside time. This was expressed through the cosmological symbolism of the *mandala*, and even an early temple like the Deogarh (5th century) was based on an elaborate *mandala* ground plan governed by strict geometrical principles. But a layout derived from a strict grid system was not unique to sacred architecture; it determined the plan of secular buildings and, as we have seen, the layout of cities. The sacred geometry had much to do with astronomical considerations.

The earliest Hindu temple is found in Sanchi (Temple 17), a square flat-roofed room with a covered portico supported by columns in front. The shape of the columns was traditional—square with octagonal variations. In India a square was the favored shape for the column; round pillars are very rare. Of the several Gupta temples from this period, namely Bhitargaon, Bhumara, and Deogarh, the last one is by far the most impressive. Built of ashlar masonry and containing a now-ruined, square tower, the most striking features of the Deogarh temple are the typical Gupta doorway framed with beautifully decorated pilasters and the three sculptural reliefs on three sides set in deeply recessed niches, framed, like the doorway, by elegant pilasters. The whole temple was designed to stand on a high plinth to separate it, as it were, from the mundane world, a conception peculiarly Hindu. Another feature that separated this early temple from Buddhist *chaityas* was the absence of great stress on the facade; while the main entrance was to the east, the other three sides were given equal architectural and sculptural importance.

The Gupta temple of Deogarh was a fine but isolated example. For the evolution of two main types of Hindu temples, later to be classed as northern and southern, we must turn to the clusters of temples in the old Chalukyan capitals of Aihole, Badami, and Pattadakal, in Dharwar. They are of great historic importance. Two in Aihole belonging to the 5th century reflect an experimental period when architects were searching for inspiration. The Lad Khan temple, a rectangular building with massive capitals and flat roof covered with stone slabs, was derived from ancient village meeting halls. The Durga temple, on the other hand, sought inspiration in Buddhist *chaityas* and has the unusual feature of a corridor going right around the temple. Its "garbha griha" ends like a *chaitya* in a semicircle. As in Deogarh, a tower marked the shrine; the preceding hall was added in the design to accommodate worshipers.

The Durga temple at Aihole; c500 AD

The Chalukya capital shifted to Badami and finally to Pattadakal where two of the finest early temples are to be found. The Papanatha (Shiva) temple (680) is distinguished by the gently curved tower, known as the northern kind, as distinct from the flat, stepped tiers of southern temples. In the Papanatha, the basic northern form is somewhat modified by tiers, each consisting of *chaitya* and fluted round *amalaka* disc motifs. Another unusual element is its length in relation to its height and width, achieved here by joining two halls together, lending it an elegant appearance. With other Gupta temples it shares an elaborately carved, framed main doorway, while a very important development is the decoration of the sides—carefully worked out and spaced niches formed by pilasters and crowned with pediments. Their decoration consists of geometric, foliate, and mythical animal designs. The Virupaksha (Shiva) temple built in 740 is more elaborate, containing a uniform south-Indian type of tiered tower. The design is more developed and the sculptures, now playing a more important role on the niches, appear at regular intervals, thus anticipating the common arrangement in southern temples of later periods. In their two temples the Buddhist *chaitya* window (horseshoe) motif becomes a common decorative feature.

About the time the Virupaksha was built, the Pallavas (625–800), impressed by the Chalukya achievement, undertook to embellish their own kingdom in the south with splendid temples. On the eastern shores of the Indian Ocean, in Mamallapuram, are to be found the first experiments by designers to discover the appropriate form—the five *rathas* built of solid stone in five different styles including some variations of the *chaitya*. The most successful among them was the Dharmaraja *ratha*—a pyramidal tower made up of diminishing terraces, similar in shape and design to that of Virupaksha. The advantages of this form were its square shape oriented in four cardinal directions and the incorporation of any number of equal parts which could be varied according to the size of the tower. The individual motifs as well as the crowning solid polygonal dome were derived from the *chaitya*.

When c700 the great Shore Temple at Mamallapuram was built, architects were able to use their experience with Dharmaraja *ratha* profitably. And yet the designers were not entirely bound by tradition. The many unusual features of the Shore Temple follow the peculiar needs of the site. The main shrine surmounted by the pyramidal, terraced *shikhara* faces towards the sea in the east so that the *linga* image could be seen by the passing ships, while a smaller shrine with less lofty *shikhara* was added which could be approached from the town in the west. The main *shikhara* also has a very slender appearance, produced by virtually stretching each tier vertically including its *chaitya* motifs. Because the temple was to serve as a landmark for sailors, its height was of great importance; even today the *shikhara* of the Shore Temple dominates the coast. Much of the temple has fallen down, but the strong enclosing wall surmounted by seated bulls exists as well as pilasters containing springing lions—a southern feature that makes one of its first appearances here. The other great Pallava temple, the Kailasanatha (Shiva) at Kanchipuram, was simply Virupaksha on a grander scale.

A unique development of the southern style took place when the Kailasanatha temple in Ellora was built for the Rashtrakutas (752–83). Made out of a solid block of rock (250 ft, 76 m long, 150 ft, 46 m wide, 100 ft, 30 m deep) separated from its surroundings, it is one of the most imaginative achievements in the history of architecture, and the supreme achievement in the field of rock-temples in India. Instead of the traditional practice of making a tunnel in the rock face, the designers decided to carve a complex two-storied, freestanding temple by working from the top downwards. The enormous range of details, such as single and multiple levels, bridges, halls, richly ornamented columns, and the great variety of fine sculptures required the most rigorous planning, for a single error could have marred the imposing effect. The whole grand impression is further enhanced by the choice of a very high plinth (25 ft, 7.6 m) for the temple.

The final achievement of the southern style was seen c1000, when the powerful Chola rulers built the high Brihadishvara temple in Tanjore. Here the enormously high *shikhara* (190 ft, 58 m) dwarfs the other components of the temple. The impression of great height is produced partly by conceiving the *cella* containing the image in two lofty stories. The niches here, a common southern feature, are deployed harmoniously and contain some very powerful sculptures of Shiva.

The development of southern temples took a new turn after Tanjore. From this time onwards the main shrine and the *shikhara* no longer interest the builders, while great ingenuity and imagination are lavished on the temple gateways which now rise to great heights. The purpose of great height for the

Right: the Shore Temple at Mamallapuram; c700 AD

The Lingaraja temple at Bhubaneswar; c1000 AD

tower gateways (*gopuras*) was to offer symbolic protection to the sacred temple precinct. The 17th-century temples of Madura and Srirangam increasingly resemble fortified cities with their concentric walls and gate-towers, and they were actually fortified against different invaders. Two other southern architectural elements deserve special mention: water tanks and handsome assembly halls standing on sometimes up to a thousand rows of pillars.

In the north, the distinguishing feature, the *shikhara*, followed along the lines seen first in the Papanatha temple in Pattadakal, and this style reached its culmination in two areas, Orissa and Khajuraho, around the 1st millennium. There is yet another important distinction between the north and the south. Although relieved by symmetrically aligned niches with sculptures, the elevations of the southern temples are generally flat; in the north, on the other hand, the elevations are elaborately articulated with alternate projections and recesses, a

principle carried on in the tower over the shrine.

The Orissan style may be best studied in the most complete example, the Lingaraja temple in Bhubaneswar. To the traditional arrangement of the main shrine with high tower, preceded by an assembly hall, were added two further halls. The basic shape of the tower is a tall spire (148 ft, 45 m) which curves slightly inwards at the top and is crowned with a fluted, bulging disk resembling the Indian *amalaka* fruit. On closer inspection we can see that the alternate projections and recesses are intensified by deep incisions of vertical lines right from the *amalaka* down to the base. The further elements are the horizontal ribs as well as the tower (*shikhara*) motifs on various scales punctuating the whole surface of the main tower, as well as sculptures filling the gaps in the recesses. The assembly hall is a square building with a pyramidal roof consisting of two groups of three tiers surmounted by an *amalaka*.

Before leaving Orissa we must mention the magnificent but

unrealized dream, the Sun temple at Konarak, of which only the colossal front hall and the Hall of the Dance remain. Dedicated to the Sun god, the temple is in the form of a handsome, 12-wheeled chariot drawn by seven pairs of horses. From the coherence of the total design to the large sculptures—richly decorated wheels and sculpted erotic couples of various sizes—the immense attention to details, however trivial, is astonishing. Built in the 13th century, it is the last exuberance of the human spirit already threatened with extinction by the invading Muslims.

In the Chandela capital at Khajuraho (950–1050), a variation of the northern style appeared. Impression of lofty heights was created by architects here in a different manner from the Orissans. First, the temple as a sacred precinct was stressed by a very high base which separated it from the surrounding plains. The sense of height is increased by the narrow, high flight of steps leading to the temple entrance. The three main elements, the shrine with its tower, the assembly hall, and the portico are all joined together as one edifice, unlike Orissan temples. A sense of airy space is created by a circumambulatory passage going right around the temple, lit by large, open balconies. The tower of the fine Kandariya Mahedeo (Shiva) temple has repeated on its four sides a number of vertical projections as smaller, variously graded scales. This, along with the deep recesses contrasting with projections, make for an intense play of light and shadow under the Indian sun, and is quite unlike the relatively unbroken surface of the Orissan temples. A further element here is the figure sculpture in several parallel rows over the base and below the tower.

Among important local variations are the temples built for Hoyshala kings in Belur, Halebid, and Somnathpur in the south, famous for their exquisitely detailed sculpture covering the surface and for their star-shaped ground plans. The stellar plan was achieved by a complex geometrical pattern of superimposed squares at angles to each other, forming a succession of related projections and recesses so strictly ordered that a circle may be drawn around them. The form of the towers of these temples is closer to the north. In a very fine example, the Keshava (Vishnu) temple (1268) at Somnathpur, the plan is based on a group of three-star towers. Profusion of delicate carvings on a temple surface is also to be seen in the north in the Jain marble temples of Rajasthan (1032–1232), the Vimala Shah and Tejahpala temples on Mount Abu. Built for affluent merchants, these white marble temples are remarkable for the "crisp, thin, translucent, shell-like treatment" of the delicate marble. The work required such care that ordinary chiseling would have been disastrous. So the carvings were produced by scraping the marble away and "masons were paid by the amount of marble dust so removed" (Zimmer, H. *The Art of Indian Asia*). Finally, another provincial style, the terracotta temples of Bengal (100–1600), has recently rewarded patient study: *see* McCutchion, D.J. *Late Medieval Temples of Bengal* Calcutta (1972).

As in Buddhism, the stress on absolute devotion to a personal savior god partly contributed to the creation of the ideal image of the Buddha and Bodhisattva, so in Hinduism, after the rise of *Bhakti* movements and the emergence of Vishnu and Shiva as the greatest gods, superseding all others, came the creation of permanent images of the two gods. Although literary references to images of gods occur very early, including the description by a foreigner of an androgynous many-limbed symbolic god (Bardesanes' testimony recorded by Porphyry, 3rd century), the earliest extant images of Vishnu and Shiva are in fact from the Gupta period, parallel to the rise of temples. An early Vishnu from the Gupta period looks strikingly like a Bodhisattva because artists applied their experience in Buddhism to the new religious art.

In Hinduism, there are two kinds of images, those worshiped at home and those in temples; we are concerned here with the art of the latter. In the temple the main shrine, over which the tower rises, is windowless, bare, and purposely austere—a repository of inscrutable mystery, darkness, and the numinous. Similarly, the main image installed there is often not primarily aesthetic in its concern. Indeed, in the greatest temples the images are purposely abstract, archaic, primitive, and often bizarre, so that worshipers may respond to them on multiple levels of symbolic meaning. But there is a whole range of sculptures, including images of gods on the outer surface of the temples, usually connected with the mythological cycles related to the particular divinity inhabiting the temple. The range of sculptures on the sides of temples—from the large images of gods and main narrative cycles portraying the *Puranas*, the Hindu sacred mythology, to the detailed geometrical, foliate, and mythical animal decorations—are all strictly ordered within a hierarchy of levels of meaning.

However, some of the greatest artistic treatments of Hindu mythology are to be found in the panels of narrative sculptures on the outer walls of temples, in a spectrum of reliefs ranging in depth from the lowest to the highest relief. In fact the evolution of narrative sculpture from Sanchi to the late Hindu period demonstrates the importance of the actual depth of the reliefs as settings for the dramatic events depicted. As artists learned to represent stories more convincingly they moved away from the early shallow reliefs of Sanchi and Bharhut to greater depth of background. In the finest examples the whole scene is often presented within a deep square niche where some figures are cut in high relief while others half emerge from the rock. These different depths combine to create a dramatic effect of light and shadow, and lead to great expressiveness under the strong, natural Indian light.

The repertory of Hindu temple sculptures is large; only some of the most striking ones may be considered here. From the outset, certain *Puranic* myths, whether they related to Vishnu's or Shiva's exploits, found favor among artists because of their sculptural possibilities. Both gods were responsible for the creation, preservation, and destruction of the universe, while Vishnu had more solar attributes and was generally life-affirming. Shiva, a more complex god embodying contrary elements—namely asceticism and sexuality—was more chthonic by nature. Both their myths relate either their benign act of creation after periodic dissolution of aeons or their fierce aspect of battling with forces of darkness—the demons (*asuras*). But while these gods destroy the evil demons they also hold out to their victims the possibility of redemption, thus indicating that these destructive acts of the god are his cosmic "play". Sculptors, faced with the problem of treating these scenes, presented them as the enactment of divine theater.

In one of the first great pieces of sculpture in the Deogarh Vishnu temple, we see the sleep of Vishnu between the dissolution of the world and its recreation depicted. He is attended by his wife Lakshmi while he sleeps on the serpent embodying time (*shesa*). The creator, Brahma, rests on a lotus springing from his navel. While other gods watch the scene, his weapons, personified here, battle with two demons. Vishnu is also associated with the notion of incarnation (*avatara*) and assumes mortal form to restore righteousness. One of the most powerful images of monumentality is to be seen in Udaigiri (*c*500), where Vishnu as a cosmic boar rescues the goddess earth from under the waters as a multitude of sages (*rishis*) sing his praise.

From a cave in Ellora (*c*600) comes a spirited depiction of Vishnu's man-lion incarnation where he destroys the demon by emerging from inside a pillar. Here the artist has chosen the moment of the fight between the demon and the god, which is treated with a great deal of movement and expression. In Ellora senses of movement and dynamism are the important developments from more static Deogarh sculpture. Other representations of Vishnu include the Krishna incarnation holding a flute, commonly seen in the south, as well as his four-armed frontal image wearing an elaborate crown and holding four attributes—conch, discus, mace, and lotus—in his four hands.

Like Vishnu, Shiva is represented in both his benevolent and fierce aspects, and with him the chthonic aspects are particularly important. Unlike Vishnu who wears a crown Shiva is always shown with the matted hair of the ascetic. His favorite weapon of destruction is the trident. Between the 6th and 8th centuries, sculptors in the area extending from Ellora to Elephanta produced some of the most remarkable groups of Shiva stories, closely related in style and unified by a common iconography. Among them, the sculpture of Shiva destroying the three cities of the demon Tripura in the Kailasa temple, Ellora, is full of movement and energy. The destruction of the demon Andhaka in the Elephanta temple is famed for its power of expression, showing the moment when Shiva pins the demon on his trident with one hand while with another he holds a cup to collect the victim's dripping blood.

At these sites there are also a number of very fine sculptures of the dancing Shiva, whose cosmic acts of creation and destruction are always presented in the form of the dance. In Ellora, the sculptor who depicts Shiva performing the mea-

The three faces of Shiva in the temple at Elephanta; c 8th century AD

sured dance, known as *katisama* in classical dance repertoire, shows him dancing before his family as well as other gods, as if in a theater. In another, Shiva does a more abandoned dance, full of grace and rhythm. In both these sculptures the artists have presented Shiva as a beautiful man and have taken special care in the treatment of his hair and personal ornament. In Elephanta there also exists the sculpture of the great three faces of Shiva: horrific, feminine, and tranquil. This bust, meant to emerge in half light and darkness because of the deeply cut niche that frames it, is possibly the supreme achievement of the period.

Other dancing Shiva figures include the famous Chola Nataraja (King of the Dance) bronzes, many examples of which exist outside India in European museums (for example, Musée Guimet, Paris). The divine dancer with her slender, graceful build and elegant fingers and toes is shown dancing on the little demon, Ignorance, while he is ringed by the conflagration that destroys the cosmos. Shiva is also represented in an androgynous form. In the case of the classical hermaphrodite, the male and female elements are blended in the figure while Indian sculptors chose to emphasize the two contrary principles by dividing the figure equally into male and female.

Among depictions of goddesses, the myth about the destruction of the buffalo demon by Devi, Shiva's wife, is the most popular. Legend has it that when unrighteousness became intolerable each god offered up part of his power to fashion the miraculous goddess who would be greater than all of them, and thus Durga was conceived. Among the several famous scenes depicting her destruction of the Buffalo demon, one at Ellora and several at Mamallapuram are most moving. In Ellora she is shown struggling with the enormously powerful demon with all the weapons presented by gods in her ten hands. The scene is characteristically full of movement and action, a favorite with sculptors here.

But the main problem artists faced was how to show a great, bloody battle in which Devi engaged in order to kill

Mahishasura and yet present her, so literature has it, as a young woman of great beauty and gentleness. In Mamallapuram this is solved, interestingly, by the choice of the moment shown: she is represented as a beautiful young girl standing demurely and the only trace of the great battle is in the severed head of the buffalo lying under her.

Apart from Vaishnava and Shaiva deities, one god dating from the Vedic period continued to draw the allegiance of worshipers. Surya, the Sun god, to whom a number of temples were dedicated from the 5th to the 11th centuries AD, including the great Konarak temple, is recognizable by his high boots and seven horses, as seen in the fine image from Konarak. We may marvel at the achievements of great power and beauty in the major relief cycles about stories of gods, but we cannot neglect more intimate treatments, especially of women, an area very close to the heart of the sculptors from the days of Sanchi. Male figures, apart from the Door Guardians, were generally vehicles of religious symbolism, and while many of these figures are very beautiful we cannot separate the beauty of these divine figures from their symbolic attributes. In other words, even in their beauty they are larger than life and remote from us. Women, on the other hand, were direct, intensely human, and represented as desirable. In Sanchi we encounter the nubile tree-spirits. In Ellora there are several memorable feminine images. Some of the finest, however, come from c10th century, and are full of grace and feeling. The sculptors were particularly adept in bringing out the soft, bare quality of flesh by contrasting it with rich jewelry and exquisite costumes, as in the striking Lady of the Tree (Central Archaeological Museum, Gwalior), a perfect translation of Kalidasa's poetry into stone.

Apart from this universal celebration of the physical beauty

One of the masterpieces of Indian erotic art: sculptured figures on the Sun temple at Konarak; 13th century

Sculpture of Devi at Ellora

The sculpture of Devi or the Goddess slaying Mahisasura, the buffalo demon, in the precinct of the 8th-century Hindu rock-cut temple of Kailasa at Ellora in western India is a truly remarkable piece of work at a site filled with many of the finest achievements of ancient Indian art—Hindu, Buddhist, and Jain. The piece is one of the twin sculptural compositions that adorn the site of the Kailasa temple, belonging to the worshipers of Shiva. The other one depicts Shiva's destruction of Tripura, the demon of the three cities. Both relate stories from the sectarian mythology of the Saivas and both relief panels treat battle scenes in which the deities are engaged in destroying the demon that has upset the cosmic order, so that the order may be restored. Both sculptures, particularly the scene depicting Devi's great battle, represent a high point in the development of Hindu iconography and its treatment in narrative sculpture as well as the treatment of the human figure, and above all in the solving of compositional problems and problems of expression. In short, this compositional piece is one of the most dramatic treatments in the history of Indian monumental sculpture.

The theme of Devi destroying the buffalo demon has been one of the most popular subjects for artists, from the rise of Hindu sculpture to the present. To Hindus it is also one of the most inspiring legends, as seen in the worship of the image in its present form in Bengal. The story of the great goddess,

Devi or Durga, as it occurs in its most complete version in the *Markandeya Purana*, is as follows: the universe is dominated by the eternal struggle between *devas* (gods) and *asuras* (demons or antigods who happen to be half-brothers of gods), in which struggle the world order is periodically upset when the demon king, through sheer willpower, gains ascendancy over the mythological gods. Then it becomes necessary for either of the supreme gods, Vishnu or Shiva, to come to

the rescue of the mythological gods and restore cosmic order by destroying the demon. On this occasion the particular demon, who took the form of a water buffalo, is so powerful that even the two supreme deities are unable to destroy him. So all the gods come together and with their concerted willpower and energy they produce a wonderous woman, the fairest one, the invincible one, more powerful than any of them. Each god gives up part of his power and his favorite weapon, such as the *chakra* of Vishnu or the *trisula* of Shiva, to this deity. Thus armed she goes forth in battle with the

◀ Devi or Durga (left) slaying Mahisasura, the Buffalo demon; in the 8th-century Kailasa temple at Ellora

▼ Shiva destroying Tripura, the demon of the three cities; in the temple of Shiva at Ellora

▲ Durga and her companions confront Mahisasura; a relief sculpture at Mamallapuram

▼ A 6th-century figure of Durga in a niche on the veranda of the Durga temple at Aiholi

demon king and his army, riding on her animal, the lion. After a great and bloody battle in which weapons fly in all directions and innumerable demons lie dying and dead, the buffalo demon is at last cornered. When finally he tries to escape from the dying buffalo form in the guise of a man, he is dealt the death blow and perishes.

The legend has been a favorite subject of Indian sculptors because of its dramatic possibilities; and only by a comparison of various versions of the theme can we fully appreciate the achievement of the sculptor at Ellora. The nature of the story offered a number of possibilities to the artist. What proved intriguing to him was the idea that although the goddess was described in the *Puranas* as invincible and even more powerful than the gods, she was nonetheless a beautiful woman in the first bloom of youth; so any suggestion of masculinity had to be avoided, even though she engaged in the most masculine of acts: making war. This contradiction led to the crucial choice of the particular moment to represent in sculpture: whether to show the aftermath of the great battle when the demon lies subdued and no carnage is evident, or whether to depict the actual battle with all its fury and ugliness.

In an early image in the Durga temple at Aiholi the powers of expression are not fully developed, and the sculptor presents a more hieratic image with very little movement as the weapons presented by various gods are placed in a symmetrical manner while the buffalo demon is a diminutive figure— hardly terrifying. It was at the 7th-century

site in Mamallapuram that artists began to consider the expressive possibilities of the story. In a less-known image from the place, now in the Museum of Fine Arts, Boston, the sculptor has concentrated on the physical charm of the goddess. This sculpture is indeed one of the most beautiful feminine figures in the history of Hindu art. The sculptor ignores the essential tension of the story; the carnage is hinted at by the muted sculptured head of the buffalo. By stressing grace the artist has chosen to sacrifice dramatic tension. In fact there are only two outstanding dramatic treatments of the theme in the early period: the better-known Durga image at Mamallapuram and the great one at Kailasa in Ellora. Their treatment of the theme is similar in some respects and yet different. At Mamallapuram, Durga and her companions confront Mahisasura who is large and menacing, whose powers are still intact, while the gods watch the spectacle. Durga is presented here as a slender, graceful maiden, and even though the sculpture is badly weathered, we can still see traces of her beauty on her face. Although feminine, she is nonetheless presented as an invincible warrior as she wields her bow and a multitude of other weapons. In the horizontal composition there is a great forward thrust from left to right which is suddenly stopped by the massive diagonal of the Mahisasura's defiant form.

This kind of dramatic treatment reaches its climax in Ellora with this wonderful composition. There is hardly any symmetry, and the dead and wounded scatter in great confusion. The sculptor also follows the text carefully by showing the weapons of Durga flying in all directions. The tension is built up by the use of a vertical composition with the gods witnessing the event from above. Here Mahisasura is not a monster but a proud heroic figure: there can be no doubt that this depiction of the buffalo demon is one of the finest in early sculpture. Although today it is difficult to say what Durga's face was like because it is so badly damaged, her striking and unusual seated posture as well as her graceful, slender form is still recognizable. If we are to take other sculptures from the period at Kailasa as an indication then her head must have been very beautiful too. In Kailasa we find some of the most beautiful faces of Shiva. Finally, it is the combination of grace, beauty, power of expression, and complex and dramatic composition that makes the Durga of Ellora a remarkable relief sculpture.

PARTHA MITTER

Further reading. Gopinatha Rao, T.A. *Elements of Hindu Iconography*, Madras (1914). Zimmer, H.R. *The Art of Indian Asia* (2 vols.), New York (1955).

▼ Shiva dancing: an example of Shiva in the Kailasa temple, Ellora, contemporaneous with Devi

Above The temple of Kailasa at Ellora, a temple of Shiva cut in the rock hillside

of women, sexual love played a central role in the literature and art of ancient India and there was no hesitation in depicting the beauty of sexual love and amorous couples. Indeed Indian literature is full of praise for the life-affirming power of physical love, and one of the great objective studies of sex was made by the Indian Vatsayana, the celebrated, 5th-century, author of *Karma Sutra*. This attitude in the secular world is mirrored in the sacred. Love plays an important role in it, although there is a dialectical relationship between asceticism and sexuality. If we remember this, it becomes easy to see why there was no hesitation in representing erotic scenes on the temple walls. The connection between religion and the erotic went back to the Kushan period in the 2nd century. However, among the masterpieces of erotic art may be mentioned two scenes showing couples kissing, the first in the Kailasa temple, Ellora, remarkable for its tender elegance, and the second from Konarak Sun temple, equally moving for a subtle presentation of a much-treated theme in India.

Indo-Islamic art under the Delphi sultanate (1210–1526). The arrival of Islam marks the end of the old order in India, at least in the north. From now on the hierarchical order of Indian society was to be deeply affected by the ideas of equality and brotherhood preached by Islam, as well as by its sheer vitality; Islam in its turn was to be affected by the caste system. By AD 712 only a century after Muhammad's death, Arabs had invaded the Indus Valley: it was about the same time as, in the West, they conquered as far as Spain. Unlike Europe, where Arab learning contributed substantially to medieval civilization, it did not leave much trace of its incursion except for an early lively account of Brahmans and their culture by the great encylopedist Al-Biruni. The Arabs did, however, carry the Hindu system of numbers westwards, to be subsequently known as Arab numerals. The Muslim adventurers, such as Mahmud of Ghazni, who followed the Arabs were mainly interested in the gold and precious stones that filled temples like Somnath in western India. It was the decisive victory over a coalition of Hindu powers in 1192 that led to the founding of the first Turkish Sultanate 18 years later. In theory the whole population had to be converted or, if they resisted, put to the sword, and initially many were probably converted. But because of the overwhelming number of the conquered people it was found more convenient to tax them, an expedient adopted in other parts of the Muslim world. Accordingly, the status of *Ah l-iqitab* (people of the book), accorded to Jews and Christians in the Middle East, was, significantly, extended to the Hindus.

The Delhi Sultanate lasted from 1210 to 1526, when it was overthrown by the Mughals. During this period architecture was clearly the most important form of artistic expression; the sultans were prolific builders both in Delhi and in the provinces where further sultanates were set up. Indian architecture underwent a profound transformation because the requirements of the conqueror were very different from those of the native inhabitants. Indeed, someone traveling in this period through both the north and the south, which remained Hindu in essence right down to the 20th century, would have been struck by the great differences between the buildings of the two areas. He would have noticed, for instance, that while on the walls of mosques the only forms of decoration permitted were geometric and abstract patterns, those details were strictly subject to the overall simple, elegant design of the building. In Hindu temples the basic design was governed by precise mathematical rules; at the same time this precision was combined with a rich decorative surface, mostly based on human figures. Even though many temples were of great height the emphasis was horizontal, in the sucessive layers of stone. In the mosques the universal use of arches to span a wide area was the rule.

The design of the mosque is dictated by the need for a prayer area for a large gathering. In its simplest form it is an open quadrangle, surrounded on four sides by pillared cloisters, the west or *qibla* side pointing towards Mecca and containing the *mihrab* or walled recess, often surmounted by a dome. Another essential architectural element is the minaret from the top of which the *muezzin*, or Muslim crier, calls the faithful to prayer. The general plan and design of Indian mosques was to a large extent determined by famous models like the great Mutawakkil mosque in Sammarra (Iraq) and possibly by later examples of the Seljuk madrasahs developed in Persia. But the great strength of Islamic architecture lies in its successful combination of certain universal elements with the regional and national peculiarities of places such as Arabia, Persia, North Africa, and central Asia. India was no exception. Because importing labor on a large scale was very expensive, India's masons and builders were employed almost from the very beginning. Indian builders, whatever their own persuasion, had until then served all traditional Indian religions equally well; with Islam they simply had to adjust their skill according to the task set before them. This led to the development of a mixed style in which the general conception was broadly Islamic while many of the details were of Indian inspiration. The Indian mastery of stone-cutting is also evident in the use of dressed stone rather than brick in the construction of mosques.

In the reign of the first sultan, Qutb ud-din Aibak (1191–1211), the earliest mosques such as the Qutb mosque in Delhi (1195) were hastily built with fragments from the destroyed Hindu temples. The use of columns of different shapes and sizes from different temples give them a most bizarre appearance but in this case faith triumphed over discretion. Nonetheless, the need for a tangible expression of the ideals of Islam remained. Work on an ambitious project was therefore begun only a few years after the hesitant start with the Qutb mosque. This was the Qutb minar, an effort of great architectural importance, built to accompany the first mosque. Ostensively in the form of a minaret for the purpose of the call to prayer, its

Right: the Qutb minar, Delhi, begun in 1199 (the top two stories were rebuilt at a later date)

scale and grandeur make it an ideal symbol of Islam's victory over unbelievers. The red sandstone tower formerly 238 ft (73 m) high, consists of four diminishing stories with projecting balconies, each differently designed with combinations of circles, flutings, and star-shaped patterns. A particularly noticeable feature of the tower is the calculated use of different textures and shapes for different levels, the bottom level containing abstract patterns, employing Arabic inscriptions of great visual beauty based on quotations from the Koran. Here, unable to use human figures, Indian artists adapted their carving skill for Islamic purposes to brilliant effect.

The succeeding sultans probably felt secure enough not to need such symbols to impress their subjects. Their buildings were conspicuously modest. A new form was introduced, however, by the second sultan, Shams ud-din (1211–36). The mausoleum, the early use of which was by the Muslim sultans of Egypt, was to be raised to supreme heights by the Mughals. Shams ud-din's tomb (1235) is a simple square edifice, three sides of which have three doorways, while the fourth, the western side, repeats the *mihrab* thrice. The deceptively rugged exterior ingeniously conceals the interior with rich decorative effect in red sandstone and white marble, using motifs of koranic inscriptions.

Alauddin Khalji (1296–1316) of the succeeding dynasty had the ambition of building a tower to dwarf the lofty Qutb. While this dream was never fulfilled he has, however, left us an elegant gateway (1305) next to the Qutb which marks the next important advance in Indo-Islamic architecture in a successful blending of Seljuk and Indian elements. The Alai Darwaza (Gateway of Victory) is also the first of the series of elaborate gateways from the Muslim period to be seen in many parts of India. The 60 ft (18 m) high monument has four doorways on four sides in the form of long and elegant arches, repeated on each side by bottom rows of smaller mock arches with perforated stone screens. The doorways lead into four spacious halls and the monument itself is crowned by a low, wide dome giving a general impression of great symmetry. The decoration as usual consists chiefly of abstract patterns, based on the Koranic text, in red sandstone and white marble.

The tomb of Ghias ud-din Tughlaq (1320–5) of the next dynasty uses marble for the first time to cover the whole dome. Apart from this delicacy of treatment the whole monument has a rough simplicity which suggests that this soldier-monarch deliberately rejected anything that hinted at needless pomp and luxury. Situated in the middle of what was once a lake and protected by massive bastions, the tomb has an unmistakable air of a fortress and may have served as such to protect the sultan's treasures from the hostile indigenous population. His grand-nephew Firuz (1351–88), equally austere but a prolific builder, founded Firuz Shah Kotla, a city on the outskirts of Delhi, although strained financial conditions allowed him only rubblework in his buildings. In the tomb of his minister, numerous cupolas appeared on the roof—a new architectural element.

By far the most spectacular architectural achievement of the Sultanate period was the mausoleum (1540) of Sher Shah, the brilliant Afghan general who drove out the Mughal Emperor Humayuan and ruled in Delhi for a brief period and became the last great Sultan (1540–5). The style is of the period of the Lodi sultans of Delhi the successors of the Tughlaqs, but the monument was built in Sher Shah's original home in Sasaram, in Bihar. The architect, Aliwal Khan, conceived it as an enormous and very complex pyramid, consisting of many levels; it rises to a height of 150 ft (48 m) and is 250 ft (76 m) wide. A columned pavilion, resting on a high base, lifts its head up straight from the waters of the artificial lake surrounding the tomb. Above the pavilion is an elaborate octagon which goes up in three diminishing stages and ends in a low, broad white dome. From the distance the mixture of solidity and elegance, the skilful manipulation of different shapes and materials such as Chunar sandstone and glazed tiles, above all the shining white dome make it a truly arresting sight. Many different styles of great originality and power were produced in the courts of local Muslim rulers. From these one example may be chosen for its sheer beauty of detail: the Sidi Sayyid mosque (1516) in Ahmedabad, Gujarat. Its reputation owes a great deal to the ornamental patterns of the perforated stone screen walls, among which the finest is possibly the brilliantly conceived tree motif by an unknown artist.

The history of painting in the Sultanate period is obscure and full of conflicting evidence, and remains so until the arrival of the Mughals. But in order to understand Mughal art it is necessary to make our way through this difficult period. The previously held commonplace belief that the Delhi sultans actively discouraged painting has ceased to convince us after important researches into the literary evidence for painting in the Sultanate, although actual examples of painting have not been positively identified.

Long before the arrival of the Turks, as early as the 10th century, the nature and patronage of painting in India was changing. The great tradition of wall-painting, which went back to Ajanta, was in decline in the north and its place was increasingly taken by small-scale works, mainly book illustrations. The increasing political uncertainties and consequent insecurity of life and wealth must have contributed to the decline in patronage. The center of activity shifted to the east, which was relatively immune from foreign raids.

This was also the age when Buddhism was in retreat all over India except in the great monasteries in the eastern Pala kingdom (c760–1142) which extended its patronage to a new Buddhist movement, the Vehicle of the Thunderbolt (Vajrayana). The new sect represented the growing importance of Tantra in Buddhism, a mystical cult which sought the highest spiritual truth through the means of the senses and through elaborate sexual rites and esoteric symbolism. The tiny paintings on palm leaves, measuring 22 in by 2 in (59 cm by 5 cm) often accompanying Vajrayana texts, reflect the secretive nature of the sect. They were not meant to be openly displayed but were kept carefully wrapped up to preserve their magic and only shown rarely to initiates. An illustration from the 11th-century manuscript Astasahasrika-Prajnaparamita (Bodleian Library, Oxford) shows the Pala artist's characteristic treatment of figures with delicate curved lines as well as his use of primary colors and avoidance of tones. Pala painting was to inspire art in Nepal and Tibet, where a complex symbolic language of pure colors was evolved. But even here the colors tend to be emblematic; red, for instance, stands for passion.

It is important to see Pala painting and sculpture together to realize the common ideal of human beauty that both sculptures and painters draw upon. The Pala artists, Dhiman and Bitpala (both fl. c900), celebrated in literature, may well have been connected with the cultural center in the great monastery at Nalanda. Both stone and bronze sculptures were executed in the Pala period, but even stonework follows metal in its linear treatment of the figure with emphasis on beautifully elaborate and curvilinear patterns incised on stone. Both kinds of sculpture, however, are distant echoes of Gupta art, al-

A Tantra painting from the 11th-century manuscript Astasahasrika-Prajnaparamita. Bodleian Library, Oxford

though they now concentrate on sensuous lines. Similarly, if for a moment we forget the Pala treatment in the above painting and take a close look at the adoring figures around the central Bodhisattva, we see how close in pose and gestures their upturned faces are to Ajanta figures. Here, however, the artist has sacrificed the naturalism and the dramatic narrative character of Ajanta art in favor of a timeless sacred icon.

Pala art provided inspiration for art in Nepal and Tibet in the successive centuries down to the present. It had no further role to play in India. Its contemporary in western India, Jain religious painting, on the other hand, had great importance for the future development of painting in India. Jain painters were provided with a greater scope for development in the 15th century when they changed from palm leaf to paper. As with Pala paintings these works had a specific religious purpose. In earlier times pious Jain merchants had often been able to bear the cost of enormous marble temples in Mount Abu and other places; the presence of Muslim powers in the north increasingly forced them to turn to more modest ways of acquiring merit for it was a pious act to commission the illustration of stories from the *Kalpa sutra* or *Kalakacharya Katha* dealing with the miraculous births of Jain saints and their conversions of unbelievers.

The paintings were modest in scope, the style deliberately rigid as befitting sacred art where any deviation from the original formula may constitute sacrilege. The three-quarter face of the figures often has staring eyes with large pupils, while the farther eye is shown crossing the facial outline. The torso resembles a triangle, while shoulders are broad and the waist extremely narrow, a formula applied equally to both sexes making it difficult for us to distinguish them. There is not the slightest trace of any borrowing from Ajanta; if the painters knew of the achievement of these caves they preferred to ignore them. Within the framework of this rigid style some of the paintings are very expressive in their austere fashion. As the 16th century progressed, the original limited palette of reds, blues, and greens was enriched by gold and ultramarine, while composition became more complex as painters learned to use scroll-like clouds and other decorative motifs from Persian art. Persian merchants, who may have introduced the art of their own country to Jain artists, possibly served as the model for the portrait of the foreign Saka king converted by a Jain teacher in the *Kalpa sutra* dated 1475 (Devansano Pado Bhandar).

The pictorial tradition associated with Jain texts affected the neighboring states of Malwa and Rajasthan, although the subject and spirit of their paintings are entirely different. They are mostly visual representations of romantic poetry; the finest example of the style and also the best known is the *Chaurapanchasika* series illustrating the Kashmiri poet Bilhana's celebrated *Forty Verses of a Thief* (N.C. Mehta Collection, Gujarat Museum, Ahmedabad) dated *c*1500. "Even today do I see the fair arms that encircled my neck, when she clasped me close to her breast, and pressed her face against my own in a kiss, while her playful eyes half closed in ecstasy",

wrote the 12th-century poet Bilhana. The mood of gentle eroticism that informs the work of this poet marks an important development in Indian literature from the 10th century onwards as the formal elegance of classical Sanskrit gives way to the intimate atmosphere of vernacular languages. Romantic love, whether secular or couched in the allegory of Vaishnava mysticism, becomes the vehicle of this new literature, which will be discussed later in connection with Rajput painting.

The *Chaurapanchasika* paintings clearly show that while the artists worked within the Jain pictorial convention the subject of love between a poet and his beloved clearly required a different treatment. The heroine Champavati's features still contain traces of Jain art such as the triangular torso or staring eyes, but the whole spirit of the work is festive, as flowering trees, her gray-blue patterned skirt, the chequered bedspread, and marble architectural detail bring relief to the traditional Jain red background. A new pictorial device introduced here, the division of the picture plane into several parts by means of a columned open pavilion that allows us a glimpse into the interior of the house, was to be used in painting for several centuries by succeeding generations of Rajput artists. The charming gait of Champavati reminds us of Indian classical dance gestures. The reflection of a long and confident Hindu cultural tradition when Hindu powers were in retreat everywhere makes us conclude that the series was executed for the rulers of Mewar, the only Hindu power to recover from Muslim domination and establish its hegemony in Rajasthan in the 16th century.

Similar in style were illustrations to the *Laur Chanda*, a romantic tale about the Hindu aristocracy composed, significantly, by a Muslim poet, Maulana Da'ud. Initially Muslim rulers, who regarded Hindus as unbelievers, made no attempt to establish cultural and social contacts with them. The Hindus on their part considered everyone outside the caste system as being beyond the pale. But as the two communities began to live side by side links were formed. The first to build the bridge were Muslim Sufis, Hindu Yogis, and leaders of the *Bhakti* movement. This common sympathy helped create a new syncretic religion, the traces of which remain in India in the form of shrines attended by both Hindus and Muslims. As the text of *Laur Chanda* embodies this new spirit, so the styles of paintings that illustrate the work represent a mixture of two styles, Gujarati and Persian.

The version in the John Rylands Library, Manchester, is a rich storehouse for the study of contemporary modes and manners, but the paintings in the Prince of Wales Museum, Bombay, are particularly remarkable for their blend of delicate colors, most unusual for the period. If we do not have any Sultanate painting, we have 16th-century paintings done for a Muslim court in western India. Nadir Shah Khalji (1500–10), the Sultan of Malwa, asked his artists to illustrate a cookery book (*Nimat-nama*) for him. The story that he replaced men with women in the kind of jobs usually reserved for men is corroborated by the paintings. The background of these pictures, showing scroll-like clouds and landscape

A scene from the Nimat-nama, the cookery book illustrated for Nadir Shah Khalji; c1500. India Office Library, London

dotted with tufts of grass, suggests a knowledge of Persian painting. The trade connections between western India and Persia may well have encouraged painters to seek employment at the Muslim court of Malwa. But what is puzzling is that these paintings also frequently incorporate figures of women derived from Jain art. Were Gujarati painters also employed to collaborate in the work as was to be common in the Mughal period? This curious mixed style is also to be seen in another contemporary (16th-century) text from Malwa, the *Miftah-al Fuzala*. These related western Indian styles from contiguous areas have some important differences but much in common, which lends support to the hypothesis that they all draw upon a common artistic background in western India. This was the general situation of painting in northern India when the Mughals arrived in the country.

Indo-Islamic art under the Mughal dynasty (1526–1757). The founder of the Mughal dynasty, Babur (1526–31), was descended from two world conquerors, Chingiz and Timur, one a Turk, the other Mongol; the culture he adopted was Persian. In 1526 Babur crushed the Delhi Sultan, and the following year the Rana of Mewar suffered the same fate; in both cases gunpowder decided the issue. With the Mughal dynasty a new era begins in India. They were Muslim but very different from the religious, austere Delhi sultans, and were to have great influence on the development of painting and architecture in India. They were intellectually curious, urbane, secular, and highly gifted individuals. Great connoisseurs of beauty, both natural and artificial, they brought a new, heightened sensibility to art and life and introduced clear principles of taste in judging works of art. The court of "The Great Mogul" (Mughal) became synonymous with pomp and circumstance. The Mughals introduced formal gardens, fountains, and the game of polo to India; their courtly etiquette was eagerly

emulated and their sartorial habits assiduously copied in the provinces—their cuisine is remembered even today. The splendor, the courtly etiquette, the wealth, all were faithfully recorded in painting, the most naturalistic in the history of Indian art. It is true that in order to maintain the high cultural standards of the Empire later emperors were forced to levy increasingly oppressive taxes, but at least in the period of the early emperors India enjoyed remarkable peace and prosperity. Babur himself was a curious mixture of blood-thirsty warrior and reflective man of letters; his autobiography is delightful to read. He was steeped in Persian culture and did not know India well enough to care for it. His early death led to a period of chaos in India when his son was driven out to Persia for a number of years.

The great age of the Mughals begins with the accession of Akbar (1556–1605) at the age of 13, destined to become one of the greatest rulers the world has seen. The great Catholic encyclopedist Athanasius Kircher (1602–80) paid a tribute to him when he stated that Akbar was renowned for "la beauté de son esprit". His age breathes such an air of confident optimism and vitality that it brings to mind an earlier one, that of the Guptas. In the 16th century Muslims and Hindus had come closer and yet the latter suffered from certain disadvantages in the Muslim state. Akbar took the decisive step of removing all the marks of inferiority, such as the poll tax, which defined Hindus as the conquered subjects. He also married into Rajput houses and made this powerful political group partners in his Empire. Although his immensely busy life left him little time for a formal education he showed lively intellectual curiosity in many things, above all in the nature of religion. At the end of his life he came to accept that all religions contained something of value, a position that brought him in conflict with the orthodox divines (*ulema*). His reign marks an advance in architecture in the spaciously constructed tomb of his father, which anticipates the style of the Taj Mahal.

But it is the architecture of the city of Fathpur Sikri, abandoned when the water supply ran out, that engages our attention. Wide, spacious terraces and courtyards separate the numerous palaces, pavilions, and shrines in Fathpur which rest on a windswept ridge somewhat elevated from the surrounding plains. The imaginative conception of the architect is brought out with clarity in the two extremes of buildings; the towering Buland Darwaza (Triumphal Gateway) whose overwhelming strength is tempered by a series of kiosks with cupolas that lighten the heaviness of the red sandstone. This gateway may be considered the culmination of the process begun with Alauddin's modest Alai Darwaza. The other extreme is an intimate and delicate little tomb of the saint Salim Chisti, with its perforated stonework of rare delicacy, giving us a foretaste of the Taj Mahal.

When the great Emperor set up his huge artistic establishment he is said to have answered the Muslim argument, that when an artist created images he was usurping God's prerogative to infuse creatures with life, with a counterargument. His

Part of the Panch Mahal, a summer palace in the abandoned city of Fathpur Sikri; second half of the 16th century

answer was calculated to silence the divines but it also indicates his mystical approach to religion. According to his friend and chronicler Abul Fazl, he stated that the very fact the artist could create likenesses of mortal creatures but not give them life made him all the more aware of God's omnipotence.

Akbar's studio was set up under the guidance of two 16th-century Persian artists, Mir Sayyid Ali and Khwaja Abd al-Samad, persuaded by Akbar's father, Humayun, to emigrate to India. This event marked the beginning of a steady flow of Muslim artists from Persia and neighboring countries to the Mughal court where they knew they were welcome. In setting up his studio Akbar naturally chose the Persian school with which he was familiar. Book illustrations, which emerged in the 13th century in Iran, owed many of their motifs, such as cloud forms or rocks and other landscape elements, to the art of China, although Persian artists had reduced the atmospheric idiom of Chinese art to charming patterns of lines and colors. Akbar, who had been taught to paint by Abd al-Samad, personally supervised the painters who were recruited in large numbers to illustrate the enormous collection of manuscripts inherited by the Emperor. There is a touching picture by the Persian master showing young Akbar offering his own work to Humayun.

The first great project was undertaken in the 1580s to relate the romantic tales of Amir Hamza, an uncle of the Prophet, in 1,700 large-sized (at least for Persian book illustration) paintings on cotton. But for a chance discovery, these works of considerable historical importance, some of them masterpieces, would have been irretrievably lost. Today 200 remain in various European museums (two main collections are those of the Österreichisches Museum für Angewandte Kunst, Vienna, and the Victoria and Albert Museum, London). It is hardly surprising that Akbar's ignorance of Indian art made him import Persian style into India; what is astonishing is the rapidity with which Mughal art cut its Persian umbilical cord and stood on its own feet. As with the architects, the majority of the painters were Indian, some definitely known to be Gujarati, who brought their own traditions with them. Indeed the unique feature of Mughal art is the happy confluence of three pictorial traditions, Persian, Indian, and as we shall see later, European.

In the *Hamza-nama* the main compositional elements are Persian, like the so-called aerial perspective, ideally suited for historical and dramatic subjects as it gave a panoramic view of the scene depicted. Another feature is the dazzling combination of pure colors in decorative patterns. These two elements

Gujarati girls drawing water from a well: a detail from a painting in the Hamza-nama; 1580s. Victoria and Albert Museum, London

been alien to the ordered sensibility of the Safavid artist. Significantly, the Indian preference for naturalism was shared by Akbar, who increasingly turned away from the pure Persian idiom because he needed a form of art to record faithfully the immensely eventful life at the court. This preference is revealed in Mughal appreciation of European art as well as in Abul-Fazl's statement that in art "even inanimate objects look as if they had life". Thus in *Hamza* we have dazzling Persian details in tiled architecture or richly patterned carpets set against men and women in violent combat with men or with supernatural beings. The realism and immediacy of the pictures is enhanced by the device of cutting off foreground figures, giving a snapshot impression of the scene. On balance, there is some loss of the abstract charm of Safavid painting; the gain is in terms of powerful drawing, fiery colors, and expressive figures which from now on are to be psychologically related.

A conqueror himself, Akbar took great delight in scenes from epics and histories. He was the first Muslim ruler to take an interest in Hindu literature. What is revealing is that when he had the great epic *Mahabharata* (finally edited in the 2nd century AD) translated into Persian, the title given was *Razm-nama* or the *Book of Wars*; this interest is clear from the 179 paintings, the majority of which deal with scenes of war and other violent activities. The frenzied actions, the great ability to show movement, the violent colors, and very complex compositions in which many figures are engaged in mortal struggle are most compelling in their peculiar expressionist, even obsessive manner. The movement, the violent clash, of colors and feverish activity in paintings of Akbar's reign have often been attributed solely to Akbar's dynamic personality, much as Jahangir's introverted nature has been seen in the restrained, delicate pictures of his period. It is no doubt true that Akbar's close personal scrutiny and active interest had much to do with the rapid progress of Mughal art. Indeed the extraordinary rapport between the emperors and their artists is rare in the history of art. But the important role of the painters and their personalities should not be underestimated, however little we may know of their specific contributions.

Although the *Razm-nama* paintings are collaborations in typical Akbari fashion, the early ones, especially 30 of them, include the signature of a tormented genius, Daswanth (*c*1550–*ob.* by 1584), whose talents were discovered early by Akbar himself. Daswanth became a legendary figure in his lifetime but his melancholic spirit eventually made him take his own life at an early age. His expressionist brush which could not be contained within the bounds of balanced pictorial composition must have had a profound effect on his contemporaries.

With Daswanth's death *c*1584 the Dionysiac element in Mughal painting gave way to the Apollonian, under the influence of the other major painter of the period, Basawan.

seem to have liberated Indian artists from a limited range of colors seen in Gujarati painting, and contributed to the development of a pictorial tradition of epic and historical narratives. But *Hamza* paintings are far removed from the delicate, magic world of decorative patterns in Persian art. The Indian artist's preference for naturalism breaks through in revealing details, like the Gujarati girls drawing water from the well in the top right-hand corner of the painting depicting the giant Zummurad (Victoria and Albert Museum, London).

The Gujarati element may also be seen in an early work of the leading painter Basawan (1556–1605) in the Cleveland *Tuti nama*, dating from this period (Cleveland Museum of Art). Naturalistic details of familiar animals rendered with loving care in *Hamza* are also more characteristically Indian. But above all, there is an important departure from the Persian tradition in the use of many figures engaged in dramatic and violent action, the very actuality of which would have

Right: A scene from the Akbar-nama, a cheetah hunt; 1590. Victoria and Albert Museum, London

Mughal Painting

The 17th century, or more precisely the period from *c*1600 to *c*1660, covering the reigns of the emperors Jahangir (1605–27) and Shah Jahan (1627–58), represents not only the greatest period of Mughal painting but one of the finest achievements in the history of representational art. Jahangir's reign saw great innovations in naturalism built on foundations laid in the previous period. In Shah Jahan's reign the gains in the mastery of representation were further consolidated but did not lead to any major innovations. Undoubtedly the central period of Mughal painting is Jahangir's reign, reflecting an unusually sympathetic interaction between the Emperor's tastes and the artists' personalities, rarely encountered in art patronage. Active encouragement of painting by Jahangir, who gave it priority over the administration of the state, helped take this art to great heights—a central event in the life of the court was the weekly inspection of completed paintings.

▲ *Officers and Wise Man* by Payag. Sterling and Francine Clark Art Institute, Williamstown

▼ *The Presentation of the Book* by Abul Hasan. The Walters Art Gallery, Baltimore

▶ *Hindu Holy Men*, a yogi scene by Govardhan; *c*1626–30. Williams Hayes Fogg Art Museum, Cambridge, Mass.

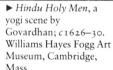

▶ *The Young Hawk and the Hunt:* an illustrated album leaf by Aqa Riza; 23×14cm (9×5½in). British Library, London

◀ *King Vulture and Griffin* by Mansur; color and gilt on paper; 39×26cm (15×10in). Metropolitan Museum, New York

Seventeenth-century Mughal painting is dominated by twin pulls, between the formal color and linear arrangements of Persian art and the new requirements of representational art at the court, whose ultimate source was European prints. The nucleus of Jahangir style is the series done in Allahabad in the 1590s when the rebel prince set up his capital there. The studio was led by Aqa Riza who preferred the Persian idiom, even though interest was shifting to European naturalism and a number of copies of European prints had been produced in this period. European naturalism enabled painters to tell stories more convincingly, introducing, for example, exploration of psychological relationships between figures, as seen in the late Akbar period painting of the dying king, from the *Gulistan* manuscript (The Walters Art Gallery, Baltimore), in which the faces, especially the king's emaciated face, are intensely individual. Secondly, a convincing background is created with natural or architectural details, occasionally ones derived from European prints. Above all, "consistent lighting" is employed, though not always consistently.

The best known Jahangir paintings are portraits, which include some very fine individual portraits as well as group portraits representing court ceremonials, historic and dynastic subjects, and animal studies which often combine acute observation of details and a remarkable perfection of finish, as seen in Mansur's *King Vulture and Griffin*. Less appreciated until recently are the picturesque "genre" scenes, dealing with the life of ordinary people far removed from courtly life, though sometimes scenes from the imperial zenana are also included. Less concerned with high finish, they are in many ways the

most fascinating and rewarding, as they give glimpses of the Mughal artist's powers of observation. Two examples are the detail of a cat from a zenana scene and a striking study of a scribe.

Jahangir's patronage, with his concentration on a limited number of masters, marks a distinct change from the large-scale workshop of Akbar. This led to the abandonment of collaboration among painters and the emergence of individual artists with their specific traits and predilections within a common idiom. One of the finest masters of naturalism is Abul Hasan, who, unlike Manohar with his studied elegance, is keen to explore the effect of light on objects, especially on fabrics. Of special interest is his sympathetic exploration of the individuality of different faces, and the softening of outlines to create more subtle naturalism, as seen in *The Presentation of the Book*. Similar concern is seen in the work of Govardhan, a fascinating and enigmatic personality. His genre scenes, notably with yogis, probe the relationship between lying and seated figures. He is unique in showing a great deal of concern with life outside the court circle. His paintings with their soft modeling of figures

and subtle erotic overtones, reflect a rather unusual sensibility; the subject of naked yogis he was so fond of painting gave him an opportunity to develop the relationship between light and shadow on the surfaces of the figures. Payag, an artist who rose to prominence in the Shah JaNan period, continues this concern for representation in a remarkably ambitious painting, bringing the Mughal art of story-telling to its culmination. In the night scene *Officers and Wise Man*, the figures are seated around a centrally placed candle, cleverly creating a single light source in the picture. His subtle combination of various light and shadow areas in the picture and skilful characterization of figures make him one of the most outstanding artists of Shah Jahan's reign.

PARTHA MITTER

Further reading. Beach, M.C. *The Grand Mogul*, New York (1978). Ettinghausen, R. *Paintings of the Sultans and Emperors of India*, New Delhi (1961). Ettinghausen, R. *Persian and Mughal Art*, London (1976). Ettinghausen, R. *Paintings from the Muslim Courts of India*, London (1976). Welch, S.C. *The Art of Mughal India*, New York (1964).

Abul-Fazl, our invaluable guide in these matters, mentions that some critics preferred him to Daswanth. Basawan was more interested in pictorial composition, in the foreshortening of figures, and in relating several figures to one another as well as to their landscape or architectural setting, such experiments probably prompted by the Mughal discovery of European art. His colors too were subtle and full of tonalities. A court scene from the *Anwar i-Suhayli* (Bharat Kala Bhavan, Benaras) gives us a good idea of the complex arrangement of figures he was particularly fond of. He had a leading role in creating the very fine series of paintings now in the Victoria and Albert Museum, London (*Akbar-nama*); among them "Akbar struggling to contain enraged elephants as courtiers anxiously watch him", captures the scene most vividly. Basawan moved away from the pure color harmonies of the Persian idiom towards consistent chiaroscuro, especially evident in the treatment of the elephants. Yet another style emerges in the work of a different painter, Miskin (late 16th–early 17th centuries), who in his interpretation of the night scene from Jami's *Baharistan* (Bodleian Library, Oxford) has made subtle use of atmospheric light and delicate colors, learnt from European art.

Akbar's concern with accurately documenting the major events in his reign encouraged the growth of the "reporting" style of painting which led to the search for a naturalistic idiom that was new in India; he himself is said to have sat for his likeness. In the 1580s when the Jesuits, keen to convert him, brought presents including Plantin's Polyglot Bible, illustrated with engravings, Akbar and his artists must have eagerly examined the Western prints. Akbar was particularly interested in Christian themes, but his own collection included secular European paintings and engravings, as well as tapestries and even a musical instrument—the organ. Engravings and other forms of art continued to pour in, even during Jahangir's reign (1605–27), notably a miniature by the leading English miniaturist, Isaac Oliver, presented by James I's emissary, Sir Thomas Roe. Dated copies of European works include Kesu's copy of Heemskerck's *St Matthew*, Nadira Banu's copy of Sadeler's *St Jerome*, and the 13-year-old Abul Hasan's fine copy of St John from Dürer's *Crucifixion* (1511). It is difficult to put dates to stages in the absorption of Western pictorial convention; the first period was probably one of wonder and experimentation, leading gradually to more selective borrowings.

European subject matter, motifs, and techniques seem to have appealed to Mughal artists; among these copies two may be chosen for their specially interesting features. A copy of a *Deposition from the Cross* based on a Raimondi print of a lost Raphael, by an unknown artist, is a striking adaptation because of its accomplished handling of colors, close to European Mannerist art. This is probably the work done for Jahangir in 1598 described by the Jesuit Jerome Xavier. A close look at the picture reveals that not only has the artist chosen the tragic theme of Deposition but that he has also filled the background with details from another painting by an as yet unidentified European painter. In Mughal painting European motifs are often combined in a particular work, sometimes in such a playful manner that to a European it would pose problems of compatibility.

There is another interesting picture showing a mythological figure holding up a dragon-shaped object (formerly S.C. Welch Collection, Cambridge, Mass.); it may well have been based on Botticelli's *Judith with the Head of Holofernes*, only in this case Judith's right arm, instead of holding a sword, is joined to the head on a salver carried by the attendant. These departures do not fail to delight us but the important question is, what permanent gains were made by these artists? Illusionistic art made a deep impression upon them, as it was to do later in Japan. Skilled at the naturalistic rendering of objects, including portraiture, they found European art challenging. The technique of representing consistent lighting through chiaros curo was easily grasped as the Persian mode of formal coloring was gradually abandoned. Foreshortening and the suggestion of distance by making distant objects small compared with the ones in the foreground were also successful adopted. But linear perspective posed the greatest challenge

A Mughal mythological figure that may have been copied from a painting by Botticelli. Location unknown

and continued to do so even in the 18th century. While the quality of Mughal painting was in no way affected by whether perspective was correctly applied or not, it is nonetheless worth pondering why they failed in its application. Although in a number of traditions it was known that distance could be suggested by making distant figures small, linear perspective, specially applied to architecture, based on precise rules governing the recession of objects in space, was a Renaissance invention. Its laws could not be comprehended through copying and Mughal artists had no opportunity to learn the theory behind them.

From the copious documentation of Akbar's reign by Abul Fazl, and because of the importance attached to painters and paintings, we know about the organization of workshops, set up on a large scale with over 100 painters including a woman, Nadira Banu (*fl.* mid 16th–early 17th century). Three-quarters of the artists were Hindus, who were picked out by Abul-Fazl for special praise. The identification of individual styles in the early period when collaboration was the rule, poses problems for us. Main design, sketch, and later corrections were reserved for major artists. For portraits, thumbnail sketches were kept in stock. Stress was laid on details such as hands, which were drawn with infinite care, an Indian characteristic since the time of Ajanta. Some Mughal painters were born in the royal household and received training at an early age. They were given drawing exercises from pattern books, beginning with simple shapes like spirals and triangles, then graduating to birds, flowers, architectural details, and finally moving on to the human form. Flower drawings were meant to develop their aesthetic sense. The beautiful finish in painting much admired in this period was obtained from careful priming of the paper and smoothing it with agate. Paper, initially imported from Persia, was produced in Sialkot, in Punjab. A drawing was created by transferring to paper a tracing made on deer skin; black chalk was used to correct drawing with red chalk. These stencils, introduced from Persia and imported in fair quantities with color indications, made possible the continued use of Persian design in Mughal art. Brushes were made from the hair of different animals; organic and mineral colors were held together on the paper by means of glue. In the final analysis the quality of work depended a great deal on imagination and talent; a master could transform the mechanical process of tracing into something pulsating with life.

When Jahangir came to the throne (1605) he already possessed a large establishment of painters, including the Persian artist Aqa Riza (*fl.* late 16th–early 17th centuries); he now inherited Akbar's studio, which consisted of a number of important painters. Basawan trained his son, Manohar (*c*1565–*c*1628). Others, like Mansur (*fl.* late 16th–mid 17th centuries) and Abul Hasan (*c*1589–*c*1650), had served their apprenticeships in the Akbar period. From the end of Akbar's reign individual works without accompanying texts, forming parts of albums, began to be assigned to each master. Also noticeable is the quietening down of the bustle and fury of

Hamza and *Razm-nama*; now colors are in low key and related in tonal values. Complex scenes with numerous figures in violent movement are given up in favor of single figures against a plain background.

The major preoccupation of Akbar, epic and history painting, was abandoned; instead, portraits, court scenes, animal and flower paintings were further developed and now became models of ordered simplicity and lyrical understatement. We know artists such as Abul Hasan, Mansur, Bishndas, Manohar, Bichitr, Padarath, and Daulat from their works; we even know what some of them looked like from a sketch by Daulat of five painters, including his self-portrait, and from a self-portrait of Manohar. Jahangir, who was happy to maintain the territorial integrity of the Empire without any further expansion, found particular pleasure in the company of his artists whom he honored in various ways. A man of great culture, learning, and sensibility, a collector and the author of a delightful autobiography, he was above all the foremost creator of the Mughal tradition of connoisseurship and taste for art as well as the criteria for judging styles and the quality of painting. He remarks on his discerning eye in his autobiography:

> my liking for painting and ...judging it have arrived at such a point that when any work is brought before me ...I say on the spur of the moment that it is the work of such and such a man. And if there be a picture containing many portraits and each be the face of a different master, I can discover which face is the work of each of them.

One of the consequences of the lively appreciation of the Mughal masters by their contemporaries was the rise of the practice of copying well-known masterpieces, which makes the task of distinguishing the real work from the fake rather difficult.

Portrait painting assumed great importance in Jahangir's reign. In the formal portraits of assembled courtiers and the Emperor a curious feature is often noticeable. In a late picture, for example the *Durbar of Jahangir* (*c*1620; Goloubew Collection, Museum of Fine Arts, Boston), we may find young courtiers mingling happily with ones long since dead. The fact is that these *durbar* scenes were not literal representations of actual events but were meant as records of the personalities of the reign. The likenesses of the subjects, based on stencils kept in stock, are so accurate that we know the rulers and courtiers from the Mughal period very well. But they were considerably stylized, as for instance where Jahangir's dignified mask-like profile is meant to convey the solemnity of the occasion at Diwan i-Khas in Agra.

Quite opposite in spirit are informal portraits such as the joint portrait by Govardhan of Jahangir and his beloved Nur Jahan, one of the great beauties of the age. One of the finest of this genre is the monarch's son Khuram's portrait in a bright amber dress against a dark emerald background holding a jeweled brooch (Victoria and Albert Museum, London). This is by Jahangir's favorite Abul Hasan who has picked out such details as his personal jewelry and patterns on his scarf and

A durbar scene: Emperor Jahangir (1605–27) receives Prince Parviz.
Victoria and Albert Museum, London

Jahangir Prefers Sufis to Kings by Bichitr; 25×18cm (10×7in).
Freer Gallery of Art, Washington, D.C.

sash with brilliant effect.

Portraitists served diplomatic purposes as well. Jahangir's second major portrait painter Bishndas was sent with an embassy to depict the likeness of Shah Abbas of Iran and was honored with gifts on his return. Some of the best likenesses of the Persian monarch are by Bishndas in the Leningrad Album (Hermitage Museum, Leningrad). Similarly, on receiving from the English ambassador Roe a work by Isaac Oliver, Jahangir presented him with his own portrait by Manohar, which survives only in a print in *Purchas his Pilgrimes*, the famous 17th-century travelogue of the Revd Samuel Purchas. Jahangir's portraitists such as Abul Hasan developed a special type of symbolic portrait expressing complex iconography and often accompanied with allegorical poems. Of the four in the Freer Gallery of Art, Washington D.C., dealing with Jahangir's imaginary encounters with other rulers, the one by Bichitr called *Jahangir prefers Sufis to Kings* is probably the most striking and complex. Jahangir is shown here sitting on an elaborately carved hourglass with grotesques carved on it symbolizing Time and representing his long life. Little winged cherubs derived from Western art turn away from him in anguish as he spurns worldly kings like the Turkish Sultan and King James I and seeks the company of Sufis or mystics.

Jahangir's autobiography testifies to his great intellectual curiosity. He had agents who scoured home and abroad for exotic people like Siamese twins and bearded ladies. Sometimes his curiosity verged on the bizarre, as when a noble of the realm, Inayat Khan, was dying from an excess of drugs and alcohol—he had a drawing made of the poor emaciated man just before his death. While his caprices need no longer hold our interest, this particular outcome was certainly a hauntingly powerful picture.

Animal painting, begun in the previous period (see the fine works in *Anwar i-Suhayli*, School of Oriental and African Studies, London) now reached new heights. Jahangir's favorite animal recorder, Mansur, made faithful paintings of a large variety of birds and animals, including the exotic zebra and turkey, as well as of hundreds of flowers and plants from Kashmir. Mansur's style is one of studied elegance and great precision, as if he carefully dissected each subject for anatomical accuracy, to be seen for instance in the Chameleon (Royal Library, Windsor) although the Cheer pheasant (Victoria and Albert Museum, London) by him is livelier. Warmth and movement in the depiction of animals is to be seen in a superlative example of Mughal animal art by the portraitist, Abul Hasan. It may seem a paradox that Mansur, famous for his animals, produced the portrait of *The Vina Player* (Edward Croft Murray Collection, London), a very fine ex-

The Taj Mahal at Agra, a mausoleum built by Shah Jahan for his wife. The mausoleum was built between 1632 and 1643 and the surrounding complex finished in 1654

ample of Mughal figure painting, while Abul Hasan, prized by Jahangir for his allegorical portraits, produced in the *Squirrels in a Chennar Tree* one of the finest animal paintings, unrivaled except for ones by Chinese artists and the great Dürer. Another animal painting worth mentioning is Padarath's *Mountain Sheep* (Chester Beatty Library, Dublin).

Shah Jahan (1627–1656), who succeeded Jahangir, is known to us mainly for the Taj Mahal at Agra, built in memory of his wife. His prodigious building activity forms a contrast to Jahangir's almost total indifference to architecture. The personal and intensely passionate intervention of his son is evident in the range and quality of the architecture of the period; the same mastery over architectural material and the art of building is to be seen not only in grand conceptions like the Taj but in exquisite cameos like the Pearl Mosque (Moti Masjid, Agra), with its perfect proportions and refinement of details.

With the Taj Mahal the climax in the art of mausoleum building is reached not only in Mughal architecture but in the whole tradition of Islamic tomb architecture. This mausoleum, consisting of a central structure with a high dome and smaller cupolas and minarets set at the end of ornamental gardens with lotus pools and fountains, is justly famous for its simplicity of conception, symmetry, and lucidity as well as for

From Squirrels in a Chennar Tree by Abul Hasan. India Office Library, London

its perfect proportions. Another feature of the Taj, unique and legendary in the history of architecture, is the very special quality of Markrana marble which changes its delicate shades in response to the atmospheric light from the rose of the Indian dawn to the pristine white of a moonlit summer night in Agra. But the Taj is no less exquisite in the details of its perforated screen and *pietra dura* work.

Among small objects of great beauty is the jade winecup belonging to Shah Jahan (1657; Victoria and Albert Museum, London). Painting, however, continued to be important in his reign. History painting was revived, some of the finest examples of which are in the *Shah Jahan-nama* (Royal Library, Windsor). Formal group portraits showing many courtiers increased in number, ranging from stiff, unimaginative hackwork to items of ingenuity and imagination. The main innovation of the period was the equestrian portrait, to be widely adopted by provincial rulers all over India within a short time. The painting by Govardhan of Shah Jahan and his favorite son, Dara, a great patron of Hindu philosophy (Victoria and Albert Museum, London), shows the mastery over line and shading achieved by Mughal artists as well as the subtle range of tones used in the work. Equestrian portraits and other forms of Mughal art of the Jahangir and Shah Jahan periods made their way into Rembrandt's collection. His delicate sketches after Mughal art, which show his own mastery of expression without destroying the essential nature of Indian works, form a fascinating chapter in the history of cultural borrowings.

With the accession of the orthodox Aurangzeb (1658–1707), painting and other arts ceased to be of importance at the court. As tradition has it, his musicians in a symbolic gesture of protest buried their instruments in the earth. This act apparently left the Emperor unmoved. In this atmosphere, painting naturally suffered. After him, increasing disintegration of the Empire led his successors to withdraw into their harems, where they continued to support an intensely romantic and gently erotic school of painting with misty landscapes, atmospheric colors, and pretty women. Gradually artists began to seek employment elsewhere while popular painters began a veritable industry of copying masterpieces.

Schools of painting flourished in the Muslim courts of Ahmadnagar, Golconda, and Bijapur from the 16th century onwards, independent of and parallel to the Mughal atelier, their independence symbolizing the resistance of these courts to the might of the Emperor in the north. The influence of the Safavid School of Persia came through trade contacts and marriage alliances: it can be seen in the landscape in the *Tarif i-Husayn Shahi* album painted for the Ahmadnagar ruler, Husayn Nizam Shah I (Bharata Itihasha Samshodaka Mandala Collection, Poona). The affluence of Golconda, partly owing to the newly discovered diamond mines, is reflected in the lavish jewelry worn by the subjects portrayed as well as in the generous use of gold.

From Golconda comes one of the most remarkable paintings, until recently wrongly identified as Mughal: Muhammad Ali's *The Poet in the Garden* (Museum of Fine Arts, Boston), which shows a great delicacy of drawing and colors. The best-known Deccani paintings are of course the portraits of Bijapur sultans and courtiers with their fully rounded forms and flowing transparent skirts. One of the most striking examples of this style is the portrait of a courtier whose powerful frame and expression is underlined by the deliberately low-key background relieved only by two bright yellow flying birds, a style that makes an interesting contrast with Mughal portraits. These important schools declined c1627, partly because the three kingdoms were gradually absorbed in the Mughal Empire.

With the decline of the Mughal Empire the center of gravity for painting shifts to the hills of Rajasthan and Punjab, although inferior works continued to flow from the metropoli-

A Deccan school miniature of a Bijapur courtier. British Museum, London

Left: Shah Jahan (1627–56) and his son Dara by Govardhan.
Victoria and Albert Museum, London

tan centers of Agra and Delhi. The Rajputs, including the fiercely independent rulers of Mewar, the chief of the Rajput clans, had ceased to resist the Mughals during Jahangir's reign. Mewar chiefs built a new capital on the beautiful Pichola lake when Chitor had to be abandoned after its sack by Akbar. The Rajputs who took office under the Mughals were obviously impressed by the naturalistic achievements of the Mughal artists; there exists a picture of the Rana of Mewar with Shah Jahan in Mughal style. From the Mughals these princes learned to appreciate portraits and every Rajput court from the tiniest to the most exalted had its portraitist for whom the rulers eagerly posed. Frequently they are represented on horseback or, for instance, out hunting wild boars in the green Aravalli hills dotted with shrubs, a passion they shared with the Mughal emperors.

As the Mughal tradition receded, however, the portraits increasingly concentrated on formal harmonies of color and line, even though attention continued to be given to the accurate likeness of the sitter. In fact the Mughal formulas of profile portraits were adapted to Rajput purposes. But while Rajput princes happily adopted Mughal costume, etiquette, and pastimes, they nonetheless never forgot they belonged to a very different tradition. Neither had the old tradition of painting exemplified by the *Chaurapanchasika* series been totally forgotten. As we shall see, it makes its appearance again in the 17th century in Mewar.

But to understand the subjects chosen by artists for the Rajput courts we must examine the deep undercurrent of mystical romanticism that flowed through the whole of India from the 10th century onwards, a form of mysticism that refused to draw the line between sacred and profane love and expressed itself through the divine love of Radha and Krishna, the love of God for the human soul. The change is seen clearly in literature: the aristocratic elegance of Kalidasa's Sanskrit was meant for the aristocratic literati, for courtly Sanskrit was not accessible to everyone. The new literature was addressed directly to the common man in the vernacular, the language he could understand. A number of religious leaders like Ramanuja (*ob.* 1137), Ramananda (*c*1370–1440), and Chaitanya (*c*1485–1533) were largely responsible for these changes. From the early centuries of the Christian era older forms of Hinduism had already been challenged by the new *Bhakti* movement, which sought a direct covenant between the devotee and his transcendental God. The Krishna of the *Bhagavad-Gita* was the perfect example of this. *Bhakti* movements swept right across India over a number of centuries and gave rise to major religious leaders and reformers, who sought to reach all people across the caste barriers. There were various different forms of *Bhakti* cults, both Shaiva and Vaishnava, but the most powerful impulse came from the myths relating to Krishna and Radha and their love for each other.

The earliest of the poets to celebrate this love were Jayadeva (12th century), Chandidasa, and Vidyapati (both in the 14th century) in the remote eastern corner of India, but their songs were heard several thousands of miles away in Rajasthan soon

after. Secular literature mirrored this new development in mystical love poetry as well as its creation of literary conventions to describe the different phases of Radha's beauty from youth to maturity and the different states of her emotions on which poets like Chandidasa loved to dwell. These conventions of emotional states crystalized into two main kinds, love in separation and love in union, both providing inspiration for Rajput artists (as well as the literary divisions of heroines and heroes into different kinds according to their emotional state). The intensely romantic Rajput society had parallels with the chivalric tradition of the feudal society of medieval Europe. In a society bound by the rules of fidelity in marriage the extra-marital love of the divine pair offered an ideal surrogate. The very ambiguities of a make-believe world in which the ruler and his beloved dressed up as Krishna and Radha with genuine mystical emotion inspired artists to treat the theme on different levels.

Here we must also raise the question why monumental sculpture was replaced in this period by painting. Earlier gods, like Shiva or Vishnu as in the cosmic image of the Boar in Udaygiri, were meant to awe the worshiper with their transcendental quality. The intention of the sculptor was to create a distance between man and god. On the other hand the Krishna of the later *Bhakti* movement was intensely human, a god whose human beauty, colorful dress, and blue-green peacock feathers could only be captured in painting. A further element entered these romantic traditions of painting. To the dictum *ut pictura poesis* should be added music. Paintings based on *ragas* and *raginis* or personifications of modes in Indian music were first seen in Jain texts, and became an important genre of expression in Rajasthan and Hill states, although Ragamala paintings are also to be found in the Deccan. In general certain conventions became popular for depicting the *ragas* and *raginis*; their iconography was, however, by no means fixed. The modes were rather points of departure which the artist used freely to make his own imaginative contribution.

There exists an early painting of the Dipak *raga* (1605) by a Muslim painter Nisaradi from Mewar, whose direct antecedent is the *Chaurapanchasika* style, although here the colors are mellower and the composition more complex. The interesting new element, which suggests Mughal contact, is the arrangement of the bottles in the niches on the wall, a feature first seen in early Mughal works such as the *Tutinama* (Cleveland Museum of Art). On the other hand the men and women here are derived from pre-Mughal western Indian art. The Lalita *ragini* painted by another 17th-century Muslim painter, Sahibdin, in 1628, in the period when the ruler of Mewar had already joined the Mughal court for some years, shows even greater Mughal contact though the picture is conventionally divided into sections by means of an open pavilion. The lover who leaves in disappointment because the lady is offended and feigns sleep is in Mughal costume, with a transparent skirt over his trousers.

Sahibdin, a remarkable artist of the period, illustrated sec-

A forest landscape from the Ramayana illustrated by the school of Sahibdin; late 17th century. British Museum, London

tions of the *Ramayana*, the *Sukar Kshetra Mahatmya*, and *Bhagavata Purana*, dealing with Krishna's life, between 1648 and 1656. These is a striking picture in the British Museum, London, from the *Ramayana* done by the school of Sahibdin which depicts a forest landscape; its most notable feature is the whole range of flowering trees, painted with great care and imagination. For us Mewar is especially interesting because we can trace the evolution of its style on the basis of dated paintings, from the *Chaurapanchasika* type to the ones done under Mughal influence. But in the final analysis it was not so much the Mughal idiom absorbing the local tradition as adding a new dimension to the old themes and manners of painting.

From the many different courts, three may be selected for their special interest. To the state of Bundi is attributed a remarkably delicate *Bhagavata Purana* (1640)—the style is a transition from *Chaurapanchasika* figures to one of graceful naturalism and gentle blend of colors. The story depicted is about the child Krishna who subdues the gigantic serpent Kaliya. Mughal influence is evident in the group of musicians in the Akbari style as well as in the ubiquitous theme of bottles in wall niches. But Bundi is more famous for the so-called "white" paintings, mainly from the 18th century, representing a new ideal of small-breasted feminine beauty, showing women with high foreheads, hair brushed back, reminding us of 15th-century Flemish paintings. It is interesting that during the height of Mughal art neither the nude nor the beauty of women ever constituted an important subject for the artists. In the Rajput courts, however, the perennial Indian concern for feminine beauty returns with renewed vigor and produces several memorable versions of loveliness. A very fine Bundi work is *Lady Yearning for Her Lover* in which the semidraped

figure of the woman and her attendant dominate a delicate warm gray, almost totally bare background (John Kenneth Galbraith Collection, Cambridge, Mass.).

The ruler Ummed Singh (1771–1819) of the neighboring state of Kotah was obsessively interested in lion and tiger hunts and his painters recorded this passion with great faithfulness. A fine example is *Raja Guman Chand Shooting Tigers* (Victoria and Albert Museum, London) where the painter has woven a fantasy world bathed in the light of the moon, reflected in the rich growth of shrubs, trees, and smooth rocks—a perfect poetic image of a tropical jungle, not familiar enough to encourage confidence, yet not too strange to be repellent.

In Kishangarh, set in the midst of an idyllic country of mountains and lakes, one of the finest developments of art based on the legend of Krishna and Radha takes place. This happened when Raja Sawant Singh (1748–57) during his brief rule in Kishangarh persuaded a highly gifted artist, Nihal Chand, to work for him. The life of this ruler, himself a gifted poet, painter, and a devotee of Krishna, reads like a romantic story, especially in his love for the musician, Bani Thani. Their love was celebrated in Nihal Chand's works in the 18th century as the earthly form of love of Radha and Krishna. Nihal Chand, whose portrait we possess, introduced a new ideal of a beautiful woman, possibly based on Bani Thani, with curved eyes, arched eyebrows, sharp nose, pointed chin, and enigmatic smile. Paintings of exquisite mannerism and delicate range of colors mark this school.

Painting made further progress in the so-called Hill states (Pahari), lying in the foothills of the Himalayas and deep in the valleys of Jammu, Kangra, and Kulu, some of the most breathtakingly beautiful parts of India. Their very seclusion protected these small princes from the devastations taking place in the north Indian plains and enabled them to create a cloistered, self-contained fairy-tale world in the 17th and 18th centuries—a world where men were eternally elegant and women eternally enchanting, poised, aristocratic, and remote.

Much of the life of these princes and princesses was recaptured in paintings from these areas. Two most important schools are the somewhat earlier Basohli and the later Guler-Kangra. The first phase of Basohli is represented by paintings based on Bhanudatta's *Chittarasamanjari*, a text which deals with various kinds of lovers and different states of love. Produced in Kirpal Pal's reign (1678–95), the unknown artist makes clever use of red and orange and of open pavilions in the *Chaurapanchasika* tradition, but he has also chosen to represent carpets in great detail. There is one among the series called *Secretly Belonging to Another* (Victoria and Albert Museum, London), representing an unfaithful wife who blames her love-bruises on the cat seen on the upper floor. The cat-and-mouse game represented by the artist echoes the dangers she faces in taking a lover. Details in the picture such as the red petticoat under a blue transparent skirt are very carefully drawn. In this period beetle wings were employed to produce certain brilliant greens.

The 18th-century artist Manaku, who did a series of paintings on Jayadeva's poem about the love of Radha and Krishna, belonged to a talented family of artists who were employed in different Pahari courts. His father Pandit Seu, originally from Kashmir, had settled in Guler, which already had a flourishing school of painting. Manaku's early style showed the influence of the Basohli tradition, but it began to change under the influence of his brother Nainsukh (c1725–c1790), who was undoubtedly one of the finest painters in this period and was responsible for introducing elements from Mughal naturalism in the hills. It is not known how Nainsukh received training in

the Mughal idiom but his accurate portraits, his composition and arrangement of different figures, and his colors and drawing all show an intimate knowledge of the techniques perfected by Mughal artists, especially those associated with the Emperor Muhammad Shah (1719–48). Nainsukh took employment under Balwant Singh, whose career he recorded with great fidelity. His works of this period, including a self-portrait, are characterized by elegant naturalism and penetrating psychological studies of his subjects. While they were affected by Mughal art, their individual style could not for a moment be mistaken for that of Mughal works. After his patron's death he was invited to join the household of the Basohli ruler, Amrit Pal (1757–76), where his brother Manaku was already employed. This important event marks a radical change in the painting of Basohli, from mannered paintings of pure warm colors to a new lyrical and graceful naturalism. Today the painting of the Hill courts is known chiefly for the graceful naturalism whose best-known example is Kangra art.

The Radha-Krishna cult was important not only in the art of the Hills but in its culture, for it was very much a deeply felt, living religious tradition. But as Hindus, whose religious approach was essentially syncretic, the Hill rulers were also worshipers of Shiva and Shakti. These deities are therefore represented in art in great profusion. There is a very powerful picture of Kali with her nocturnal and chthonic attendants from the small state of Chamba.

Pahari rulers, like the Rajputs, sat frequently for their portraits; among a whole variety of portraits, one may be chosen as a particularly fine example of the genre. For sheer formal harmonies the portrait of Raja Ajmat Dev of Mankot (Victoria and Albert Museum, London) is unsurpassed in the careful arrangement and interrelation of each shape and color. At the same time it is not entirely a formal exercise, for the subject is very much a living person who sits smoking his *hookah*. The artist has been able to capture the elegance and culture of these small courts with rare economy.

However interesting these works may be, the major concerns of the painters are still the subjects of love, divine and secular, and beautiful women in various activities and guises. It is in Kangra ruled by Sansar Chand (1775–1823) that we find the last magnificent vision of feminine beauty in Indian art; Kangra comes to mind first when we think of this type of ideal, but it was shared by artists in all the courts in the late 18th and early 19th centuries. Unlike the women of Basohli or even Kishangarh, those of Kangra are a delicate balance between the ideal and the real; their limpid dark eyes, delicate noses, aristocratic features, and elegant figures make them entirely convincing as real, desirable women. They are the result of synthesis between Mughal naturalism and the Indian artist's search for ideal feminine beauty whose roots go back to the *Yakshis* of Sanchi. We do not know who created this image in the Pahari region, but it had a very powerful influence and was so widely copied that today the Kangra type of beauty suffers from overexposure.

The miniature from the series Secretly Belonging to Another; late 17th century. Victoria and Albert Museum, London

Even if today we fail, rightly, to be moved by the unimaginative reproductions of this kind of art, we must not underestimate the value of the original impulse. Sansar Chand's great interest in art and his enormous collection of paintings are mentioned by contemporary European visitors to his court. It was the happy combination of his unusual interest in painting and the presence of a number of talented painters in the region that created the intensely vital art movement in Kangra which lasted until Sansar Chand himself fell from power. Among his artists were the descendants of Nainsukh and Manaku, namely Khusala, Fattu, and Gaudhu (all active in the late 18th and early 19th centuries), suggesting the continued participation of this talented family in the development of Pahari art. To give a final instance of this exceptionally productive period there is a beautiful example of Kangra art dating from the 1780s, *Radha sees Krishna with the Cow-girls* (Bharat Kala Bhavan, Benaras), which epitomizes the whole period in its evocation of spring with red, pink, white, and yellow flowers, birds, mango trees, and above all, in the celebration of the beauty of the two women, Radha and her girl friend.

Westernization. As patronage began to dry up in princely courts because of political upheavals which began to affect even the remote areas, artists faced the problem of making a living; some began to find work elsewhere, especially with the English employees of the East India Company. The centers of what might be called the Company Style were Murshidabad, Patna, and Lucknow; the artists made conscious attempts to modify their own tradition in view of the demand for naturalism by the English and even received suggestions about perspective and other conventions. There are many natural history drawings in the India Office Library done by Indian artists for the English. (An Indian artist did sketches for Sir Charles Malet when he visited Ellora in the late 18th century.) There are instances of artists dealing with scenes from contemporary life, both European and Indian. There was also a very interesting and flourishing tradition of bazaar paintings at Kalighat in Calcutta, which produced some lively and often amusing accounts of daily life among the Sahibs and the natives. This situation continued until the middle of the 19th century when new art movements followed the westernization of the rising elite and the growth of national political consciousness.

The profession of artists in India, as in Europe before the Renaissance, was not a socially exalted one. Therefore the initial impact of Western ideas among the elite was restricted to literature and did not include the visual arts. When Western academic art became the medium of instruction for artists, the traditional artist classes did not have much share in it; from now on art became the prerogative of the educated. Both European architecture and painting had begun to spread in India from the late 18th century. The trend of neoclassical architecture set by the East India Company was taken over by English residents and then by Indians, as country villas of affluent Bengalis with classical facades sprang up everywhere in Bengal. Portraits in oils were commissioned by Indian aristocrats from itinerant European artists.

The first Indian artist who saw great possibilities in using western techniques to represent a realistic scene was Ravi Varma, *fl.* 1874–1905. His fame soon spread all over India, helped by the issue of cheap prints of his oils. Ravi Varma's paintings, based mainly on ancient literature of India, suffered from a self-conscious manner common to 19th-century academic history painting in Europe; his heroines had the air of well-brought-up young ladies taking part in an amateur theatrical production. Actual art schools of the English kind were set up in India in an entirely separate context in the 1850s, to train artisans. Industrial revolution, it was generally recognized, had caused serious damage to traditional industries in India as it had done in the West. The present art schools in Britain owe their origin to the need felt to teach artisans the correct principles of design in the aftermath of the Great Exhibition of 1851. This idea was extended to India but without any significant result.

Meanwhile as the 19th century came to a close, after more than 50 years of westernization which had helped India to enter the modern age, the search for cultural identity began. This was a period of immense intellectual ferment in the major cities, especially Calcutta, epitomized by the universal genius of the poet Rabindranath Tagore (1861–1941), who gathered around him the rising groups of Bengali intellectuals.

The Calcutta Art School, in existence since 1854, had been concerned with imparting English academic art education which included the study of Classical antiques and the nude. At this point a committed artist, E.B. Havell (1861–1934), arrived as the head of the Calcutta Art School. Havell, like several other famous English men and women who had adopted Indian culture as their own, had a crucial role to play in the future development of art in India. A meeting between him and Abanindranath (1871–1951), Tagore's nephew, whom he subsequently inspired, led to the founding of a national style of art, the Bengal School. Discarding drawing from the antique as well as from life in the Western manner, Abanindranath sought to derive his style from a combination of styles that did not imitate nature, notably Mughal and Far Eastern art. The Bengal School represented the reaction to Ravi Varma's westernization and the search for cultural roots, and yet Abanindranath's own work suffered from his early training in Western academic art and excessive eclecticism. But his role was that of teacher and inspirer rather than a major creative force, and he certainly inspired a whole new influential group of painters, soon to spread to different parts of India—notably Nandalal Bose (1882–1966), the Ukil brothers (born c1900), Deviprasad Roychaudhury (1899–1975), and Abdur Rahman Chughtai (born 1899). Deviprasad became a powerful figurative sculptor. Chughtai applied the "archaeological" style of the Bengal School to his own Islamic and Persian heritage and created a mannered style full of erotic overtones and languid Beardsleyesque lines.

Reactions against the Bengal School came with the news of the achievements of modern European artists, who had similarly revolted against Renaissance naturalism. In 1922 an important exhibition of modern artists took place in Calcutta, which included works by Klee and Kandinsky. Even in Abanindranath's family two people disagreed with him. His brother Gaganendranath (1867–1938) found that decorative elements of synthetic Cubism provided him with the means of realizing his own visions of fantasy landscapes and interiors, some of which are delightful in their delicate color combinations. Abanindranath's uncle, the great Tagore, took up painting in 1928 when he was 67 years old. A catalyst in his case was probably Freud, but it was Klee's *jeux d'esprit* that struck a sympathetic chord in Tagore. His art began in the form of doodles and patterns made out of part of the writing he crossed out, and had the character of ink blots used in Rorschach tests.

Another artist, Amrita Sher-Gil (1913–41), who spent her early years in Europe and had been trained in France, evolved a style balanced between formal simplification and naturalistic treatment of figures, reminiscent of Gauguin. The simplicity and dignity of her peasant studies are very moving. George Keyt (born 1901), a Ceylonese, had close emotional ties with India and translated from Sanskrit poetry. He recaptured the ancient Indian ideals of voluptuous womanhood and tender eroticism, paradoxically through the idiom of Cubism. But it is significant that he chose the decorative qualities of synthetic Cubism rather than the austere fragmentation of the analytical period. In fact the solid volumes of his women are distinctly reminiscent of Léger's tubular women.

The dialectic between tradition and modernity in the form of international contemporary styles is the problem that still faces the Indian painter. It was given the most compelling solution by probably the only genius of this period, Jamini Roy (1887–1974). He went through the usual phases of academic painting in Calcutta Art School as well as a revivalist Bengal School period, but a profound spiritual crisis led him to seek expression in the popular and folk art of Bengal. He created powerful images of the primitive Santals, containing radical simplifications and touches of tender eroticism. His later phase became more austere and included some moving interpretations of the life of Christ—seen as a spiritual hero in the eyes of a Hindu artist. Gradually coming to accept that art should be within the reach of ordinary people, he set up his workshop with pupils and assistants, producing collaborations with his assistants and denying that art should be concerned with individual expression.

Kashmir, Nepal, Tibet, Ceylon. Among the immediate neighbors of India belonging within its cultural sphere, Kashmir's greatest period was between *c*600–1350, when fine works of art and architecture were produced as well as the great historical treatise *Rajatarangini*. In the fluted columns and tympana with triangular pediments enclosing trefoil arches, belonging to the *stupas* of Parihasapura, the echoes of Classical art through the mediation of Gandhara are evident. These elements and other stylistic features from the Gupta period were

Mother and Child by Jamini Roy (1887–1974)

A Buddhist stupa with added eyes near Katmandu, Nepal

carried over to Hindu temples as exemplified by the famous
Sun temple of Martand, set impressively in the midst of a
valley on a high plinth with double pyramidal roof and with
porticoes that allowed solar rites. The sloping roofs and projecting gables of the small Shiva temple at Pandrenthan, on the
other hand, remind us of European buildings mainly because
of the adaptation of the roof to the cold climate. The "lan-
tern" ceilings of Kashmir temples made up of overlapping
squares are another interesting architectural feature of the
area. Sculpture too shows Gandharan elements; bronze
figures and stone pieces such as the fine tricephalic 9th-century
Vishnu from Avantipura are worthy of note.

Nepalese architecture, which employs much wood and
brick and provides carvings and paintings on its walls, had
been praised by ancient Chinese pilgrims. In Nepal, as in other
areas outside India proper, the umbrellas assumed increasing
architectural importance in the *stupas*. A unique feature in
Nepal was the introduction of two eyes on the *stupa* to suggest that it represented the cosmic man—a feature extended to
the great Hindu temple of Pashupatinatha (Shiva) at Katmandu. The well-known bronze and brass sculpture and the painting tradition of Nepal represent a vigorous and imaginative
development of the style and iconography of Pala Vajrayana
art. In the Museum of Fine Arts, Boston, an early masterpiece
of the 12th century, showing Buddha surrounded by the *mandala* of eight great Bodhisattvas and deities of the Vajrayana
pantheon, is characterized by sensitive drawing and great delicacy of colors. The same Museum contains a gilt copper figure
of a ten-armed cosmic (Vishvarupa) image of Vishnu.

In Tibet, as in Nepal, Buddhism was introduced by monks
from the Pala kingdom but here it was superimposed on existing shamanistic cults. Situated on cultural crossroads, Tibet's
art absorbed elements from two great traditions, Chinese and
Indian. *Stupas* (*chorten*) here take the form of a square base
with bulbous middle part—a form that occurs over an area
extending to Java. The type of architecture, however, that we
immediately associate with Tibet is the fortress-monastery
such as the Potala at Lhasa built of sun-dried bricks, whose
doors and windows become somewhat smaller at upper levels.
Sculptures include gilded bronze figures from the Vajrayana
pantheon. Wall-paintings include the famous 10th-century
works in the Tung Huang area but the best known Tibetan
paintings in the West, for example those in the Victoria and
Albert Museum, London, are the sacred banners (*tankas*)
which represent *tantric* cults through erotic imagery and an
esoteric language of pictorial forms. Elements like landscape
background owe much to China while in general the colors
are pure and glittering in their undiluted brightness.

Ceylon's history begins with Ashoka's conversion of King
Tissa (247–207 BC); the history is scarred with successive
Tamil invasions which led to the abandonment of once flour-
ishing capitals, Anuradhapura and Pollonaruva. Ceylon,

The statue of Parakrama Vahu I wielding the yoke of administration,
at Pollonaruva, Ceylon

which remained Theravadin (*Hinayana*), produced some very important examples of Buddhist art. A typical early example of early Buddhist architecture, the well-documented brick-work *dagoba* (*stupa*) of Ruanveli, whose base, drum, and mast are precisely proportioned, lays special importance on the ringed spire of seven umbrellas, an important departure from the early practices in Sanchi and elsewhere. Its impressive height is in accord with the enormous square base with four outer altars. Begun in Dutta Gamani's reign, the relic in this *stupa* rests in a chamber which has access from the outside. While there are a number of striking colossal Buddhas here, it is the great image of Dutta Gamani that impresses us with its austere grandeur. The simplicity and almost archaic power of these colossal figures as well as other sculptures in Ceylon owe as much to Theravada doctrine as to the character of the massive boulders from which these images are carved.

It is with the reign of Parakrama Vahu I (AD 1164–97) that we associate the architecture of Pollonaruva. The seven-storied Sat Mahal Pasada, the temple containing the tooth relic with its simple exterior of ashlar masonry broken only by decorative bands, and the famous circular Wata-da-ge shrine with Buddhas facing four directions are the three major buildings. Here the columns used in the Nissanka Lata Mandapeya are designed in the form of lotus with stalk which gives them a most unusual appearance. The colossal sculpture of Parakrama Vahu I wielding the yoke of administration, carved out of a large boulder, is comparable in dignity to the earlier one of Dutta Gamani. The finest wall-paintings in Ceylon occur in Sigiriya, the fortress capital of Kassapa I (479–97). The style and treatment of celestial maidens, half-hidden in clouds, owe much to Ajanta but here line takes precedence over tone and color. The composition, colors, and expressive quality of these paintings are also more limited. Examples of South Indian temple tradition and bronze sculpture are associated with the invading Cholas. A fine example of sculpture is the colored brass Pattini Devi (British Museum, London).

Conclusion. The history of Indian art and architecture spans nearly 5,000 years, during which period great and radical changes took place in the form, style, and subject matter of art, and yet there was a coherence and unity underlying these changes, reflecting the specific and recognizable civilization that evolved in this subcontinent. In the ancient period, the mainsprings of art were the two religions, Buddhism and Hinduism, which found dominant expression in sacred monumental architecture and narrative sculpture, notwithstanding the fact that Ajanta represented the highest achievement in painting for the ancient period. In the Islamic period, particularly the Mughal period, the main interest shifted to small-scale paintings, even though there are abundant instances of fine buildings from this age, not to mention the Taj Mahal, acknowledged to be a universal wonder. Interests may change and new forms may replace old ones but there flows through history a clear and unwavering concern with subjects of human interest and a lively curiosity about the minutiae of nature. It is true that Indian interest in nature was never objective to the same extent as Greek empiricism, but it was no less intense. Also, outside the orbit of Greek civilization perhaps no other tradition offered so many variations on the theme of the nude, so many versions of feminine beauty, from the nubile *Yakshis* of Sanchi to the slender princesses of Pahari painting. With the arrival of the British, Indian society underwent a profound change. This also affected art, leading to the spread of a style deriving from European academic art of the 19th century. But even today, when little trace of traditional art remains, the human subject has continued to engage the attention of the artist.

PARTHA MITTER

Bibliography. Archer, W.G. *India and Modern Art*, London (1959). Archer, W.G. *Indian Paintings from the Punjab Hills* (2 vols.), London (1973). Barrett, D. and Gray, B. *Indian Painting*, London (1978). Basham, A.L. *The Wonder that was India*, London (1954). Brown, P. *Indian Architecture*, Bombay (1968). Desai, D. *Erotic Sculpture of India*, New Delhi (1975). Gascoigne, B. *The Great Moghuls*, New York (1971). Getty, A. *The Gods of Northern Buddhism*, Oxford (1914). Hambly, G. *Cities of Mughal India*, New York (1968). Kramrisch, S. *The Art of Nepal*, London (1964). Kramrisch, S. *The Hindu Temple* (2 vols.), Calcutta (1946). O'Flaherty, W.D. *Hindu Myths*, London (1975). Pal, P. *The Arts of Nepal* (pt 1), Leiden (1974). Paranavitana, S. *Art of the Ancient Sinhalese*, Colombo (1971). Parimoo, R. *The Paintings of the Three Tagores*, Baroda (1973). Rao, T.A.G. *Elements of Hindu Iconography* (4 vols.), Delhi (1971). Rowland, B. *The Art and Architecture of India*, London (1953). Singh, M. *Ajanta*, Lausanne (1965). Snelgrove, D. *The Image of the Buddha*, London (1979). Tucci, G. *Tibetan Painted Scrolls* (3 vols.), Rome (1958). Volwahsen, A. *Living Architecture: Indian*, London (1969). Zimmer, H. *The Art of Indian Asia* (2 vols.), Princeton (1955).

16

SOUTHEAST ASIAN ART

**A Dong-son lamp-holder from Lach Truong; c 2nd century BC
height 13cm (5in). National Museum, Hanoi (see page 278)**

THE countries of Southeast Asia—Vietnam, Laos, Cambodia, Thailand, Burma, Malaysia, Singapore, and the two island republics of Indonesia and the Philippines—have been markedly influenced by their neighboring cultural zones, the Indian subcontinent and China. Yet, to varying degrees, they have also produced their own distinctive art forms, though these have not necessarily been confined within their present political boundaries.

The earliest surviving forms of art, described as Dong-sonian after a site in Vietnam, date from the 2nd century BC onwards. Bronze drums, for example, demonstrate something of the nature of one apparently indigenous tradition: a combination of geometric motifs, clearly derived from Eurasiatic connections, and almost naturalistic "drawing". Other items, for example figurines and a 5 in (13 cm) high lamp-holder based on a kneeling figure, from Lach Truong (National Museum, Hanoi), demonstrate an understanding of three-dimensional work.

The typical Dong-son artifact is a single-ended, waisted drum, cast in a bronze alloy with high lead content either in a stone mold or by the *cire perdue* method. On the largest examples the tympanum, usually at least 3 ft (1 m) in diameter,

has concentric rings in linear low relief showing geometric motifs, sequences of birds, animals, or other creatures, and scenes of plumed figures dancing, pounding rice, or playing on mouth organs; others strike gong-chimes or drums of the Dong-son type. The innermost motif is a multi-pointed star which often has stylized faces in the spaces between the points. On the curved section below the tympanum plumed figures, in boats, are often depicted. Similar figures, or dancing warriors, are also to be found in panels on the body. They may carry spears, play musical instruments, or parade with the sort of pediform axes still used in southeast Asia as ritual weapons, especially among the Konyak Naga on the India-Burma border. Some of the drums have three-dimensional frogs mounted on the tympanum. It is suggested in Chinese texts of later date that the drums were used in rainmaking ceremonies.

The Dong-son culture had links with the bronze-using people of Shih-chai-shan, Yunnan. Bronze drums and pediform weapons, as well as certain decorative motifs, are common to both but the Yunnanese sites have yielded much three-dimensional art, including groups of small figures arranged as tableaux on the tympana of the drums. It seems that

The modern countries and main sites of artistic importance of Southeast Asia

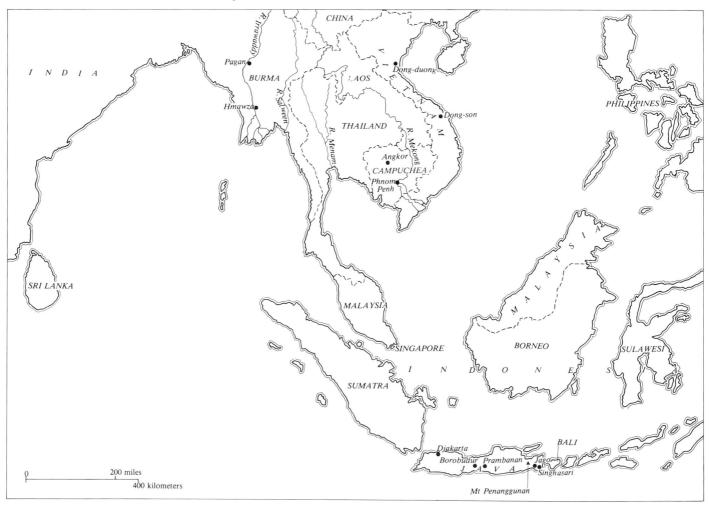

A sacred bronze drum, known as the Moon of Pejeng; height 180cm (71in). Panataran Sasih temple, Pejeng

these contacts date mostly from the Western Han period (206 BC–AD 26) when the Chinese proper were in the process of gaining control of the region.

The Dong-son culture is also found in eastern Southeast Asia, in Malaysia, and in parts of Indonesia, which has produced the largest known bronze drum, the Balinese "Moon of Pejeng" (Pura Panataran Sasih, Pejeng). Six ft (1.8 m) high with a tympanum 5 ft (1.6 m) in diameter, this drum belongs, like other Dong-son drums found in Indonesia, to a late phase of the Dong-son culture, in the early centuries of the Christian era, when traders and pilgrims traveling between the Far East and India began to use maritime routes rather than those by land across central Asia along which journeys were being interrupted by nomadic hordes. From the 1st century AD onwards this seabound traffic led to the development of entrepôts, controlled by local rulers, where Indian goods and, later, Indian ideas began to make an impact upon indigenous cultures.

There is sufficient evidence to prove that goods traveled from one end of Eurasia to the other. A lamp from Pompeii was found at Pong Tuk, Thailand (National Museum, Bangkok). Jewels and amulets from the Roman Orient have been excavated at Go Oc-Eo in the Mekong Delta—a trading complex linked to the interior by a system of canals—and seals and signet rings have also been found there (now in the National Museum, Ho Chi Minh City).

A number of Buddhist images, from the Korat Plateau, the coast of Vietnam, eastern Java, and the island of Sulawesi, have been compared with types from Amaravati in southeast India, Sri Lanka, and Gupta India, but the tendency now is to date them later, after AD 400, though B.-P. Groslier argues for

a considerably earlier date (3rd century AD) for an extremely fine Buddha from Sulawesi (Museum Pusat, Djakarta). Another splendid example comes from Dong-duong in Vietnam, which later became a major Buddhist center (National Museum, Hanoi). Clearly of northern Indian inspiration it may have been the model for images found in the interior of mainland Southeast Asia. Its date is certainly later and it may have been manufactured locally.

But for the most part, all we know of the first stages of Indian influences in Southeast Asia comes from Chinese accounts of the region. They mention the kingdoms of Funan (possibly a version of the modern Khmer *phnom*, "mountain") and Lin-i, in the Mekong Delta and central Vietnam respectively, and another in west Java. The texts also mention temples and images but these have not yet been located.

It is from the final period of Funan (AD 200?–560) and its successor, Chen-la (560–700) that the earliest statuary and shrines come: they are linked with a Vaishnavite ruler, Rudravarman (AD 514–?39). Terracotta heads framed by false windows are known from Nui Sam in Vietnam (National Museum, Ho Chi Minh City) and a group of statues from Phnom Da, near Angkor Borei (National Museum, Phnom Penh) which seems to have been his capital. The group includes two images of Krishna holding up the mountain, one in a manner derived more from the eastern Mediterranean than India, and a Harihara (the gods Shiva and Vishnu combined in a single figure) which may be a little later in date. A great eight-armed image of Vishnu has its hands and their attributes supported on a horseshoe arch, perhaps because the artists were unsure whether the local stone was strong enough for a figure larger than life size.

The skill of local sculptors is shown in a horse-headed deity from Kuk Trap and in two Harihara figures from Prasat Andet and Sambhor Prei Kuk (both in the National Museum, Phnom Penh). A headless female figure from the latter site and a Lakshmi (wife of Vishnu) from Koh Krieng, both with rounded breasts and both in the National Museum, Phnom Penh, suggest the influence of an Indian prototype rather than a local one on which sloping breasts usually featured. An Avalokiteshvara (the compassionate Bodhisattva who has vowed to defer his own attainment of Buddhahood until all sentient beings have attained Nirvana) from Rach-gia (now in the Collection Didelot, Paris, France), who stands with each foot on a lotus, and standing Buddhas from Tuol Prah Theat and Vat Romlok show something of the Sarnath classical manner of Gupta India (AD 320–540), but their faces are Southeast Asian. It may be that we are witnessing in them the beginning of a development by which royalty and Buddhahood became subtly but increasingly identified.

Although images from Phnom Da seem to have been housed in a kind of artificial grotto, the earliest surviving buildings are probably the brick tower at Prah Theat Tuoch and a sandstone structure at Ta Keo, Ashram Maha Rosei, which was probably derived from a Pallavan prototype and which left no Cambodian successor. Both would have been covered in stucco, as were the many buildings of Sambhor Prei Kuk where surviving sandstone lintels give some idea of later Chan-la decoration. They bear garlands of flowers and jeweled swags whose ends are swallowed by *makara* (crocodile-like sea monsters) and sometimes inhabited by dwarfs and deities: they prefigure the lintels of the classical Khmer manner and support the view that the overthrow of Funan by Chen-la (*c* AD 555) was in fact the Khmer breaking free from their possibly Indonesian overlords. The little statuary surviving from the period displays a further evolution from figures in very high relief with a supporting arch, worked from the back as well as from the front but still not truly three-dimensional, towards fully freestanding figures. Female images show increasing stylization, but the number of male images declines, perhaps because of an increase in Shaivism with its aniconic *linga* (a more or less stylized representation of the phallus, usually set on a base, the *yoni*, which symbolizes the vulva), later the specific embodiment of Khmer kingship.

To the northeast of Funan/Chen-la, Lin-i gave way to the kingdom of Champa (*c*AD 400–1640). Several pieces of statuary from the important religious center of Mison show affinities with pieces from Malaysia: with the Buddha found at Dong-duong in central Vietnam these may have led on to later Khmer developments. Elements that were to characterize later Cham art—especially in the adornment of altars—are encapsulated in a pediment with a reclining Vishnu and in a beautiful pedestal for a *linga* which is decorated with relief figures of hermits and of a very lively dancing girl doing the splits (both in the National Museum of Cham Sculpture, Da Nang). The affinities with Malaysia suggest that the arts of both areas shared a common origin in the Indian school from which Pallava art stemmed.

Similar features are also to be seen in the early pieces from Indonesia. Following the collapse of Chen-la, political developments in Indonesia led to the emergence of firstly a new maritime power, Srivijaya, based on Sumatra, and secondly a land-oriented kingdom among the Khmer, with its center around Angkor-Siemreap. At the same time, the Shailendra dynasty, which probably had links with the rulers of Funan, came to power in central Java and initiated the great period of temple building which produced Borobudur, Kalasan, and the Prambanan group.

Apart from isolated Buddha images and crude figures of Vishnu from west Java in "international Pallava" style, the earliest surviving evidence for Indianizing cultures in Indonesia is in the temple groups of Dieng and Ungaran, both volcanic sites with buildings in a simple manner. Their affinities are generally with southern India, though Chandi Bima, Dieng, combines a *shikhara* type superstructure (the towerlike structural form characteristic of northern Indian temple architecture) with *kudu* (horseshoe-shaped niches on the bodies of temples) of south Indian style and human heads, jewels, or vases in the niches. All these buildings, as well as the two earliest from east Java, Badut (now tentatively dated to

the 10th century), and Sanggariti (with a spring-fed well in its *cella*) are Shaivite. Related images of deities have the *vahana* in human form; only the head is the shape of the appropriate animal. (The *vahana* is the animal upon which a Hindu or Buddhist deity is believed to ride. Shiva rides the bull Nandin; Vishnu, the eagle Garuda.)

A fine group of images from Chandi Banon, near Borobudur—of Shiva Mahadeva with Nandi, Ganesha, Mahaguru (the bearded, pot-bellied teacher), Brahma, and Vishnu with Garuda—shows that Javanese sculptors were capable of carving figures larger than life, in stone, with considerable virtuosity: Vishnu is over 6 ft (2 m) tall (Museum Pusat, Djakarta). Evidence of metalworking is provided by a number of Buddhist images (in the Museum Pusat, Djakarta), including a ten-armed Avalokiteshvara in bronze and a curious pair representing Shiva and Paravati, made of gold, found near Dieng. But even the largest surviving metal figure, a silver-plated bronze Avalokiteshvara (33 in, 83 cm high), gives no real idea of the very large works that odd fragments suggest once existed: we must look to stone figures for glimpses of the achievements of Javanese makers of monumental images.

Fine examples of such images can be found in the complex of buildings of which Borobudur is the center. They date from *c*800. Chandi Mendut and Chandi Pawon, 1.8 miles (3 km) and 1 mile (1.75 km) respectively to the east of Chandi Borobudur, form with it a single, linear complex. They have entrances facing northwest. The Borobudur reliefs show that it was originally approached by the eastern one of its four staircases.

Mendut has a single *cella*, reached by a flight of steps, with small *jataka* panels on the outer walls—stories telling of the Buddha's many previous existences before his final attainment of Enlightenment which marked the end of the necessity for him, in common with all other beings, to undergo reincarnation. On the inner walls of the porch are large panels in low relief showing Hariti (on the entrant's left) and either Panchika or Atavaka on the right (an ogress and an ogre converted by the Buddha from child-eating to child-protection). On the panels of the plinth, decorative patterns alternate with angelic figures who gesture upwards to the body of the temple. Its outer walls portray, in large vertical panels, Lokeshvara and the Eight Mahabodhisattva, a group not otherwise known in Indonesian art. Side-panels show Buddhist female deities. Inside the *cella* are three colossal seated figures, Buddha with Lokeshvara and Vajrapani to his right and left; they form a triad facing the entrance. A pair of niches to either side probably housed figures of Jina-buddhas to form a pentad with the central image. (Jina-buddhas are the five Buddhas associated with the five directions—the cardinal points and the zenith—and who, unlike ordinary Buddhas who strive for Enlightenment through millions of lives, have existed as Buddhas from the beginning. They are a feature of *Mahayana* Buddhism and seem to have been introduced about the middle of the 8th century AD.) The central image is shown in *dharmachak-*

An aerial view of the temple of Borobudur; c800 AD

A relief scene from Borobudur: Queen Maya traveling to the Lumbini grove where the future Buddha will be born

ramudra: on a throne, seated "in the European manner", with two deer and a wheel, the usual indication of the First Sermon.

The *cella* of Pawon is now empty. Its exterior reliefs, however, depict wish-granting and wealth-bestowing trees, money-pots, *kinnara* (a fabulous creature, half man, half bird, who served as a celestial musician), and bearded dwarfs, all of which suggest a connection with Kuvera, god of riches and of the merchant community—a reminder of the capital resources that must have been required for the construction of the main temple, one of Buddhism's greatest shrines.

Borobudur essentially consists of walled galleries, arranged in four tiers of squares with stepped ("redentate") corners, on a base which provides a broad circumambulatory. Above the squares are three circular platforms with 72 small *stupas* in concentric rings round a larger central *stupa* on a circular base. At the center of each side is a stairway which leads to the top, passing through elaborate archways in the gallery walls. The sides of the temple (403 ft, 123 m long at the base) are oriented to the cardinal points.

There is a striking contrast between the square terraces—richly carved on their inner faces with narrative reliefs, their walls crowned with miniature *stupas*, jewels, and niches which house seated Buddha figures—and the bare circular platforms with only the *stupas* housing seated Buddhas. The Buddhas in the niches are appropriate to the quarters. Each is distinguished by its *mudra* (hand gesture): Akshobya, earth-touching, East; Ratnasambhava, gift-bestowing, South; Amitabha, meditation, West; Amoghasiddha, fear-dispelling, North. The niches on top of each side of the fourth terrace have Vairochana (the Illuminator), disputation. The figures under the brick-lattice *stupas* on the circular platforms are in

the preaching *mudra*. The existing circumambulatory was added later to the original structure, as is shown by the fact that it conceals a set of 160 panels carved with reliefs based on the *Karmavibhanga*, a text dealing with rewards and punishments for good or evil actions. Some of the reliefs are incomplete, which suggests that the addition was made while the building was still under construction.

Each of the walled galleries carries reliefs on its inner faces concerned with various aspects of Buddhism and the Buddha. On the inner wall of the first gallery one tier presents the life of Shakya-muni (Prince Siddhartha of the Shakya kingdom) up to the preaching of the First Sermon. Below this, previous lives are depicted, as they are also on the outer wall. Higher galleries show further previous lives and also carry a most important set of reliefs giving an account, based on the *Gandhavyuha* and the *Bhadracari*, of a Mahayanist pilgrim's search for ultimate truth—the symbolic meaning of the central *stupa*. This is the final release from the effects of *karma*—the inexorable law whereby the deeds of beings determine their future incarnations—so vividly portrayed on the concealed reliefs at the foot of the monument.

The 1,200 carved panels constitute a major achievement of pictorial narration, a Javanese invention without parallel in India. It is tempting to speculate on its relationship with the *wayang beber*, a pictorial scroll, held and unrolled by a reciter who tells the story depicted on it by enacting the parts of the various characters. It was first reported in east Java by a 13th-century Chinese traveler; now only one survives in central Java.

The virtuosity of the artists and sculptors who worked on the monument was a worthy match to the ingenuity of those who planned the symbolic layout of this great shrine, a highly sophisticated *mandala* in stone. But there is little agreement as to how it should be interpreted, or about its relation to the dynasty presumably responsible for its erection, the Shailendras, Lords of the Mountain.

Another *mandala* pattern is to be seen at Chandi Sewu, Prambanan, probably a century later in date. The central temple here, based on a cruciform ground plan, evidently housed a Mahayanist pantheon of an Adi-Buddha (a transcendental form epitomizing the concept of Buddhahood) with attendant *dhyani*-Buddhas, Bodhisattvas, and their Taras (savioresses who help beings to cross the Ocean of Existence to Enlightenment). Surrounding the main shrine are 240 minor ones arranged in four rows, each with 13 standing figures in relief on the outer walls. Each housed one or more images: one has niches for 41. The complex covers an area of 607 by 541 ft (185 by 165 m) and is surrounded by a wall with entrances at the cardinal axes guarded by giant *dvarapala* (guardians and gatekeepers). None of the images from the main temple has survived, and the few stone ones from the minor shrines have not yielded their precise functions.

Another variant of the *mandala* is to be seen in the double complex of Chandi Plaosan, near Sewu. On the walls of the main buildings (which seem to have housed Buddhist triads, as at Chandi Sari, accompanied by the eight Mahabodhisattva) are figures of donors. The outer walls were adorned with heavenly figures, again arranged in two series as at Sari. The statuary and reliefs from the complex are characterized by finely cut features and benign expressions. A number of monks' heads in stone have also been found.

The principal Hindu monument of central Java, the Shaivite complex of Lara Jonggrang, Prambanan, probably dates from *c*900. Here three shrines of cruciform ground plan, dedicated to Brahma, Shiva, and Vishnu, from south to north, face east towards three lesser structures which house their *vahana*. A simpler version of the central temple stands at either end of the north–south axis which runs between these two groups. The whole stands in a walled compound 360 ft (110 m) square, with gates at the cardinal points. This in turn is enclosed by another wall, with sides of 728 ft (222 m) with cardinal gates set in projecting salients. Within the space thus created were 224 minor temples, about 46 ft (14 m) high (for comparison, the Shiva temple is 154 ft, 47 m high) arranged in four rows. A third wall lies eccentrically about the temple enclosures which are located in its southwest sector. The gates in the outermost walls lie on the cardinal axes and are therefore set irregularly within it.

The *cella* of the main temple contains a four-armed image of Shiva (9.8 ft, 3 m high). The wall behind the image is carved with a low-relief pattern which probably derives from a Chinese silk hanging. Similar carvings are found at Sewu. The subsidiary *cellae* house Mahaguru, Ganesha, and Durga. The main image is of no great artistic merit, though the carving of the details of dress, jewelry, and attributes is fine. The complex's ritual center is not under this main image as we

The shrine of Shiva in the complex of Lara Jonggrang, Prambanan

A relief scene from the Ramayana, at Lara Jonggrang; c900 AD

would normally expect but in a small shrine set in the angle between the temple body and the south wall of the main access staircase.

The four staircases are topped by towered arches with *stupa*-like finials, behind which is the entrance to the *cella* with a great *kala*-head in relief surmounted by a triple gad-rooned *stupa* motif. Similar *stupas* crown the exterior wall of the circumambulatory and the architraves of the six-storied tower above the central body of the temple which is divided horizontally into two zones, with 24 niches in each, which once held statues.

The exterior of the main plinth of the temple is elaborately decorated with niches containing celestial beings in groups of three, alternating with dancers and musicians. Below these are other ornaments, the most important—because peculiar to the site—being a lion, in a niche, flanked by celestial trees, which have pairs of animals, rams, hares, deer, monkeys, geese, peacocks, or *kinnara* at either side of their trunks.

The base of the body of the temple has 24 panels with seated figures who are believed to be the various forms of the regents of the quarters. On the inner wall of the balustrade are relief panels, noticeably different in style from the Borobudur reliefs, illustrating scenes from the *Ramayana*, the story of how the deity Rama and his wife Sita are exiled, how she is carried off to Ceylon by the demon Ravana, and how Rama, accompanied by an army of monkeys, among them Hanuman, defeats the demons and recovers his wife. These panels take the story as far as the arrival of the monkey army on Ceylon. The narrative continues on the balustrade of the Brahma temple. The Vishnu temple has reliefs telling of the youthful adventures of Krishna.

At about the time Borobudur was under construction (at the end of the 8th century) Prince Jayavarman (the second, according to the Khmer king list) went from Java to Cambodia, and set up a new dynasty there with the *linga* as its palladium. (The kings of Champa had earlier instituted such a system, the royal *linga* having a name linked to that of the ruler.) At first this royal symbol seems to have been installed on some natural eminence which was treated as Mount Sumeru, the world axis. But the absence of suitable eminent sites in the central Cambodian region led to the construction of an artificial temple-mountain, to serve as the axis of the kingdom and hence of the world. To construct such a temple and an associated system of waterways, both to portray Ocean (which was believed to surround the world) and to irrigate crops on the plains surrounding the capital, became the prior responsibility of Khmer rulers.

There is evidence to suggest that a temple of the Cham type was the first model, but Khmer builders soon evolved a style of their own. Other influences came from Srivijaya, suzerain over parts of Malaysia, and from the lower Menam Basin which, once part of the maritime kingdom of Funan-Chen-la, now constituted the kingdom of Dvaravati. Here flourished a Buddhist art derived from eastern India which favored the use of stucco and terracotta, and probably a vigorous secular

tradition, suggested by some striking genre heads. Images of Buddha and Bodhisattva in both stone and bronze survive. Of the latter, an Avalokiteshvara from Chaiya, showing him in royal attire, is a major achievement of Mahayanist art. This school provided the basis for Khmer Buddhist art which reached its royal climax in the complex of Angkor Thom and Bayon.

No doubt Jayavarman, the Cambodian ruler from Java, brought ideas with him, and possibly also artisans, for there are demonstrable Javanese elements and motifs in early Khmer art. The preoccupation with mountain shrines also had Indonesian analogs. This influence may explain why, after a series of temporary capitals in the region north of the Tonle Sap, Jayavarman set up the royal shrine on Mount Kulen, about 19 miles (30 km) northeast of Angkor. Called Kruh Prah Aram Rong Chen, in a form reminiscent of a step-pyramid, it is thought to have once housed the palladium. But the site was certainly unsuitable for a capital, and the king returned to Roluos.

From here Jayavarman's second successor, Indravarman (877–89), a scholar-king, was to develop further these hesitant attempts to found a great central and symbolic city. His first act, significantly, was to create a great artificial lake, Indratataka, whose waters filled the moats of the temple of Prah Ko, then those of Bakong, the royal temple-mountain, of Prasat Prei Monti, the palace, and finally, imbued with both divine and royal essence, flowed through the rice fields. At the same time, boats from the great lake were given access to the capital and great quantities of stone for building temples could be easily transported from the quarries in the hills to the north of the complex.

The temple of Prah Ko was dedicated to the royal ancestors in 879. Within its great enclosure two rows of three towers set on a single terrace housed images of Indravarman's precursors, males in the front row, females in the rear. Because he was probably a usurper, his symbolic claim assumed more importance.

The grouped towers were decorated in carved stucco, with branched foliage, monsters supporting rings in which small figures swing, and lotuses. Lower down the wall sandstone slabs are carved in high relief with figures of protective deities whose rich jewelry, like the bristling hair of the male figures, suggests a Javanese origin. Lintels show horsemen among the foliage, surmounted by half-length worshipers; the scenes on the pediments remain unidentified.

As a central mountain to house the royal *linga*, Bakong was dedicated in 881 and set the pattern for subsequent royal foundations at the center of the Cambodian capital. Five superimposed terraces, faced with sandstone, held in place by stone elephants at the corners, represent the layered worlds of the cosmos. Various small towers housed protective deities and possibly the lords of the planets, often portrayed in Khmer sculpture. Subsidiary buildings round the base included one with an image of the king. The topmost *cella*, on a terrace 49 ft (50 m) above the ground, housed the *linga*. The

The Neak Pean Shrine, Angkor

Architectural symbolism is of very great significance in Southeast Asia. An example is provided by one of the smaller monuments, Neak Pean, "Entwined Serpents", which was erected by King Jayavarman VII (1181–1219). It is situated on an artificial island with stepped stone embankments and stone elephants at the corners, in the (now dry) great lake he constructed to the east of Prah Khan, a temple housing an image of his father as the Bodhisattva Lokeshvara. An inscription tells us that Lake Jayatataka is "like an auspicious mirror, colored with jewels, gold, and garlands. At its center is a prominent isle, its charm derived from the basins that surround it, cleansing from the mud of sin those who come into contact with it and serving as a boat to cross the ocean of existence".

In the middle of this island is a square basin with stepped stone sides at whose center is a circular islet surmounted by a small sanctuary. Four subsidiary basins are set on the flanks of the main tank, with chapels on the cardinal axes of the shared embankments. The stepped base of the islet is surrounded by a pair of serpents, their entwined tails to the west, their separated,

▲ The central pool and the main shrine

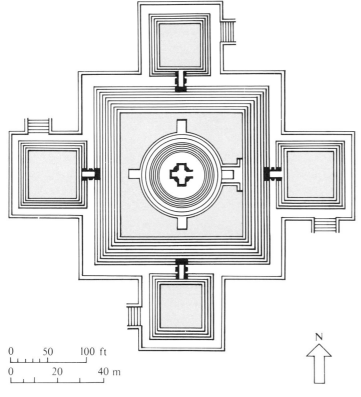

0   50   100 ft
0   20   40 m

N

▲ A ground plan of the artificial island, sanctuary, and main shrine at Neak Pean. The boundary wall of the complex is not shown

▶ The east front of the central sanctuary at Neak Pean and the entrance to the shrine. The panel above the door shows the future Buddha cutting his hair. The approach leads between the heads of entwined snakes

▲ The west front of the central sanctuary. The main panel shows Lokeshvara with petitioners. Above him the Buddha meditates under the Bodhi tree

Above right The north front of the sanctuary. Above the doorway is the Great Departure. Below, Lokeshvara is flanked by seated Bodhisattvas with heavenly figures above and laymen below

Below left The northwest corner of the sanctuary. Set in the angle is Airavata, the three-headed elephant of Indra, surmounted by a rearing lion

▼ The remains of another three-headed elephant and surmounting lion. The lion symbolizes the Boddha Lion of the Sakyas as well as the Lordship of Space

hooded heads to the east: hence the name. A causeway between the heads gives access to the platform, on which a base in the form of the corolla of a 16-petalled lotus supports the sanctuary. The shrine, two-storied with a lotus finial, is cruciform in plan, just a simple *cella*: the image is missing. The entrance is on the east where the doorway is crowned by a tympanum on which Siddhartha is depicted cutting his hair. The false doors have tympana showing the Great Departure (north), the Enlightenment (west); the south tympanum is defaced. The sanctuary was originally open on all four sides, but later panels, showing aspects of the Bodhisattva Lokeshvara, were added to block three of the entrances. At the same time tricephalic elephants, similar to those of Angkor Thom but surmounted by rearing lions instead of human riders, were set in the angles of the building. ▶

The four axial chapels on the main embankment are so set that only the part from the bottom of the tympana upwards is visible. Vaulted structures rising somewhat above the level of the embankment form tunnels into either face of it, their entrances set in flamboyant frames. The sides have carved tympana and stepped-back pediments. The whole structure is crowned by a four-sided pillar, with rounded top, and paneled sides with reliefs of the Bodhisattva. Healing is the motif of all the narrative carvings. In each chapel a pipe within the structure terminates in a lotus basin surmounted by a female bust. The outer end, above a circular lotus platform with a pair of footprints cut on its upper surface, forms a gargoyle. The one to the east is a magnificently carved human head. The others, notably inferior as works of art, are a lion's head (south), a horse's (west), and an elephant's (north). Pilgrims bathed under them to cleanse themselves ritually from physical or spiritual imperfection.

◄ The central pediment of the south outflow shrine. In the lower panel Lokeshvara blesses petitioners

▲ One of the four minor shrines housing the outflow tunnels. They are all covered with figures of Lokeshvara

▼ On the east outflow is this magnificently carved human head

▲ On the platform on the eastern cardinal axis Lokeshvara, as the horse Balaha, rescues the shipwrecked merchants

▼ The complex of Neak Pean is surrounded by a wall. At its northwest corner stands this elephant, another symbol of Space

Four platforms on the cardinal axes within the main basin once supported stone objects. Those on the west and north have disappeared. To the south are the remains of groups of *linga*; the inscription quoted above also speaks of "thousands of *linga*". The eastern platform, facing the entrance to the shrine, supports a colossal horse, made from carved stone blocks, to whose body human figures cling. The group represents a well-known Buddhist story. A party of seafaring merchants is wrecked on an island inhabited by ogresses who take them to husband and then, mantis-like, devour them. The merchant Simhala calls on the compassionate Avalokiteshvara, who protects from every peril: shipwreck is specifically mentioned, a fact suggesting a mercantile cult. The Bodhisattva appears in the form of a flying white horse to carry the survivors to safety, a somewhat curious version of the "boat to cross the ocean of existence". Similarly, King Jayavarman, through his patronage of Buddhism and his self-identification with the Bodhisattva, brings the Khmer people to salvation.

The layout of the monument as a whole is modeled on the Buddhist sacred lake Anavatapta which is believed to lie high in the Himalayas. There Buddhas, Bodhisattvas, arhats, and ascetics bathe, while from its four banks the four great rivers of the world, including the Ganges, flow through gargoyles, lion, elephant, horse, and bull, to bring the fertilizing waters to mankind, just as the beneficent king provides irrigation for his realm and its inhabitants. The similarity with the royal *tirtha* of Java and Bali is obvious, though there is no exactly parallel shrine. Neak Pean is also, indeed, unique in Cambodia. Common to the two cultures is the concept of the mountain, associated so closely with kingship, as the source for the vivifying waters.

ANTHONY CHRISTIE

Further reading. Coedes, G. *Angkor: an Introduction*, Hong Kong (1963). Christie, A. "Natural Symbols in Java" in Milner, G.B. (ed.) *Natural Symbols in South East Asia*, London (1978). Finot, L. and Goloubew, V. "Le Symbolisme de Nak Pan" *Bull. Ec. Franc. Extr. Orient*, vol. 23 (1925) pp401–5. Glaize, M. "Essai sur la Connnaissance de Nak Pan après Anastylose" *Bull. Ec. France. Extr. Orient*, vol. 40 (1940) pp351–62.

existing structure is of the 12th century, but the decoration is consciously archaizing. There are two enclosure walls and two moats, the latter crossed by east–west causeways to the main gates which show the earliest surviving examples of *naga*-balustrades—a feature of classical Khmer sculpture. The *nagas* (snakes) are being hunted by the freestanding Garudas. The wall of the fifth terrace is carved with scenes which have become too worn for identification but are evidence of an amazing skill in the depiction of movement.

Once again the manner points to Javanese inspiration. Indeed, B.-P. Groslier has even compared Borobudur and Bakong; it is at least tempting to believe that Indravarman wished to build a dynastic temple to rival that of the Shailendras from whom Jayavarman had sought to set Cambodia free. The king himself is shown at Bakong, flanked by two of his wives: another innovation of the period, though there are already signs of the standardized formulae that dominate later art. As Groslier writes: "By this time we find the whole Khmer order of society perfected. Under Indravarman, Jayavarman II's work took root; Angkor has been founded and will continue to grow."

Two elements of symbolic art remained to be created: the quincunxial central shrine and the cloisters to house long panels of reliefs, but both are present in embryo.

The central tower on the top terrace was shortly joined by four others to make a five-fold top characteristic of Sumeru. This appeared by 893, at Bakheng, the central temple of Indravarman's successor Yashovarman. Bakheng is a masterpiece of cosmological symbolism on a far greater scale than Bakong, from which it evolved. Yashovarman's lake Yashodharatataka, six times the size of Indratataka, relied on the natural flow of the Siemreap River to fill a system of moats on the periphery of his capital, with its amazingly sophisticated cosmic temple on a natural hill at the center. It presents the seven tiers of Mount Meru with its 33 gods (the number of towers visible from the middle of any side). One hundred and eight subsidiary towers—this number being the product of 4 and 27—subsume the four phases of the moon and the 27 lunar mansions; another combination represents the 60-year cycle of Jupiter. It is an astronomical calendar in stone.

Within another 70 years the final element of Khmer architecture was added. At Prei Rup (dedicated in 961) the subsidiary terraces had long, stone chambers with tiled roofs on timber frames—the prototypes for the cloister galleries of Angkor Wat. This period also saw further examples of the freestanding images of the kind noted at Bakong, including brilliantly conceived monkey wrestlers, presumably from the *Ramayana*.

To this same period belongs the gem of Khmer architecture, Banteay Srei, dedicated in 967, not by a king but by a royal Brahmin, Yajnavaraha. A Shaivite shrine, it is built on a miniature scale: the central one of its three main *cellae* is only 33 ft (10 m) high, but it is richly ornamented, with many elements drawn from earlier phases of Khmer art. Niches set in foliated panels, where dancers and animals flit among the leaves,

A niche figure at Banteay Srei

house exquisite flower-carrying nymphs in deeply cut relief. The tympana display scenes from myths and legends, like theatrical sets with carefully posed actors. Masques probably formed part of court entertainment at this time, as they did until recently. Statuary of the period shows some return to anatomical reality after a phase of stylization. Freestanding figures of the Bakong-Koh Ker type are found: Shiva seated with his consort Uma or Parvati, his eyes open and sensual, his lips fleshy, seems to preside over a true paradise on earth.

At the beginning of the 11th century, at Ta Keo, the continuous cloister was to be constructed, on the second terrace, which also had an impressive *gopura*-like entrance on the east and lesser gateways on the other three sides (a *gopura* being a gateway surmounted by a towerlike structure). The quincunx was set on the fifth platform somewhat towards the western end of the enclosure. This is the final form of the temple-mountain, a masterpiece, and one of the finest buildings in the Siemreap region.

Of the same period are the remains of a colossal bronze Vishnu: head, shoulders, and two right arms of a reclining figure which must have been about 13 ft (4 m) long. Now in the National Museum, Phnom Penh, its original location was on a plinth, probably in the form of the world serpent Shesha, in a pool in the West Mebon, an island set in the Western Baray, the great reservoir that lies to the west of Angkor Thom. The image was constructed in sections by the *cire perdue* method and was once encrusted with gold, while jewels and enamels were used for the eyes. A Shiva head, also in bronze, gilded, with encrustations of leadglaze, 12½ in (32 cm) high without its chignon, from Por Loboeuk (now in the Angkor Conservation Depot, Siemreap), bears further testimony to the skill and mastery of Khmer metalworkers, so little of whose work has survived.

Stone images were of secondary significance, though from these we are forced to judge Khmer glyptic. Although Khmer sculptors had shown an early interest in producing genuine work-in-the-round, after eliminating various supporting devices they chose to develop the frontal poses of images on thick legs, with little attempt to reproduce natural anatomy.

The Chams, who inhabited the area that now constitutes central and south Vietnam, were more inclined to model poses other than frontal. This was undoubtedly the result of using altars with a reredos and retable, open on three sides, with the main image at the back surrounded by guardian figures, subsidiary divinities, animals, worshipers, and donors. All these faced towards the principal image, forcing the artists to consider non-frontal presentation. The Chams were also most successful in portraying movement, a skill found less often among the Khmer: those responsible for the Khmer reliefs were exceptional.

In architecture, the Chams almost exclusively used brick for their buildings, reserving sandstone for ornamentation in the earliest and, usually, best examples, where it is confined to door-frames, pilasters on the corners of the body, and accent pieces on the superstructure which rose by repetitive and decreasing stories. Blind arches, without the tympanum found on Khmer buildings, project over door or facade: their fronts are carved with foliage and bear a monster head at the peak, curiously reminiscent of central Javanese temples.

The great 9th-century temple complex at Dong-duong is Buddhist, although Champa was generally shaivite and may well have been the source for Khmer Shaivism. Brick *stupas* are of a grooved cylindrical form and seem to be of Chinese origin. The decorative style is complex, but the sculpture's impressive vitality is informed with the illusion of movement. Buildings at Po Nagar and Mi-son, dating from a couple of centuries later, show a renewed interest in discrete ornamentation on elegant structures whose tall silhouettes seem to be outlined by stone flames. The sculpture, in contrast with the almost primitive vitality of that of Dong-duong, is restrained but sensual. Parts of an enormous altar from Tra-kieu (National Museum of Cham Sculpture, Da Nang) on which a frieze of dancers and musicians, cut deeply in blue-gray sandstone, honor the god embodied in the *linga* supported by the altar. On another pedestal the female dancer has become an arabesque in stone. This marks the apogee of Cham art which slowly declined as the Vietnamese, moving inexorably southwards, gradually swamped the small centers of Cham culture. The area as far south as Hue was annexed by 1306, the area to Cap Varella by 1471. The last Cham temple, Po Rome, is usually dated to the mid 17th century, when the last parts of

Champa, many of whose inhabitants had adopted Islam, came under Vietnamese rule.

On the other side of the Khmer Empire the Mons of Dvaravati continued to develop various forms of Buddhist art and architecture, some of which found their way into Cambodia from the 11th century onwards. Their relic shrine was a brick cube, surmounted by receding stories with figures set under arches and often with a galleried circumambulatory set on a terrace of Khmer type. With the addition of stucco decoration this became the model for later northern Thai architecture. Two Buddha figures also evolved in Dvaravati: the standing Buddha wearing a single garment with both arms held out symmetrically, and the seated figure, meditating under the hood(s) of a coiled *naga*. When Buddhism became the state religion towards the end of the Khmer Empire (late 12th century) they provided two important icons.

The image with pendent legs did not enter the Khmer repertory, but was favored in central Java, where it may have appeared earlier than it did on the lower Menam.

But above all, it was as a source for *Hinayana* Buddhist art that Dvaravati and the succeeding Thai states were important, once the Khmer had fallen. And to this repertory the Mons of Burma made a major contribution, most significantly after Anawratha (1044–77) had incorporated them into a united Burma with its great Buddhist center at Pagan. Other components came from the Pyu who had long practiced *Mahayana* Buddhism, with some elements from Hinduism.

It was from an amalgam of Pyu, Mon, and Burman that a new art and architecture were to emerge. The Pyu developed tall, cylindrical *stupas* of brick, crowned with a bell-like finial with a central spire. The plinth was shallow, stepped, and circular. A typical example is the Baw-bawgyi at Hmawza, nearly 164 ft (50 m) high.

The Pyu temple was either rectangular in plan, with a single entrance facing an image set against the rear wall, or consisted of a square central block, with relief images on each face

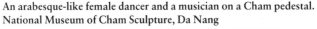

An arabesque-like female dancer and a musician on a Cham pedestal. National Museum of Cham Sculpture, Da Nang

opposite doorways in each of the four walls. At the Pyu site of Hmawza, the Bebe Paya represents the first type while the Lemyethna, which may be of slightly earlier date, represents the second.

The East Zegu at Hmawza, perhaps a little earlier in date, demonstrates the earliest true arch in Southeast Asia. The arch has no place in Khmer or Javanese architecture. But its use by the Pyu in the 8th century undoubtedly made possible the barrel-vaulted, two-storied structures of brick found in Pagan 200 or 300 years later.

From the Pyu period (3rd–9th centuries AD) come a number of stone images of Vishnu and some bronze Bodhisattvas, as well as Buddhas carved in stone relief which seem to belong to the *Theravada* tradition (Hmawza Museum, Hmawza; National Museum, Rangoon). Ashes of the royal dead were housed in fine stone urns; but the people had to rest content with pots. Reliefs reveal that arcaded Buddha figures were set round the drums of *stupas*. Another type of shrine consisted of two slabs with Buddha images in relief set several feet apart at either end of a narrow brick terrace marking a place where Buddhas are said to have "walked and talked".

After Anawratha, King of Pagan (1044–77), captured the capital of the western Mon, Thaton, in the mid 11th century, Mon culture contributed to the development of architecture. In part they transmitted influences from the artistic reservoir of Dvaravati and from Sri Lanka, with which they had direct contact and where *Theravada* Buddhism was already flourishing. The Mon had a tradition of temple shrines, of which the Nan-paya at Pagan is a fine example.

The Burmans probably acquired their Buddhism in large part from the Pyu and the Mon. Their own contribution to the amalgam was the cult of Nats: nature spirits. Once they were innumerable but by the time of King Kyanzittha (1084–1112) the total had stabilized at 37. The Buddha was sometimes treated as their chief. They were often housed in special shrines on pagoda platforms, as at the Shwezigon.

The leaders of the nature spirits, the Mahagiri Nats on Mount Popa in central Burma, were provided with shrines at the Sarabha Gate of Pagan. They show the typical low pilasters and molded architraves of Pagan buildings, almost all of which are brick built with a stucco engobe (embellishment). The Pyu *stupa* was adapted so that the terrace became more important, the body reduced in scale, and the spire greatly elongated and emphasized. Around this structure, which was treated as the core of the Lemyethna, a circumambulatory was created, its doors set at the cardinal points of the outer walls. Entrance corridors were added to these, with richly elaborated frontispieces. The angles of the roofs were accented with spires derived from that of the central mass.

By this process of development the Pagan builders produced their major achievement: the Ananda pagoda. It is still a center of worship, with its great standing Buddhas, its countless small reliefs of *jataka* and other themes—many carrying the inscriptions in the script of the Mon that prove their responsibility for this school of Buddhist architecture.

Most of the thousands of shrines at Pagan and in its neighborhood are variants of the two forms—*stupa* and shrine—with subsidiary buildings which were libraries or monasteries. In 1287, under Mongol attack, the site was abandoned, but Burmese Buddhist art and architecture had been established.

While Anawratha's successors had been filling Pagan with further elaborations of the Burmese style, Khmer art and architecture was approaching its climax under a new dynasty which had come to power in 1080. In 1113 the great-nephew of the founder, Suryavarman II, embarked on a great campaign of military and architectural aggrandizement. There was no space in the existing capital area for a new temple and surrounding enclosure to form a whole new city, but a site was found, on the royal road from Baphuon to the Tonle Sap, for a spectacular temple-mountain: Angkor Wat. Its construction occupied most of Suryavarman's reign (1113–50).

Its main facade faced west, the direction of the setting sun, the region of Death; perhaps symbolic of the temple's role as a shrine for the dead king in his apotheotic form. The enclosure is rectangular, surrounded by a moat more than 195 yds (180 m) wide, fed from the Siemreap River. An embanked road, flanked by *naga* balustrades, crosses the moat to the main gate, which reproduced the facade of the actual temple building. At the end of a paved road is a three-tiered pyramid whose central tower rises to a height of 230 ft (70 m). The three tiers have corner towers and central pavilions preceded by steps. The main tower with the *cella* is linked by pillared galleries to the entrance pavilions of the quincunx. A triple staircase links the western entrance of the first tier to that of the second: these pillared galleries are covered by corbeled vaulting. The whole structure is consciously designed to appear as a pyramid to the approaching worshiper. By means of correctly judged ratios between access and facade, the calculated staggering of the succeeding terraces towards the east, and increases in height, the builders avoided giving any sensation that the structure was falling towards the viewer. All these elements, as well as the layout of the site, had been present at Baphuon: at Angkor Wat they achieve perfection.

The whole of the stone surface is covered with decoration. Storiated pediments, lintels, and doorposts portray gods and heroes: capitals and gallery cornices have lotus friezes; the walls have heavenly dancers in low relief (set against carved panels whose patterns derive from textiles)—almost 2,000 of them and each one different in detail from the others. The gallery linking the entrances and corner towers of the first tier has pillars in place of the outer wall to allow light to fall on the inner wall which has a series of scenes carved in low relief, about 6 ft (2 m) in height and more than 1 mile (1.75 km) in overall length. Apparently these reliefs are meant to be read counterclockwise, a characteristic of funerary rites, supporting the view that Suryavarman intended the temple as his mortuary shrine. One whole panel is dedicated to Yama, ruler of the underworld, judging the dead. Other scenes are based upon Vaishnavite themes: the churning of the ocean, Krishna stories, and episodes from the *Mahabharata* and the *Ramaya-*

Angkor Wat, Suryavarman II's temple-mountain; early 12th century; a view across the moat

na. One panel of great interest shows the king himself, at first seated in his court, and then sitting on a royal elephant leading his army.

The reliefs, which were certainly gilded and possibly colored, are the ultimate fruition of an art that began at Borobudur and was further developed at Banteay Srei and at the temple-mountain of Baphuon. Chinese elements have been detected, but, as P.S. Rawson has pointed out, the mode of expression owes much to the dance. This, in combination with umbrellas, banners, weapons, and scarves, gives an amazing sense of movement. The relief is very shallow, about an inch deep, but complex sequences of overlapping curves create a convincing sensation of depth: in its conception the whole work is painterly. The galleries must be ranked among the greatest examples of relief art in the world.

It was perhaps some realization of his father's achievement that led Jayarvarman VII (1181–1219), towards the end of his reign, to attempt the creation of a Buddhist shrine to rival Angkor Wat and to occupy the center of the royal domain. This was the Bayon. Built on the site of a city founded more than a century earlier by Udayadityavarman II, it was surrounded by a great wall, more than 10 miles (16 km) long, with five gateways and bridges across the moat, more than 110 yds (100 m) wide. The bridges have balustrades of gods and demons holding serpents, a vast representation of the churning of the Ocean with the Bayon as the churnstick. The bridges also represented the rainbow path which links heaven, the royal microcosmic enclosure, and earth, the surrounding kingdom of the Khmer. The gate pavilions were topped with triple towers carved with huge faces, the great artistic innovation of the reign to be repeated on the 54 towers of the central temple. The faces, gazing out to the cardinal points, are those

of the King as the compassionate Bodhisattva Lokeshvara.

His temple-mountain consisted of a galleried structure in the form of a "Greek" cross surrounding a central platform with a circular shrine and 12 subsidiary radiating chapels. The original cross was then modified by the addition of extra galleries to form a rectangle enclosed within another gallery. The subsidiary towers rise over the intersections thus created, des-

Jayarvarman VII's temple at Angkor, the Bayon; carved faces of the King as Lokeshvara

ignating shrines which may have represented the provinces of the Empire. Out of this forest of stone the main tower rises to a height of 140 ft (43 m). The whole structure was, however, subjected to a number of modifications—some seemingly capricious—during the course of its construction, so its meaning cannot be properly analyzed.

Two galleries carry reliefs, showing episodes in the life of the King and the history of his military campaigns: amazingly vivid scenes of everyday life in a profusion that lacks the controlled elegance of reliefs at Angkor Wat. A new element of naturalism is present, and at least one attempt at aerial perspective possibly made under Chinese influence.

But the resources that built the Bayon and a host of other vast buildings diverted labor from the basic economic activities of the state. Jayavarman's desire to glorify the dynasty through Buddhism probably contributed to both the downfall of the dynasty and the replacement of the royal *Mahayana* Buddhism by *Theravada* Buddhism. But Jayavarman's memory is preserved in his inscriptions, which record buildings, roads, and bridges; in buildings themselves; in several splendid stone statues, which include the so-called Leper King (Angkor Thom, Siemreap), the Lokeshvara from Prah Khan, probably a portrait of the King's father (National Museum, Phnom Penh); in a seated Buddha from the shaft under the center of the Bayon; and, above all, in the portrait head of the King himself, a worthy tribute in stone to a ruler who employed so much of that material to the glory of Buddha as king (both in the National Museum, Phnom Penh).

In Java, towards the middle of the 11th century, the seat of power seems to have shifted from the center to the east of the island. Thereafter, no more great unified complexes were to be built, though certain centers were developed, often in the Cham manner as found at Mi-son.

Typical of this tendency are Panataran (the name meaning something like Pantheon) and Mount Penanggunan which has more than 80 shrines, including two constructed round sacred fountains. Jalatunda (977) has a rectangular basin, filled with water from the mountain, is identified with Sumeru, with its multiple peaks. The water gushed from a fountain with one central and eight subsidiary spouts, its base encircled by a serpent, into the main basin through holes in slabs carved with themes from the *Mahabharata*, undoubtedly of dynastic significance. Under the basin lay a burial casket.

At Belahan a similar structure, which was originally part of a larger complex, is believed to be the burial place of King Airlangga who was portrayed there as Vishnu on Garuda (Mojokerto Museum). The monument, dated to 1049, takes the form of a brick basin in the bed of a stream. Set in its back wall are three niches surmounted by heavenly clouds with figures. In the center stood the Vishnu image with the king's principal wives, Shri and Lakshmi, installed on either hand. From a spout in Garuda's left hand, a jar held by the goddess in the southern niche, and the breasts of the northern deity, water falls into the basin and then makes its way down to the fields below.

An analogous shrine lies in front of the famous Goa Gajah cave, with its witch mask over the entrance, near Bedulu in Bali. Here water spouts from the breasts of six female figures. Many other examples of spout-figures are known from Java and Bali.

The small pool in the Panataran enclosure, dated to 1415, has animal panels, though not all can be identified. The complex itself contains buildings dated from 1197 to 1454 and appears to have been dedicated to Shiva as Lord of the Mountain. On the southwest slopes of Mount Kelut there are three successive courtyards with the main shrine nearest the peak—a layout characteristic of temple enclosures in present-day Bali where it is held to be of east Javanese origin. The first enclosure has a ceremonial entrance and a large platform whose walls are decorated with relief panels. Most of the figures are in profile, the style is semi-naturalistic. In the second enclosure is the so-called "Dated Temple" (1369), its *cella* standing on a low plinth with an entrance on the northwest and three false doors. The reconstructed roof is in three receding double tiers surmounted by a cubic top. In the same enclosure is another, roofless, structure, whose *cella*, this time on a high plinth with an ornamented staircase, is decorated below the cornice with the bodies of great serpents supported by nine regally attired figures holding priest's bells.

The main shrine, in the third enclosure, has a projection on the front with two stairways leading to the circumambulatory. The guardian figures, just over 6 ft high (1.9 m) with backs decorated with animal reliefs, are dated to 1347. The walls of the first terrace are divided by pilasters which carry *Ramayana* reliefs, but only the episodes involving Hanuman and the monkey army. They are treated in silhouette and are reminiscent of shadow theater. On the second terrace long panels show scenes from the life of Krishna in a much more naturalistic manner. The third terrace, on which the main *cella* was set, has alternating winged serpents and winged lions. This platform encloses the remains of an earlier brick structure of unknown date. At the corners of the *cella* are male deities; females are in niches on the walls, serpents between: probably another system to indicate Sumeru.

Other temples of similar style are found in east Java, mostly serving as the mortuary shrines of kings and their immediate kin. Among them is Chandi Jago, of the late 13th century, set on two terraces with the *cella* towards the rear of the upper one. Images from this, now in the Museum Pusat, Djakarta, show that it housed a pantheon with an eight-armed Amoghapasha (a form of the Bodhisattva Avalokiteshvara) as the central figure—an interesting feature because no fewer than five bronze plaques, about 8½ in (22 cm) high, dedicated by King Kertanagara, are known, which display the same group of 14 figures (Museum Pusat, Djakarta; Royal Tropical Institute, Amsterdam; Ethnographic Museum, Leiden). So too does a great stone relief, over 5 ft (1.6 m) high, from central Sumatra and now in Djakarta (Museum Pusat). According to an inscription dated 1286, this was brought from Java by a prince who was to marry a Sumatran princess. An enormous stone Bhairava (a horrific deity in the Buddhist tantric tradition) also came to Djakarta from the same site in Sumatra; the image is thought to represent the mid-14th-century King Adityavarman of Sumatra. Indeed, everything points to considerable cultural exchange between Java and Sumatra which appear to have shared a royal tantric cult.

The reliefs of Chandi Jago which, unusually for Java, run counterclockwise, include a Javanese version of the Sanskrit *Panchatantra* animal fables, the story of Kunjarakarna and various adventures of the Pandavas. Native, Buddhist, and Hindu elements were included in the cult which seems to have been strongly salvationist. The temple's statuary, in late Pala manner, differs stylistically from the reliefs. It may belong to a major rededication of the shrine about a century after its original foundation.

The tower type of temple is exemplified by Chandi Kidal, of the mid 13th century, where the story of Garuda's search for nectar to buy his mother's freedom from the *nagas* is depicted: another east Java redemption theme. The *cella* housed a theomorphic image of King Anushapati as Shiva, a typical posthumous royal portrait.

At Singhasari the surviving building was unfinished, though the images for the outer niches were in place, before they were all, except the figure of Mahaguru, removed to Leiden (Ethnographic Museum). The figure of the goddess Durga—a fierce form of Uma, the consort of Shiva—slaying the buffalo-demon is a magnificent piece. The straddled posture, unknown in other Javanese examples and certainly improper in contemporary Javanese behavior, suggests eastern Indian influence, but the technique of carving does not. Uniquely, the *cella* of the temple is located in the plinth; the apparent shrine is an empty cube, without entrances, which is linked to the *cella* and to the superstructure by special openings in its floor and ceiling. The plan is probably of ritual significance in view of the preoccupation with mystery religions which characterized the Singhasari dynasty (1222–92).

Statuary reached new heights during the later East Javanese period. A Chakrachakra (so-called on the rear of the image—a ferocious form of the god Shiva, naked and hung with skulls and severed heads, sitting on a jackal; Ethnographic Museum, Leiden) from Singasari epitomizes another aspect of royal tantrism, while the colossal guardian figures, some 12 ft (3.7 m) high, indicate the confidence with which the sculptors of the period handled great blocks of stone. A beautiful image in very high relief against a background throne, depicts Prajnaparamita, Perfection of Wisdom, meditating with crossed legs and with hands in *dharmachakramudra*, the gesture of setting in motion the Wheel of the Law—that is, of preaching the Buddhist doctrine (Ethnographic Museum, Leiden). To the left of the crowned and bejeweled figure a lotus supports her palm-leaf book: her face portrays the tranquillity brought by transcendental wisdom. It is believed that the image is a portrait statue of Queen Dedes who was concerned in the violence that brought her husband to power and to found the

The goddess Durga slaying the buffalo-demon, from Singhasari, Java; 13th century; height 175cm (69in). Ethnographic Museum, Leiden

Singasari dynasty in the first half of the 13th century.

Another genre of sculpture is shown by the remarkable seated Ganesha, originally from Jimbe on the banks of the Brantas River (now in Bara village, near Blitar in east Java): in Java this god often guarded river-crossings. The almost-square figure, dated on the rear of his skull-adorned plinth 1239, is deeply carved so that the shadows emphasize the mass. He is richly bejeweled and crowned: his trunk lifts a sweetmeat from his skull-bowl. On the back of his great head and across his shoulders is a vividly carved *kala* head (the depiction of the face, without its lower jaw, of a mythical monster with apotropaic head): the protector is himself protected.

The royal portraits are generally shown in the guise of Hindu or Buddhist deities, but the human hands are usually without attributes. In the case of King Kertarajasa (1293–1309), founder of the Majapahit dynasty, the main attributes are Vaishnavite, but the upper right hand bears not a conch but a snail emerging from its shell. Some pieces, such as a royal pair from Jebuk, Tulung Agung, Kediri, while clearly deriving from a Shiva-Uma group, achieve a markedly informal air which makes us regret that so little of the most attractive work in terracotta has survived.

Conclusion. The development of art and architecture in Southeast Asia from the Dong-son period to the 14th century reflects the various elements that contributed to it: native,

Indian, and especially in the case of Vietnam, Chinese. Their influences varied over the centuries and so too did the cultural forms in which such influences were manifested. Indian influence was predominant in religious iconography; Chinese influence was central to the development of ceramic art in Vietnam and Thailand; while Chinese export wares were, and still are, in great demand in Southeast Asia, not only among the plains-dwellers but also among the various hill-peoples. Native influences determined the practice of portraying dead rulers and their kin in the guise of Hindu or Buddhist deities, a practice that can be linked with the carving of ritual images in wood among such groups as the Ngaju Dyak of Sulawesi or the people of Nias off the coast of Sumatra.

During the 13th and 14th centuries the cultures of Southeast Asia became increasingly independent of those of their great neighbors while differences between areas of Southeast Asia became more marked, though the influence of one region on another was often of great importance. A clear example of the latter is the influence of the Thai style of Ayudhya upon post-Angkorian Khmer art which resulted from sackings of the Kampuchean capital in 1353, 1393, and finally in 1431, the end of the Angkor period. Sometimes a much older tradition, long encapsulated within strongly Indianizing art and architectural forms, reemerged. The two 15th-century shrines on the slopes of Gunung Lawu in central Java, Candi Sukuh and Candi Ceto, with their terraced layouts and unroofed shrines—in many ways reminiscent of religious structures in the Pacific—represent such a development.

Changes in religious patterns also played their part. The shift from *Mahayana*, court-supported, Buddhism—ostentatious, demanding expensive monuments—to the *Theravada* school with its simpler requirements had a profound effect. The spread of Islam in Indonesia and Malaysia, as well as in parts of Champa, became increasingly significant in the 14th and 15th centuries. Though Islam was unable to repress wholly a vigorous iconic tradition—in Southeast Asia it inherited a culture rather than imposed one—its spread certainly decreased the demand for many artistic skills. An example of Islamic culture based on inherited forms is provided by the typical Southeast Asian mosque, usually without a minaret, which owes much more to the Javano-Balinese multi-roofed temple than to the Middle Eastern domed building. In the wake of Islam, Hinduism almost completely disappeared, save in Bali and Lombok where it can still be observed, though in a highly modified form, and in the royal courts of the Buddhist kingdoms of mainland Southeast Asia, where Brahmins are required to provide rituals, coronations for instance, for which *Theravada* Buddhism makes no provision. But although *Theravada* rejected the conspicuous monumentality of earlier monarchical Buddhism, it still required craftsmen to carve and gild monastery buildings or to adorn them with glazed tiles and complex ceramic finials. Chinese influences

played an important part in the development of later Buddhist architecture. In Vietnam, where *Mahayana* Buddhism continued to flourish, together with Taoism and neo-Confucian cults, the arts of the court were strongly influenced by Ming China. Elaborate royal palaces, tombs, and dynastic temples were constructed, though little has survived the recent years of war.

Throughout Southeast Asia painting appears to have increased in importance, perhaps as the decrease in royal patronage produced a decline in sculpture and statuary. Only the simplest images were required, and these, more often than not, in a consciously archaic style. Narrative art, once in bas-relief, as in the great panels of Borobudur or those in the cloister of Angkor Wat, took the form of mural paintings, especially in the areas of Thai influence. And painting was the art form in which European influences were first experienced in the mid 19th century. At first, individuals such as the Javanese Raden Salah (1814–80) went to study in Europe, but gradually colonial powers instituted art schools under European directors.

Although the intention may have been to develop the native tradition, increasing evidence of western influence can be detected, though this may have been a natural outcome of the search for new idioms to express contemporary ideas. Certainly, there has been a marked swing towards secular subjects to be seen most clearly in the work of those artists in Bali who, between the wars, came under the influence of such Westerners as Rudolf Bonnet (b. 1927), Miguel Covarrubias (1904–57), and Walter Spies (1896–1947). Their pictures show a great simplification of forms and a proliferation of non-mythological themes. Further changes were brought about by the various independence movements, when artists played a part in the anti-colonial struggles. Ideological considerations led to an interest in popular and folk art, as well as in the search for new, non-Western idioms, to express Third World ideas and ideals. There is yet little sign of new art forms for the older Asian religions, but there are some interesting indications that those concerned with Christian art feel free to interpret this in Asian forms rather than in those evolved in Western Europe.

ANTHONY CHRISTIE

Bibliography. Boisselier, J. *La Statuaire du Champa*, Paris, École Française d'Extrême-Orient (1963). Boisselier, J. *Thai Painting*, Tokyo (1976). Boisselier, J. *The Heritage of Thai Sculpture*, New York (1975). Frederic, L. *The Temples and Sculpture of Southeast Asia*, London (1965). Groslier, B.-P. *Angkor: Art and Civilization*, London (1966). Groslier, B.-P. *Indochina: Art in the Melting-pot of Races*, London (1962). Hejzlar, J. *The Art of Vietnam*, London (1973). Holt, C. *Art in Indonesia: Continuity and Change*, Ithaca (1967). Kempers, A.J.B. *Ancient Indonesian Art*, Cambridge, Mass. (1959). Luce, G.H. *Old Burma, Early Pagan*, Locust Valley, N.Y. (1969). Ramseyer, U. *The Art and Culture of Bali*, Oxford (1977). Rawson, P.S. *The Art of Southeast Asia*, London (1967).

17

CHINESE AND KOREAN ART

A Famille Rose decorated plate; 18th century. Ashmolean Museum, Oxford (see page 331)

ALTHOUGH it is often said that China has the longest unbroken cultural tradition in the world, there are evident changes within that culture in the relative values of the visual arts. Chinese art displays no simple evolution from primitive beginnings to a mature artistic tradition. Indeed, there is at least one clear change of direction. In a very simple analysis, we can find a change from an "object oriented" culture of the early ritualistic societies of the Neolithic and Bronze Ages to the "painting and calligraphy honoring" culture from the Han period (*c*200 BC). From then on, although emphases and fashions change the basic evaluation is unchanged and the position of calligraphy and painting as "fine" arts is never questioned. This implies a radical change in cultural outlook just before and during the Han dynasty (206 BC–AD 221) for which there is both literary and archaeological evidence.

Before the Han period, society and its culture had been centered on a ritualism stemming from the ruler which controlled all aspects of life. In the earliest periods of the Neolithic settlement (4th millennium to 18th century BC) aesthetic considerations seem to have been of no great importance except in the making of ceramics, particularly those associated with burial rituals. Funerary pots seem to have been the most important works of art produced by these peoples.

The Bronze Age cult of ruler and state required grand objects and explicit symbolism and the Chinese produced magnificent bronzes which, in their symbolism, come closer to the expressiveness of "fine" art. But as ritual fell away in import-

Important centers mentioned in the text

ance toward the end of the Chou dynasty in the 3rd century BC, the casting of bronzes took its place among other crafts; this change coincided with the development of writing styles and the aesthetic consideration of calligraphy, itself regarded as a parent of the art of painting in China. Almost from the time of its appearance in the last centuries of the Chou dynasty painting was regarded as the one true art, with its close relation calligraphy. The art of painting has many roles, from the recording of likeness in portraiture, the creation of decoration or symbolism in bird and flower painting, to the expression of religious, poetic, or philosophic themes leading almost to abstraction. In China the separation of these roles is quickly marked and classified so that the aristocrat of the painter's world is at the poetic, philosophical abstraction end of the spectrum, and the decorative recording arts of portraiture and flower painting are at the other. This severe classification of subject matter had its basis in literary scholastic judgments, for to the scholarly meritocracy who became China's ruling class these judgments seemed natural.

The concern of scholars with both painting and poetry throws light upon the tradition which evolved, and helps to explain its cohesion. Culture is cumulative and China's emphasis on honoring the great, spread a strong web over the whole culture and kept alive a tradition of painting which in its limitation of materials and techniques might, at first consideration, appear over-restrictive. The wish to stay within the tradition was not a slavish copyist's instinct but a desire to remain in good company. The artist expressed his individuality within the tradition and the great artist enriched that tradition for future painters.

With the notable exception of images for the Buddhist church, sculpture never recommended itself to Chinese artists as a mode of anything but monumental expression. There must be many explanations for this but perhaps the most powerful is that it would be unthinkable that a scholar-artist should work with materials other than ink, paper, and silk. This would preclude the recognized "fine" artist from working in sculpture. As an extension, this same scholarly artist-patron would have no interest in artistic work produced by an artisan—except again in the context of Buddhism. There was indeed in Chinese civic and domestic architectural planning no need of sculpture; the great sculpture of China was produced for a church that has its roots in India, where sculpture was the chief medium of expression. The Chinese sculptor followed a foreign tradition to produce images, but this tradition did not take root in China.

The other applied arts of China, so highly regarded abroad, should be considered as the furnishings and trivia of a highly sophisticated and diverse society. In so far as they satisfy the eye and are made for their looks they can be considered as art but they never, after the inception of expressive painting, play anything but a minor role in China's visual culture.

Pottery of the Neolithic period (4th millennium–18th century BC). The Neolithic peoples of north China took a lively interest in the decoration and shape of pottery. This pottery is the only surviving expression of their artistic style although we know, from fragmentary remains, that they made basketry and wove silk and ramie. These materials do not survive the long time (some 8,000 years) of burial; we have to look to pottery for glimpses of current ideas of beauty and style.

The population of Neolithic China was widespread over the north and east of China. The early center of a culture given the type name of Yang Shao seems to have been in the Wei river valley, and here at the Pan P'o site (Sian) and the nearby settlement at Miao Ti Kou we find the potters already making a range of shapes: simple bowls and pointed based jars, which are of a rough cord-marked ware, and also decorated ware of fine-bodied pottery painted with slip in red, white, and black; the motifs are either of a geometric type or a stylized representation of fish and human faces. Further east, as this people spread along the valley of the Yellow River, we find similar shapes and decorated pots, but in each local area the decoration differs, and flower-derived designs are introduced in a non-repeating elegant design of curving lines and areas of dark and light.

Yet further to the east in the region of present-day Shantung and to the north and south of this region a related Neolithic people, given the type name of Lung Shan, also made distinctive pottery, sometimes also slip-decorated. They greatly enlarged the vocabulary of shapes to include composite forms, which necessitated luting together different parts, and it is clear that during the 4th and 3rd millennia BC the potter's wheel was developed in this eastern area of north China. This innovation made possible the production of very thin-bodied wares which were burnished, fired, and "reduced" to produce a glossy black pottery, only occasionally decorated by the addition of a pastry-type trimming. This very sophisticated pottery was the artistic tradition of the later Neolithic people who seem to have been closely related at least in their craft work to the metalworkers of the succeeding period.

While the metal culture peoples of the central and eastern area were overwhelming the Neolithic peoples of the central Yellow River area, there were many Neolithic settlements in present day Kansu for which the potters made most handsome painted urns and bowls—footed bowls—for their burial pits at the famous sites of Pan Shan, Ma Chia Yao, Hsin Tien, and Ch'i Chia P'ing. These late Neolithic decorated pots are the richest in the painted pottery tradition, the motifs moving from a formalized spiraling movement of Pan Shan to animal designs and even models of human heads in the round forming the cover of the jar. This is a style that died only as the area was eventually overrun by the Han.

The Bronze Age (18th–3rd centuries BC). The flowering of art more nearly in the sense of an expression of some culturally meaningful ideas in a visually memorable form came with the perfecting of bronze-casting techniques and the elaboration of the ceremonial culture during the Shang dynasty (c1766–1122 BC). The question of the origin of the bronze culture and

A large Neolithic slip-decorated jar from Pan Shan in modern Kansu. Ashmolean Museum, Oxford

the proposition that the apparent absence of copper or tin artifacts may point to the importation of bronzecasting as a technique, is one that awaits further study. But as with the Neolithic peoples it is possible from evidence, particularly of weaponry, to suppose that at least part of the answer to the possible origins lies in the area to the northeast, the Baikalia region. The motifs, decoration, and shapes of the surviving bronze vessels are certainly all "Chinese" in character and were evolved to take part in a very specific cultural ceremonial. At least by the mid Shang period (14th century BC) the state of Shang was "Chinese". There was a written script, part hieroglyphic, part phonetic, which is recognizable as the ancestor of the present-day script; the shapes of the ritual vessels of these early people have in many cases been preserved, in a modified form, in the shapes of the traditional pottery, down to the present day. This was a typical Bronze Age society, with powerful warrior kings, a highly developed ceremonial, which included the sacrifice of humans and animals, particularly dogs, and enormous funeral pomp associated with the royal house. The mass of the population were to all intents still living a Neolithic life.

Thus the art of this society which survives in the durable materials of bronze and jade is exclusively associated with the ruling class and appears to have an overpowering ceremonial significance. With this in mind we can appreciate the exquisite productions found at the capital site of Anyang, especially in the royal tombs at Hsiao T'un. The full vocabulary of vessel shapes cast in bronze had been developed by this Anyang period (14th–12th centuries BC) and indeed some shapes were already on their way out. So this is the classic period of Shang bronze.

The decoration cast into the bronze was of two very different styles: one a simple representational style as seen in the animal masks and human faces, very telling and surprisingly

A bronze tripod caldron (ting) of the mid Shang period, decorated with dragons and a t'ao t'ieh mask. Ashmolean Museum, Oxford

tender; the other a stylized animal forming either a ferocious mask, the *t'ao t'ieh*, or a processional band around the vessel. This last style was the one developed and elaborated during the Shang period. The little one-legged *k'uei* dragon with a snout, horns, and ears seems to be the basic unit of much of this decoration. Confronted, a pair can become a very effective monster mask, albeit without a lower jaw. Although this *t'ao-t'ieh*, as it came to be called, has been interpreted as a symbol of greed, we can only guess the meaning of this motif. During the last two centuries of the Shang period the richness of the relief and surface texture was at its height. The animal character of the decoration was still fierce and the background developed a rich texture of spiral whorls so that even small ritual bronzes have an imposing monumentality and express a period style of solemnity and richness.

In a quite different way jade-carving, the other ceremonial art, bears this same period character. Following the simple style of bronzes, there are large numbers of small realistic representations of animals and birds, usually pierced as though for attachment to a thread or fabric. These are in the form of flat slips of stone cut into a silhouette shape, very simply incised and often called "amulets" for no very firm reason. Alternatively this very precious material was used for the ritual disks, possibly developed from Neolithic rings.

These have been given the general titles of *pi* and *huan* in Chinese and are associated with burial ritual and the ceremonial for the sacrifices to heaven. In the Shang period these ceremonial shapes seem to have been undecorated and to have held a meaning inherent in their shape and material which itself has a special place in Chinese culture.

Probably derived at this time from the Baikal area, the true nephrite jade has never been found within the greater China borders. This perhaps accounts for some of the mystique attached to it. However this may be, the very subtle qualities of toughness and the smooth, lustrous, unglassy surface and coolness to the touch have attracted the Chinese craftsman and connoisseur throughout the ages, and it is significant that jade had already taken this place in the culture of China in the Bronze Age.

Although there is a change in dynasty title with the overthrow of the Shang by the Chou (1111 BC), who would appear to have been their neighbors and possibly even relatives, the early years of the new dynasty saw little change in the general character of the crafts commanding attention. However, with territorial expansion and the enfeoffment of princelings to rule subsidiary states, regional styles emerged presenting a rich picture, still largely concentrated in bronze vessels. The appearance of birds in the decoration lends a lightness to the animal relief, while the dragon evolves to resemble a four-legged lizard or a serpent; the use of either of these variants leads to a totally different surface decoration. The serpentine interlaced dragon of the north, eventually studded with semiprecious stones, makes a rich textural effect in contrast to the elegant lizard dragons of the south, curling their way over a finely cast rhomboid decoration of interlocking square whorls. This introduces one of the favorite juxtapositions of the Chinese designer, sinuous line over an angular geometric motif.

To the south, in the state of Ch'u, was a foreign culture which became increasingly influential. It was strongly animistic, and gave birds, snakes, and antlers a special significance. There must have been for these people a vivid mythology in which real and imagined beings mixed freely, and from the aesthetic viewpoint this was one of the generating areas of the

An incised jade pendant of the Shang period. British Museum, London

visual arts. From this area comes lacquer-painted wood, pottery, and more rarely bronze, in which a poetic vision of life is expressed in terms not entirely allied to ritual. The style is free and elegant with loose, yet controlled lines and brilliant color which is striking and entirely characteristic. This whole culture of the southern state greatly influenced the northerners; and indeed the complex variety of this period, picturesquely known as the Warring States period, is only just now beginning to be understood. For clearly there were also people to the west in Szechwan, partly cut off from the central valley but aware of the crafts of the main culture; there were also very different people further southwest who rose to cultural maturity under the Han. And in the far north and west there were people in close contact with nomads and their crafts.

The Han period (*c*200 BC–AD 221). The 400 years of the Han dynasty, with the important preceding short Ch'in dynasty, saw the establishment of a recognizable nation-state covering an area bearing some relation to the China of today, except that the control of the east coast area was still unsure. The union of the Warring States of the last years of the Chou dynasty was achieved by the Ch'in in 221 BC under the "First Emperor", who called himself just that, Shih Huang-ti. This great administrative genius coordinated a road system, city building, and a defensive wall system in the north. The so-called Great Wall is a complex aggregation of various parts, which had existed in part as interstate boundaries. The arts of the Ch'in dynasty have not yet been fully investigated but the united country embraced a wealth of artistic traditions which began to make themselves felt during the Han period.

The Han dynasty is often referred to by the Chinese as possibly the finest, if not the greatest, of their history. It was certainly one of splendid experiment and achievement in many directions. In the arts, painting became a true means of artistic expression—or perhaps it would be fairer to say it was the first time in which there were ideas and concepts which required painting for their expression. As we have seen, before the Ch'in-Han period, the chief cultural requirements had at first been ritual objects which were produced in jade and bronze, and then status objects again of jade, bronze, and lacquer in which were embodied some elements of the cult and ritual of the earlier dynasty.

The Han emperors brought under their control a wide area which included many subcultures, not only the imaginative and poetic culture of the Ch'u people, the myths of Szechwan, and the whole compendium of legends of the center and north, but also the much less understood cultures of the outlying areas of present-day Yunnan in the southwest and of the nomadic far north. Although the central government was at some pains to unify beliefs and to codify "religion" as part of the unification program, the few remains of painting on lacquer or on cloth give clear evidence of a richness of ideas which do not appear in the *Shih Ching*, the official record of the period. Painting became explicitly the prime means for expression of a complex of ideas whose symbolic meaning is

The banner found in the tomb of Lady T'ai; 1st century BC. Changsha Museum

not fully comprehensible today.

However, one can now point to specific examples of quality painting in this period. Firstly in the tombs of the Marquis of Tai, his wife, and son, at Ma Wang Tui, Changsha, Hunan, painted hangings were found draped over the coffins, in fine condition, as was everything in the tomb. A painted cloth has also been found in the same area. The hangings appear to represent the four layers of existence: the heavens, the sun, the moon, and heavenly beings; the mundane world of the dead; limbo; and at the bottom of the banner the netherworld. The whole design is composed with the wreathing lines and dragons of the bronze and jade decoration of previous centuries but with the addition of rich colors and, particularly in the upper portion, a feeling for atmosphere. In the middle portion

Chinese Bronzes

Casting bronze by the piece-mold method was the traditional craft of the Chinese metalworker in the Bronze Age (c18th–4th centuries BC). The most beautiful and elaborate objects were the ritual vessels found buried in grand tombs. These vessels, an important element in the rituals of the day, were quickly classified by shape and decoration all of which had names, often recorded in inscriptions. The shapes are associated with the preparation and serving of food and wine, an important part of the ceremonial. The decoration is to be seen as an expression of ideas and beliefs behind that ritual. This is particularly true of the earlier pieces produced before the 11th century BC.

The metal alloy used is unusual because it contains lead (its constitution: copper, 73 percent; tin, 12 percent; lead, 12 percent). The method of casting bronze by multiple piece molds is complex and requires great skill from the potter, for he must produce an accurately keyed mold which can be assembled, into which the bronze can be poured, and then the mold removed. Neolithic potters achieved considerable expertise and must have been the major craftsmen in the development of the new bronzecasting technology. So accurate was the casting that Chinese metalworkers did not customarily tool their bronzes after casting; all the decoration was cast in the mold.

▼ A wine vessel (*yu*) of the Shang period in the shape of a tiger with a human being. Musée Cernuschi, Paris

Above A mirror-back from the Warring States period (481–221 BC); diameter 14cm (5½in). Museum of Far Eastern Antiquities, Stockholm

▲ A wine vessel (*yu*) of the early Chou period, late 12th–11th centuries BC. Height 23cm (9in). Freer Gallery of Art, Washington, D.C.

▶ A shallow bowl (*p'an*) of the Shang period, 13th–12th centuries BC. Diameter of rim 33cm (13in), depth 12cm (5in). Freer Gallery of Art, Washington, D.C.

Below right A vessel for storing liquids (*pien hu*) inlaid with silver; 4th century BC; height 31cm (12in). Freer Gallery of Art, Washington, D.C.

The vessels of the great period, mid to late Shang (14th–12th centuries BC), are elaborately decorated and sturdy in form. Their motifs are exclusively animal ones though they may be real or mythological. The chief animal is the *k'uei*, a little snouted two-legged creature always shown in profile. At an early date it developed ears and horns and a very pronounced eye. The mask, called a *t'ao t'ieh*, also dominates earlier pieces. It may appear as a mask in its own right or as a composite of two *k'uei* placed face to face at a join in the molds. These two motifs are enriched by a surface texture motif, a squared spiral (*lei wen*) and a growing vocabulary of animals: deer, elephant, fish, cicada, and felines. The human face, which gives such a haunting effect to rare bronzes, is perhaps the most vivid example of the power of the mixture of real and mythological in expressive art.

The role of the bronze vessel changes gradually from ritual to status symbol and this is reflected in both motifs and shapes. They become more varied and are freely used. Birds with curving plumes and crests were popular in east China and quadruped feline creatures or serpentine dragons make their appearance in the north and more metropolitan region. Shapes were often exaggerated or became almost domestic. Abstraction from the curving line to a plant scroll completed the change of character. Writhing snakes and bird-head motifs in undercut and cut-through style required the *cire perdue* casting method which Chinese craftsmen adopted and used as it was needed, though the source of their knowledge of this technique is not known. The logical development was to a decorative art in which inlay and gilding played an important role. The line possible in silver and gold inlay on bronze produced some of the most elegant metalwork ever made in China.

MARY TREGEAR

Further reading. Barnard, N. and Sato, T. *Metallurgical Remains of Ancient China*, Tokyo (1975). Rawson, J. *Ancient China, Art and Archaeology*, London (1980). Watson, W. *Ancient Chinese Bronzes*, London (1962).

of the Lady Tai Banner (Changsha Museum) a skill in portraiture is evident, for the lady shown with her retinue is undoubtedly the lady of the tomb herself. The body in this tomb was so well preserved that we can make this assertion with unusual confidence.

Many of these characteristics of painting style can be seen in the remains of wall-paintings in the brick and stone tombs of the period with their detailed characterization of the figure painting, their lively observation of animals, and their use of sinuous brush strokes. Pictorial composition was still at the experimental stage: the allover placing of the elements of the picture read from bottom to top, to denote foreground to background. Problems of scale are unimportant at this time and where hills and trees are introduced, though beautifully expressed in a formalized style they "read" with no relationship of scale to figures and animals.

The brushwork and the quality of line are free and assured and have a fascinating strength—not surprising, for this is the era of the "draft script", that free but mannered calligraphy, often miscalled "grass script". The invention of the chancery clerks, it was quickly taken up by scholars. Thus during the Han period calligraphy became an "art" form with many well-recognized variants of script, and with it was developed a system of aesthetics which though simple could be sophisticated.

The aesthetics of calligraphy seem to have been expressed in moral rather than artistic terms. The equation of aesthetic quality with moral value is one ever after present within Chinese culture. This is partly due to the critical vocabulary and the literary tradition within which aesthetic writing is framed, but it also reflects the Confucian doctrine that "rightness" is an all-embracing term which can be applied to all judgments. The Chinese also had a penchant for classification which led very early to the naming and defining of the various calligraphic styles: for example, the Seal script (large and small), the Li or formal script, Hsing or running hand, and finally the draft or clerkly script. Each style has its own distinct character and use and the great masters of each style quickly entered the lists of artists.

The applied arts of the Han period begin to represent the paraphernalia of aristocratic life. The needs of ritual were now quite subordinate to the decorativeness and showiness of the object. Made in gilt bronze, or bronze inlaid with decorative stones, vessels are sometimes the traditional ritual shapes but characteristically the more utilitarian *hu* (storage jar) shape and the *tou* (stemmed covered bowl) became popular. The incense burner in the form of a mountain landscape, the *po shan lu*, caught designers' imaginations and was clearly important in the varied new religious rituals now practiced. Buddhism had come to China in the 1st century and at about the same time Taoism became formalized and ritualized, creating a need for objects and regalia to match the fully developed iconography of Buddhism. The consequent multiplication of materials and shapes is evident and the use of showy material is one of the features of the period. The chief materials used were bronze, both gilt and inlaid; lacquer, which is painted in the lively swirling styles originating in the southern states of the Warring States period; and carved jade, which retained throughout the centuries something of the mystique of earlier periods, although its use was increasingly decorative.

Weaving was also important during this period, with silk thread fully developed and indeed exported to the Middle East and very fine fabric woven into gauzes and handsome damask cloth of self-colored pattern. This was sometimes further enhanced with a multicolored silk embroidery in chain stitch in swirling design as a counterpoint to the rhomboid designs of the woven fabric.

The more outlying areas of the Empire brought special flavors to the visual arts. In Yunnan the kingdom of Tien claimed descent from the Han royal house but was clearly a quite different society. It had an obsession with bulls, perhaps to the point of worshiping them as we can see in the marvelous animal bronzes and cowrie containers covered with vivid village scenes. In artistic expression these people owed little to the metropolitan traditions, apart from the technique of fine bronzecasting. To the northwest in western Kansu, at the gateway to the central Asian trade routes, there had always been settlements from Neolithic times, and by the middle Han period this was a cosmopolitan area where some of the earliest Buddhist monastery settlements were to be established at Tun Huang in the 3rd century AD. The Chinese skills of bronzecasting had also traveled to the northwest, for the finds of a cast bronze cavalcade of horses and riders with chariots show a typical Chinese chariot and mounted horsemen, apparently originally silk dressed. This lively portrayal of the large horses from western Asia predates the T'ang ceramic tomb figures by many centuries but is evidence of the Han interest in foreign cavalry horses—and also perhaps further evidence of the Chinese preoccupation with the tribes on the western borders, an ever-present source of both trouble and trade.

In the mountains of Szechwan, now controlled by the metropolitan Chinese government, the expression of ideas in the arts has survived most happily in the carved soft stone and stamped brick panels. These range from fanciful mythological scenes depicting beliefs beyond the canon of "official" stories and beliefs that appear in the written literature of the period, to those showing ordinary scenes of hunting and salt-mining. There are also occasions when the world of mythology meets the everyday world which again seems characteristic of the expressive arts of the time. Contrasting in style are the well-cut and compositionally "tight" stone reliefs of the Shantung area, notably at the Wu Liang Tz'u. Here the traditional stories are told in pictures of bold, flat, low relief and striking silhouette, in compositions constructed, as were the paintings, to be read from bottom to top, showing recession without respect for scale. Chinese influence extended further to the north at this time through Manchuria and into north Korea, as we know from the famous tomb found by the Japanese at Lo Lang. The Han period marks the colonization of this area and the introduction of Chinese customs of burial, architecture, and perhaps of potting.

Architecture, although never regarded as an art in China, was developing in important ways in the Han period. The traditional technique of building, with stone footing, wooden pillar, and beam had developed over many centuries. In the late Chou dynasty the introduction of ceramic tiles and the consequent increased weight of the roof led to the development of the distinctive Chinese bracket taking the load from a wide span on to the columns. By the end of the Han period the engineering of these brackets seems to have been fully explored and the disposition of one-story buildings around courtyards had become established; from then onwards, with elaborations, this was to be the style and the tradition. Also in the Han period fire-baked brick and stone for building and for facing the traditional heavy beaten earth walls were introduced. It seems they were used primarily for tombs, whose barrel vaults were constructed underground, or for defensive walls, either for cities or for the huge and composite Great Wall.

Although there were later technical innovations, the main characteristics of traditional Chinese architecture of all types were established during the Han period, and Chinese settlements of the time must have looked similar to those of the 19th century, if simpler. The requirements of these buildings were the same: there was no great opportunity for interior wall decoration, except in the temples and tombs, and there was little felt need for or use made of sculpture, except the monumental type. The great exception to all these observations was the decoration and furnishing of the Buddhist temples and monasteries which began to be built toward the end of the Han dynasty.

Korea to the far north of China was inhabited by Neolithic peoples until the northern part of the peninsula was conquered by the Chinese during the empire-building period of the Han. A Chinese army of occupation was established at Lo Lang, and for a while at least the Koreans were under the control of Chinese rulers, learning for the first time something of Chinese language and culture. Evidence for this is preserved in the tomb of the period at Lo Lang. The famous painted lacquer basket with its scenes of filial piety found in this tomb is certainly a Chinese object and there is little, as yet, to show a local culture which was surely present as is shown in the early Koguryo tombs of Pyong Yang.

Northern and Southern dynasties (AD 220–581). With the collapse of the Han dynasty China moved into a period known as the Northern and Southern dynasties. As the name suggests

A Han period Chinese painted lacquer basket found in a tomb at Lo Lang in Korea, then under Chinese colonization. National Museum of Korea, Seoul

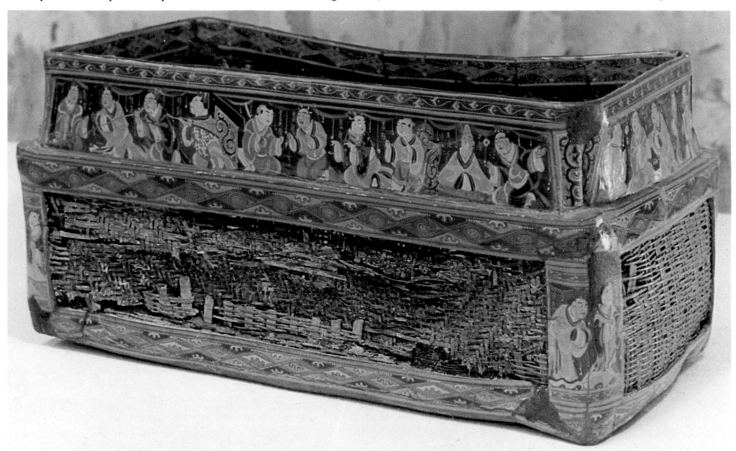

there were a number of autonomous states, each with its own court and coterie of artists. Very little survives of the painting and calligraphy of this period. However, it is the period of the great Buddhist cave temples, and the lavish sculptures and wall-paintings in them have been preserved. The cave temples are all situated in the northern states and so must represent the arts of the Wei and the Northern Ch'i. The painting and sculpture are, however, iconic in concept; this is new in Chinese art and must be regarded as a foreign inheritance. The sculpture in these caves is an unusually rich production by Chinese artists in this medium.

Although a considerable output was achieved in China in the service of the Buddhist church, little of the style spills over into secular art. In the south, the state of Chin has left us one artist, Ku K'ai-chih, both in the records and perhaps only indirectly represented, but nevertheless characterized, in at least one handscroll. This court artist seems to have been largely concerned, like all his contemporaries, with portrait painting. But it is also clear from their writings that the conception of the possibilities of painting as an expressive art were being explored perhaps more felicitously in theory than in practice and the treatise of Hsieh Ho (c AD 500), though terse to the point of obscurity, clearly carries some subtle understanding of the special quality of painting as an art.

Hsieh Ho's *Ku Hua P'in Lu* enumerates the six principles essential to the judgment of great painting:

First, spirit resonance which means vitality; second, bone method which is [a way of] using the brush; third, correspondence to the object which means depicting of the forms; fourth, suitability to type which has to do with the laying on of colors; fifth, division and planning, that is, placing and arrangement; and sixth, transmission by copying, that is to say the copying of models. (Acker, W.R.B. *Some T'ang and Pre-T'ang Texts on Chinese Painting*, Brill (1954) p4.)

These principles were probably based on an earlier set perhaps devised to assess the excellence of calligraphy. This may explain the apparent use of technical terms, now difficult to interpret but probably current at that time. The first principle seems at its simplest to refer to that quality in any painting which we may assert to be "alive" as opposed to "dead"—the quality in fact without which all other excellences are worthless. The second principle refers to the "strength" of brushwork, a quality that has nothing to do with the weight of the brush line but to its tensile quality, the ability of the artist to transmit his nervous and muscular control through the brush and the ink. This is a significant quality in calligraphy but equally in painting in China because of the use of the same media. The brush and the ink must always be the controlling factors and the manner of their use the main medium of expression.

The third and fourth principles seem somewhat mundane and must refer to a need for verisimilitude; remembering that this was a period of portraiture this need is clear. The fifth principle, of the composition of the painting, is interesting for from the few fragments of silk painting and from the wall-paintings of the period, it is clear that ideas of composition were forming. Even the beginnings of the great preoccupation with landscape painting which later formed the main theme of Chinese painting are visible in the surviving stone reliefs and wall paintings. The sixth principle seems to refer to the method of learning from copying models, and the consequent adherence to tradition.

These principles form a brief introduction to a short treatise on the major artists, past and present, arranged by classes of excellence as is the custom in so much Chinese critical writing. Unfortunately none of the work of the artists listed in the first and second classes remains and the critical assessment can give us no clear idea of their style. Ku K'ai-chih appears in the third class.

Perhaps the clearest hint of the style of the figure painters of the period comes through the surviving stone relief carvings. The simplest is a stamped brick wall found in the Yangtse area and preserved in Nanking Museum. It depicts the sages seated under trees. The men each sit under a tree in a mode of "figure and tree" group which survived for a long time. Each unit is slightly different but the treatment of the flowing line and the stylized tree is common and builds a quiet but moving composition which is almost two-dimensional and may have been taken from an ink painting original. The other very striking example is the stone sarcophagus now in the William Rockhill Nelson Gallery in Kansas City. Here the scenes show stories of filial piety with figures now really within a landscape setting, though still very stylized. Here is some indication of a tradition developing to express current poetic mythical themes.

Apart from painting and calligraphy the chief applied art of this period, about which surprisingly little is known, is the pottery of the eastern area, the state of Chin. In the northern part of Chekiang slow but steady progress was made through a succession of kilns in the making and perfecting of the elegant gray stoneware with a green glaze which was to be one of the technical and artistic achievements of the Chinese potter. From the 3rd to the 6th century potters in this area made strong pots in a great variety of shapes for everyday use. They also made a heavy well-potted stoneware for burial furniture, ornately decorated at first, later undecorated but bizarre in shape. These pots, with a gradually developing glaze, were the antecedents of the famous celadon wares of the 12th and 13th centuries.

As little is known of the arts of northern China apart from that produced for and preserved in the Buddhist temples and monasteries, it is hard to trace the links between China and Korea at this time. Indeed the only clear links are those of the Buddhist arts, sculpture, architecture, and bronze images, which occur in Korea apparently in a completely Chinese form. However, it is possible to see some distinctive Korean characteristics in the painting remaining on the tomb walls of the Tomb of the Dancers, at Tung Kou, Manchuria, or the vivid tortoise and snake preserved at the Namdo in Pyong Yang, the capital of Koguryo (37 BC—AD 668). Both these examples reflect a style of painting already seen in China but, particularly in the case of the dancers, there is something new in the color and formal arrangement—a characteristic angularity and sharpness which recur throughout the centuries. The tortoise and snake, a Chinese motif for the Black Warrior symbolizing the north, presents a nice contrast in style and marks another Korean style of sinuous line and delicate drawing which recurs often in decorative arts. While Koguryo is noted for its painting, Paekche is rich in Buddhist remains. The state of Old Silla with its capital at Kyongju was known by the Japanese as the "Land of Gold". Its goldsmiths produced the famous gold crowns found in the Kum Kwan-ch'ong tomb, and other rich gold jewelry. Jade was also a treasured material in Korea and the distinctive comma-shaped pendants, called by the Japanese *Magatama*, appeared at this time. The Japanese were very interested in the southern Korean state and many of the craft styles of Old Silla reappear in Japan.

The T'ang dynasty (618–906). By the 6th century in China the Sui state was subjugating the other kingdoms; ruler Sui

A gold crown from the Kum Kwan-ch'ong tomb; 5th–6th centuries AD. National Museum of Korea, Seoul

A section of the engraved side of a gray, stone sarcophagus; height 61cm (24in); c AD 525. William Rockhill Nelson Gallery, Kansas City

Wen-ti reunified the country and laid the foundations for one of the classic great dynasties of China—the T'ang. Artistically the Sui was a southern dynasty, but foreign motifs flourished and experiments were made particularly in large glazed ceramic figurines. Colored glazes were not yet used but the massive cream and brown guardians excavated at Anyang (Palace Museum, Peking) mark a move toward a tradition which flourished at its most flamboyant in the next 300 years.

The 300 years of the T'ang dynasty are ones of artistic vitality and great innovations, sophistication of patronage, and riches, but are poorly recorded in the arts. We know from literary references that painting became a major art, not only in the metropolitan life of palaces and great houses, but also in the temple building of the period, during which Buddhism was very influential. Great artists are recorded and were clearly treated with respect. Stories are preserved of the uncannily lifelike quality of their work: paintings of horses which galloped away and dragons which flew off into the clouds. Portrait painting was of importance, as one would expect in a time of affluence, and the giants such as Han Kan (*fl.* 742–56), Yen Li-pen (*ob.* 673), and Chou Fang (*fl.* 780–810) have cast their shadows down the ages. It is most unlikely that any of their actual work has survived but no doubt some of the copies of copies preserve something of their style. They show a refined and wiry drawing, and a strength of composition unknown before.

Probably our best clue to the special quality of figure painting at this time is to be gained from wall-paintings in the few tombs of the period that have been carefully excavated. In particular there is the tomb of the Princess Yung T'ai, made in AD 706 to be the burial place of a young girl murdered in a court intrigue and buried in state several years later by her father when he regained the throne. This is therefore an imperial tomb decorated by the court office, whose business this was. The court office was usually headed by a notable artist of the day. Thus the well-preserved wall-paintings in the processional way to the tomb chamber (now in Sian Provincial Museum) have a special interest. Their main subject is an extensive procession of guards (military and civil), servants, and retainers along both walls of the passage leading to the tomb chamber and culminating in a finely drawn group of ladies of the Princess' own household. These paintings show an assured representation of gently moving figures arranged in groups which have a most convincing spatial relationship to each other. The depth of the group is not ambitious and the painting of the figures, as opposed to the drawing, is little more than a "coloring in". However, the strength and confidence of the line remain in the mind's eye and must be regarded as an example of the current style of figure drawing.

We should remember that court tomb decoration at this time reflected the changed status of the emperor, who was now only a member of the aristocracy and not always of the most prestigious family. So although an imperial tomb would be planned with care and skill by the court artist, there was now no theocratic element in the position of the royal family to require a funerary art that differed from the seriously composed art for the living.

In terms of painting this can be demonstrated in the consideration of landscape painting. In the same tomb there are passages of ambitiously planned landscape, palace and hunting scenes carried out in color with some bravura. The piling of mountain on mountain and the placing of animals among trees again show an interest in spatial composition and hint at the solution of many problems which had previously remained unsolved. But a comparison of these landscapes with the famous painting called *The Flight of Ming Huang* in the National Palace Museum, Taipei, shows the difference in quality between tomb painting and that of real life. In the Ming Huang painting the composition is ambitious and spatial relationships are worked out with care. The painting is in fresh blues and greens with touches of bright vermilion making a beguiling picture of an idyllic mountain valley. Indeed it has been suggested that far from depicting a desperate flight of an emperor, this is the scene of an aristocrat's pleasure excursion. This ambiguity of subject and mood highlights a later critical view of this type of painting as superficial and decorative.

The 8th century was a period of great artistic vitality which saw two of the very great artists of China, Wu Tao-tzu and Wang Wei. Wu (*c*680–*c*740) was a marvel of his time, a man of great energy and enormous output if we are to believe even some of the stories told about him. He decorated temples and palace buildings with figures, animals, landscapes, and religious scenes, and his vitality of line became a legend. Indeed this is all that is left for no certain paintings survive and only few somewhat crude stone engravings after his style have been preserved in ink rubbings. However, his reputation was such that a school of figure painters long traced their ancestry to him, and he remains the foil to his contemporary, the retiring poetic Wang Wei (699–759). Wang Wei is credited with the foundation of the school of ink landscape painting which was to become the basis of much of the serious painting of China for the next millennium. The discarding of color and the development of the sensitive use of ink on silk or paper marked a decisive change of style which had a lasting influence on Chinese painting and aesthetic ideas.

Apart from these important developments in landscape painting, the earlier half of the dynasty saw a great output of Buddhist art, painting, sculpture, and bronze, to decorate the many temples built on the mountains of China. This is the period of rich patronage of both the Buddhist and the Taoist churches, and the vogue for pilgrimage to the newly designated holy places of China. In many cases these were at places hallowed by time, which had had some special significance to the native animistic religions, but which were now marked by Buddhist and Taoist buildings. Unfortunately for a study of the temple arts, the fierce anti-Buddhist iconoclastic movement of the early 840s has left little of the buildings or their contents. Thus the chief remains are again remote cave temples and again in the north of the country.

The Flight of the Emperor Ming Huang; 8th century; ink and color on silk; height 56cm (22in). National Palace Museum, Taipei

The great capitals at Ch'ang-An and Loyang, planned and built by Sui Wen-ti and his son, became under the T'ang the first splendid cosmopolitan centers of the Far East. Uighur Turks, Sogdians, and foreigners from further west were visitors and traders in the flourishing cities. Cosmopolitan richness is evident in all the applied arts of the time: silver and gold vessels which show a marked Sogdian character and thus preserve the strong tradition of Sassanian art; the use of glass, rare in China and always apparently under foreign influence; and the more traditionally Chinese crafts of silk weaving, lacquer, and pottery in a colorful variety of styles. Recent finds in Turfan of woven brocades and embroidered damasks as shoes and fragments bear witness to a flourishing silk industry which drew its inspiration for design from outside China but produced a style that is readily recognizable as of the 7th and 8th centuries in China.

The lacquer wares of the T'ang dynasty, richly painted or inlaid with a showy mother-of-pearl and amber decoration, aptly show the period style and accords with the general ideas of the court. The collection of lacquer wares preserved in the Shoso-in in Nara gives some indication of the range of possibilities of the medium at this time. The delicately painted landscape on the *pi-pa* (lutes) and the elegantly inlaid furniture contrast with the richly inlaid mirror-backs. The latter are an example of the use of lacquer as a material for inlay on a metal ground. It also appears that carved lacquer was a technique developing during the latter part of the T'ang

dynasty. The earliest example known is the lacquer-painted leather armor from Miran in which disks were cut into the lacquer to show successive layers of different colors. This must be regarded as the forerunner of one of the major lacquer techniques developed by the Chinese.

In ceramics a similar taste for the colorful and lively resulted in the traditional funerary pottery being made of colored glazed earthenware, an idea and probably a technique borrowed from the Middle East but made so completely Chinese that many authorities question its origin. The tomb models of people, animals, and buildings were made for a purpose similar to those of the previous dynasties: representations of the household and equipment to be enjoyed by the dead. But in fashionable metropolitan society they also became status symbols for the living and were paraded before burial as a show of wealth and position. Thus for a few years they became more than funeral objects and although they cannot quite be classed as sculpture, the finest examples do have some quality of modeling and vitality which appeals directly to people of quite another age. By the very nature of their mass production and the reason for their manufacture these tomb models must stand in somewhat the same position to the fine arts as do the tomb wall-paintings.

In the main line of potting in China, that of the high-fired wares, the T'ang period sees the further development in the north from the firing of a white-bodied ware to the production of true porcelain by the 7th century. In the south, in Chekiang, the gray-green stoneware was refined, reaching the elegance of the Yueh ware of Shang Lin Hu by the 9th century. Apart from these are the handsome black-glazed stonewares of the north, sometimes with a striking gray or purple splash, and the start of the long-lasting kilns of Hopei which specialized in slip decoration of a buff-bodied stoneware, known under the generic term of Tzu Chou ware. Pottery is not a localized craft in China, and with the unification of the country and the establishment of an immense consumer market in the two capitals there was a rapid growth in the circulation of all notable wares. In turn this led to the imitation of popular types in all the major kilns; and so diversification became complex and increased from this period onward.

The great richness and inventiveness associated with the T'ang period arts probably more rightly belongs to the mid T'ang and particularly to the reign of the Hsuan Tsung Emperor (847–60). For, with the recurring troubles that followed his reign, the country, and the patronage on which the arts depended, became more unsettled. We know little of the details of late T'ang dynasty art and it would be wrong to assume that quality fell away. It was, rather, that the character changed as once again the country was divided under separate courts during the 10th century.

The Five Dynasties period (907–60). Although no actual scrolls remain from this period it is clear from their persisting reputations that there were great painters during this very influential century. Such giants as Fan K'uan (*fl.* 990–1030), Li Ch'eng (*fl.* 940–67), Tung Yuan (*fl.* 947–70), and Chu Jan (*fl.* 960–80) have been regarded with awe by painters of later centuries. They were versatile court artists who could be asked to paint portraits, Buddhist paintings, and decorative work, but nevertheless earned their reputation in the exacting art of ink on silk landscape painting. With their contemporaries they developed the magnificent large mountain landscapes which have been given the name of "master mountain" compositions. Their pictures seemed to their contemporaries to embody much of the current thought of the literati concerned with ideas of Taoism and the place of man within the world. These ideas can be dramatically demonstrated by placing man in mountain surroundings; and the magnificent mountains of north and east China, with their cloud-wreathed peaks and streaming waterfalls, became the models for the classical painting of the 10th- and 11th-century painters.

At first these large paintings were grand in scale and concept, whether they were derived from the gaunt northern landscape or the softer southern hills of Kiangsi. Human beings occasionally appear but seem to be ants creeping through an overpowering terrain, not at home in a paradise like their T'ang predecessors. The rocks are huge and usually build up to a towering center block of background, dominating the picture but divided from the nearer scenes by a wreath of cloud, itself creating a sense of mystery and unexplained distance. Incidentally, the cloud perhaps also disguises a change of distance, for the falling eye-level of the composition was

still fairly simply applied and a large step was often hidden by the cloud. The mid-to-foreground of the picture would then be composed in two or three levels but never approaching very close to the viewer. Five Dynasties' pictures, known only from copies, are typically remote in feeling and express the grandeur of nature at its most dramatic and eternal. There is no expression of weather in these paintings, except for the snow of winter and the bare trees of the north, compared with the grassy slopes of the southern artists and the leafy trees of a more hospitable climate. No effects of light and storm are used. This is understandable in an aesthetic concerned with the expression of the eternal reality of nature.

With the brief establishment of regional courts in the 10th century and the southern court at Nanking, the kilns of the Chekiang area came into prominence once more with a very refined production of gray-green high-fired wares at Shang Lin Hu. This considerable group of kilns, at least 25 around the lake, made varied qualities of this gray-green ware, but the best was called Yueh ware. The name derives from the old name of the area, the state of Yueh running down the east coast of China. This lovely pottery has a finely ground gray

A Yueh ware ewer; 10th century; height 20cm (8in). Ashmolean Museum, Oxford

body, strongly but often thinly and elegantly potted, sometimes quite plain but often decorated with a very fine incised line in bird and flower decoration which shows faintly through the thin, blue-green glaze. These wares were very highly valued in their time and praised in the writings on tea which was then becoming popular. The gray-green ware was thought to be the most suitable for tea cups, in contrast to the white wares of the north, which, also of a fine and elegant quality, were valued as wine cups but thought too anemic for the pale, greenish tea.

It is interesting that pottery was from now onward a collector's item and worthy of note by poets and scholars who even graded the wares from the more notable kilns in order of preference. This patronage must have a great deal to do with the variety and quality of pottery production in China. It was paralleled by an interest in all the minor arts which provided objects for the wealthy and cultured man's house: those of the jade-carver, the bamboo-carver, the ink stone maker, and to some extent the metalworker. This seems to be the start of the cult of the scholar's taste which encouraged the elegance and restraint so often associated with Chinese taste in the applied arts, but which is only one of the strands of a much more complex thread. As we have seen in the account of the T'ang period, the wealthy had a taste for the showy and the rich. This taste persisted and is evident in all periods of affluence and was indeed reflected in the peasant arts of all periods, in their love of bright color and ebullient decoration. However, with the establishment of a scholar class, an influential patronage grew for restrained design, elegance of form, and above all for a high-quality technical workmanship. Not for the Chinese scholar the Japanese cult of the faulty or the "simple"; sophistication and perfection seem to guide the eye of the gentleman.

Korea under the Koryo dynasty (918–1392). For Korea this was a period of relaxation in China's influence with the establishment of the Koryo dynasty. The arts of Korea nevertheless still show some family resemblances to those of China. It is, however, noticeable that painting in Korea remained an applied art in the sense that all surviving works are portraits of the most formal kind or specifically Buddhist iconographic subjects. Likewise sculpture, which plays a relatively important role in Buddhist artistic expression, was produced in monumental size in the earlier part of this era. It is in the smaller craft arts of metalwork and ceramics that the style of the period is most clearly seen. This is a style both conservative and experimental, in which we are aware of the precursor but also of the inventiveness and innate lightness of touch of the Korean craftsman. The graceful metal forms inlaid in silver with landscape scenes seem to be specifically Korean in both form and character of decoration; so are the mother-of-pearl inlaid lacquers and perhaps most strongly the celadon glazed ceramic.

Early in the Hu period (993–1150) some of the most elegant green-glazed wares of any part of the Far East were made in

A Korean inlaid celadon bowl; 10th–11th centuries. Collection of G.St.G. Gompertz

the tunnel kilns of Koryo. They are in some way related to the 10th-century Yueh wares of north Chekiang, but the character has been subtly changed; for the Korean celadons have a softness and gracefulness of form combined with a softness of blue-green glaze which sets them apart. In the 12th and 13th centuries the Korean potters evolved a technique of decorative inlay into the leather-hard body of the pot. This involved a fine incising of the decoration which was then inlaid with colored clay, dark gray and white. The whole was then covered with the lustrous blue-green glaze which resulted in a muted three-tone decoration. In the earlier examples this decoration is sparse and graceful, much as was seen in the silver inlaid bronzes. Later the designs became more crowded and clumsier and degenerated into stiff and trivial decorations. The latest move by the Koryo potters (1250–1350) was the introduction of underglaze metallic oxide painted decoration. In Korea this seems to have started with the use of underglaze iron painting which gives a dark brown color, appearing black under the celadon glaze overlying it. Copper and cobalt were quickly added to the repertoire to match but not to imitate the experiments being carried out in China; indeed Korean potters may well have been in the lead in these technical experiments with metallic oxide underglaze painting.

The Sung dynasty (960–1279). The relations between China and her northern and western neighbors in the period of the Sung dynasty is of great importance in political and social terms. In the visual arts this is a period of unrest, division, and ultimate reunification. First the Chin Tartars troubled the north and gradually overran the country north of the Yangtse

Sung Ceramics

A highly developed taste for and understanding of pottery is one of the characteristics of Chinese artistic taste. It has had a profound effect on the position of pottery within the culture of the country and indeed upon the status and quality of potting throughout the world, to the extent that in English one of the words for high-quality pottery is "China".

In such a craft, technology and design go hand in hand, for the material and techniques of production largely control the finished results. One of the great contributions of Chinese potters was the development of a high-fired stoneware and matching glaze. Body and glaze both contain a high proportion of some form of alumina and silica which provide the strength and fusibility of the fired clay; the natural melting temperature of such a clay would be far above the reach of a potter's kiln and so a flux of potassium or calcium is added to lower the melting point to within the 1,200–1,350°C level, within the range of a kiln. Even this temperature is difficult to achieve and hold for the required time—a problem that had to be overcome by the kiln builders. At first they developed a simple up-draft pit kiln, which in east China gave way to a more effective single chamber down-draft kiln. By the 13th century this in turn was extended to produce a climbing multichamber kiln, effectively a chain of down-draft kilns, similar to the *noborigama* used in Japan today. The Chinese "dragon" kiln is a tunnel in which successive fires are lit to maintain a strong up-draft on a sloping site.

A whole group of monochrome stonewares all with a gray body and iron-bearing glaze have come from all over China, reaching their greatest quality in the Sung period (11th–13th centuries). The reduction firing, common to all stoneware production in China, has produced all the green, blue, gray, and even dark brown/black colors of the glazes, and also the gray body. These wares share a feeling of great strength on handling and a distinctive smoothness of glaze, not usually shiny but glossy. An affinity with jade in handling quality and even in looks was obviously appreciated, and beautiful simple wheel-made forms were developed to make some of the classics of ceramic art. The two greatest wares are perhaps the Ju ware of the Kaifeng area in the 11th and 12th centuries and the Lung Ch'uan celadons of the 13th and 14th centuries.

◄ A Lung Ch'uan celadon bowl. Diameter 14cm (5½in). Percival David Foundation, London

Below left A Ju ware cup and stand. Diameter 17cm (7in). Percival David Foundation, London

▼ A Ying Ch'ing cup and stand; height 9cm (3½in). Collections Baur, Geneva

The white-bodied wares, developed in parallel but a little later in north China, have their own quality and indeed their own forms. Early in taking their inspiration from imported silver wares, the potters made a thin-walled ware with an elegant finish of the lip and foot which are features of the pre-porcelain white wares. The most elegant among many such white wares is the Ting which has an ivory tinged glaze and a thin but not translucent body. Although translucency had been achieved by the 7th century, it was some time before it was exploited, especially for wine and food vessels. The Ching-te-chen kilns have made porcelain production their speciality from the 11th century until the present day. Here they have made some of the world's finest white porcelain; characteristically it is a pure white body with a pale bluish translucent glaze called Ying Ch'ing. The decoration current in the Sung period (960–1279), of an incised line under the glaze, acquires a special quality when used on this translucent material.

In a country in which pottery was used for all domestic purposes, it is natural there should be a tradition of strong, heavy-grade wares. Notable among "folk" potting are the slip-decorated jars, bowls, and pillows, first made in the north and called Tzu Chou wares and then produced in countless kilns throughout the country. Painting in slip under a transparent glaze produced some of the strongest graphic decoration in the world. This tradition was the basis for the later cobalt oxide underglaze traditions of the famous "blue and white".

Another local potters' tradition is the "tea ware" of Fukien. Coming originally from the Chien Yang area of west Fukien it has a chocolate-colored body and a thick brown glaze in which impurities caused a streaked effect called "hare's fur". The bowls from these kilns were used for tea drinking in the Ch'an (Zen) sect of Buddhism—popular in the Hangchow area temples of the 13th and 14th centuries. The association of the bowls with the ceremony was so strong that the Japanese, who came to China to learn the teaching and traditions of Zen, took the bowls back with them and called them *Temmoku* after the area of the temples (T'ien Mu Shan) in which they had found them. This is the generic term for all imitations of the Fukien wares.

MARY TREGEAR

Further reading. Gompertz, G. St G.M. *Chinese Celadon Wares*, London (1958). Gray, B. *Early Chinese Pottery*, London (1953). Palmgren, N., Steger, W., and Sundius, N. *Sung Sherds*, Stockholm (1958).

Above A Ting ware bowl. Diameter 28cm (11in). Percival David Foundation, London

▲ A *Temmoku* "hare's fur" bowl; diameter 10cm (4 in). Ashmolean Museum, Oxford

River. In 1124 the Southern Sung court was set up in Hangchow and remained until the late 13th century when the Mongols, under Genghis Khan, conquered both the Chin and the Sung to reunite the country under foreign rule. This makes the assessment of the culture of the country complicated; for example it is difficult to trace the course of the arts of the influential north China area during the Chin occupation.

The applied arts of the Sung dynasty as a whole have acquired a special reputation for superb craftsmanship and elegance of design. This reflects the scholar gentlemen's taste, which was also that of the court in this unusually cultured period. Although present in all aspects of design from architecture to jade-carving, this special taste can be most clearly seen in the ceramics of the period. Although ceramics were a minor art, they represent for us most faithfully the taste of the Sung, for the pots are among the few completely reliable remains from the period.

The scholar taste is typified by the elegant monochrome stonewares and porcelain. First came the northern wares of Ting, Ju, and Chun, to be followed by the southern Lung Ch'uan celadons, Fukien Temmoku ware, and Ching-te-chen Ying-Ch'ing porcelains. The creamy white wares of the Ting Chou kiln area were thinly potted and incised or impressed with a floral or fish motif, then coated with a thin, transparent, ivory-colored glaze and the finished ware was warm-toned and elegant. The finer-quality pieces are translucent.

This was the most favored ware of the 11th century, but it was superseded by Ju ware in the 12th. Made at kilns near the capital at Kaifeng, Ju is a gray stoneware with a green-gray glaze and epitomizes the sober but sensitive taste of the scholar. These highly prized wares were made in shapes either reminiscent of the old ritual bronzes or in simple ceramic bowl forms, their chief beauty being their nicely balanced shape and rich glaze. In Sung times the glaze on a gray stoneware was thickly applied and fired in a way that left many small bubbles suspended in the glaze, thus giving it almost a third dimension, accentuating its thickness as the light is diffused within it. The addition of a crackle for a short time during the mid Sung period seems also to have been a device to accentuate the thickness of the glaze. It had the additional fascination of

A Sung dynasty Ju ware bowl; diameter 17cm (7in). Percival David Foundation, London

similarity to the flawing in jade.

Indeed the quality of texture and translucency of the thick feldspathic glazes of the gray stoneware tradition of the Sung often come very close to the qualities of nephrite. The southern wares came into their own in the late 12th and 13th centuries; Lung Ch'uan, Chekiang celadons, and the frail-looking Ying Ch'ing porcelains of Ching-te-chen are the descendants of their northern counterparts in style and quality. Only the Temmoku wares of Fukien seem to have a new quality to add to the black glazes of the north. These fascinatingly glazed, dark-bodied wares were the local product of a kiln at Chien Yang, central Fukien, which were adopted by the Ch'an (Zen) Buddhist sect temples which flourished in that district in the 13th century. Thus this ware has achieved a reputation as "tea ware" and engendered a whole style of potting associated with tea ceremonies both in China and Japan. The body and glaze are heavily ferruginous and have been fired in an oxidizing atmosphere, but the glaze has impurities in it which can result in lovely "hare's fur" or "oil spot" effects. The popularity of this ware is exemplified by the number of imitations made at other kilns, both in central and northern China; in each case the clay is dissimilar and the resulting ware, though clearly close in spirit, can be distinguished.

The everyday wares of the north, notably the large group known as Tzu Chou, are made of sturdy gray stoneware with ingenious decoration under the glaze involving the use of slip, either as a painting material or as a coating through which the design is incised. These boldly decorated wares with an iron or copper underglaze decoration, which were initiated in the south, reveal the continuing interest in decoration found in the north of China in most periods.

The first century of the Sung dynasty, although politically hazardous, saw particular activity in the sphere of painting. The court at Kaifeng attracted the greatest artists of the period and with Imperial patronage, notably of the Hui Tsung Emperor, an Academy was formed which gave official artists a parity with other academicians and court officials. This recognition brought with it all the benefits of honor and risks of stultification which similar systems have demonstrated throughout the world. At first the great landscape school of the 10th century blossomed with such masters as Kuo Hsi (c1020–90) carrying through the classicism of the earlier masters in a baroque style. His paintings have survived only in copies, but they show a virtuosity which matches his reputation among contemporary critics. This massive style of painting seems to be both the culmination of a century-long tradition and a solution to the problem of creating a landscape "in which one can walk about", the ambition of the scholar-artist-official of the period. It provides, with its complex composition, a variety of experience for the viewer which is almost overwhelming.

It also bears within its enormous richness the seeds of the experiments of the 12th and 13th centuries. Perhaps directly associated with the taste of the academy-court artist the paint-

From a Northern Sung dynasty painting: Fishermen by Hsu Tao-ning. William Rockhill Nelson Gallery, Kansas City

Bamboo Branch by Wen T'ung (fl. 1049–79); ink on silk. National Palace Museum, Taipei

ing of the mid 12th century also brought to the fore a style of small-format painting which is so to speak a detail of the previous massive paintings. Here the painter brings all his observation and understanding of the natural world—landscape, birds, flowers, or bamboo—down to the scale of an album leaf or slightly larger, a format that demands a new and special technique of composition. This can be most clearly demonstrated by the bird and flower compositions of the court of the Hui Tsung Emperor. The surface pattern of the composition has now been brought into play and a new dimension is in the hands of the painter. The interplay of space, line, and form becomes the special concern of the bamboo painter and the bird and flower painter. The development of a sophisticated surface composition—the so-called "one corner" arrangement—and the sensitivity to near-balance and off-balance produced some of the most delightful paintings in this category.

Landscape painting seems entirely to change its *raison d'être*. The philosophy of the Taoist-poet is replaced by the more romantic artist creating a world of a specific atmosphere of soft sadness, weeping mists, and evening light. The painters of the Southern Sung court at Hangchow were the heirs to the mid-12th-century Kaifeng court. The link was the artist Li T'ang who, as an old man, was appointed director of the new academy in Hangchow. As a younger man he had developed a new brush style and compositional interest, parts of which influenced other artists. In line with the new self-consciousness of composition came a conscious invention and naming of brush strokes, to such an extent that in Southern Sung court painting the brushwork and ink tone (ink "play") could almost become the subject of the painting. But never wholly, for Chinese painting never takes the full step to abstraction. However, Li Tang's "axe cut" stroke, a chopping harsh brush stroke executed with the side of a brush full or half-charged with ink and swept sharply down, was one of the first of the tradition.

The greatest exponents of this school of painting were Hsia Kuei (1180–1230) and Ma Yuan (1190–1224), contemporaries and shining lights of the later Southern Sung academy. They could handle small or large, and especially horizontal compositions and embody the great aphorism of the period "to represent 1,000 *li* of space in one foot of silk." This expression of space was very influential among the Japanese painters of this and later times. The Chinese artists had such a sureness of touch in the handling of ink tone that it became a very expressive medium, capable of evoking not only space, but also color and texture. Moreover paper was now often the chosen base for painting, offering a wider scope for ink texture than silk.

The elegancies of the court artists of the 13th century were carried further by the great Ch'an (Zen) artists of the period. Both Mu Ch'i (*fl. c*1269) and Liang K'ai (*c*1140–1210) appear to have been trained in the academic styles of their day, but their religious experience and motives for painting took them along different paths. In their work, preserved in

Early Spring by Kuo Hsi

This large landscape in the National Palace Museum, Taipei, Taiwan, is painted in ink and slight color on a tea-colored silk. The evocation of a dry, early spring season in the mountains is an elaborate composition of vignettes of life and scenery ranging from fishermen on the river side to a temple half way up the mountain and a far receding valley to the left. It seems to be a composite memory of more than one landscape which has been constructed in the style of the rich post-classical period of painting: Kuo Hsi (*c* 1020–90) has composed the picture by the traditional means of a series of eye-levels, in this picture not always extending right across the panel so that we view it in a series of steps to either side of the central column. Each scene is actually at eye level, carefully observed and expressed quite directly with a free but well controlled brushwork.

A disjointed effect is avoided by the other traditional tool of the Chinese painter: the surface composition is sensitively balanced by both line and tone. Kuo Hsi likes to use a swirling, curving line which gives this composition a movement swinging our eyes up the picture and carrying them smoothly from one scene to another. The use of tone in such an ink painting—for the color is very slight and in touches of green and brown—serves to compose the surface so our eyes are enticed and held. Quite unlike a European painting in which atmospheric tone is all important, a heavy tone and strong contrasts being reserved for the foreground, accents in Chinese painting are placed at crucial points over the surface of the painting, often in conflict with the requirements of recession. It is in the control of these two modes of composition, the balance of eye-level recession, of linear and surface composition, that the mastery of this style of painting rests. *Early Spring*, masterpiece as it clearly is, is one of the earliest large scroll paintings to survive in the original. This makes it one of the chief touchstones and reference points in the study of Chinese painting.

MARY TREGEAR

◀ Two details from *Early Spring*: *above* waterfalls and temples among mountains, from the right-hand side; *below* fishermen on the river side, from the bottom left corner

▶ *Early Spring* by Kuo Hsi; 158×108cm (62×43in), 1072. Painted in ink and light color on a tea-colored silk scroll. National Palace Museum, Taipei

Japan, the marvelous ink and brush control is used to express a vibrant life in all objects, living or inorganic. Mu Ch'i can express the weight, color, texture, and form of persimmons as readily as the extraordinary peace of the Kuanyin in meditation, while Liang K'ai expresses the texture and movement of a monk's robe and a humorous insight into the psychology of the monk himself.

Thus 13th-century south China seems to have produced a school of painters of sensitivity and self-awareness using techniques of a very high order, either in the service of a romantic, elegant sadness or of a lively Buddhist cult. It is not clear what happened in the north after the Chinese court had left. It seems possible that painters continued to work and more than likely that they worked anonymously; several paintings of distinction have been put forward as belonging to the period and they reflect a tradition of minute observation and unself-conscious concern with all aspects of life. They have been

classed as genre paintings, but they include landscape painting of a serious kind, not of the grand school but borrowing much of the technique and calmness of those masters.

The Yuan dynasty (1279–1368). It may well be that the fusing of two general lines of painting, the sophisticated and the minutely observed, generated the great art of the 14th century. Much is made, traditionally, of the peculiar position of the official in a highly organized bureaucratic society when that society is controlled by a foreign head of state. The choice facing the Confucian scholar official was either a career in the service of a foreign regime or a self-imposed retirement from the capital to the simple life, probably on the family estate. Such was the position when the Mongols conquered China in 1280 and Kublai Khan set up a capital at Khanbalik, or Peking. The position of the Chinese intelligentsia was given one more complicated twist. The Yuan government now

A detail showing bamboo stems from an album painted by Wu Chen in 1350; National Palace Museum, Taipei

headed a united country, but under the domination of an uncultured but very strong foreign clan. A great number of potential officials decided to retire from service and the painters among this class probably found themselves with time to practice their art. They were in no way restricted and were in contact with each other but living away from the center that would have been their natural milieu in other times.

So the enrichment of the painters' outlook, brought about by the unification of the country and a renewed awareness of the grand traditions of the North, coincided with an unusual isolation of the artists, who at the same time were able to concentrate on their art free from concerns of court or patronage. This is an almost unique set of conditions and one to which the richness of the artistic output of the period is often ascribed. It is certainly true that during the 70 years of the Yuan dynasty some half-dozen great painters were active and produced work that has influenced Chinese artists to the present day.

Chao Meng-fu (1254–1322), a cultured and successful official, calligrapher, and painter, whose wife, Kuan Tao-sheng (1262–c1325), was also an accomplished painter of bamboo, stands out as the scholar artist who did not retire but who fulfilled his career and painted perhaps in the "court" style of the day. There was in fact no academy, but Chao Meng-fu and his son continued the scholarly Northern court tradition of thoughtful landscape painting and quiet observation. Wu Chen (1280–1354) and Li K'an (1245–c1320), individuals of great power in painting, worked in a style of fluent brushwork, both favoring bamboo as a subject although Wu Chen also excelled in marvelously free landscape painting. There is something here of the Southern courtly style in the brushwork and in the nature of the landscape for these artists tended to congregate in the lower Yangtse area—the Nan Chiang area in the south and Anhui in the north. Again and again the landscapes are of low hills, lakes, and rivers painted in the wet, smooth ink tones of Wu Chen or the silvery, dry ink of Ni Tsan (1301–74). This artist was a real eccentric with a restricted but clear-sounding genius. His style, his composition, and indeed the spirit of his uninhabited landscape haunted painters over the centuries, although none have quite matched the necessary asceticism to catch his spirit.

Of the group of great artists Wang Meng (1309–85) was probably the least accessible and so less obviously influential although his work was much admired by 17th- and 18th-century masters. Wang Meng painted bravura compositions, constructed in the classic style but treated in a completely individual style, densely worked and textured to a richness not usually tolerated in China. The absence of sky in some compositions is an experiment not repeated until the 18th century.

Finally we cannot leave this creative half-century without looking to Huang Kung-wang (1269–1354) and his Fu Ch'un mountain handscroll (National Palace Museum, Taipei). This magnificent landscape, the work of a 70-year-old artist, is the apotheosis of his style. With economy of brush but marvelous variety of handling he builds up a landscape immediately at-

A Yuan dynasty porcelain jar; height 39cm (15in). Cleveland Museum of Art

tracting and absorbing. This scroll became the greatest treasure to artists through the centuries and the opportunity to see and study it was a matter of pilgrimage for such varying painters as Shen Chou (1427–1509), Shih T'ao (1630–1707), and Wang Chien (1598–1677). This painting seems to stand as a beacon: it synthesizes the materials and tradition of the classic Northern court style and shines a light over the school of Wu painters who follow, through to the 17th century.

Thus the Yuan dynasty period is astonishingly rich in individual painters. Their work, perhaps in the original in some cases, comes through to the present day with great clarity and has been respected and admired by all artists in the intervening centuries.

The Yuan court of Mongol administrators was uninterested in the literati arts of south China but took a lively interest in the applied arts: jewelry, metalwork, ceramics, and silks. Here it is likely that their knowledge of Middle Eastern art was influential. Portraiture became very important and some Imperial portraits have survived. These have the straightforward boldness of the record of a grandee who requires a likeness of himself and his accoutrements. As always with Chinese portrait painting, however formal, the character of the sitter is there, although there may be little interest in solidity of form or nuance of color.

For the furnishing of aristocratic houses, craftsmen produced metalwork of silver and gold, engraved and inlaid. The use of precious metals in China for bowls and other vessels is often regarded as a foreign-style craft. However, it was a consistent if not very flourishing craft from the T'ang period onward. Chinese metalworkers always tended toward casting as their first choice of technique, using turning and beating only when essential. Consequently their work sometimes has a bizarre appearance, achieved as it is by a combination of techniques. But in the 14th century a love of decoration and richness lent itself to rather heavy pieces which could take encrustation with semiprecious stones. The Mongol rulers were familiar with the metalwork of the Middle Eastern craftsmen and had a taste already formed for this work.

But in the matter of porcelain the rulers were introduced to a new material. The kilns at Ching-te-chen in Kangsi were in strong production by the fall of the Southern Sung and were making high-quality white porcelain and developing techniques of underglaze decoration. Although most ceramic production was for home use, the Chinese increasingly used porcelain in trade. Not all the trade porcelain came from Ching-te-chen, for the ports used were Canton and Ch'uan Chou on the Fukien coast. As there were already kiln areas developed in the south, a certain proportion of the porcelain exported came from the vicinity of the port. However, the products of superior quality were all from Ching-te-chen. This trade went to Japan, the Philippines, Indonesia, Malaya, India, and the Middle East, notably to Hormuz on the Persian Gulf and Cairo in Egypt.

In modern times a considerable quantity of the very best 14th-century blue and white decorated porcelain has been found in Damascus, Syria, and there is some discussion of the route of entry for this. It may be that an overland route was used for special cargo although the Chinese have always preferred water transport for ceramics. This porcelain can be of the most exquisite quality of drawing on a strong, heavy-bodied pot or dish. The control of cobalt is clearly almost complete. The vocabulary of decoration is elaborate and follows a style usually explained as a combination of motifs from Near Eastern and Chinese sources. The Chinese tendency to arrange a design on a vessel in parallel bands is adopted for blue and white decoration, though the zones vary in width. The apparently inconsequential choice of motifs to fill the various bands is a fascinating aspect of Chinese decorators' art. There seems no good reason for the juxtaposition of the complicated motifs on the blue and white vases dated 1351. However, a tradition soon grew up for certain motifs to take certain positions, though these may vary from time to time and be one of the clues to dating.

Coming very close to the underglaze decorated porcelain is the lacquer ware of the Yuan. Most striking are the monochrome, dark brown to black wares in exquisite shapes, which epitomize the work of the lacquer makers of Chekiang, centering around the Shouchou district. Here the beautiful sheen of the material was left to speak for itself, but in this period the *ch'iang-chin* inlay technique was also used in a most striking style.

The Yuan dynasty, though short, was one of great stimulus

Returning Home from a Spring Outing by Tai Chin; ink and light colors on a silk scroll; 170×80cm (67×31in). National Palace Museum, Taipei

not least in the sphere of town building and particularly in palace architecture. The Mongols were interested in city planning and built a capital city at Peking, which they called Khanbalik, and made an imperial palace, a walled city which has been incorporated in the Ming and Ch'ing building now known as the Ku Kung (Old Palace), or Forbidden City. Recent excavations of the northwest corner of the Yuan Palace have uncovered a massive wall and gateway, similar to those gateways in the wall that has been preserved.

The Ming dynasty (1368–1644). It was not long before the Mongol rulers lost their drive and power. Revolts started among the Chinese and eventually a peasant leader was successful and formed a new dynasty to which he gave the name of Ming (bright). To mark the change from a foreign rule and to celebrate the real reunification of China the capital was at first moved to Nanking, literally Southern Capital. Much of the spirit of the new dynasty looked back to the glories of the past, particularly to the Han and T'ang when China had been strong, unified, and a nation. With a largely unlettered court of strong men the country was culturally without a center. Moves were made by the court to entice artists and scholars to serve the emperor. Confucian philosophy regained its vigor, but the attempted academy never was established and indeed those artists who did go to court were regarded with some suspicion and scorn.

Even this very simple estimate of the situation explains a little of the complex positions of the painters at the start of the dynasty. There was a group of artists painting in Chekiang who followed the style of Li K'an, Wu Chen, and the Southern Sung academy painters with an elegant, wet ink style and sweeping compositions. One or two of these, notably Tai Chin (1380–1452) stayed only briefly at court. Realizing that intrigue and courtly pastimes were not for him, Tai Chin returned to his native Chekiang for the last 20 years of his life, creating many fine paintings in the Hsia Kuei-Ma Yuan school but on a large scale which was to become characteristic of early Ming painting. His painting of river boatmen (Freer Gallery of Art, Washington, D.C.) is one of the major works of Chinese painting which has perhaps survived in the original. The fragility of scroll painting and the assiduous copying of all masterpieces has created a problem of connoisseurship in the study of Chinese painting which must always be in mind when considering works of great masters. However, as the period more nearly approaches our own it is at least likely that masterpieces may be judged to be originals and to that extent the whole appreciation of painting takes on a new and more exciting flavor. Tai Chin used color but in the texture of the ink painting of his great works there is a clear indication of the different character that finds its way into most early Ming painting. There is a panache and freedom of brushwork exploiting the larger format, and the self-conscious composition of the Southern Sung artists is loosened.

Closely allied to the Che School and yet worlds away from them were the court artists proper of the early Ming. These were the men who made their entire reputation at court, who painted to the needs of the court and were indeed professional painters. Lu Chi (*fl. c*1560) is perhaps the greatest exponent of this art; using mostly the bird and flower subject he created magnificent compositions which have much of the meticulous observation evident in the painting of Sung Emperor Hui Tsung (1082–1135), but once again the tight control of the composition has been relaxed and the subject is allowed to dictate the movement. Also it is clear that the birds and flowers are painted in their own surroundings so that the atmosphere is of a wild place rather than the rarified setting of the perfect bird on the perfect branch.

So much of Chinese decorative painting is romantic in style that we must differentiate between the romanticism of the Northern Sung, that of the Southern Sung, and now the broader warmth of the Ming. These court artists are not by any stretch of the term literati painters, but neither are they journeymen decorators of whom there were always a great many in China. But they are serious artists working within a genre which was much admired at this and every other time, except by those whose judgment of art was strictly moralistic.

By contrast and in conflict with the Che School painters were the group who are associated at first with Wu-hsien, present-day Suchow. These were painters consciously in the mold of the classic artists of the Yuan. They knew and respected the older paintings and took seriously the precept that artists should study the masters before branching out on their own. The first great artist of this group, called the Wu School, is Shen Chou (1427–1509). Shen Chou was an eclectic in the best tradition of the literati painters; his earlier work imitates the masters of the Yuan, whose works he would have known, for he lived in the same area where they had worked only a century before. He did, however, develop a strong style of his own which has been regarded as the best of the middle Ming. Shen is one of the dozen or so great painters in China who still have influence, in his case for his effortless, straightforward brushwork and telling compositions in which the human being is often the focus and seems to be the artist himself. This introduction of the painter into his own picture gives it an immediacy which, with the poem often also added by the artist, makes this both a private work and one that speaks directly to the viewer. This directness is a new twist to the literati tradition—the poet-painter is both speaking to the viewer and inviting him into his vision. The small painting of the poet singing on the cliff top (William Rockhill Nelson Gallery, Kansas City) is a marvelously vivid example. The poem says:

> White clouds encircle the mountain waist like a sash
> Stone steps mount high into the void where the narrow path leads far.
> Alone, leaning on my rustic staff I gaze idly into the distance.
> My longing for the notes of a flute is answered in the murmuring of the gorge.
>
> (Sickman, L. and Soper, A. *The Art and Architecture of China* p177.)

Directly we are there and identify with the figure in the landscape in a way quite different from any other landscape with figures previously produced in China. Another aspect of this use of a figure is shown in his large landscape in the style of Ni Tsan (National Palace Museum, Taipei). Although some of the brush and compositional style of Ni Tsan is echoed, Shen Chou has knitted the landscape together in a solid interrelationship of rock and tree shapes, avoiding the special ascetic sparsity of Ni Tsan and the creation of space and light of

Landscape Painting

There are many strands in the web that unites the varied styles of landscape painting of the scholar class of China across the centuries. These include brushwork—personal ink mannerisms, the ways of painting trees and rocks—but the strongest link is in the use of modes of composition. Early in the development of landscape as a serious subject for the painter a method of composing in depth was evolved and accepted as traditional. This method has been called the "rising eye-level", a system of successive eye-levels which allowed an expression of depth in a tall format; it is the conventional perspective of Chinese landscape painting.

The surface composition of these paintings, the way in which the composition is tied to the edges and in which it can be read, is something common to all paintings composed within a rectangular frame but which has a special character when the painting is not in color. In surface composition the edges

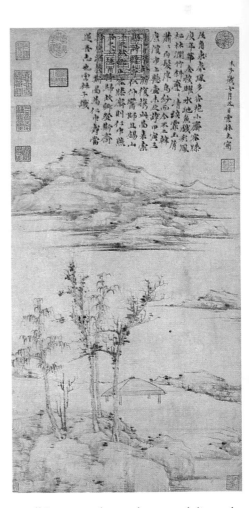

▶ *Jung Hsi Studio* by Ni Tsan; height 74cm (29in). National Palace Museum, Taipei

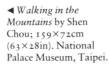

◀ *Walking in the Mountains* by Shen Chou; 159×72cm (63×28in). National Palace Museum, Taipei.

are all-important but understressed; lines of trees and mountains intersect and touch the edge at carefully devised spots. It is often upon the success of this composition that the feeling of balance within the picture depends. The balance of the surface is worked to a large extent independently of the in-depth composition; in the largely monochrome tradition of China considerations of tonal recession can be ignored in deference to surface balance. The eye is led around the surface of the painting by accent of tone and line.

The balance of surface and depth composition was a major interest for many Chinese painters. From this aspect alone the painting *Walking in the Mountains* (National Palace Museum, Taipei) by Shen Chou (1427–1509) shows a closely knit composition of interlocking spurs of land composed by the rising eye-level method. An overlay of lines from the trees and the figure firmly ties the composition of the surface to produce a sturdy equilibrium characteristic of this artist. He regarded himself as within the tradition of the 10th-century painter Tung Yuan whose landscape *Festival Invoking Rain* (National Palace Museum, Taipei) is organized more loosely on the rising eye-level, interlocking spurs method. In this calm and open composition the trees and bushes

◄ *Festival Invoking Rain* by Tung Yuan; 145×163cm (57×64in). National Palace Museum, Taipei

▼ *Dwelling in Ch'ing Pien Mountains* by Tung Ch'i-ch'ang; height 217cm (85in). Cleveland Museum of Art

are accents and guides to the eye, gently leading the attention over the surface which here is not governed by a network of lines.

Between the time of Tung Yuan and that of Shen Chou many experiments had been made with techniques of composition. An example that relates the two masters is the *Jung Hsi Studio* (National Palace Museum, Taipei) by Ni Tsan (1301–74). Here the rising eye-level, interlocking spur composition has been "stretched" to the point at which the islands almost do not interlock. Contact with the edge of the painting is subtle and the judgment of the points of contact and the division of the line are carefully made to avoid splitting the composition. Trees in Ni Tsan's painting are important as elements to direct the eye-lines of the surface and also to act as a strong tie to strengthen the surface within the frame. They are indeed controlling the central part of the picture. Shen Chou admired Ni Tsan's work and borrowed many of his composition techniques, notably the use of trees in the foreground. A simple comparison of these three artists seems to place Shen Chou between the other two. His was not the last word on this interplay of ideas: his pupil Wen Cheng-ming (1470–1559) took up Ni Tsan's composition seemingly in a purely eclectic spirit in his *Spring Landscape* in color. Closeness to the earlier painting is limited to the formal composition, for by the use of full color Wen Cheng-ming here produces a very different painting. The blues and greens of the landscape cancel the traditional tonal composition of the surface. Quite apart from the recession qualities of the color of which the painter was apparently unaware, he is unable in color to use the techniques of accent by tone which ink painters had developed since the time of Tung Yuan.

Tung Ch'i-ch'ang (1555–1636), the great analyst and student of classical painting, makes a clear comment on the aspects of landscape painting under discussion in his landscape *Dwelling in Ch'ing Pien Mountains* (1617; Cleveland Museum of Art). This painting, with its interest in painting itself as a subject of painting, summarizes much of the special nature of the Chinese scholar landscape school. For although the evocation of a scene remained a primary reason for painting, Tung saw the reinterpretation of other painters' work as of equal interest for the artist. Here the bones of the painting are evident and the way in which the composition is constructed is as much the subject of the painting as is the representation of a mountain landscape.　　　MARY TREGEAR

Further reading. Loehr, M. *The Great Painters of China*, Oxford (1980). Sullivan, M. *The Birth of Landscape Painting in China*, London (1962).

the earlier artist. But more outrageously, he has introduced a figure quietly walking through the landscape who becomes the focus of the picture. Comparison with the single figure in landscape of Ma Yuan (National Palace Museum, Taipei) gives us a clue to the special dimension of these Shen Chou figures, which seem to invite the viewer to identify with them and to look at the landscape from inside the picture rather than from a distance.

Wen Cheng-ming (1470–1559) was contemporary with and lived in the same general district as Shen Chou, and they are inevitably associated in the Wu School. However, they were quite different personalities and produced very different work although they were both members of the literati class and worked from an eclectic base. Such was the variety of the 14th-century Old Masters from whom they could claim descent that Wen Cheng-ming, fundamentally a decorative artist interested in color and texture and even light and atmosphere, could fit into this very loosely grouped School. Wen and his large family were the generators of the later (16th and 17th century) Wu School which did move away from the intensity of vision and personal experimentation of Shen Chou into calmer waters and large and impressive landscapes.

Two of the great 16th-century painters were Ch'iu Ying (c1494–c1552) and T'ang Yin (1470–1523). They do not quite fit into the tidy grouping of painters as professional, court or literati artists. Ch'iu Ying was originally a journeyman painter, not an educated man and therefore not easily accepted as a named artist. But he was a great natural artist and so spectacularly beautiful was his painting that he became popular and has been influential ever since. His large oeuvre has been grossly swelled by copyists and imitators but we must believe that he painted a wide variety of subjects. He is best known for his palace genre scenes and his colored landscapes. These last link him to the Wu School in its more decorative aspect.

T'ang Yin was quite a different case. He was a disgraced scholar who seems to have "dropped out" in a very modern fashion but who, in his more sober periods, painted so beautifully, in the traditional literati style with an added personal comment, that he must be accounted a major artist. Chinese aesthetic assessments are apt to see signs of moral lapses revealed in the artists' work. Thus in assessing T'ang Yin it would seem that the natural elegance of the painting has been confused with degeneracy. However this may be, his output was small and his paintings rare.

The recording and preservation of the work of these two nonconforming artists is a small hint of the movement taking place in the art world of China toward the end of the Ming dynasty, a movement to loosen the admittedly not very strong bonds of tradition. No strong academy was formed in the Ming dynasty, the most highly respected artists all lived away from court, so there was in no sense an establishment, other than the Wu School, to which serious artists aspired. The Wu School gradually held under its umbrella a wide variety of artists but the tendency seemed towards a colored decorative

style retaining a Yuan/Northern Sung composition. This tendency was noted and caused disquiet to the scholarly who admired the solemn grandeur of the 12th-century Old Masters and their followers in the 14th century. Tung Ch'i-ch'ang (1555–1636) and his friend, Mo Shih-lung (fl. 1567–1600) were the leaders of the discussion and together they wrote on the theory and philosophy of aesthetics until Mo Shih-lung's death.

Tung Ch'i-ch'ang was a rare and complex artist, an analyst and theoretician. He was interested in the construction of paintings and in the relationship of one painting to another. A Confucian scholar by training and a Ch'an Buddhist by conviction, his treatises on painting are interesting to read. Unfortunately he is best known for his strictures, notably those inherent in his classification of the Northern and Southern Schools. But more fruitful is his idea of transformation, the process by which an artist expresses what he sees in brush stroke and composition. For Tung this came to be the central interest of painting.

The early 15th century was the period of the major building of the Forbidden City—the Imperial Palace—in Peking. The Yung Lo Emperor (1403–25) moved the capital north after a struggle for power with his nephews which left him with a very shaky power base in the Southern capital of Nanking. Having moved to his own fief in the north he planned and started to build the large enclosed palace we know today. This is a rectangular walled compound, enclosing the Yuan palace; the buildings are carefully aligned on a north–south axis and consist of a series of ceremonial halls each approached across an awesome courtyard. To the east and west of these are a series of court offices with the domestic courtyards and living quarters for the Emperor to the west and the women and children of the court to the east. Officials of the court lived outside the walls but close to the palace which was the winter residence of the Emperor. Various princes and other members of the Imperial family had palace residences in Peking and it became the custom to have a summer residence up in the hills out of Peking to escape the dry heat. This Imperial building in the traditional wooden pillar-and-beam style, but with more and more elaborate roof bracketing to take the wide sweeping tiled roofs, is an example of a widespread building activity in China. It is characteristic that neither the style nor the technique and materials of building had changed since the T'ang dynasty.

The interior of the houses of the increasingly wealthy new merchant class and the rich bureaucrats must have become more and more colorful and rich-looking. There is a general heaviness of style, carried through from the Yuan period in which furniture was solidly constructed of dark, polished wood.

Ceramics, always an important minor art, saw a stylization of the underglaze blue of the Yuan period. Imperial patronage

Clearing after Snow in a Mountain Pass by T'ang Yin; scroll, ink and light colors on silk; 71×35cm (28×14in). National Palace Museum, Taipei

A bowl of the Cheng Hua period (1465–88) with floral underglaze blue decoration. Percival David Foundation, London

of the kiln at Ching-te-chen, where a government office was established to manage the considerable orders required by the palaces alone, led to a more obvious progression of styles of decoration. There was such a strong element of fashion that motifs come and go in succession in the highest quality wares, only to survive and become combined in the provincial wares of south China and Annam. During the Ming dynasty the high quality products of the Ching-te-chen kiln were marked with the reign and dynasty on the base of the piece. Thus a few of the reigns have become noted for the special qualities of the wares produced for them. Probably the Yung Lo reign is the first great period; the pots are close in style to Yuan pieces but still unmarked, and are of very high quality. The floral scrolls are rich and generously drawn, the leaf and flowers dominating the stem. The figure and animal painting of this period can be vigorous and of the highest quality. Pieces tend still to be massive.

The Hsuan Te reign (1426–36) is the next notable porcelain period in which exquisite blue and white porcelain was produced. It was of a more delicate design in which the floral scroll is dominated by the line of the stem; the leaves and flowers were reduced and became accents to the sinuous curve. During this period too, the glaze became finer and less blue, marking a gradual but continuous move toward the perfection of a clear shining glaze through which the intense cobalt blue would shine at its brightest in the 17th and 18th centuries. The Cheng Hua reign (1465–88) is famous for its delicate small pieces, perhaps most notably the *tou-ts'ai* or "fighting color" pieces in which the transparent pale-colored overglaze decoration is superimposed on and completes the underglaze blue decoration. This so-called enamel or overglaze decoration gradually superseded the underglaze blue, but not completely until the 18th century. Throughout the Ming period potters experimented with the rich palette of five colors—red, green, yellow, blue, and purple—which they had at their disposal.

Three other periods need to be mentioned in relation to ceramic wares. The Cheng Te reign (1506–22) saw a vogue for painting in double outline and the decoration often included an inscription of good wishes or an Arabic Koranic quotation. This last reflects the Muslim Eunuch's influence at court for this reign. The Chia Ching period (1522–67) is notable for colored and blue and white pieces; the decoration is now more informal, even light-hearted, probably marking the enlargement of the market for these wares within China. No longer the prerogative of the court and the very wealthy, they must now have been the most common decorative materials.

The overseas trade in porcelain was growing and in the late 16th and 17th centuries considerable quantities were sent to Europe to start a vogue which gathered momentum and became immense in the 18th century. Europeans were partial to blue and white porcelain and this trade supported the production of blue and white in China at a time when Chinese taste was moving toward polychrome decorated porcelain. The Wan Li Emperor (1573–1620) presided over one of the last of the cultured courts of the Ming dynasty. During his reign Ching-te-chen produced some very fine thin and elegant wares presumably for domestic use, in contrast to the heavy, handsome wares exported to Europe.

Lacquer became very popular during the Ming period, particularly carved red or black lacquer. Polished red lacquer has a particularly beautiful voluptuous quality when carved in the generous style of the early Ming. The depth of lacquer and soft richness of carving are unequaled in any other period, and reflect the quality of contemporary aristocratic taste. With rather heavy simple jade carving, rich silks, heavy, dark wood polished furniture, and opulent bird and flower painting, the 15th-century interior could be one of great richness. With the passing years the richness increased as more and more decorative material was produced in cloisonné enamel, painted enamel, carved ivory, amber, jade, hard stones, and such exotics as rhinoceros horn. The decoration tended to become more complex and the scale diminished so that where in the late 14th and early 15th centuries most media show a relatively large design on a simple-shaped object, as time passed this character changed and shapes became more bizarre. Gradually the clutter was enlarged; the amassing of wealth, though halted or redistributed to some extent at the downfall of the dynasty, must be regarded as a continuing movement through to the 18th century. The scholar's taste in the midst of this worldliness was for beautiful, simply-made but elegant material, and so monochrome glazes appear, simpler forms of carving in bamboo, ivory, and rhinoceros horn. This last material was a favorite among the superstitious for not only was it thought to be an aphrodisiac, it was also regarded as a sure indicator of poison. Hence the vogue for cups of this material. This quickly developed into a style of carving in a shape adapted to the short horn of the Java rhinoceros.

Korea in the Choson and Yi periods (1392–1910). Although Korea was invaded from Japan during the Yi period (in 1592) and a specifically Korean script had been invented and adopted (in 1446) Korea remained culturally close to China.

Nowhere is this more evident than in the visual arts.

After the development of plain and inlaid celadons by the Koryo, potters turned their attention to a white-bodied stoneware with underglaze decoration. This closely follows the move in the Chinese pottery trade, but it is thought that the Koreans may have led the way with the use of copper oxide under the glaze, which when satisfactorily fired (reduced) produces a red. However this may be, it is clear that the 14th century saw the initial experimentation and exploitation of the underglaze technique with the three metallic oxides, iron, copper, and cobalt. The Koreans had their own graphic style, closely following the flower painters' style of the period. They tended to use decoration sparingly and to great effect on the full-bodied shapes they were making in heavy white stoneware. The Korean potters always seem to have one eye on the Chinese craftsmen but never became subservient to them in either technique or style.

In the more homely wares of the earlier part of the Yi period the Koreans developed the Pun Ch'ong wares. In many ways these have an affinity with the northern wares of China and Manchuria, the Tzu Chou or Liao type of slip and incised decorated gray stonewares. In Korea the gray body is incised or impressed with simple decoration and the whole is then lightly brushed with white slip. This will effectively inlay the decoration, leaving a distinctive streaky white surface on the warm, gray body, which is then glazed. Pun Ch'ong wares are also more traditionally decorated with slip decoration, both painted and incised and also with iron-painted underglaze decoration. This ware has a great influence on Japanese potting, notably of Karatsu, but the relationship with Japan is that of inspiration or even actual teacher; with China there seems a less obvious but quite persistent link. Likewise with lacquer the Koreans continued the mother-of-pearl inlay techniques of the Chinese, and during the 14th to the 16th centuries produced boxes, trays, and chests of a bold, rich design if not of exquisite workmanship. Another inlay technique which is solely Korean is that of insetting the surface of boxes and small chests with sheets of horn painted with bright colors. The painted side is set inside and the translucency of the horn lends a richness to the coloring. These are truly folk art pieces, but attractive and typical of the Korean genius for unsophisticated, colorful works of art.

During this long period painting emerged as a major art. As in China the Koreans had both professional and literati painters, although they were organized differently. Both schools owed their original character to the Chinese. However, there were very few Imperial patrons of the arts and so painting was not centered around an academy, nor were there the scholar-official schools of the 14th or of the 16th and 17th centuries, so influential in China. In the early centuries of Yi, the Office of Painting, established in the Koryo period, continued and many artists were trained there. The only great Imperial patron was Prince Anp'yong who amassed an important collection including Chinese Sung and Yuan paintings. However, he died young and his collection was dispersed.

The outstanding Korean painters of the earlier period, the 15th and 16th centuries, were professionals. An Kyon (1418–?), a protégé of Prince Anp'yong, was trained in the Northern Sung and Chao Meng-fu styles. His most famous work, *The Fairyland Seen in a Dream* (or *Spring Dream*; private collection), was painted for his patron and shows his academic style. An Kyon was the first master of the Yi period and his work was much admired. Yi Sang-jwa (1465–?), a follower of An and a specialist in the Hsia Kuei, Ma Yuan style, is a typical professional painter of the early Yi. He rose from humble beginnings to become a painter in government employment; his painting is close to Chinese styles. Many painters are recorded, all in this school, specializing in portraiture, bird and flower, bamboo, and most strikingly in Buddhist painting where Zen styles predominated.

The contrast with the later period, the 17th to the 19th centuries, is striking, for at this time the literati painters of Korea came to the fore and painted in the styles of the Chinese Wu School and the Individualists of the 17th and 18th centuries. However, the Korean artists added their own characteristic of a persistent genre setting in any painting containing figures. A certain informality already noted in Korean paintings as compared with their Chinese forerunners is quite clear in the later paintings. There is also a love of grotesquery in the painting of rocks, which become jagged and abrupt, and trees, reduced to dashingly abbreviated symbols.

Chong Son (1676–1769) stands out as one of the great artists in this style. He was a theorist and teacher who produced practical guidebooks to his style. His landscapes depict actual beauty spots in areas around Seoul and particularly in the Diamond Mountains. Later followers of this style are the brothers Kim Tuk-sin (1754–1821) and Kim Sok-sin (1758–?), each painting both landscape and genre scenes with figures reminiscent of the Southern Sung painter, Hsia Kuei (1180–1230).

Korean calligraphy was affected by the introduction of the Korean script Han'gul. However, the educated literati class continued to use the Chinese script in an elegant if somewhat weak style. The Han'gul script, regarded as a plebeian and illiterate mode, was nevertheless developed by the court ladies into a cursive script of some distinction.

Ch'ing dynasty (1644–1911). At the beginning of the 17th century culture in China was at a low ebb as the dynasty fell into disorder and degeneracy, to be overrun by the Manchu rulers from the north who founded the Ch'ing dynasty. Once again a pattern was set of a foreign imperial power, but this time the rulers were uncultured and admired Chinese ways. Chinese bureaucrats and literati were encouraged and indeed the administration of the country was run in tandem. Thus coinage and official seals had Manchu writing on one side and Chinese on the other. All official posts were in duplicate (Manchu and Chinese) and strenuous efforts were made to make official life attractive to the Chinese scholar. Three successive courts under the K'ang Hsi (1662–1723), Yung Cheng

Steep Rock Formation by Chong Son (1676–1769). National Museum of Korea, Seoul

(1723–36), and Ch'ien Lung (1736–96) Emperors fostered good living, serious philosophical thought, and cultural activity.

However, of even greater importance in the consideration of the visual arts is the rapid enlargement of private wealth. Great merchant houses were established based on commodities such as silk and salt. A vivid picture of the gradual demise of one of these large families is drawn in *The Dream of the Red Chamber*, the first modern-style novel written in China in the 18th century. It was therefore a more complex society within which artists functioned. Firstly there were the artists who retired from official circles for political reasons. Amongst these must be placed two of the great Individualists Chu Ta (Pa Ta Shan-jen) and Shih T'ao (Tao Chi).

Chu Ta (1626–1705), a fine exponent of Ch'an (Zen) painting, was a minor member of the Ming royal family and an eccentric who retired to live in a monastery. In the tradition of Ch'an artists he was a literati-trained painter who used his great skill in the handling of ink and paper in intense paintings of birds, flowers, and landscape. Much has been made of the isolation of Chu Ta, but although he lived a solitary life, he was in touch with such contemporaries as Shih T'ao. The Ch'an tradition has always been a dynamic but limited force in Chinese art. The particular style of composition and concept of brushwork used remained constant. The one unusual

aspect of Chu Ta's work is his landscape painting, which curiously shows a clear understanding of and interest in Tung Ch'i-ch'ang's analytical work on the composition of landscape. Chu was one of the very few artists to follow up Tung's experiments with landscape painting and to try to clothe them in the warmth and life of his brushwork.

Shih T'ao (1630–1707) was a quite different personality. Cast in the mold of Shen Chou, he was a dedicated painter and devout Buddhist, with no taste for official life. Shih T'ao was an educated and sophisticated scholar, well acquainted with the Old Masters but with such originality of vision that he very soon imbued everything he painted with his own romantic view of the world. He developed all the classic techniques of *ts'un* and dots but used them in color or on such a scale as to change their character. As a painter Shih T'ao was

Left: Waterfall on Mount Lu by Shih T'ao (1630–1707); hanging scroll, ink and light colors on silk; width 64cm (25in). Tokyo National Museum

A landscape by Chu Ta (1626–1705); 24×28cm (9×11in). Honolulu Academy of Arts

the antithesis of Tung Ch'i-ch'ang whose theorizing he distrusted, for where Tung classified and sought to dissect, Shih saw the unity of painting and relied on nature for his inspiration, the expression of which was his sole objective. Thus he attacked Tung Ch'i-ch'ang's theories of "transformation" and stressed that the only starting point for a painting was the observation of nature.

Although Chu Ta and Shih T'ao were so opposed in outlook it is salutary, from our distance, to see within what a short focus this opposition took place, for both would stand by the literati concept of the artist as based within the tradition of the Old Masters. Each was to some extent eclectic in his method of work, but Shih T'ao represents the greatest liberation in his personal expression of the artist's vision. This is a clear illustration of the narrow scope within which Chinese painters worked. There is never any suggestion that new materials or format should be used, no experimentation with the media such as the Japanese indulged in. So that where we acknowledge an outstanding individual, he is always within the broad framework of the accepted styles and forms of painting established over the previous seven centuries.

Having introduced the 17th century and the new dynasty with two great masters traditionally regarded as of astonishing originality, we must step back to the orthodox school represented again traditionally by the four Wangs. These four artists follow the Wen Cheng-ming school of colored, massive landscapes. The eldest of the Wangs was contemporary with Shih T'ao, with whom he was acquainted and whose work he admired. Although no great innovators themselves these artists at their best seem to embody all that is positive in the theories of Tung Ch'i-ch'ang; they followed the old traditions with sincerity and intelligence but they were also able, within narrow confines, to produce individual work of some power. Indeed Wang Yuan-ch'i (1642–1715) came close to cubist expression. He experimented with ideas of solid form in a way that has never been further explored. This inhibition from development of ideas of an abstract nature—color, form, or line—is one of the striking characteristics in Chinese painting.

A spirit of experiment, however, was alive among the painters in the flourishing cities of Suchow and Yangchow. Here the personal wealth of some of the great families encouraged the collection of all sorts of artifacts including paintings. The patrons were not traditional, well-informed, scholarly gentlemen but successful businessmen with uncultured eyes. They were intrigued by originality, and the "different" quality in works of art fascinated them. In an almost modern situation painters sought to differ from each other and gained the title of Eccentric Groups of loosely connected artists, such as the Eight Eccentrics of Yangchow or the Four Hsinan Masters who seemed the epitome of highly successful fashionable collectors' artists. These men do not fit into the pattern of court, professional, or scholar painter thus far examined. They were men of education and culture, but they painted for a market outside their own circle and were financially successful in their painting.

Thus a new artist entered society in the 18th century and he has been there ever since. Nineteenth-century and especially 20th-century painters are of this type: they paint in much the same way as the European artist, for an unidentified clientele of collectors. The concept of schools and even of the scholar-painter must be reconsidered, for although traditional scholars and painters certainly existed through the 19th century, the mainstream of painting now flowed through the Eccentric or Individualist painters. The differentiation between these two categories is much a matter of degree and standing; the Individualists were all major artists schooled in the classical tradition, each forming a personal style of such power that it could stand alone. The Eccentrics, by comparison, were lesser artists who evolved a completely personal style of expression; but each worked in a limited field so that while their painting is easily identifiable by style, they have not inspired later painters to develop their ideas further. The differentiation amounts to a subjective assessment of the germinal quality of the painting.

There were few great painters in the 19th century. Jen Po-nien (1840–95) was a lively bird and flower painter who used a spiky brushwork and attractive color. He was an influential painter who led the way to a style of painting both decorative in its use of color and capable of expression in the brushwork. Jen Po-nien had contemporaries who painted in a similar style and this became established as one of the major styles of the late 19th and 20th centuries—for bird and flower painting was a popular subject for some of the major artists of this period of change in Chinese society.

A few names stand out amongst the artists working in the first half of the 20th century: Wu Ch'ang-shih (1844–1927) who painted in a strong ink style, often painted bird and flower but also landscape and bamboo; he in turn influenced Ch'i Pai-shih (1851–1957), one of the best-known of 20th-century painters. This long-lived artist was an instinctive painter who often painted brilliantly. He was heir to the Ch'an tradition, but in his art used elements from other old decorative traditions both of meticulous and free painting.

Ch'i was one of the minority of his generation of artists who did not travel abroad. Hsu Pei-hung (1895–1953) went to France as did Lin Feng-mien (1901 or 1906–) and they brought back elements of European art, the concept of "drawing" as then practiced in art schools. This led to the curiously anthropomorphic animals of Hsu and the concept of color of the French Post-Impressionists translated to a delicate freedom when used in the Chinese tradition. Other artists, notably Fu Pao-shih (1904–65), went to Japan and joined the experiments of the Japanese artists with texture and paper. Fu Paoshih appears to paint in the tradition of Shih T'ao but more blandly. He was interested in historical styles and painted figures in a T'ang style, curiously at variance with his romantic landscapes. In this versatility he was matched by Chang Ta-ch'ien who has done much archaistic work but has also painted delightful paintings in his own personal style. Chang was one of the first artists to study and transmit the

Birds and Branches by Jen Po-nien (1840–95); ink and color on paper; 66×46cm (26×18in). Ashmolean Museum, Oxford

great wall-paintings at Tun Huang and introduce his countrymen to the great heritage of the early Buddhist paintings. In this he stepped outside any role of painter yet practiced in China. Indeed the 20th century has seen much change in the role and the production of artists who now seem to occupy a position closer to that of the artist in the West. The work of the traditional painters shows their links with the traditions within which they still work. Contemporary arts present such a wide spectrum that a different criterion is required for their discussion, but Chinese painting as an art form is alive and as expressive as ever of the society of which it is part. As that society evolves, so painting will inevitably change.

As the Ch'ing dynasty ran its course the decoration and furnishing of houses became more and more elaborate. Craftsmen were kept busy producing exquisite toys and decoration for the wealthy. This increase in personal wealth was one of the major influences of the period. Ceramics remained the staple material for all eating vessels and Ching-te-chen the major kiln area for the production of porcelain. The court

reestablished its factories; the government official overseeing Imperial orders became a notable person and his name was recorded. Thus the official in the brilliant K'ang Hsi reign (1661–1720), Tsang Ying-hsuan, fostered the production of brilliant blue and white ware decorated with figure scenes taken from the woodcut book illustrations so popular at this time. These scenes often depict characters from plays such as the *Hsi Hsiang chi*, a Yuan drama. The K'ang Hsi period also saw the finest of the Famille Verte decorated porcelains; the colors in overglaze were of the group called Five Color in the Ming. The tendency was toward the refinement of the colors which became paler as they were applied over the bright transparent white glaze. The potters devised a technique of overglaze decorating on a biscuit fired porcelain which resulted in a richer coloring as the reflection of light through the primary glaze was cut out. The on-the-biscuit Famille Verte represents a class of pottery of the curious style becoming more popular in collectors' circles. For the rich of Soochow by no means restricted their collecting to paintings but amassed extensive holdings of pottery, bronze, jade, lacquer, enamel, and textiles.

Among the visitors to the K'ang Hsi court were foreigners from many countries, and the Jesuits sent their missionaries to court in Peking where they were tolerated as mathematicians. One of the Jesuits, Guiseppe Castiglione (1688–1716), caught Imperial attention as a painter; trained as he had been in the Italian schools, he attempted an amalgamation of styles with the Chinese. He was known in China as Lang Shih-ning and painted in Chinese format with ink and color on silk or paper. His exquisite flower paintings, stiffly organized and entirely un-Chinese in feeling, were appreciated for their "lifelike" drawing as indeed were his paintings of horses and figures. This artist, who worked in the Yung Cheng and early Chien Lung periods, stood at the head of a style of hybrid painting which found favor with the decorators at a time when Europeans were engaged in an extensive trade with China and later with Japan. The trading companies set up by Holland, Spain, Sweden, and Britain maintained a trade through Canton in ceramics, lacquer, and silk, with other commodities such as spices and tea, sufficient to affect the manufacture of these things in China. Chinese craftsmen evolved a style and vocabulary of decoration which they associated with work for foreigners and which they did not employ on objects specifically for their own use. This is one example of an export style of which there are others in China, for they made for the Islamic market in the Far East and Near East as well as for the Europeans. It is therefore understandable that foreign ideas of decoration for each specific market should be regarded as something apart from that used in work for the home market.

During the short Yung Cheng reign (1723–36) the overseer at the Imperial factories of Ching-te-chen, Nien Hsi-yao, ordered the production of a beautiful series of archaistic wares in the style of the Sung court wares of the 12th and 13th centuries. Ju and Kuan type wares were produced and cherished in the early 18th century. The body of these wares

was usually white porcelain which lightens the overall effect of the thick crackled glaze. The similarity with the earlier pieces is striking, and shows a fine understanding of Sung aesthetics. Also in the Yung Cheng period a very delicate "boneless" style of overglaze decoration was introduced using the new palette of Famille Rose. This marked the introduction of a crimson color, derived from colloidal gold, and an opaque white derived from arsenic, both used in low-fired overglaze decoration. Both these colors came from Europe and their use is a rare example of technical innovation being accepted from outside China at this time.

Following this very brief period was the long reign of the Ch'ien Lung Emperor (1736–96). During his era the most notable official at Ching-te-chen was T'ang Ying. The kilns during his term of office reached the technical peak of their production, indulging in the tricks of imitating of other materials in ceramic to such a standard that it is difficult to distinguish even porcelain "brocade-covered books" except on touch. This period of very ornate taste finds its treasures in the elaborate gilded and carved wares, the brilliant technical feats mentioned and, relatively rarely, blue and white or perfect white porcelain faultlessly decorated in tightly designed motifs.

As we have seen at other periods, Chinese taste is not monolithic and so in the 18th century the scholar-gentleman demanded a less showy but nonetheless exquisite ware. To meet this demand came typically the brown basalt-type ware of I Hsing, a fascinating ware of unglazed brown clay which could be carved and modeled. It caught the eye of both the Japanese (Bizen) and English (Wedgwood) potters. In some respects this sophisticated cult of a rough-looking ware has parallels with the Sung cult of tea wares. The Ch'ing scholars also affected carved bamboo on their desks in a similar attempt to attain a simplicity not present in the other rooms of their houses. After this period Ching-te-chen, though still producing fine workmanship, was not such a consistent kiln, and indeed ceramics in general in China seems to have suffered a lack of strong patronage, reflecting the gradual disintegration of society and loss of confidence in artistic judgment which marks the 19th and 20th centuries. In the 20th century good quality porcelains have been and still are made at the great kiln sites, albeit still in the traditional style with little reference to the movements in design originating in Japan and the Scandinavian countries. However, as Chinese technical achievements are still inspiring such potters the wheel still has time to come full circle.

A similar line of technical perfection linked to elaborate decorative taste may be traced in the many applied arts furnishing the great houses of the 18th and 19th centuries. Carved jades and hard stones approximated to jewelry, immense boulders of jade carved as a landscape were treasured by the very rich and intricately carved tinkling hanging rings on ar-

The Monkey of Cochinchina by Lang Shih-ning (1688–1716); color on silk; 190×84cm (75×33in). National Palace Museum, Taipei

chaistic vases were popular with collectors. The gentleman scholar collected lapidary carved desk screens, water pots, and snuff bottles; the latter, developed from the small medicine bottle of plain porcelain, became a vogue in the 18th century with the introduction of snuff from Europe. Snuff bottles were indeed made in every material and technique in this later period.

The craft of enameling metal, used in the Ming dynasty in the cloisonné enamels, was enriched if stylized in the Ch'ing. The cloisonné enamels, made in the Soochow region of China, became heavy and solid pieces with, at their richest, gold cloisonné and colored enamels. These objects, usually in archaic bronze shapes, reflect in their decoration the motifs used in ceramic Famille Rose wares. The heavy gold outlining of the color gives an added glamor to the Imperial pieces. By contrast the development of the so-called Canton enamel produces a delicate effect. This technique of laying enamel on the surface of a metal vessel and firing the whole to achieve an effect similar to the Famille Rose porcelain of the period was developed in Canton although the metal bodies were made in the Hangchow district of north Chekiang. This very skilled work was developed as a substitute for porcelain, supposedly to be stronger and so to travel more safely. In fact although it does not fracture as porcelain, it is susceptible to stress and chipping and stands wear and tear much less kindly.

Curiosities naturally find a place in the urban society of the 18th and 19th centuries, such as carvings in rhinoceros horn, a rare material which has some of the warmth, lightness, and translucency of amber. Bamboo root carving is a weird affectation of the period, almost an objet trouvé cult, but the root is aided by carving and by composition. This same aesthetic is evident in the gardens of the period which were already traditional. Grotesque stones had for many centuries been used to form the focus of a landscape in miniature, and stones were collected from all over the kingdom. Some of the best-preserved of these gardens are now in the palaces of Peking, and in Hangchow and Canton. Here the idea of a garden as a symbolic landscape is carried through in a formalized layout including the rock mountain and possibly water with flowers and plants often provided in containers.

These gardens were furnished with bamboo, lacquered or porcelain furniture in the form of stools, and tables used either as seats or stands. Inside the house the chief furnishing material was still dark wood but this was becoming rarer and its place was taken by rosewood. Southern grandees liked to use marble and mother-of-pearl inlay in furniture and in most areas bamboo chairs and tables became fashionable. The sheer wealth of material to be contained in a house made the construction of shelves and cabinets essential and this is the time of the irregular display shelving associated in Europe with the chinoiserie vogue.

As always the scholar's room was usually different with a restrained use of color and an insistence on exquisite workmanship and materials. Here we find the elegant bookbinding, in silk brocade with ivory or jade fittings, and all the paraphernalia for the viewing of scrolls—the weights for hand-scrolls, the stick to hang the long scroll, the weights to keep it still—all made with minute taste. The Chinese gentleman at this time used a toggle much as the better known netsuke; he carried a fan, often a card case and tobacco and pipe. These could be made in ivory, wood, or any hardstone, for the Chinese love of material for its own character is always present. However, in times of affluence the tendency to torture material is exaggerated. Hence the intricate carving of ivory until it splinters, the use of one material to imitate another noted especially in porcelain, and the minute carving of jade until it is paper thin and loses its weight and sense of strength. This, often regarded as a failure of taste visible in many cultures with the rise of the rich middle class, was the companion to the loss of direction seen in painting of the later 18th and 19th centuries. It seems to mark a loss of judgment in so many directions. The patrons, in this case the rich aristocratic and mercantile upper classes, apparently largely subscribed to a taste insecurely grounded in tradition and governed by a feeling for display. These two sterile qualities do not together give a craftsman enough inspiration or impetus to keep his craft more than technically alive. The admiration for technique, an essential ingredient for the appreciation and patronage of craft, is however not enough. Remembering that no personal reputation was possible, for Chinese craftsmen were normally anonymous, the craftsmen must rely on the interest of the buyer, however remote, to spark their interest in design and help to form a taste even within themselves.

It is possibly this same set of circumstances in different degrees that are at play today. There is no doubt that traditions and techniques are still alive; the interest now lies in the character of patronage. This question, recurrent in most present-day societies, awaits an answer in China where the visual arts still play a very important role in everyday life.

M. TREGEAR

Bibliography. CHINA: Cahill, J. *Chinese Painting*, Geneva (1960). Cahill, J. *Hills beyond a River: Chinese Painting of the Yuan Dynasty*, New York and Tokyo (1976). Cahill, J. *Painting at the Shore: Chinese Painting of the Early and Middle Ming*, New York and Tokyo (1978). Chang, K.C. *Archaeology of Ancient China*, New Haven (1977). Lee, S.E. *A History of Far Eastern Art*, London (1964). Medley, M. *The Chinese Potter*, Oxford and New York (1976). Sickman, L. and Soper, A.C. *The Art and Architecture of China*, Harmondsworth (1971). Siren, O. *Chinese Painting*, (7 vols.) London (1956–8). Sullivan, M. *The Arts of China*, Berkeley (1977). Sullivan, M. *Chinese Art in the 20th Century*, London (1959). Valenstein, S. *A Handbook of Chinese Ceramics*, New York (1975). Watson, W. *Ancient Chinese Bronzes*, London (1977). Watson, W. *Cultural Frontiers in Ancient East Asia*, Edinburgh (1971). KOREA: Chewon, K. and Kim, W.Y. *Arts of Korea*, Seoul (1970). Gompertz, G.St.G.M. *Korean Pottery and Porcelain of the Yi Period*, London (1968). McCune, E. *The Arts of Korea*, Tokyo (1962). Ministry of Culture and Information of South Korea *The Ancient Arts of Korea*, Seoul (1970).

18

JAPANESE ART

Catching Fireflies by Eishosai Choki; c1794. British Museum, London (see page 352)

JAPANESE art is easy to define, being the art produced in the islands that form modern Japan. Until 1945, Japan was never controlled from outside. In the prehistoric period cultural links with East Asia were close, but she never owed practical allegiance to a continental power. In the early historical period we are uncertain in some cases whether artistic monuments are the work of native or East Asian artists (for example, the 8th-century AD frescoes at the Horyuji Temple). Since then, no major work of art produced in Japan is by an immigrant. Examples of important Japanese artists working abroad are equally rare—until the later 19th century AD, Sesshu is the only example and he only for a short time. Japanese art is therefore very self-contained, though ideas usually originated from outside.

Japan's geographical position encouraged both general isolation and dependence on East Asia. Until modern times the only country easily reached was Korea, and that by a stormy sea-crossing of some 120 miles (195 km). So cultural ideas from China and northeast Asia came slowly and often acquired a Korean slant before settling down in semi-isolation. That is why Japanese art, though superficially like Chinese or Korean, usually has a strong character of its own.

This character was influenced partly by the danger and impermanence of life. Most Japanese were threatened by earthquake, landslide, typhoon, tidal wave, or fire. Hard stone for buildings and monuments was largely absent, so culture developed in a setting of wooden, easily replaced buildings, divided inside by light, paper-covered screens. Arts tended to the small, the light, and the replaceable. In no other advanced culture have paper, wood, and lacquer played so important a part.

After the 7th century AD there were no important immigrations into the islands, and the character of the people developed in isolation. A gentle melancholy overlaying a core of tortured violence may derive from their physical situation; a deep love of nature and of the strongly marked seasons is strengthened by their accessibility in semi-openair houses. But their unerring sense of mostly unsymmetrical design seems to be innate, as are their craftsmanship and feeling for materials.

The preliterate period (c10,000 BC–mid 6th century). Japan's preliterate period lasts until the introduction of higher Chinese civilization in the mid 6th century AD—an age without writing or firmly recorded history. The islands formed part of a Northeast Asian cultural area, with advanced pottery, woodwork, textiles, and metalwork, but no higher civilization in the Chinese sense.

The main interest for students of the visual arts is the magnificent *Jomon* pottery, which gives its name to the Japanese neolithic (c10,000–300 BC). It was produced by a culture of gatherers and hunters. Basically a simple earthenware, fired at low temperatures to a dull red or black, a fantastic variety of shapes and decorations were developed, dominated by the cord-impressed pattern (*Jomon*) displaying extraordinary inventiveness, energy, and plastic sense. These qualities were later to be overlaid by Chinese civilization, but they remain under the surface of Japanese art at all periods. *Jomon* figurines of fertility goddesses, with protruding breasts and huge, blind science-fictional eyes, display a barbaric force unsurpassed in Asian plastic art. The great vases with their elaborate openwork superstructures and impressed and incised abstract patterns are monuments of vitality.

Similar power is found in the red pottery *haniwa* figures of the Great Tombs (*Kofun*) period, c AD 250–552. These tombs of the great are proof of a more elaborate social system, able to organize builders and craftsmen in large numbers. The guardian *haniwa* were placed on the outsides of the often huge moated tumuli. Their cut-out eyes give them a deathly quality which recalls some 20th-century Western painting and sculpture. Buddhism introduced in the mid 6th century diverted these plastic qualities into sculpture, and ceramics were thereafter more restrained.

Of early painting, only murals on inner rock walls of 5th- and 6th-century AD tombs survive. They are boldly done with simple pigments, usually red, black, blue, and yellow. But the technique employed was primitive and they are often painted straight on to the rock face. The emphasis is on geometrical patterns, but there are also human figures under parasols, recalling contemporary Chinese and Korean murals but obviously copies at second hand or after verbal descriptions. Simi-

Centers of artistic importance

SEA OF JAPAN

HOKKAIDO

HONSHU

Tokyo (Edo)

Kamakura

Kyoto

Osaka Nara

SHIKOKU

KYUSHU

PACIFIC OCEAN

0   200 miles

200 kilometers

The inner shrine of the great shrine at Ise, rebuilt every 20 years since at least the 8th century AD

lar patterns and figures, the latter like children's "stick" drawings, are engraved or cast on the bronze bell-like objects called *dotaku* which date from the preceding *Yayoi* period (*c*300 BC–AD 250), when Japan adopted the settled rice-growing life of East Asia, creating conditions for the growth of specialist arts and crafts. (*Yayoi* is the name of a Tokyo archaeological site.)

Aesthetic continuity between the Preliterate Age and successive periods is found in architecture associated with Shintoism, which originated in the *Yayoi* period. Shinto, "the way of the gods", pays respect to "gods" called *kami*, which can represent natural forces like wind, a mountain, or a tree, the personality of any dead person, the spirit of a craft or profession, or the spirit of Japan herself. The *kami* are rarely represented artistically, hence there seems to be little Shinto art. But since the Japanese conceive Shinto more as an expression of their national character and beliefs than as a conventional religion, most Japanese art can in a sense be considered Shinto.

Incised drawings on *dotaku* and *haniwa* models of buildings show that the simple, strong architecture still used today in Shinto shrines began in the ordinary buildings of these early periods. The great shrine at Ise has been ritually rebuilt in its ancient style every 20 years since records began in the 8th century AD. Its simple structure and strong association with the natural woodlands around it are typical of much Japanese architecture in later periods, and seem to have no continental origin. The extended beams of the pitched roof, crossing into

an X-shaped projection, are found now only on Shinto shrines and older rural buildings.

Early Buddhist and courtly culture (552–1192). The Japan into which Buddhism arrived at the beginning of her recorded history, in AD 552, was apparently unified, except for the Ainu in the north, according to the earliest records, and therefore ready to receive a more complex civilization. By the time of the death in AD 621 of the religion's first great patron, the Regent Prince Shotoku, Buddhism was the established religion of Japan, coexisting with the tolerant Shinto worship. With Buddhism came the arts, ceremonies, literature, and philosophy of a great world religion, and inevitably the Chinese system of writing and theories of government. Japanese patrons of the arts were now educated nobles and priests, so a concept of the higher arts began to emerge. This was intensified by the move to the first settled capital, at Nara, in AD 710—modeled on the Chinese capital at Ch'ang-an, and surrounded by the ever more influential Buddhist temples—and taken even further after the founding of the Heian capital (Kyoto) on yet grander lines.

Buddhist sculpture in Japan was for long dependent on Korean and Chinese patterns—the search for a truly national style stretched into the mid Heian period (*c* AD 900). Nevertheless these early centuries produced much of the greatest surviving Far Eastern Buddhist sculpture, movingly innocent at first, later grandly cosmopolitan.

Though sculpture from the 10th century onwards was

almost always in wood, in earlier times bronze, clay, and lacquer were also much used; but suitable stone for carving was almost entirely absent. These materials were painted or gilded, though such decoration rarely survives. To have developed a monumental sculptural tradition without stone was a great achievement.

Early Buddhism in Japan was aristocratic and elitist—the superior man could aspire to Buddhahood through contemplation. The earliest carvings are therefore mainly single figures or triads of Buddhas and Bodhisattvas in contemplative poses, such as the 8th-century gilt-bronze figure of the Bodhisattva Maitreya in the British Museum, London. The half-bare torso, the calm smile, the sweet face, the detached but not forbidding attitude are typical of this time—witnesses

A detail of a wooden Bodhisattva in the Hall of Dreams in the Horyuji Temple, Nara; gilded wood; height of statue 6ft 5in (1.97m); 7th century

of the hope that the new religion brought to the hard realities of life. Bigger examples in wood are the Bodhisattvas in the Koryuji Temple (Kyoto) and the Chuguji nunnery near Nara.

Next to the Chuguji is the Horyuji, the oldest surviving Japanese temple (founded by Prince Shotoku in the early 7th century) and in effect the world's oldest museum. Many of the sculptures of this primitive period were preserved here, including a series of 47 bronze contemplative Bodhisattvas, all different, and the unique standing wooden Bodhisattvas known as the Kudara Kannon and the Kuze Kannon. The exaggerated but graceful proportions and mysterious, inward smiles of these figures must have impressed the early Japanese converts even more than they impress today. There is much of Korean sculpture in them, but only in Japan have such old wooden figures survived to the present.

With the founding of the Nara capital in AD 710, the metropolitan civilization of T'ang China reached Japan. The tableau of clay figures of the Death of the Buddha in the pagoda of the Horyuji (c AD 710) strives to emulate the complex stone groups and rock temples of T'ang China. More ambitious 8th-century clay guardian figures in the Hokkedo hall of the Todaiji Temple have a confident, classical internationalism, unique to that age but nowhere else so well preserved. These athletic figures complemented the increasing grandeur of the great Buddha images, culminating in the 52 ft (16 m) high bronze Vairocana in the Todaiji. This is hardly, in its much repaired state, a beautiful image, but it indicates a high level of metal technology in the mid 8th century.

Sculptural modeling from lacquer was usually done by soaking it into thick cloth over a wooden frame, and then finishing it with more lacquer. The liquid medium gave lightness and an unprecedented refinement of facial expression, at its most moving in the central face of the three-headed, six-armed divinity Ashura in the Kofukuji Temple, Nara (AD 734). The largest lacquer sculpture in Japan is the 12 ft (3.5 m) standing figure of the Bodhisattva Fuku Kenzaku Kannon in the Hokkedo of the Todaiji, a masterpiece of withdrawn compassion. The elaborate halos, scepters, and jewelry are features that came to dominate Buddhist sculpture in later periods when strong religious inspiration had disappeared.

While Buddhist sculpture expressed the higher traditions of Asia, there lingered a more vigorous and barbaric strain from the nomadic peoples of the Steppes, whose culture had entered Japan by way of Korea. The big 8th-century wooden *Gigaku* masks, many of which are preserved in the Horyuji, were used in a dramatic temple dance of burlesque character. The extrovert liveliness of these masks seems secular in spirit. After the Nara period *Gigaku* was replaced by *Bugaku*, a court entertainment. The masks continued the vigorous tradition of the grotesque, but were smaller, more comical, and often had moving parts.

Right: The head of a clay guardian figure in the Todaiji Temple, Nara; 8th century; height of statue 330cm (130in)

Japan's second permanent capital city, called Heian (modern Kyoto), remained the center of politics for almost 400 years (793–1192) and of art for nearly 1,200 years. New sculpture was needed for the many temples that grew up around the city, and to supply images for the new sects imported from China. Of these the *Shingon* (a mystical and esoteric sect) was artistically important. Its concept of a universe populated by countless divinities encouraged a vivid art, depicting them separately or in schematic groups. The latter were better suited to paintings (called *mandalas*) but sculptural schemes exist, notably in the Toji Temple (Kyoto). Here the massive, square-chested central figure of Fudo, the Immovable, sitting on rocks and surrounded by groups of guardians and divinities, is typical of the early Heian monumental style. A technique of carving most of a figure from one great block of wood came to prominence, and the result was often heavy, in the Chinese late T'ang style.

In the 11th century a major innovation in technique combined with deepening confidence in native Japanese taste to usher in the greatest era of Japanese sculpture. The method was the *Yosegi*, by which a figure was built up in small pieces, each carved to suit the grain, then covered with gesso and gilded or painted. Greater expressive flexibility gave even the largest sculptures lightness and movement. The founder of this style was Jocho (*fl.* 1022–57) whose masterpiece is the 10 ft (3 m) high seated figure of the Buddha Amida in the Phoenix Hall of the Byodoin Temple near Kyoto. The cult of Amida, the Merciful, who would lead all believers into his Western Paradise, was becoming the one most congenial to Japanese sentiment. The sweet face carved by Jocho is peaceful and withdrawn, gazing with recognizable humanity at the devotee. The half-relief figures of divine attendants in the Buddha's great halo and the bigger ones round the walls of the hall are by members of Jocho's school: their graceful movement is a new feature in sculpture.

In spite of natural disasters, Japan has preserved the oldest surviving wooden buildings of the Far East. Up to *c* AD 900 buildings reflected Chinese and Korean architectural styles which can no longer be seen in their original countries. Because wood and light plaster were used (the only durable parts being ceramic roof tiles and beam-ends), the grandiose was rarely attempted. The exception is the Main Hall of the Todaiji, Nara, built to house the Great Buddha. The hall, a 17th-century two-thirds-sized rebuilding of the original, is the biggest wooden structure in the world. Its double-roofed style is found in the 7th-century Golden Hall of the Horyuji, which is the oldest building in Japan and reflects contemporary Korean styles, as does the slightly later, irregularly stepped pagoda of the nearby Yakushiji Temple. A quieter, Chinese-derived taste of almost Grecian proportions is preserved in the 8th-century main halls of the Shin Yakushiji and Toshodaiji temples (Nara). The Horyuji's octagonal Hall of Dreams, built in 739, is a perfect and unrepeated achievement.

Direct continental influence diminished after AD 900. A more native style grew up to suit the refined but not austere tastes of the Kyoto aristocracy. Surviving examples include the complex symmetrical pagoda of the Daigoji Temple built in 951, its worldly elegance heightened by the red painted timberwork, and the Phoenix Hall of the Byodoin (Uji), built in 1053 and made to resemble the shape of a phoenix with extended wings. Originally a palace, its galleries connect the wings to the main building, half enclosing a garden and lake, in the secular aristocratic style of the later Heian period. Both buildings use a complicated system of roof-beams and brackets which interlock to form a functional but decorative story above the main pillars and below the roof tiling, a feature much used in later times.

Few paintings have survived from before the mid 11th century, and most are on hard surfaces—walls, wooden doors, pillars, shrines, and even musical instruments. Only a handful of paintings on paper, hemp, and silk remain from these early centuries. But our sketchy knowledge was increased by the discovery, in 1972, of murals in a late-7th-century tomb at Takamatsuzuka in the Asuka area. A non-Buddhist tomb, but decorated well into the Buddhist age, it provides evidence of artistic continuity. On the walls are scenes of attendants in procession, mostly in greens, reds, and yellows with strong black outline, and vigorous portrayals of the animals guarding the four quarters. The mixture of Korean and Chinese styles suggests a typically Japanese synthesis of foreign culture. Mineral pigments, like those on continental murals, and prepared wall-surfaces show that full technical competence had been reached.

The 8th-century Buddhist murals of the Horyuji were almost entirely destroyed by fire in 1949. They depicted four Buddhist paradises peopled by hosts of heavenly beings. They were monuments of the T'ang style, grave, elevated, and graceful, done in clear double outline of red and black, and rich colors dominated by black, purple, dark red, and yellow. Foreign artists may have contributed, but in the Nara period over 100 official painters were maintained, most of whom must have been Japanese. From that time onwards there were nearly always official painters. The pigments of the Horyuji murals were used on wooden panels and pillars in the Daigoji pagoda (951), but elevated gravity was turning to a more Japanese sweetness, and the heavenly beings have considerable humanity. This process had gone further in the paradise scenes, now set in a very Japanese landscape, on the mid-11th-century doors of the Phoenix Hall. These are the last great monuments of wall-painting on solid surfaces. The true Japanese style which emerged was happier, with warmer, lighter pigments on paper or silk.

In the later Heian period better techniques of mounting paper and silk as hanging- or hand-scrolls encouraged the development of more native styles and formats. The period 1050 to 1300 was the great age of Buddhist painting—elevated, sentimental, warmly colorful, sensitive in line.

The esoteric *Shingon* and the popular Amidist sects provided most of the inspiration and subject matter. The numerous divinities—benign, fierce, or mysterious—of the *Shingon*

The octagonal Hall of Dreams in the Horyuji Temple, Nara; built in 739

doctrine were best portrayed in painting, where their complicated iconography could be more subtly expressed and balanced, than in sculpture. The big, mid-11th-century painting of Dai-itoku-myoo (Museum of Fine Arts, Boston) and the famous "blue" Fudo (Shorenin, Kyoto) are splendid examples. The former makes the blue-bodied, three-faced, many-armed-and-legged god, seated on a green bull, into a powerful yet beautiful image. The blood-red fiery halo at once symbolizes energy and provides the perfect decorative pattern for the background. This work shows the new features that give strong flavor to Heian and Kamakura Buddhist painting—supple black line, freely done in a semicalligraphic style, use of eggshell-white under the colors to give them depth, lavish detail in the brocades, and the use of cut gold leaf

(*kirikane*) on the body ornaments, scepters, etc. *Kirikane* laid on in complex patterns became the main element of many paintings by the Kamakura period (1192–1333), transforming them into semi-sculptural golden images.

The comforting Amidist doctrine stated that the Buddha Amida would take all his believers at death to his Paradise of the West. From the 11th century onwards many sumptuous works were commissioned by temples and rich patrons showing the great Buddha, with hosts of divine attendants and musicians, descending to earth to receive the soul of the believer (whose thoughts would be turned to his savior by the unrolling of the hanging scroll before his eyes as he lay dying). The greatest is the 12th-century triptych at the Mount Koya temples (Wakayama Prefecture). The central figure glows with

Buddhist Kamakura Sculpture

Buddhist sculpture in Japan reached the last and greatest of its peaks in the Kamakura period (1192–1333). Supreme technique in wood carving, a vigorous military culture, religious fervor, and a rediscovery of earlier sculptures combined for about 150 years to produce one of the world's great artistic achievements.

As so often in art history, the confidence of a new dominant class combined with rediscovery of long-past ideals to produce originality and vitality. The Kamakura military dictators had destroyed the effete Kyoto aristocracy; hence physical strength displayed in the rippling torsos of ferocious Buddhist figures became aesthetically desirable. The wars they fought destroyed the ancient temples of Nara. Rebuilding and the repairs of 8th-century carvings showed 13th-century sculptors a vigor long forgotten. As the almost dormant court culture was swept away, new, more humane styles from Sung China were imported and copied. The soft, very human figure of Dainichi by Unkei is very close to Sung Buddhist painting. At the same time, new, more popular Buddhist movements rose to replace the rarified aristocratic *Tendai* and *Shingon* sects. An age of

deep faith produced the endless comforting images of the Buddha Amida or the Bodhisattva Kannon, 1,001 images of whom were sculpted for the Hall of the 1,000 Kannons in Kyoto in the 13th century.

In the 11th century, the *yosegi* (multiblock) method of construction was developed in order to make bigger wooden images quickly. Craftsmen produced different parts under the direction of a master carver. But the effect was still refined, aristocratic calm, as in Jocho's 10 ft (3 m) high Amida of AD 1053. The 26 ft (8 m) Kongo Rikishi (AD 1204) of Unkei and Kaikei uses this technique in a new way to extend the physical limits of wood carving and to produce dynamic movement and power. The draperies are released to move where the sculptor wished. An 8th-century figure of Shukongo Shin from the same temple served as inspiration, but there is much less freedom in its body and garments. The vitality of the Kamakura sculptures is further enhanced by the *gyokugan* technique of inlaying eyes in crystal lined with paper on which the pupils were painted. Most pieces were brightly painted and gilt, but only traces of pigment normally remain.

◄ The portrait statue of Uesegi Shigetusa. 13th century; painted wood; height 70cm (28in). Meigetsuin Temple, Kamakura

▲ The humane, aristocratic face of the Amida made by Jocho in 1053. Height of statue 300cm (118in). Byodoin Temple, Uji

◄ The portrait statue of Muchaku by Unkei; 1208. Height 194cm (76in). Kofukuji Temple, Nara

► The Dainichi Nyorai made in 1176 by Unkei in the joined-wood technique. The eyes are inlaid with crystal. Height 101cm (40in). Enjoji Temple, Nara

Truth to nature is the keynote of the age. Sculpture was made for new militaristic patrons instead of for the aristocracy, or for vigorous new sects such as *Jodo* or *Shinran*. Although they were not strictly speaking human, every Buddha, divinity, or guardian was carved with an intense awareness of the human face or body. Vigor and violence, as in Jokei's superbly muscular guardian Kongo Rikishi, was balanced by the sweetness and humanity of the Buddha Amida, the major object of worship of the *Jodo* sect. The terrifying contortions of Koyu's judge of hell, Shoko-O, have their answer in the truly monumental calm of the great Buddha of Kamakura, which was, unusually, cast in metal sections which are the bronzeworker's reply to the multi-block technique.

Great sculpture portraits of real people were also a feature of the age, reflection of a new humanity. The figure of the formidable Uesegi Shigefusa is a rare secular example, but there are many masterly portrayals of religious figures. Unkei's magnificently weighty life-size carving of Muchaku combines dignity with a powerful sense of the real person, while pathos and spirituality are combined in the portrait of the priest Chogen.

LAWRENCE SMITH

Further reading. Kuno, T. *A Guide to Japanese Sculpture*, Tokyo (1963). Mori, H. (trans. Eickmann, K.) *Sculpture of the Kamakura Period*, London (1974).

◄ The great Buddha of Kamakura, cast in 1252 by Ono Goroemon. Bronze; height including dais 14.9m (49ft). Precinct of Kotokuin Temple, Kamakura

▲ The head of Shoko-O by Koyu; mid Kamakura period; painted wood; height of statue 102cm (40in). Ennoji Temple, Kanagawa prefecture

kirikane, while the garments of the attendants are painted in deep, rich colors, their bodies in pink-shaded white. All are unified by the white, swirling clouds on which they descend. This was the compositional prototype for many *Amida Raigo* (Descent of Amida paintings).

The Kamakura period (1192–1333) continues this tradition to *c* AD 1300, after which Buddhist painting slowly loses its conviction and becomes mere image-making. The Kamakura colors are more somber, the compositions more rational, reflecting the serious spirit of the age. A favorite figure of this period was Jizo, saver of souls. He was an aspect of Amida, usually shown as a compassionate shaven-headed monk holding a staff and a sacred jewel. His human face suited the naturalistic tendencies of the age; the use of *kirikane* with somber colors on his robes gave a restrained, introverted richness. The dynamism characteristic of this period was better expressed in sculpture and in the narrative handscroll.

Patronage of the arts in the period 900–1150 was dominated by the Kyoto aristocracy and by the big temples around Kyoto. Lessening Chinese influence after AD 900 encouraged new and more Japanese styles of architecture, sculpture, painting, decorative arts, and literature, patronized by these classes, and especially by the controlling Fujiwara family.

Domestic architecture became intimate; fragile sliding screens covered with paper (*shoji*) and portable folding screens (*byobu*) were used to divide open-plan floors, which were now raised above the ground on low stilts. Literary references mention that these screens were decorated with scenes of the natural world, especially of landscapes in the four seasons and the 12 months, and of views of beauty spots. They were called *Yamatoe*, "Japanese pictures", as opposed to *Kara-e*, "Chinese pictures", most of which must have been grand, imaginary mountain landscapes like the one preserved on the leather of a lute from the mid-8th-century repository called the *Shosoin* at Nara.

Yamatoe depicted the round-hilled, intimate landscape of the Kyoto/Nara area with strong feeling for the changing seasons, humanized by the addition of domestic buildings and people in ordinary occupations. The earliest surviving examples are the Buddhist Paradises set in the four seasons on the doors of the Byodoin. All the features of the style are already present—the viewpoint above the foreground, looking across to the far hills; the simple black outline with clear, mostly unmixed colors; the water, expressed by closely set, black lines representing ripples; the loving detail of the trees, flowers, people, and wild creatures; and the lack of sustained perspective and proportion between parts of the composition. This is an intimate art, the sky almost omitted by the high horizon. It reappears in folding screens of landscapes with religious figures, like the 11th-century ones from the Toji Temple, Kyoto. These were used in Buddhist ordination ceremonies. By this time the Japanese view of nature was thought elevated enough for such purposes, and it forms the basis of all subsequent schools in native taste.

At this period the small-scale *Yamatoe* paintings were illustrating calligraphic albums of poetry, none of which survive. In the 10th century a fully Japanese calligraphy had emerged. Important as calligraphy was in Chinese civilization, the Japanese had never excelled at the square hands which were most to Chinese taste. But with the development, from very simplified forms of characters, of a syllabary called *hiragana* to express Japanese sounds, a very cursive and liquid calligraphic style grew up. Its greatest executants were often Heian court ladies, whose menfolk by convention kept to Chinese. The poetic, feminine nature of this style suited the short nature-dominated poems called *Waka*, which could be written with a few movements of the brush. From the 12th century onwards survive *shikishi*, collage sheets of carefully matched, dyed papers, on each of which a poem was written. These rank among the most elegant productions of Heian court civilization. Such was the status of calligraphy in Japan that these survived where the paintings did not. Album paintings illustrating these sheets survive only from later periods, but their style was certainly the basis for the handscrolls which were the next to develop.

The *Tale of Genji*, written *c* AD 1000 by Lady Murasaki, was the greatest of the prose romances which were copied in *hiragana* in the form of handscrolls from the 10th century onwards. They came to have illustrations attached, one section of writing succeeded by one picture as the scroll unrolled from right to left. These *emakimono* (picture handscrolls) differ technically from the only earlier surviving picture scroll, the 8th-century *Ingakyo* (version in the Jobun Rendaiji Temple, Kyoto). This was a life of the Buddha, in a fairly primitive style; the columns of writing in square characters ran continuously along the bottom of the scroll but the columns were too short to allow the freedom necessary for a good *hiragana* hand.

The earliest remaining *Genji* scroll sections (some are in the Tokugawa Museum, Nagoya) show a fully fledged illustrative style in the early 12th century. The point of view is almost vertically above the buildings, into which we peer as though they were roofless. The beams of the buildings themselves are represented by carefully ruled lines without foreshortening. The story is emotionally and symbolically illustrated, because emotionally subtle situations appealed to the aristocratic readers. The faces are perfunctorily done—two slits for the eyes, a hook for the nose; women's feelings are expressed through the black windings of their long hair. Colors are rich, with purples, dark yellows, oranges, greens, and dark reds—a regal palette which hardly recurs in later Japanese art.

Later Buddhist and feudal culture (1192–1573). The mid-12th-century civil wars of the Taira and Minamoto clans ended in the victory of the latter and the end of the courtly age. Their leader, Yoritomo, was a provincial military man. In 1192 he was appointed *Shogun* (generalissimo) and moved the effective capital to the small eastern town of Kamakura. This government was feudal. In place of governors appointed by a Kyoto bureaucracy, Japan was controlled by local lords loyal to Yoritomo.

Art was never so capital-oriented again. Centers of culture grew up in the provinces, and the arbiters of taste were now the men of action. Art became more naturalistic and energetic, less exquisite, often more concerned with ordinary people. Gradually Zen Buddhism came to dominate other sects intellectually, and the Muromachi period (1392–1573) was the greatest period of Zen art.

The years 1150–1350 saw also the flowering of that most Japanese art form, the narrative or descriptive handscroll. Increasing interest in new things, places, and ideas extended subject matter, and styles became more varied to suit them. Ever-longer continuous sections were painted with masterly organization, while textual sections became smaller. In the 14th century the ability to organize a long composition declined, and the bands of clouds found on earlier works become long, formalized bars linking sections of the narrative in a very arbitrary manner.

The late Heian style, used for courtly novels and collections of poems (c1000–1192) became less distinguished in the Kamakura period (1192–1333), but its spirit continued in the *hakubyo* "white drawing" style, done in thick, lustrous ink, heightened with lacquer, on a pure white paper. This uniquely Japanese manner was almost calligraphic. The sinuous, jet-black strands of the ladies' hair formed the main element of design.

There was little interest in the common people among the aristocratic patrons of Heian art, though recent discoveries of very racy caricatures of artisans under the borders of mounted Buddhist paintings suggest a hidden tradition. This came into the open during the Civil Wars, notably in the vigorous crowd scenes of the *Story of Ban Dainagon* (Sakai Collection, Tokyo) which, significantly, may have been the work of the court painter Mitsuhiro, c1150. The nervous graphic style of the figures and the individuality of the faces began a tradition which still persists. Other good examples are *The Legends of Mount Shigi* (Choyosonshiji, Nara) from the 12th century, and the 14th century *Fukutomi Zoshi Emaki* (Cleveland Museum of Art).

In illustrating war stories based on the recent civil wars, the pictorial organization needed to handle large crowded scenes of action reached its zenith. The section of the 13th-century *Story of the Heiji Rebellion* (Museum of Fine Arts, Boston) illustrating the burning of the Sanjo Palace in Kyoto is a masterpiece of movement fitted into a narrow format to make a satisfying design. Carefully ruled lines of buildings frame the scene and give it stability. The brown roofs, seen from above, form thick bars unifying the composition. Across the bottom left pour charging horsemen and soldiers, painted with lively detail. The top right is filled with the horrifying flames and smoke of the burning palace, both turned into beautiful patterns of white edged with red. Another monument of this type records the Mongol invasions of 1274 and 1281, and *The Latter Three Years' War* of 1347 is one of the last great handscrolls (Tokyo National Museum).

Much beauty and sheer entertainment was insinuated into Buddhist and Shinto scrolls recording the horrors of hell, histories of saints, and the founding and miracles of temples and shrines. In the latter the *Yamatoe* landscape style reaches its zenith, best of all in the lovingly recorded landscapes of the *Life of the Monk Ippen* by En'i, AD 1299 (Kankikoji, Kyoto).

A detail from an illustrated scroll of the Tales of Genji; 2nd half of the 12th century. Tokugawa Reimeikai Foundation, Tokyo

Unusually on silk, it tells of Ippen's apostolic wanderings over Japan, depicting in lyrical detail the actual landscapes of each area and the lives of the people. There is a touch of Sung Chinese rationality in these scenes, but there is no doubt that the Japanese of this period deeply revered their country's fabric. Such feelings originated in Shinto but it was a new pride in localities and their gods that revitalized religious painting. The *Suijaku* doctrine, that Shinto gods were manifestations of Buddhist divinities, further encouraged it. Apart from handscrolls, there are many hanging scrolls from the Kamakura and Nambokucho periods (1192–1333 and 1333–92) showing shrines and temples set among their native landscape and peopled with large figures of their guardian gods.

The greatest of the Shinto works is the *Kitano Tenjin Engi* (Kitano Shrine, Kyoto). The largest of all the scrolls, over 20 in (50 cm) in height, it records the life of Michizane, the 9th-century scholar who died in exile, and the building of his shrine. Dated to 1219 its main interest is the lively detail of human life and nature, but selection of pictorial material simply for the sake of the composition is beginning to show. People and animals, as well as trees, rocks, and buildings are placed on the page with a monumental certainty which is the mark of Japanese decorative genius. The line tends to become ornamental in itself, and brilliantly warm, unmixed colors are laid on in clearly separated patches. Here are premonitions of the *Rimpa* style of the 17th to 19th centuries. They are seen more strongly in the mid-14th-century *Life of the Monk Honen* (Chion'in, Kyoto); an enormous work in many scrolls. In some sections the *Yamatoe* style of rounded hills is simplified to almost concentric bands of gray ink, blue, green, and gold.

Until the 12th century, brush ink outline in *Yamatoe* and Buddhist painting had been sensitive and supple, but undynamic. During that century there emerged in Kyoto a high level of skill in pure ink sketching of *Shingon* divinities for iconographic purposes, particularly at the Toji, Ninnaji, and Daigoji temples in Kyoto where big collections of such sketches remain. Good as they were, a more dynamic line, influenced from China and Korea, developed at the Kozanji Temple at Takao near Kyoto. The most famous product of this school (the temple was that of the semimystical Kegon sect) is the late-12th-century set of scrolls of animals called the *Choju Giga*, a series of satires on contemporary clerical life. Done in ink without color, the line is freer than ever before, and ink shading is used to suggest volume and movement. The scene of frogs and rabbits wrestling is a representative enthusiastic satire of the world of men. They are attributed to a monk, Toba Sojo, after whom such works are often called *Tobae*.

The possibilities of brushwork are carried further in the slightly later Kozanji scrolls of the lives of the Kegon monks Gisho and Gengyo, romantic tales of adventure and love. The colors are kept deliberately light, so that the emotional and varied pictorial line can be properly seen. Ink wash was also blended with gold, green, and blue to give tonal range, a

technique adopted in later painting. Their artist, the monk Enichi-bo-Jonin (*fl. c*1210–30) also did a memorable hanging scroll of the Kozanji patriarch Myoe, seated in meditation among the local woodlands. The thick, expressive line of both trees and rocks gives flowing unity to this mystical vision of man in the natural world.

The Takuma School of Buddhist painters (named from their founder, Takuma Tameuji who worked in the late 10th century) were inspired from the 12th century onwards by influences from Sung China. In place of the simple lines and formal backgrounds of Kamakura Buddhist painting, they employed a nervous line with less decoration and often backgrounds of Chinese-style ink landscape. The panels of 12 divinities attributed to the late-13th-century Takuma Shoga (Toji Temple, Kyoto) are splendid examples of this energetic style. Gnarled portraits of the Buddhist apostles called *Rakan* were supplied by this school and continued as late as the early 15th century by *Mincho*.

The strong individualism of the *Shogun* Yoritomo and his captains favored realistic portraiture. The standard was set by the works of the courtier Fujiwara Takanobu (*ob.* 1205). Of his three large-scale portraits surviving in the Jingoji Temple at Takao near Kyoto, the most famous is of Yoritomo himself: the lean face with its hard steely eyes is unforgettable. The black mass of the formal robes of his seated figure throws more attention on the face. The handscrolls of portraits of previous emperors, courtiers, famous horses, and even prize ritual bulls also express the naturalistic spirit of the age.

Portraiture, both in painting and sculpture, was one of the glories of Kamakura culture. From the 14th century the inspiration and power of Buddhist sculpture and painting declined and some of the native ability to model plastic figures and faces went into masks. A more subtle style was used for the masks of the *No* drama, a restrained, static form of poetic dance-play which developed in the 14th century. Delicate expression was achieved by both refined carving and very sensitive painting over thick gesso. The masks were for stock characters, for example a young woman, and could reflect and project the changing moods of the actor himself.

Zen Buddhism encouraged every man to discover both his own Buddha-nature and the nature of existence through contemplation and action. It appealed in some measure to all the influential classes: the aristocracy for its aesthetics, the priests and scholars for its seriousness (though it was far from solemn), the fighting *samurai* for its sharpening of the intuitive action in martial skills. Zen was thus by accident of the times fitted to achieve cultural dominance in the Muromachi period (1392–1573) when all three classes were powerful.

Zen's most enduring monuments in Japan are its temples and gardens; most of the greatest are in Kyoto. In them, the formality and comparative grandeur of Heian and Kamakura buildings and gardens were forgotten. The large Zen temple was a collection of restrained buildings, never ostentatious even when big, each walled in its own garden, set along tree-lined or walled avenues. The most famous is the Daitokuji,

The portrait of Yoritomo by Fujiwara Takanobu (1142–1205). Jingoji Temple, Takao, near Kyoto

A mask of a young woman used in No Drama; c1800. British Museum, London

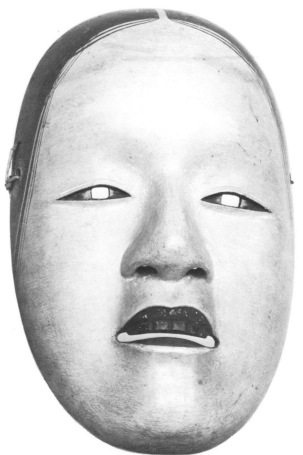

Kyoto, a very large complex of sub-temples and a cradle of Zen arts during the Muromachi period.

The gardens are all designed to help contemplation; none have flowers, so they seem fresh in all seasons. The biggest are the "borrowed landscape" type where the surrounding hills are included in a design of lakes, hillocks, and foliage. The best known are at the Golden Pavilion and the nearby Ryoanji temples. At the latter is also the most famous of the rock gardens, a small enclosed space viewed from a veranda, consisting now of only a few mossy rocks set in a sea of raked pebbles, although it once included a few trees. The importance of the garden reaches its peak in the Kyoto Moss Temple, a landscaped fantasy of mossy undulations set round water under trees, where the buildings are almost unnoticeable.

The Golden Pavilion and the Silver Pavilion, both secular in origin, are the monuments of upper-class domestic architecture of Muromachi Kyoto. The first was the house of the abdicated *Shogun* Yoshimitsu from 1395 to 1408. It has, unusually, three floors instead of one and is, uniquely, covered in gold leaf. From its upper floor the Zen devotee could contemplate, overlooking a lake and "borrowed landscape" of superlative beauty. The Pavilion itself is of the lightest structure and overhangs a still lake on which it appears to float. The Silver Pavilion (Ginkakuji) is associated with another arbiter of taste, the *Shogun* Yoshimasa (in power from 1449 to 1474). Faced in plain wood, it is the epitome of the restrained Zen taste of the period.

In the gardens of the Silver Pavilion was perhaps the first example of a Tea House with a four-and-half-mat floor (approximately 80 sq ft; 7.5 sq m). The Tea Ceremony originated in austere Zen devotions in China, but in Muromachi Kyoto it became a gathering of cultivated friends, in conditions of carefully planned simplicity, to drink tea in a prescribed manner and to discuss the utensils used, the architecture of the house, the flower arrangement, and the painting or calligraphy, usually in ink only, decorating the alcove called the *tokonoma*. Its artistic importance is that it formed the aesthetic framework in which men of taste met and agreed on their tastes. It gave a unifying aesthetic to a number of related arts. Naturally, in this developed form it included much that was not originally Zen.

In the Chinese-dominated artistic milieu of Muromachi Kyoto the ink painting traditions of China inevitably made a rather delayed entry into Japanese art. Ink painting was one way by which a Zen priest could search for reality, and the idealized Chinese landscapes themselves, like the rock gardens, inspired meditation. The existence of new patrons who appreciated Chinese art deeply inspired a flowering of this painting in 15th-century Japan: it was found on the sliding screens of Zen temples, on hanging scrolls hung in the Tea Houses, and handscrolls and albums perused by connoisseurs.

The pioneer attempts at monochrome painting in the late 13th and 14th centuries are unexciting by Chinese standards but by 1415 at least one masterpiece, a hanging scroll on the Zen parable *Catching a Catfish with a Gourd*, had been pro-

Part of the Daitokuji Temple complex in Kyoto

A rock garden, in the Daitokuji Temple complex, Kyoto; constructed in 1509

duced, by Taiko Josetsu of the Sokokuji Temple, Kyoto, which was an early center of this art (the painting is now in the Myoshinji, Kyoto). It shows already the Japanese fondness for subtly graded ink-and-color washes which are decorative rather than symbolic. This tendency continues in the works (all attributed) of his pupil Tensho Shubun (*fl. c*1426–65) whose visit to Korea may account for his deep interest in spatial depth and recession. A splendid landscape by his pupil Tenyu Shokei (Tokyo National Museum) has the characteristic division into a foreground of rocky outcrops, pavilions, and trees, a middle ground of water, mist, and dimly seen spits of land, and a far distance of almost vertical mountains, edged in blue wash. Other artists in Shubun's general style are Gakuo (*fl.* 1504–20), Bunsei (*fl.* mid 15th century), and Kenko Shokei (*fl. c*1478–1506).

Misty effects in wash reach their apogee in the sliding screens of Soami (*ob.* 1525) in the Daisen'in, and in another set of about 1491 in the Shinjuan attributed to Jasoku II (both sub-temples in the Daitokuji, Kyoto). The *fusuma* (sliding doors) of this treasure house of ink painting are the earliest surviving of this form, done in continuous compositions across four paper-covered doors. The beginnings of other landscape ink styles are found there too, including the dynamic *haboku* (ink splash) style, which originated in China. A whole landscape is suggested with a few powerful splashes of ink, done in a high moment of Zen-induced concentration.

Haboku was one of the styles mastered by Shubun's pupil, Sesshu Toyo (1420–1506), considered by the Japanese to be their greatest artist. Of all Japanese painters Sesshu was unusually grave and serious. His characteristic line is weighty, his ink shading solid, his landscapes rational and convincing: his study visit to China probably accounts for all this. The famous landscape scroll in the Mori Collection (Mori Museum, Chofu) is a work of a complex unity, equaled only in China. In the magnificent large sketch of the famous scenery of Ama-no-Hashidate (Kyoto National Museum) he transfers his elevated vision from imaginary to real landscape.

In the late Muromachi period the only great Zen ink painter is Sesson Shukei (*c*1509–*post* 1589). Working independently in northeast Japan, consistently inspired by Sesshu's works, his technique is deliberately rough but his works impress by their deep religious sincerity.

In the 15th century two schools were established which were to dominate official painting until the mid 19th century. Members of the *Tosa* School had been artists to the Court for some time (they claimed the School had begun in the 13th century) and were guardians of the *Yamatoe* tradition in handscrolls, albums, and decorative screens. Their best-known member was Tosa Mitsunobu (*ob.* *c*1521) who in 1502 painted an excellent version of the *Kitano Tenjin Engi*, thus putting himself firmly among the masters of the handscroll tradition.

The *Kano* School begins with Kano Masanobu (1454–90) who became head of the academy of the Ashikaga *Shoguns*. An Amidist, his appointment broke the Zen dominance of ink painting and opened the way for the secular decorative *Kano* manner. His few surviving works are mostly in the Daitokuji temple, which remained a center of *Kano* style for over a century after his death; they show strong contrasts between thickly outlined and hatched rocks and trees and delicately graded mists which are already beginning to take on a significance which is more decorative than representational.

His son Motonobu (1476–1559) developed the style further, decorating whole rooms with large-scale birds, trees, and figures in landscape backgrounds, and fixing the technical repertory of the school. His masterpieces are the sliding doors of the Daisen'in (in the Daitokuji, Kyoto) and of the Reiun'in (in the Myoshinji, Kyoto). Motonobu used more color than earlier ink painters. His marriage with Mitsunobu's daughter marked the partial union of the *Tosa* and *Kano* schools, their

Landscape with a waterfall by Sesshu (1420–1506); ink on paper. Marquis of Hosokawa Collection, Horishige

future cooperation, and the mutual influence of their styles. An important result was the use of gold washes in ink screen compositions, leading to the Momoyama period outburst in this genre.

The age of secular urban culture (1573–1867). The Momoyama period (1573–1615) was one of strife and great vitality. Three unaristocratic leaders, Oda Nobunaga (1534–82), Toyotomi Hideyoshi (1536–98), and Tokugawa Ieyasu (1542–1616) unified the country after the turmoil of the late Muromachi. Nobunaga ended the long stalemate of a century of civil wars by decisively shifting the balance of power toward one dominating alliance of feudal lords loyal to him. Hideyoshi completed the reunification of the country, began a system of fierce central control, and led Japan's first foreign adventure by invading Korea. Ieyasu followed him, destroyed the last resistance to central rule, and laid down an elaborately bureaucratic system of government, controlling almost every facet of life, which lasted until 1867. He also expelled most Europeans, suppressed Christianity, and took the first steps that led Japan into isolation. These men in their castles and palaces became the new art patrons. Hideyoshi's splendid Momoyama Castle gives its name to the period 1573–1615. The arrival of European traders and missionaries, the invasions of Korea (1592 and 1597), and trade with China and southeast Asia temporarily extended the horizons of the Japanese people. From now on the dominant class in the arts were the *samurai* and the great merchants, whose attitudes merged to form a middle class with tastes of unprecedented refinement.

In 1603 Ieyasu founded his Tokugawa Government and moved the capital to Edo (modern Tokyo), leaving a powerless court at Kyoto. The period up to 1867 is called after Edo (or Tokugawa after Ieyasu's family name); in the city itself a modern-style consumer society grew up. Although a vigorous popular culture flourished in Edo, Kyoto remained the center of both traditional and most new schools of art.

In 1639 the Tokugawas banned Christianity and imposed isolation from the outside world. A few licensed Dutch and Chinese traders, restricted to Nagasaki, brought a trickle of books and paintings from their countries which were seized on by Japanese artists as the basis for new schools, but the general mood of the period was inward-looking, with an emphasis on the minor and applied arts—prints, lacquer, metalwork, miniature carving. Higher artistic talent went mostly into painting, and schools proliferated, with complex interrelationships.

The building of castles was the great architectural development of the Momoyama period, necessitated by perpetual wars in which gunpowder was used for the first time. A castle typically consisted of a huge mound faced by tall walls consisting of great stone blocks. An inner moat surrounded a smaller but similar walled moat on a higher level and this supported the main wooden structure which soared in roofed stories in between, like a broad pagoda. Such were the Momoyama Castle (now Osaka), Nagoya, and Himeji. The prototype was Nobunaga's great Azuchi Castle (built 1576–9) on the east side of Lake Biwa, of which only the foundations now remain.

These spectacular castles inspired an unusually exuberant art. But with characteristic duality, Japan also saw at this time the height of the Tea Ceremony, under its greatest Tea Master, Rikyu, inspiring temple and domestic architecture of serene quietness. The Katsura Palace in Kyoto, for example, is a perfect fusion of restrained building and carefully planned gardens; it was designed by the Tea Master Kobori Enshu (1579–1647). New types of quiet yet forceful pottery were developed at this period for the Tea Ceremony—the Raku ware of Kyoto, the Ignand Shigaraki wares from the east of Kyoto, and the Shino and Oribe wares of Mino province.

The brilliant screen style of painting, which lasted until the late 17th century, was created by Motonobu's grandson Kano Eitoku (1543–90). Used at an early date in the great castles, its features are strong line, bold composition (such as a tree spread over the whole of a wall), brilliant colors, and much use of gold wash and gold leaf as background. Interest is focused on the foreground. Such is the cypress tree, of almost brutal power, its great brown trunk set against a gold leaf background, painted by Eitoku and now in the Tokyo National Museum.

Eitoku's sons Kano Mitsunobu (1565–1608; not to be confused with Tosa Mitsunobu) and Takanobu (1571–1618) and his pupil Sanraku (1559–1635) continued the decorative tradition of which the *Kano* School had a monopoly challenged only by Hasegawa Tohaku. After Eitoku's death more em-

The moss garden of Katsura Palace, Kyoto, designed by Kobori Enshu (1579–1647)

phasis was placed on the details of foreground objects, and a quieter style developed for domestic and temple apartments, such as Mitsunobu's suite in the Kangakuin (Miidera Temple, Otsu) where the faded gold backgrounds unify the main room with an intimate richness.

In the earlier 17th century *Kano* activities diversified into decorative work, ink painting, and genre. The new generation worked on the great Nijo Palace in Kyoto, and Nagoya and Edo castles. Its members included Kano Koi (*ob.* 1636), Sadanobu (1597–1623), and the brothers Tanyu (1602–74), Naonobu (1607–50), and Yasunobu (1613–85). Tanyu came to lead the school and dominates its later history. He and his brothers produced powerful ink painting for Zen temples, as did Naonobu's son Tsunenobu (1636–1713). They became official painters at Edo, while Sanraku and his pupil Sansetsu (1590–1651) remained at Kyoto where they produced fine decorative work. The painting at Nagoya Castle shows the strains imposed on artistic invention by such vast commissions.

The later history of the *Kano* school is of decline and academic dullness. Many good Edo-period painters trained with them but then founded new schools.

The *Kano* school did not dominate ink painting until the mid 17th century. In the Momoyama period (1573–1615) there were many groups of ink painters retaining a sense of

elevation typical of the Muromachi period, many of them *samurai* devoted to Zen. The most important were Unkoku Togan (1547–1618), in the tradition of Sesshu and founder of the Unkoku School; Soga Chokuan (*ob. c*1610), founder of the new Soga School characterized by vigorous brushwork; Hasegawa Tohaku (1539–1610), possibly the most gifted of Japanese ink painters; and Kaiho Yusho (1533–1615), who displays great intellectual power. Both Tohaku and Yusho produced semidecorative screens using both ink and gold washes with great seriousness; and Tohaku's colored screens at the Chishakuin, Kyoto, are the greatest of the age.

In the next generation two individualists stand out from *Kano* orthodoxy: the swordsman Miyamoto Niten (1584–1645), and the calligrapher Nakamura Shokado (1584–1639). Both emphasized abbreviated dynamic line, though Niten could handle washes with great skill.

The increasing importance of urban dwelling in the great cities of Kyoto, Osaka, and Edo led almost inevitably to an art for ordinary people. During the 16th century the *Yamatoe* style landscape screen with strong bands of gold cloud linking parts of the composition was adapted to include townspeople at work and play; especially in crowds at festivals. The artists were often of the *Kano* or *Tosa* schools. Eitoku himself is credited with panoramas of the sights of Kyoto, each revealed through breaks in gold clouds (this popular type of composi-

Cypress: an eight-fold screen by Kano Eitoku (1543–90); color on gold-leafed paper; 170×460cm (67×181in). Tokyo National Museum

Shino Ware

The appreciation of pottery was the most advanced aesthetic skill acquired by a devotee of the Tea Ceremony. In 16th-century Japan certain styles of pottery were developed in response to the demands of these Tea Masters, and one of the most admired was Shino ware. With whitish glazes, Shino was made in Mino Province (modern Gifu prefecture) in the area round Tajimi and Toki, northeast of Nagoya. The name comes from the great incense connoisseur and Tea Master Shino Soshin (1440–1522). But he lived before the pottery itself was made; the association seems to have been the mistake of a later period.

The aesthetics of the Tea Ceremony were unified by quietness, sobriety, and balance. Depth was sought in unpretentiousness. The ceramic tea-bowls themselves stood at the center of this taste; they were appreciated not only visually, but also through the lips during tea-drinking, and through handling when emptied. Qualities of texture, weight, and balance were therefore much appreciated and were extended from the Shino bowls, such as the famous Deutzia Trellis Bowl (Mitsui Collection), to the other necessary utensils. Of these the most impressive was the water-jar (*mizusashi*) used to carry cold water into the tea-room for transfer to the kettle for heating.

The shape of this jar, like all Shino pieces, was deliberately distorted, away from perfection, on a slow-moving potter's wheel. The indentations and ridges of the body, and the irregularities of the rim, gave the piece a personality different from any other. This was not at all an act of self-expression, like that of a Western art potter, for the Japanese craftsman knew he would always remain anonymous. What was important was that the piece had solidity and coherence as well as variety. Only intense familiarity by a connoisseur would reveal whether those qualities were sufficiently present to maintain interest and admiration over a long period.

The iron-bearing clay of Shino was local and relatively unrefined. It was a natural white, but baked, when unglazed, to a subtle, restrained yet glowing orange-rust color, and parts were usually left unglazed so that this color could be appreciated. In this particular water-jar a triangular patch has been left for that purpose, but the color also shows in much subtler streaks where the glaze has drawn back in firing. To achieve this, the glaze was applied with inspired carelessness. The feldspathic glaze is thick, milky, but slightly translucent. It is soft and varied to the touch and has that "wet" appearance

which was so much prized. It seems to grow out of the body, giving a feeling of unity. Any tension between body and glaze would have disturbed the aesthetic calm of the Tea Ceremony.

Shino was fired slowly in cool and technically inefficient kilns. It was therefore not possible to predict the final result exactly, and it individuality was most admired. Even the pinholes in the glaze, regarded as a fault in more polished types of pottery, were regarded as a virtue. Many of these qualities of body and glaze seem to mirror in white the low-fired Black Raku pottery of Kyoto, which at the same period was an even more admired Tea Ceremony ware.

The design was painted with a brush to the body in an iron-bearing slip before glazing. It fired to a restrained bluish-gray, but where the glaze was very thin or not applied at all it burned to mixtures of red, brown, and purple, as seen in the triangular patch on this piece. The design is sketchy and suggestive. To the Japanese it shows clearly reeds crossed by the wind on a riverbank and a man in a boat above them. So the surrounding space is filled with the suggestion of water, and the rim acquires a hint of a distant bank or far hills. Such a design responded to the contemplation it would receive at the Tea Ceremony. In some pieces, the design was applied over the bulk of the piece. It would then fire bluish-gray in color, and this type was called Gray Shino.

LAWRENCE SMITH

Further reading. Fujioka, R. (trans. Morse, S.C.) *Shino and Oribe Ceramics*, Tokyo and New York (1977).

Above left A Black Raku tea bowl decorated with plum blossom; early 19th century; diameter 13cm (5in). British Museum, London

◄ A Shino food bowl decorated with a motif of grass; 18th century; diameter 20cm (8in). British Museum, London

► A Shino water-jar of the Momoyama period (1573–1615); height 18cm (7in). Cleveland Museum of Art. Notice the triangular patch left unglazed

tion was called *Rakuchu-Rakugai* "in and outside the Capital").

Depictions on some screens included Europeans, mostly Portuguese and Spanish missionaries and merchants, evident in Japan after 1549 and a source of curiosity. Paintings of this sort are called *Namban* art (*Namban*, "southern barbarians", means foreigners arriving via the southern sea routes).

The prominence of the standing human figure in Western art probably encouraged the emphasis given to fashionable women in mid-17th-century popular paintings. The most striking are the Matsuura screens in the Yamato Bunkakan Museum, Nara, showing stylishly dressed women, all attention devoted to the details of their dress and to their attractive faces. This world of painting—human, frivolous, joyously sensuous—is called *Ukiyoe*, "pictures of the fleeting world". Born in Kyoto, it moved to Edo in the late 17th century where its highly idealized view of the *demi-monde* inspired the first genuinely original style from the metropolis. *Kano* traditions dwindled, and some *Ukiyoe* artists like Hishikawa Moronobu (*ob.* 1694) and Miyagawa Choshun (1682–1752) signed themselves "*Yamatoe* artist".

The fame of *Ukiyoe* woodblock prints has obscured the excellence of the painting, some by artists such as Choshun and Utagawa Toyohiro (1774–1829) hardly known from prints. These artists excelled in painting beautiful women and their admirers in simple, often indoor settings. The Kabuki theater inspired many great prints but few good paintings. Distinguished work in both prints and paintings was done by members of the Kaigetsudo studio (early 18th century); by Katsukawa Shunsho (1726–92), Hosoda Eishi (1756–1829), and the two semi-*Ukiyoe* individualists Katsushika Hosusai (1760–1849) and Kawanabe Gyosai (1831–89).

In the mid 17th century the publishing industry began to produce single *Ukiyoe* prints and picture books (*ehon*) of the gay world, and a little later of the Kabuki theater and its actors. The new art drew on a 1,000-year-old tradition of textual woodblock printing, until then little used for pictorial purposes. The artists who designed for these works did not cut the blocks or print them. The art resulted from a unique cooperation of artist, craftsman, and publisher.

Early *Ukiyoe* prints were produced in black line only, sometimes hand-colored: they were dominated in the late 17th century by Hishikawa Moronobu and his school (specialists in book illustration), and in the early 18th century by the Torii School who popularized the actor-print, and the Kaigetsudo group, whose large, bold prints seem to have been made as cheap substitutes for their vigorously colorful paintings of beautiful women of the day. In the 1720s pink and green color blocks were first effectively used by Torii Kiyomasu (1706–63) and Okumura Masanobu (1690–1768). In the 1760s the full-color "brocade print" (*nishikie*) developed in the hands of Suzuki Harunobu (1724–70) and Isoda Koryusai (*fl.* c1760–80) to great heights of *faux-naïf* erotic fantasy. The late-18th-century works of Torii Kiyonaga (1752–1815), Kitagawa Utamaro (1753–1806), and Hosoda Eishi (1765–1829) are

A Beauty painted by Torii Kiyonaga (1752–1815). British Museum, London

the pinnacles of the form. The actor-prints of Shunsho, Toshusai Sharaku (*fl.* only 1794–5), Utagawa Kunimasa (1773–1810), and the young Utagawa Toyokuni (1769–1825) are outstanding.

The years 1790–1850 saw the production of many deluxe prints called *surimono* illustrating poetic subjects and using very finely graded color blocks, *gauffrage*, and applied gold, silver, and mica, used as greetings cards. They indicate the refined taste of the Edo middle classes. The master designers of *surimono* included Shuniman (1757–1820), Hokusai (1760–1849), Shinsai (1764?–1820), Hokkei (1780–1850), and Gakutei (1786?–1868).

In the early 1830s Hokusai first used European Prussian

Blue in his landscape series *Thirty-six Views of Mount Fuji*. This strong color, previously unavailable, made more varied landscape prints possible. Hokusai, Ando Hiroshige (1797–1858), and Keisai Eisen (1790–1848) all produced landscape prints of great verve and sensitivity. They were widely sold and greatly influenced later landscape painting.

After 1842, prints of heroic and legendary subjects became popular. The leader of this movement was Utagawa Kunyoshi (1797–1861) with his dynamic three-sheet designs.

The *Tosa* School continued to paint in the courtly style and Tosa Mitsuyoshi (1539–1613) in the late 16th century produced traditional works like his *Tale of Genji* album (Kyoto National Museum) in which each page is a masterpiece of detailed, richly colored romanticism. The static atmosphere of these album sheets recalls the miniatures painted for Indian courtly patrons (*see* Indian Art). In the 17th century Tosa Mitsuoki (1617–91) took advantage of the strong nostalgia in Kyoto for its classical past to extend the scope of the school to include bolder decorative screens and bird and flower hanging scrolls of exquisite refinement, but his *Tosa* successors lacked vitality.

One *Tosa* artist, Jokei (1599–1670), formed an Edo branch called *Sumiyoshi*. Its best artist was Sumiyoshi Gukei (1631–1705) whose varied works included elements of the *Tosa*, *Kano*, and *Ukiyoe* styles. Much of his work was done in Kyoto; after his death his school settled in Edo, subdivided, and produced little work of note.

In the early 19th century, an antiquarian spirit and a growing interest in Japan's Imperial past found expression in the *Fukko Yamatoa* (Revival *Yamatoe*) school. Its leading lights were Reizei Tamechika (1823–64), Tanaka Totsugen (1768–1823), and Ukita Ikkei (1795–1859). Tamechika studied and copied ancient handscrolls, but his own work is shot through with contemporary decorative romanticism. This movement contributed to the unified *Nihonga* style after the Imperial Restoration in 1867.

The founder of the style used by the *Rimpa* School was Tawaraya Sotatsu (*ob.* 1643?), though the school's name derives from its greatest member, Ogata Korin (1652–1716). A Kyoto fan painter by trade, Sotatsu was the first artist to accept the native decorative tendency completely; he created a style in perfect accord with Japanese temperament. It was basically *Yamatoe*, but with thicker line or brilliant patches of color without outline. One special technique was to drop a color on to the wet surface of another color, producing a marbled effect. *Rimpa*'s essence was strong composition, best suited to screens, sliding doors, and fans. The prototypes are Sotatsu's screens of the wind and thunder gods, one green and one white, rampaging against a gilt background enlivened by smoke done in a dazzling welter of black, green, and rust inks (Kenninji, Kyoto). Sotatsu and his pupils used the studio name I'nen, which appears on many screens brilliantly decorated with clumps of flowers on a gold-leaf background.

After the deaths of Sotatsu and his pupils most members of the School were individual painters who admired and adopted the style. The greatest was Ogata Korin (1658–1716); his screens of irises in simple blue and green on a plain gold background (Nezu Museum of Art, Tokyo) and of flowering plum trees overhanging a broad blue-and-brown stream flowing out to engulf the viewer (Atami Art Museum), are high points of Japanese decorative style. Other *Rimpa* painters were Watanabe Shiko (1683–1757), Shirai Kagei (*fl.* 1740–50), Sakai Hoitsu (1761–1828), Suzuki Kiitsu (1796–1858), and Nakamura Hochu (*fl.* c1795–1818). Hochu simplified flowers and rocks almost to abstract forms. *Rimpa* declined in the later 19th century but its ideas dominated much 20th-century *Nihonga* work.

Most schools of Japanese painting after Korin degenerated into academicism, but this decline was relieved by individualists such as Ito Jakuchu (1713–1800), Soga Shohaku

Two landscape panels by Yosa Buson (1716–83), a member of the Bunjinga movement. Museum für Ostasiatische Kunst, Cologne

(1730–81), and the Zen painter Hakuin (1685–1758); by the *Nanga* movement; and by the *Maruyama/Shijo* School. They all produced an unexpectedly healthy climate for painting in the later Edo period.

The term *Nanga* ("Southern painting") was used to denote all foreign styles filtering through the licensed port of Nagasaki. Dutch prints, oil paintings, and watercolors had wide influence on spatial composition, but little of importance was produced by those working in Western styles, who were called *Ranga* ("Dutch painters"). The *Obaku* School, on the other hand, consisted mainly of Chinese priests of the neo-Zen *Obaku* sect, who used strong line and simple color with underlying seriousness and pioneered the use of plastic shading. The so-called Nagasaki School itself excelled in the late Ming/early Ch'ing decorative bird and flower style as taught by the Chinese Ch'in Nam-Pin who painted in the city from 1730 to 1733. Kumashiro Yuhi (1712–72), and in Edo, So Shiseki (1712–86) worked in this manner.

Most important was the *Bunjinga* (scholar painting) movement, which attempted to emulate the depth of Chinese landscape and flower and rock painting done by the Confucian scholar class called *Bunjin*. The models for such painting were at first only low-grade works such as the landscapes of the Chinese Nagasaki resident I Hai, and woodblock-printed Chinese albums, especially *The Ten Bamboo Studio* (British Museum, London) and *The Mustard-Seed Garden Manual* (Museum of Fine Arts, Boston). Hence *Bunjinga* lacks the astringent brushwork, subtle washes, spatial depth and complex construction of the Chinese models. Instead, the early

Bunjin such as Gion Nankai (1677–1751), Sakaki Hyakusen (1698–1753) Yanagisawa Kien (1706–58), and Nakayama Koyo (1717–80) developed a sort of abbreviated Chinese landscape with very free line and often patches of arbitrary decorative color. A tendency to paint actual places in Japan produced the glorious fantasy landscapes, part real, part imaginary, which are the great achievement of the school. Masters of this style are Ike no Taiga (1723–76), Yosa Buson (1716–83), Uragami Gyokudo (1745–1821), and Aoki Mokubei (1767–1833). Buson's deep love of nature led him into a more native lyrical style.

In the early 19th century artists like Tanomura Chikuden (1777–1835) and Yamamoto Baiitsu (1783–1856), with access to good Chinese originals, produced distinguished work of a genuinely "scholarly" nature. In Edo, the movement was dominated by Tani Buncho (1764–1841) and Watanabe Kazan (1793–1841), both very eclectic. After 1850 only the great individualist Tomioka Tessai (1836–1924) rescued *Bunjinga* in its turn from academicism.

In the painting of the Edo period one element had been lacking—a sense of the need to paint the natural and human worlds from life. This was provided by Maruyama Okyo (1733–95) who learned from both Western and Chinese models, as well as from the *Kano* School which educated him. Okyo himself achieved most in large-scale screen composition, an art form he revived. His insistence on sketching from life inspired his successors, especially the Mori family animal-painters Sosen (1747–1821), Tessan (1775–1841), and Ippo (1798–1871). Okyo's brilliant brushwork in ink was excelled

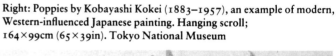

Below: A detail of a flower scroll painted by Matsumura Keibun (1779–1843). British Museum, London

Right: Poppies by Kobayashi Kokei (1883–1957), an example of modern, Western-influenced Japanese painting. Hanging scroll; 164×99cm (65×39in). Tokyo National Museum

only by that of his greatest pupil, Nagasawa Rosetsu (1755–99).

A soft, atmospheric style in landscape and bird-and-flower sketching called *Shijo* was introduced by Matsumura Goshun (1752–1811), who joined Okyo in mature years after training with Buson. Followers of Goshun's style were his brother Matsumura Keibun (1779–1843), Okamoto Toyohiko (1773–1845), and Shibata Gido (1780–1819).

At the end of the 19th century the late *Shijo* artists Imao Keinen (1845–1924) and Takeuchi Seiho (1864–1942) contributed major elements to the synthesized *Nihonga* style. The atmospheric washes, free brushwork, and simple sensuousness of the style made it the natural one for 19th-century artists. Other schools gradually adopted it, including *Ukiyoe* artists in their figure work (notably Hokusai, Eishi, and Utamaro), the successors of Kishi Ganku (1749–1838) who originally favored a very chunky line, and the school of Hara Zaichu (1750–1837) who used Okyo's spatial construction.

The great technical skill in woodblock-cutting was put to use for illustrated books from the late 17th century onwards. They included albums of poems interspersed with sumptuous plates like Utamaro's *Ehon Kyogetsubo* (Book of the Moon-Mad Monk; example in the British Museum, London), and books of designs by famous artists, alive or dead, perhaps to be used by students. The designs are usually boldly placed across an opening. Some show great refinement of graded color and extraordinary imitations of actual brush strokes. Among the best are the *Taigado Gafu* after Ike no Taiga, and from the *Maruyama/Shijo* School, *Suiseki Gafu* after Sato Suiseki (*fl. c*1800–30) and *Chinnen Gafu* after Onishi Chinnen (1792–1851); (examples in the British Museum, London).

Westernized industrial culture (1867 to present). The opening of Japan to foreigners in 1853 and the establishment of a Westernizing government in 1867 broke old patterns. Since then the major influences on Japanese art have been Western. In the Meiji period (1867–1912) technical competence in oil painting was certainly achieved but it is doubtful that any work done then is internationally significant, though in Japan the French-inspired paintings of Asai Chu (1856–1906), Kuroda Seiki (1866–1924), Fujishima Takeji (1867–1943), and Aoki Shigeru (1882–1911) are admired. With increasing confidence in the medium, however, artists of real vitality and Japanese inspiration emerged, among them Umehara Ryusaburo (b. 1888) at his best in big, colorful landscapes with thick line, simple color, and powerful design, influenced by Cézanne.

In the early Meiji period, native styles of painting began to decline under the force of the impact of Western methods (with the great exception of Tessai), but a movement soon sprang up to preserve them, culminating in the foundation of the Japan Art Academy in Tokyo in 1898. The Academy's leaders were Yokoyama Taikan (1868–1958), a great virtuoso in ink, inheritor of *Kano* and Chinese techniques, Shimomura Kazan (1878–1930), reviver of ancient *Yamatoe* styles, and Hishida Shunso (1874–1911), a neo-*Shijo* artist. In Kyoto, Takeuchi Seiho (1864–1942) successfully combined *Shijo* with Western elements and from these strands there grew a new style called *Nihonga*, opposed to Western painting (*Yoga*). It flourishes to the present. It is colorful, simple in line, supremely confident in design, subtle in emotional feeling, decorative in intent in the *Rimpa* traditions, and it maintains a high level of native craftsmanship. But its restricted scope suggests that the great painters of the future will be those who achieve a new Japanese synthesis of Western oil painting.

LAWRENCE R. H. SMITH

Bibliography. Akiyama, T. *Japanese Painting*, Lausanne (1961). Doi, T. *Momoyama Decorative Painting*, Tokyo and New York (1976). Hillier, J. *The Uninhibited Brush: the Shijo School*, London (1974). Lane, R. *Masters of the Japanese Print*, New York (1962). Miyagawa, T. *Modern Japanese Painting*, London and Tokyo (1967). Mizuo, H. *Edo Painting: Sotatsu and Korin*, Tokyo and New York (1973). Mizuno, S. *Asuka Buddhist Art: Horyuji*, Tokyo and New York (1975). Mori, H. *Sculpture of the Kamakura Period*, Tokyo and New York (1975). Ooka, M. *Temples of Nara and their Art*, Tokyo and New York (1975). Tanaka, I. *Japanese Ink Painting: Shubun to Sesshu*, Tokyo and New York (1975). Yamane, Y. *Momoyama Genre Painting*, Tokyo and New York (1974). Yonezawa, Y. and Yoshizawa, C. *Japanese Painting in the Literati Style*, Tokyo and New York (1974).

19

EARLY CHRISTIAN ART

The ivory throne of Maximian; 6th century. Museo Arcivescovile, Ravenna (see page 368)

EARLY Christian Art is not a style term, like Baroque, nor the art of an historically identifiable period, like Carolingian Art. The label describes the artistic production of the centuries between Classical Antiquity and the Middle Ages. At first sight it is a fallow period, when Classical forms slid into medieval formulae without any positive gains. Under scrutiny, however, the period emerges as a crucial one in European art, for its historical conditions ensured that Christianity accepted and continued antique cultural values.

By the 3rd century Christians in the Roman Empire had begun to borrow the art forms of their pagan contemporaries for the decoration of meeting-rooms (churches) and tombs. Such patronage of the arts received a great impetus in 312 when Constantine the Great decided to continue the policy of tolerating Christianity rather than trying to destroy the religion by persecution, as had been systematically attempted by the Emperor Diocletian at the end of the 3rd century. This Edict of Milan initiated the erection and decoration of more permanent and magnificent cult-buildings than had previously been possible for a religion illegal and devoid of large numbers of wealthy adherents. Constantine embraced other religions as well as Christianity. His encouragement of Christianity was politically surprising, for Christians must have formed a very small proportion of the Roman population. His decision must therefore have been due to personal conviction.

Christianity did expand quite rapidly during the 4th century, and was declared the official State religion by Theodosius in 392. Yet in this century the Imperial families and aristocracy tended to be eclectic (or opportunist) in religious affiliations and preferred to subscribe to a mixture of cults, committing themselves to baptism only on their death beds. This sort of religious syncretism can explain some of the iconography of 4th-century art and was a disincentive to any radical departure from traditional pagan traditions in style.

After 400, the Church became increasingly institutionalized, and theologians began to define attitudes towards art.

Centers of Early Christian art discussed in the text

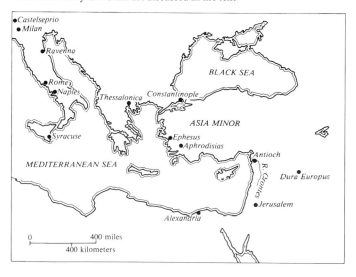

The exuberance of 4th-century art was trimmed, in favor of more dogmatic iconography and a more imposing figure-style. This shift in taste had its social counterpart in the "ascetic movement" and growth of monasticism, and for some art historians marks the end of true Early Christian art. This is probably a too subtle period distinction, but it does have the merit of finding an end for it. As it is, the term overlaps with early Byzantine art in the east Mediterranean and with the Dark Ages in the West. Alternative ends proposed for the period are the accession of Justinian (527) or the coronation of Charlemagne (800).

Not only is the chronological range of the term a matter of disagreement, but the kind of art subsumed within it is ambiguous. The period includes some notable non-Christian masterpieces, such as the Dioscurides manuscript (Nationalbibliothek, Vienna; Cod. med. gr. 1) or the portrait sculpture of Ephesus.

Most Early Christian art has been lost. The fundamental problems of when, where, and how Christian art began can only be explored, not solved. The period can hardly be characterized; it is easier to savor its random survivals.

Few early Christians encouraged artistic production, either through indifference or actual hostility. Their feelings were serious—serious enough for an undercurrent of hostility to persist for the next few centuries and to erupt in the 8th century as Iconoclasm, the attempt to stamp out religious figurative art in Byzantium. Iconoclasm was state policy for over a century. The early Christian opposition had several sources. The Jewish tradition of the Second Commandment against graven images was accepted into Christianity although the Jews themselves in some communities had relaxed the prohibition from the end of the 1st century. Paganism was also a factor, for the Christians were for some centuries a small sect outnumbered by many varieties of pagans who all had in common the worship of a statue or visible cult-object. Some pagans had seen this as a weakness of their religion, and tried to excuse the images on symbolic grounds. The Christians were able to attack these practices as idolatry, and to emphasize the spirituality of their own religion—but only so long as they avoided such representations themselves. Spanish Christians did specifically ban idolatrous art in churches (at the Council of Elvira, c300). Another attitude which discouraged art was the apocalyptic nature of the religion: the world was about to end, and the Gospels preached the need for repentance before the end of the world. What relevance or interest could art have for the committed? Apart from intellectual or emotional considerations, Christians before Constantine did not necessarily belong to a social class that patronized artists; and the various times of intensive persecution must have worked against the production (or survival) of art.

Despite radical opposition to art, the visual arts—a prominent feature of Classical culture—percolated into churches and Christian settings. The earliest firm evidence of Christian art comes from Italy and from the extreme eastern frontier of the Roman Empire in the first half of the 3rd century.

The Roman catacombs. The catacombs supply the greatest area of surviving painting from the period, though no art historian would maintain that Christian art owed its creation to underground communities in them. Certain limitations must be recognized before assessing this evidence.

The catacombs lie outside the walls of Rome, for Roman law required that the burial of the dead should normally take place outside the city. Wealthier families built masonry tombs, as along the Appian Way; presumably these subterranean passages represent the communal burial places of lower social groups. The relatively better-off Christians could afford to buy more space, and to excavate modest family vaults. Instead of using just a grave in a passage (the Latin term was *loculus*), these families could excavate a chamber (*cubiculum*), and could sometimes ornament the tomb with a framed setting (*arcosolium*). It is in these more pretentious *cubicula* that most of the painted decoration occurs.

The ground at Rome was volcanic and easy to tunnel into galleries. The passages were first dug at one level, and later extended by tunneling downwards, sometimes to depths of 30 to 50 ft (9 to 15 m). Bodies were inhumed at each level in boxes in the walls, closed by slabs or bricks, and sometimes accompanied with inscriptions. Such inscriptions are in Latin and Greek, and so indicate a Christian community of mixed nationality. This method of excavation means that the highest *loculi* are the earliest; the most recent graves are at the present floor level. Sometimes several phases of workings can be distinguished, which has been of assistance in dating-studies.

Since the catacombs began as passages, it is clear that their original function was for burials, though possibly the tombs did receive annual commemorative visits. The theory that the catacombs were excavated as churches can be dismissed, since no suitable chambers were ever cut.

The organization of "the cemetery" was attributed to Pope Callixtus (elected *c*218). A date *c*200 for the catacomb of St Callixtus accords well with the archaeological examination by P. Styger. In all, about 40 sets of catacombs were cut around Rome, and catacombs are not limited to Rome but are also known from Naples, Syracuse, and the Roman East. Present opinion on the Roman catacombs sees the first excavations as *c*200, but the earliest paintings not much before *c*250. The catacombs continued in use after the Edict of Toleration, but fell out of favor in the early 5th century, partly from feelings of insecurity outside the walls after the sack of Rome in 410, but also because they had been superseded by large cemetery Basilicas and the use of churches for housing relics.

The evidence from catacomb painting is therefore limited in its chronological range (after *c*250), in its function (as purely sepulchral art), and in its social range (for the lower classes). There was the further limitation that since the cult was illegal, to avoid confrontation with authority, inoffensive and traditional symbols were often used. However, the murals allow some insights. The style of all the paintings is fairly uniform; color and line is used to suggest solid figures in illusionist settings, but the level of execution makes them the im-

The Good Shepherd, a wall-painting in the catacomb of St Callixtus, Rome; *c*250

poverished successors of 1st-century works of Pompeii and Herculaneum. Catacomb painting does not differ in style from contemporary pagan art, but is limited in quality due to the third-rate artists Christian patrons were only able to afford.

The subject matter of catacomb art was Christian, and so its content was new in the history of art; but the visual language in which its message was encoded took the same form as existing pagan art. Its nuances could therefore only be fully understood by the convert educated in Christian literature and ritual. The basic message conveyed was similar to that of pagan art—the theme of salvation—but, for the new religion, this promise was only made to those who believed in God. Salvation meant escape from death through the promise of an afterlife. The promise was illustrated through a small number of images: by symbols, such as the fish (for Christ) and the orant (probably the praying soul of the departed), or by Old Testament witnesses of the promise of God, such as Jonah, Daniel, Sussanah, Noah, and others, or by a limited repertory of New Testament scenes, mostly concerned with the miracles of Christ, such as the Multiplication of the Loaves and Fishes, the Raising of Lazarus, and others. The same theme of salvation was illustrated in pagan art by a range of mythological stories taken to prove the afterlife, such as those concerned with Achilles, Phaethon, or the daughters of Leucippus.

The early Christian repertory was probably suggested to artists by the examples of salvation featured in Jewish and Christian prayers, notably those used in the office for the burial of the dead. This role for the prayer of the *commendatio animae* is widely accepted by scholars while admitting that their texts were not established before the 9th century.

Jonah under the Gourd Tree, a marble sculpture of c250–75;
31×46×18cm (12×18×7in). Cleveland Museum of Art

The catacomb painters made no attempt to clothe the new iconography in a new artistic form. The shift from pagan to Christian art lay not in appearances but relied on the initiation of the spectator. This conclusion from the evidence of the catacombs seems confirmed from the fragmentary material in other media and in other parts of the Roman Empire. A good case is a recently discovered set of small marble sculptures (Cleveland Museum of Art) which were probably carved in western Asia Minor in the third quarter of the 3rd century. Apart from a set of family portrait busts, there are five symbolic figures, freestanding, and cut in a lively, Hellenistic style. A spectator might identify one figure as a river god, but the Christian would have seen that this reclining man was Jonah under the Gourd Tree and that four of the pieces represent the popular catacomb cycle of the Salvation of Jonah. The sculptures are a symbolic representation of the Fall of Man, his Redemption, and Rewards in Paradise. The fifth figure of the group could be identified by Christians as a Good Shepherd (with reference to John 10: 1–16), whereas the same piece would be quite meaningful to a pagan as a Hermes or as a symbol for Philanthropy.

Analysis of iconography is therefore the best means of discovering the nature of innovation in Early Christian art. It can be stated that if a Christian scene reflected some parallel theme in existing late antique art, then the established form was taken over. Many cases can be adduced: angels derive from Victories; Apostles, Prophets, and some types of Christ derive from standing Pagan Philosophers; Evangelists from Seated Poets; Eve from Venus; Jonah from Endymion; David from Orpheus; the Creation of Man from the myth of Prometheus; and more.

The question to ask is: where and when were these artistic adjustments made? The low-grade artists of the catacombs are not likely to be the actual innovators as these paintings are no more than an accident of survival. The Cleveland sculptures seem closer to a moment of invention. Unfortunately most of the art of the major eastern Mediterranean cities from the 3rd and 4th centuries is lost.

The answer to the question of origins may be different for Old and New Testament subjects. Old Testament illustration could have a long tradition, for the Bible was translated into Greek in Alexandria in the 3rd century BC, and the hellenized Jews of this city might have commissioned illustrated manuscripts of the Septuagint. Book illumination might have been the medium in which the new iconography was generated. There is no straightforward evidence to decide this controversial point, for the earliest surviving Old Testament books with pictures belong to the 5th century, by which time books were in the new codex form (invented c100), and the earlier *rotulus* format was superseded (a format less suitable for painted illustration).

Dura Europus. The evidence from the city of Dura Europus is important here. This was a Hellenistic settlement which became a Roman frontier garrison on the Euphrates. It was partially excavated in the 1930s, and the finds are now shared between the National Museum, Damascus, and Yale University Art Gallery, New Haven. It was found that the citizens abandoned the area around its walls c256 in the face of a threatened Persian invasion. Among the buildings evacuated was a synagogue, and a structure built as a house but which had recently been converted into a church. Both the synagogue and the church are datable to before 256.

The wall-paintings of the synagogue belong to the early 3rd century. The subjects are partly symbolic (like the Temple with the Ark) and partly narrative (like a Moses cycle and other scenes, which are however selected with a purpose in mind, the declaration of the salvation of the Jewish people). Some of these images did enter Christian art, notably the Sacrifice of Isaac, but never in precisely the same form as in the Dura synagogue. It is clear that the Jews of the Diaspora did have a cycle of Old Testament pictures, for Dura Europus cannot be unique. Whether such illustrations were disseminated in monumental or miniature form, and whether they occurred before the 3rd century, is unknown. Christian artists probably made borrowings from the Jewish tradition (whether or not it was older than Christian art), but they did not take over the entire cycle.

The canon of the text of the New Testament was only established in the mid 2nd century, in fact not very long before the catacombs. Catacomb painting already shows a uniformity of treatment and composition—standard formulae such as Daniel between the Lions. The conversion of the house at Dura Europus into a church and the fitting and decoration of one of its rooms as a baptistery dates from the 230s or 240s. The baptistery's paintings are therefore contemporary with the earliest catacomb art. The paintings—such as the Good Shepherd and Adam and Eve above the font, and the Healing of the Paralytic, Peter walking on the Water, and the Three Women at the Sepulcher (?) on the walls—give evidence of a Salvation cycle at the eastern limits of the Roman Empire with some individual scenes treated in the same form as the catacombs. It may be concluded that New Testament illustration was in a state of elaboration in the 3rd century with some consistency throughout the Roman Empire.

The medium in which scenes were developed and disseminated is unknown. It follows that any suggestion about the place or places where Christian art began, or among which social class, must be conjectural. But the simplest solution is to suppose that those classes who had traditionally commissioned funerary monuments or expected to worship in a decorated environment did continue to patronize artists after their conversion. This situation would explain the continuation of traditional patterns of art. Possibly such patrons were the less radical members of the church, selecting their religious beliefs with circumspection and without exclusiveness. A striking case of late Roman religious eclecticism is given by the Emperor Alexander Severus (222–35), who placed in his household oratory (*lararium*) statues of such figures as deified Emperors (only the most noble selected) and other sacred persons including the philosopher Apollonius of Tyana, Christ, Abraham, Orpheus, and Alexander the Great.

Early Christian sculpture. The medium in which the best quality Early Christian art has survived is in marble sculpture, predominantly in sepulchral work. The sequence of datable sarcophagi from Rome gives some picture of the patronage of wealthier Christians during the years when the cult developed from proscription to convention.

A sarcophagus now in the church of S. Maria Antiqua in the Forum at Rome is a fine example of the possible level of achievement of pre-Constantinian art. It was probably made to stand in some grand *cubiculum* in the third quarter of the 3rd century. The relief is deeply cut, and the figures stand against a traditional pastoral background. There are scenes of Jonah and the Baptism of Christ, and figures of the Good Shepherd, an orant woman, and a man seated in the pose of a philosopher. The faces of the latter couple are blocked out; the figures must have been intended for use for donor portraits. One explanation for this lack of finish is that workshops kept sarcophagi in stock, to be finished off with the portraits of the purchaser, and that in this case (as in some others) the necessity for a quick burial prevented the final carving. It is not, however, necessary to deduce this pattern of trading; the individual sarcophagus might have been ordered in advance of death, and the portraits left unmade so that a record of the mature donors could be made in due course, or the portraits might be left incomplete for more superstitious motives.

The 4th century saw a substantial increase in the number of Christian sarcophagi; this occurred despite a probable overall decline in marble carving in the period, due to the dislocation of workshop traditions in the political upheavals in Rome in the 3rd century, and perhaps also due to concern about the Second Commandment. The Roman sarcophagi after the Edict of Toleration (312) extend the Christian use of art. In addition to the message of individual salvation, there is the new theme of the triumph of the Christian Church as an institution. In style, these sarcophagi reflect the taste of the Imperial family and the aristocracy.

During the reign of Constantine (*ob.* 337), a number of "frieze" sarcophagi were produced whose style is an incongruous deviation from Hellenistic traditions; the frieze is a row of gesticulating mannequins. Though the iconography is difficult to read, the figures portray a mixture of Old and New Testament scenes, most with a reference to salvation. With their stiff and awkward attitudes, oddly proportioned bodies, and lack of expressions, these figures are inspired by Tetrarchic art, and, more directly, by the new reliefs on the Arch of Constantine (315). The technique is not ineffective in conveying a spiritual message: these are salvation prayers "frozen into stone".

In the second half of the 4th century the more traditional values of the Roman aristocracy reasserted themselves. It is as if artists were required to copy the reused panels on the Arch of Constantine, rather than those of their own time. The grandest production was the sarcophagus of Junius Bassus (Vat-

A sarcophagus in S. Maria Antiqua, Rome; c250–75. The faces of the central figures are uncarved

The marble sarcophagus of Junius Bassus; c359. Vatican Museums, Rome

ican Museums, Rome) who died at the age of 42 in 359. The inscription on the lintel records that he was Prefect of the City, and baptized on his deathbed; he is a typical member of the wealthy aristocracy. The front of the sarcophagus is divided into two horizontal registers; each scene is framed by ornamented columns. The central pairs of columns in both registers are decorated with putti climbing vines, a clear reference to the pagan Bacchic paradise. The Biblical scenes have two themes: God's promise of salvation after suffering, and the triumph of Christ and the Apostles after suffering. The message conveyed is of the immortality promised to Christians, and of the triumph of the Church. The sarcophagus is primarily a declaration of Church teaching rather than a memorial to an individual. A later 4th-century sarcophagus, now in S. Ambrogio in Milan, emphasizes even more emphatically the triumph of the established Church.

With the departure of the Christian court patrons from Rome to Milan and then Ravenna at the end of the 4th century, sarcophagus workshops declined due to lack of support. The 4th-century production of high-quality sculpture was not, however, confined to Rome, but is matched in several cities of the eastern Mediterranean, particularly in Asia Minor at Aphrodisias and Ephesus. At Constantinople production is more varied; some sarcophagi worked in limestone are no more than inferior copies of Italian models, but there are outstanding productions, such as a child's sarcophagus in Istanbul Archaeological Museum on which are carved well-modeled

angels in the traditional style of Hellenistic Victories. Theodosius (379–95) and Arcadius (395–408) could find sculptors able to produce cochleate columns to proclaim the importance of New Rome as successor to the Old. Stone and metal sculpture continued in the East to be a major medium to at least the 6th century, when, however, the Marmara and other quarries apparently ceased production.

The religious syncretism of the Junius Bassus sarcophagus is conspicuous on a monumental scale in two mausolea built by the children of Constantine: his own mausoleum, part of the complex of the church of the Holy Apostles in Constantinople, is not preserved. The church of S. Costanza in Rome was erected for Constantina between 337 and 354, and probably decorated with mosaics in the 350s. A second domed, centrally-planned structure at Centcelles, near Tarragona, in Spain, can in all probability be attributed to the mid 4th century as the mausoleum of Constantius (ob. 361). Both monuments have survived, but with no more than fragments of their original magnificent decorations. The dome mosaics of S. Costanza were removed in the 17th century, but had been previously drawn and described. The Centcelles cupola is a wreck, with some discernible elements. Both domes received a mixture of Biblical scenes and pagan funerary elements, such as a river scene with fishermen at Rome and a hunting scene in Spain. The surviving mosaics at S. Costanza, in the ambulatory vaults, have no overt Christian message, and include panels with Bacchic putti. These mausolea with their expensive mosaic vaults (the idea of using mosaic in vaults was a fairly recent innovation in Late Roman art), and marble-clad walls show the ostentatious taste of the new Christian aristocracy. This is the use of pagan art forms in the service of yet another religion.

Early Christian art in the 5th century. The 5th century was a turning point in Early Christian art, perhaps a deliberate reaction to the 4th-century pattern of art. The rise of the ascetics and monks did not prevent the investment of wealth in expensive architecture and fittings, but the Church does seem to have imposed limitations on iconography, and a concern with subject matter probably influenced its stylistic treatment. Stern statements on the Christian use of art were penned by Paulinus of Nola in Italy and Nilus of Ankara in Asia Minor. Nilus condemned the decoration of a church with hunting scenes or fishing scenes and the like as "childish and stupid". Instead he recommends the representation of a cross and pictures of Old and New Testament themes as "the mark of a firm and manly mind". Such theologians began to ask art to perform a serious purpose, such as the instruction of the illiterate in the Bible or the inducement to prayer. Under such thinking the Church began to perfect the use of art as a didactic instrument and as a vehicle for the propagation of the faith.

The new spirit is found in the Papal mosaics in the vast Basilica of S. Maria Maggiore in Rome, decorated by Sixtus III (432–40). The original nave and sanctuary mosaics thus date from the time of the Council of Ephesus (431) at which the status and nature of the Virgin Mary was defined. This issue explains the unusual iconography of the triumphal arch (the lost apse mosaic represented the Virgin); Mary is shown as the Queen of Virgins. The Adoration of the Magi is unique in showing Christ not as usual seated on his mother's lap, but isolated on a throne between two standing figures, Mary (?) and the Church (?). There is no representation at all of the Nativity of Christ. Art here is therefore not employed to tell a narrative, but is used with dogmatic intent. This use of art as theology has influenced the mode in which the subject matter is expressed. The figures are hieratic, set against a gold ground and without an illusionist setting; this marks a new stage of religious art.

The mosaic panels in the nave show Old Testament episodes, and are also selected with some purpose. For example panels near the altar incorporate liturgical elements (such as Abraham meeting Melchizedek). Several other themes are woven into the cycle: the panel of Abraham meeting the Angels has typological references to the Trinity (underlined by the new motive of the mandorla), and to Mary through the antetype of the Annunciation to Sarah. The general sense of the program is as usual Christian salvation and triumph, but perhaps the individual panels were expected to be used by pilgrims as vehicles of their individual prayers, as recommended by Paulinus in his foundation at Nola. The nave panels are not homogenous in style, for some are in the tradition of the late Antique, others more in the hieratic form of

the triumphal arch. This variation is probably due less to the content of the scenes than to the nature of their models. Some compositions may be 5th-century inventions, but others had already gained a conventional appearance after a few centuries of use. S. Maria Maggiore is a key monument for an understanding of the interaction of themes and styles at the point when antique art is becoming medieval. In terms of purely artistic expertise it is less remarkable, since, like S. Costanza, the scenes are too small and too high to be read from the floor.

The problem of scale was treated more satisfactorily in monuments of the mid 5th century in Ravenna and Thessalonica. The interior decoration of the Orthodox baptistery in Ravenna is crowned with a dome composition showing the Apostles around the Baptism within a medallion. It is a scheme probably adapted from a circular pavement composition with personification of the Months known in late Roman floor mosaics, and it is successfully adapted to the size of the building. Even more impressive is the scale of the cupola mosaic of the Rotunda, or church of S. George, Thessalonica. The building was a Tetrarchic mausoleum, built by Galerius c300, though not used for his burial, and was converted into a

Abraham meeting Melchizedek, a mosaic panel in S. Maria Maggiore, Rome; c440

The Antioch Chalice

Found accidentally in 1910, buried (reportedly) in the region of Antioch-on-the-Orontes (now Antakya, Turkey), this cup is unique in technique and form among known chalices of the early Church. Soon after its discovery it became the center of a heated controversy when extravagant claims were made for its origin in the time of Christ (which put it in a category of objects not unlike that of the Turin Shroud).

The Antioch Chalice (Metropolitan Museum, New York) consists of a plain inner silver cup cradled in an openwork silver gilt outer container on which 12 figures are engraved within a trellis of vine scrolls. The first study (by G.A. Eisen) appeared in 1923 with the title: *The Great Chalice of Antioch on which are depicted in sculpture the earliest known portraits of Christ, Apostles, and Evangelists.* The publication, as lavish as its claims, hinted that the inner cup was the Holy Grail and dated the outer cup to *c*50, making it about two centuries earlier than any other known Christian works of art. But while the use of a cup at the Last Supper was sanctioned by the words of Jesus as reported in Mark 14:23, it was believed in the early Church that this was made of onyx and was kept in the church of the Holy Sepulcher in Jerusalem and shown to pilgrims, at least in the 6th century. Also, the legends of the Grail as the cup used at the Last Supper and by Joseph of Arimathea to collect the blood of Jesus belong only to the late Middle Ages. But the most common reaction to the publication of the Chalice's discovery was to condemn the whole cup as a modern fake.

The authenticity of the Chalice was only finally established in 1954 by scientific tests. Its subject matter, date, and place of manufacture still need to be decided. No doubt all of one period, the Chalice has a surface that is worn, broken, and corroded. The central figure on each side must be Jesus. On one side, he is apparently beardless and sits on a chair that encloses his head like a halo; he holds out his right hand in a gesture to indicate that he is speaking, and holds a scroll in his left. He is acclaimed by other seated figures, presumably his Apostles though none of them can be individually identified by attribute or portraiture. The suggestion has been made that this shows Christ giving the keys to Peter and Paul, but there are no keys to be seen. The scene may be Christ teaching his Apostles (perhaps at the time of the Last Supper). The other side may be more specific; again Christ sits among Apostles, but this time he is bearded and has a lamb to his left and below his feet

there is an eagle standing on a basket of grapes. The references are more obviously to the eucharist, to the sacrifice of the Lamb of God, and to the Resurrection. Perhaps this side shows the resurrected Christ in heaven at the time of the Last Judgment. Presumably, the purpose of the decoration was to refer literally to the use of the chalice for holding the wine of the eucharist, and metaphorically to the significance of the rite for the religion.

It was the profile of the Chalice with its low base and deep cup as well as the use of openwork that led to the dating to the 1st

▼ The Antioch Chalice, the side of the beardless Christ; height 19cm (7in); diameter of rim 15cm (6in); diameter of base 8cm (3in). Metropolitan Museum, New York, Cloisters Collection

century, for Roman cups of similar appearance are known. The usual shape of the 6th-century chalice is seen, for example, in another find from the same region now in the Cleveland Museum of Art or as represented on a eucharist bread dish, the Riha paten (Dumbarton Oaks Research Library and Collection, Washington, D.C.): on this, a chalice and a paten together with skins for water and wine are set on the altar used by Christ to give the wine and bread of the eucharist to the Apostles. The Antioch Chalice is, despite its profile, most likely to date from the 6th century. The most similar treatment of figures and vine scrolls are found on the ivory throne of Bishop Maximian of Ravenna of the mid 6th century (Museo Arcivescovile, Ravenna).

The Chalice appears to lack any stamps which would have guaranteed the quality of its silver and possibly have revealed its place

of production. Now damaged after its burial underground, the Chalice was not originally a work of delicacy and refinement. Syria was an active region in the production of art, but it was declining in the 6th century. There is, therefore, a case for supposing that it was a work of the silversmiths of Antioch.

Doubts have been cast on the truth of the find-spot of the Chalice and the accompanying objects. The other pieces are now also in the Metropolitan Museum and appear to be of a 6th-century date: a silver cross, a silver paten, a pair of bookcovers,

Above left The Riha paten; diameter 35cm (14in); 6th century. Dumbarton Oaks Research Library and Collection, Washington, D.C.

◄ A silver-gilt chalice showing Apostles, from the Hama Treasure; height 17cm (7in); diameter of rim 14cm (5½in); 6th century. The Walters Art Gallery, Baltimore

and another bookcover. This could well be the church plate of one community, but there is the odd coincidence that in the same region in 1910 another large silver treasure surfaced, the so-called Hama Treasure, much of which is now in the Walters Art Gallery, Baltimore. The suspicion has been voiced that all these silver objects belonged to churches in the Christian cult city of S. Sergios (now called Risafe), and that they were either found there through clandestine diggings or were hidden underground at various spots in the region by Christians fleeing from the advancing Arab army in the 7th century. Whether or not the Chalice was actually found in Antioch, its attribution to the art of the city must be considered seriously. It would then show that important provincial cities like Antioch played some part in the formation of Early Christian art.

R. CORMACK

▲ A silver-gilt bookcover found with the Antioch Chalice; 28×23cm (11×9in); 6th century. Metropolitan Museum, New York

► The Antioch Chalice, the side of the bearded Christ. To the left stands a lamb and below an eagle on a basket of grapes

Apostles surrounding the Baptism of Christ, the dome of the Orthodox baptistery, Ravenna; c450

church c450. The best preserved register is the lowest zone of the cupola in which are shown groups of standing martyrs (originally these surrounded a medallion of Christ at the apex). The figures are highly modeled but generalized portraits, set against fantastic architecture, and each one was identified by an inscription with his name and month of commemoration. The influence of the liturgy on this program is clear—the mosaics are a visualization of the calendar of the Church year.

It is easier to piece together a "vertical" development of Early Christian art than to understand the "horizontal" situation across the Roman world at any precise point in time. Although Italy, and especially Rome, suffered from a series of political crises and military attacks from the 5th century onwards, causing it to enter a Dark Age, many cities in the eastern Mediterranean enjoyed stable, even prosperous, conditions. The subsequent destruction of nearly all the Early Christian monumental art of Constantinople, Jerusalem, Antioch, and Alexandria (to name only the largest cities) has removed the possibility of assessing the contribution of their artists or even regional traditions to the creation of an international language of Christian art. Yet communications between

cities were good, and the wealthiest patrons could travel and observe church art all around the Christian Roman Empire. Not only emperors traveled; Archbishop Maximiam of Ravenna had seen Alexandria and Constantinople. Any analysis in terms of discrete regional styles or isolated local traditions would therefore be absurd—attempts to confine "illusionistic" style to Alexandria or "frontalism" to Antioch must be rejected. Yet the survivals from two prosperous cities of the period, Ravenna and Thessalonica, intimate that within the international language of art, some local circumstances may cause variations of style, and local themes and interests may emerge in iconography. The development of regional traditions, however subtle, raises the possibility of these influencing other cities. It is unlikely that all innovations should be attributed to artists in one center, for example Constantinople. The course of Christian art was not determined by such polarities as the Orient or Rome; but at present it seems impossible to offer a refined interpretation of the stages through which it developed.

Ravenna at the beginning of the 5th century was a seaport on piles, traversed by canals. It had been designated headquarters of the Roman fleet on the Adriatic by Augustus. Today the sea has receded from the port, then named Classis. When Theodosius died in 395 he left Arcadius to rule the East, and Honorius in Milan to rule the West. Honorius decided c402 to move the court to Ravenna, but developed a site a few miles inland. This "new town" was better placed for contacts with Constantinople than either Milan or Rome.

The monuments of Ravenna belong to three historical stages: in the first the city was developed as an Imperial capital, and the artists and their models must have originated outside, from, for example, Milan, Rome, or Constantinople —the situation might be compared with the building of St Petersburg in the 18th century. As in the new Russian capital, the buildings of the first generation were probably somewhat tentative and modest, and only with the second generation's confidence in survival was Ravenna enriched and ornamented, here too by a female ruler, Galla Placidia, half sister of Honorius (ob. 423) and regent for her son Valentinian III. She died in 450. The process of enrichment is exemplified by the baptistery of the Orthodox cathedral, an insubstantial octagonal building of the beginning of the century which received its new interior decoration of marble, stucco, and mosaic in the middle of the century. The mosaic workshop was probably also employed on the mosaics of the mausoleum of Galla Placidia; its style is so much a development of late antique art in Italy that there is no need to postulate the presence of artists from the Greek East; the artists more probably came direct from one of the extensive mosaic operations underway in Rome.

The second stage of Ravennate art dates from 494, when control of the city fell into the hands of the Goth Theodoric—

Right: Apostles surrounding the Baptism of Christ, the dome of the Arian baptistery, Ravenna; c500

his rule was recognized by Constantinople from 498. Theodoric died in 526, but control of Ravenna was only regained by Constantinople in 540 when Justinian's commander Belisarius entered the city. The rulers of Ravenna from 494 to 540 were Arian Christians. Whereas Orthodox theology stated that the human and divine natures of Christ coexisted, the Arian belief (anathematized in 381) was that the essence of the divine and human parts of Christ were different (so there was a time when Christ was not).

The Arians built a new cathedral and baptistery, and the mosaic decoration of the dome of the latter survives (c500). It copies the Orthodox baptistery directly, but, in contrast, the style is simpler and more linear, and the iconography reduced and simplified. Paradoxically, although the execution of the later mosaic may be less subtle, the differences can be characterized in terms of progress rather than decline. The composition is more literal and empirical, and so gains in clarity and effectiveness. The comparison is an example of the general trend in Early Christian art away from the classical values of plasticity, individual portraiture, and emotional expression, which leads not to loss of expressiveness, but to a new positive medium for the portrayal of Christian dogma and attitudes. The artists of the Arian baptistery and those of the New Testament cycle in the Arian foundation now called the church of S. Apollinare Nuovo but originally dedicated as the Church of Christ, seem closely related to Roman art, almost to the simplicity of catacomb art.

The third stage of the art of Ravenna, the Byzantine period, lasted from 540 to 568, but the city continued as an Exarchate until the Lombards took over in 751. The mosaics of this stage, as for example in S. Vitale, completed c548, show many elements derived from the Greek East, but Italian traditions are not submerged. The panel of Abraham meeting the three angels seems to be a development of and reaction to the similar scene at S. Maria Maggiore. The mosaics of Ravenna develop a distinctive tradition, but are not isolated in their time.

Thessalonica, too, was developed as a luxurious "new town" in the mid 5th century, when the Prefect of Illyricum moved from Sirmium to safer headquarters. The mosaics of the Rotunda were probably executed by a workshop sent by the Emperor from Constantinople. Thereafter local mosaicists of the second half of the 5th century were influenced by its dome. As a result designs were developed locally out of a work of international status. For example, mosaic panels in the church of S. Demetrius, which show this local cult-saint as the object of citizens' prayers, represent him standing against an architectural setting—the format obviously derives from the martyrs in the Rotunda. Under stylistic comparison the settings for S. Demetrius are seen to be simplified and reduced, but not without new features. The building in front of which he stands is not an idealized church sanctuary, as used in the Rotunda, but a representation of a structure peculiar to Thessalonica, the silver *ciborium* of S. Demetrius, which stood like a tabernacle in the nave of this church. Both Ravenna and Thessalonica did then develop local traditions out of a wider international vocabulary of art, but these did not develop precisely in parallel or at the same rate.

With the accession of Justinian (527) and establishment of Constantinople as the most dominant center of art, the period of experimentation in Early Christian art may be considered to end. In Italy from the mid 6th century down to c800 there were few significant developments, despite major transplants of Byzantine painting, as at various times in S. Maria Antiqua in the Roman Forum and in the church of S. Maria at Castelseprio.

It has to be emphasized that too little art of the period has survived for description and interpretation to be much more than a reflection of modern attitudes and prejudices. While the achievements of the period are seen at their most impressive in monumental painting, mosaic, and sculpture, yet portable objects were produced in expensive materials—gold and silver plate, ivory panels, and illuminated manuscripts. Possibly such glorifications of God were the real purpose of Early Christian art. As it is, Maximian of Ravenna has left no record whether he prized his ivory throne more or less than the mosaics of S. Vitale.

R. CORMACK

Bibliography. Grabar, A. *Christian Iconography: a Study of its Origins*, London (1969). Perkins, A.L. *The Art of Dura-Europos*, Oxford (1973). Volbach, W.F. *Early Christian Art*, London (1961). Wixom, W.D. "Early Christian Sculptures at Cleveland", *Bulletin of the Cleveland Museum of Art*, Cleveland (March 1967).